THE UNCOMFORTABLE PEW

MCGILL-QUEEN'S STUDIES IN THE HISTORY OF RELIGION
Volumes in this series have been supported by the Jackman Foundation of Toronto.

SERIES ONE: G.A. RAWLYK, EDITOR

1 Small Differences
  Irish Catholics and Irish Protestants,
  1815–1922
  An International Perspective
  Donald Harman Akenson

2 Two Worlds
  The Protestant Culture of
  Nineteenth-Century Ontario
  William Westfall

3 An Evangelical Mind
  Nathanael Burwash and the
  Methodist Tradition in Canada,
  1839–1918
  Marguerite Van Die

4 The Dévotes
  Women and Church in
  Seventeenth-Century France
  Elizabeth Rapley

5 The Evangelical Century
  College and Creed in English Canada
  from the Great Revival to the Great
  Depression
  Michael Gauvreau

6 The German Peasants' War and
  Anabaptist Community of Goods
  James M. Stayer

7 A World Mission
  Canadian Protestantism and the Quest
  for a New International Order,
  1918–1939
  Robert Wright

8 Serving the Present Age
  Revivalism, Progressivism, and the
  Methodist Tradition in Canada
  Phyllis D. Airhart

9 A Sensitive Independence
  Canadian Methodist Women
  Missionaries in Canada and the Orient,
  1881–1925
  Rosemary R. Gagan

10 God's Peoples
   Covenant and Land in South
   Africa, Israel, and Ulster
   Donald Harman Akenson

11 Creed and Culture
   The Place of English-Speaking Catholics
   in Canadian Society, 1750–1930
   Edited by Terrence Murphy
   and Gerald Stortz

12 Piety and Nationalism
   Lay Voluntary Associations and
   the Creation of an Irish-Catholic
   Community in Toronto, 1850–1895
   Brian P. Clarke

13 Amazing Grace
   Studies in Evangelicalism in Australia,
   Britain, Canada, and the United States
   Edited by George Rawlyk
   and Mark A. Noll

14 Children of Peace
   W. John McIntyre

15 A Solitary Pillar
   Montreal's Anglican Church
   and the Quiet Revolution
   Joan Marshall

16 Padres in No Man's Land
   Canadian Chaplains and the Great War
   Duff Crerar

17 Christian Ethics and Political Economy
   in North America
   A Critical Analysis
   P. Travis Kroeker

18 Pilgrims in Lotus Land
   Conservative Protestantism in
   British Columbia, 1917–1981
   Robert K. Burkinshaw

19 Through Sunshine and Shadow
   The Woman's Christian
   Temperance Union, Evangelicalism,
   and Reform in Ontario, 1874–1930
   Sharon Cook

20 Church, College, and Clergy
   A History of Theological
   Education at Knox College,
   Toronto, 1844–1994
   Brian J. Fraser

21 The Lord's Dominion
   The History of Canadian Methodism
   Neil Semple
22 A Full-Orbed Christianity
   The Protestant Churches and Social
   Welfare in Canada, 1900–1940
   Nancy Christie and Michael Gauvreau
23 Evangelism and Apostasy
   The Evolution and Impact
   of Evangelicals in Modern Mexico
   Kurt Bowen
24 The Chignecto Covenanters
   A Regional History of Reformed
   Presbyterianism in New Brunswick
   and Nova Scotia, 1827–1905
   Eldon Hay
25 Methodists and Women's
   Education in Ontario, 1836–1925
   Johanne Selles
26 Puritanism and Historical
   Controversy
   William Lamont

SERIES TWO: IN MEMORY OF GEORGE RAWLYK
DONALD HARMAN AKENSON, EDITOR

1 Marguerite Bourgeoys and Montreal,
  1640–1665
  Patricia Simpson
2 Aspects of the Canadian
  Evangelical Experience
  Edited by G.A. Rawlyk
3 Infinity, Faith, and Time
  Christian Humanism and
  Renaissance Literature
  John Spencer Hill
4 The Contribution of Presbyterianism
  to the Maritime Provinces of Canada
  *Edited by Charles H.H. Scobie
  and G.A. Rawlyk*
5 Labour, Love, and Prayer
  Female Piety in Ulster Religious
  Literature, 1850–1914
  Andrea Ebel Brozyna
6 The Waning of the Green
  Catholics, the Irish, and Identity
  in Toronto, 1887–1922
  Mark G. McGowan
7 Religion and Nationality
  in Western Ukraine
  The Greek Catholic Church
  and the Ruthenian National
  Movement in Galicia, 1867–1900
  John-Paul Himka
8 Good Citizens
  British Missionaries and Imperial States,
  1870–1918
  *James G. Greenlee and
  Charles M. Johnston*
9 The Theology of the Oral Torah
  Revealing the Justice of God
  Jacob Neusner
10 Gentle Eminence
   A Life of Cardinal Flahiff
   P. Wallace Platt
11 Culture, Religion, and Demographic
   Behaviour
   Catholics and Lutherans in Alsace,
   1750–1870
   Kevin McQuillan
12 Between Damnation and Starvation
   Priests and Merchants
   in Newfoundland Politics,
   1745–1855
   John P. Greene
13 Martin Luther, German Saviour
   German Evangelical Theological
   Factions and the Interpretation
   of Luther, 1917–1933
   James M. Stayer
14 Modernity and the Dilemma
   of North American Anglican
   Identities, 1880–1950
   William H. Katerberg
15 The Methodist Church on
   the Prairies, 1896–1914
   George Emery
16 Christian Attitudes towards
   the State of Israel
   Paul Charles Merkley
17 A Social History of the Cloister
   Daily Life in the Teaching
   Monasteries of the Old Regime
   Elizabeth Rapley
18 Households of Faith
   Family, Gender, and Community
   in Canada, 1760–1969
   Edited by Nancy Christie

19 Blood Ground
   Colonialism, Missions, and the Contest
   for Christianity in the Cape Colony
   and Britain, 1799–1853
   Elizabeth Elbourne

20 A History of Canadian Catholics
   Gallicanism, Romanism, and
   Canadianism
   Terence J. Fay

21 The View from Rome
   Archbishop Stagni's 1915
   Reports on the Ontario Bilingual
   Schools Question
   *Edited and translated by
   John Zucchi*

22 The Founding Moment
   Church, Society, and the
   Construction of Trinity College
   William Westfall

23 The Holocaust, Israel, and
   Canadian Protestant Churches
   Haim Genizi

24 Governing Charities
   Church and State in Toronto's
   Catholic Archdiocese, 1850–1950
   Paula Maurutto

25 Anglicans and the Atlantic World
   High Churchmen, Evangelicals,
   and the Quebec Connection
   Richard W. Vaudry

26 Evangelicals and the
   Continental Divide
   The Conservative Protestant Subculture
   in Canada and the United States
   Sam Reimer

27 Christians in a Secular World
   The Canadian Experience
   Kurt Bowen

28 Anatomy of a Seance
   A History of Spirit Communication
   in Central Canada
   Stan McMullin

29 With Skilful Hand
   The Story of King David
   David T. Barnard

30 Faithful Intellect
   Samuel S. Nelles and
   Victoria University
   Neil Semple

31 W. Stanford Reid
   An Evangelical Calvinist
   in the Academy
   Donald MacLeod

32 A Long Eclipse
   The Liberal Protestant
   Establishment and the Canadian
   University, 1920–1970
   Catherine Gidney

33 Forkhill Protestants and Forkhill
   Catholics, 1787–1858
   Kyla Madden

34 For Canada's Sake
   Public Religion, Centennial
   Celebrations, and the Re-making
   of Canada in the 1960s
   Gary R. Miedema

35 Revival in the City
   The Impact of American
   Evangelists in Canada, 1884–1914
   Eric R. Crouse

36 The Lord for the Body
   Religion, Medicine, and
   Protestant Faith Healing in
   Canada, 1880–1930
   James Opp

37 Six Hundred Years of Reform
   Bishops and the French Church,
   1190–1789
   *J. Michael Hayden and
   Malcolm R. Greenshields*

38 The Missionary Oblate Sisters
   Vision and Mission
   Rosa Bruno-Jofré

39 Religion, Family, and Community
   in Victorian Canada
   The Colbys of Carrollcroft
   Marguerite Van Die

40 Michael Power
   The Struggle to Build the Catholic
   Church on the Canadian Frontier
   Mark G. McGowan

41 The Catholic Origins of Quebec's
   Quiet Revolution, 1931–1970
   Michael Gauvreau

42 Marguerite Bourgeoys and the
   Congregation of Notre Dame,
   1665–1700
   Patricia Simpson

43 To Heal a Fractured World
   The Ethics of Responsibility
   Jonathan Sacks

44 Revivalists
   Marketing the Gospel in
   English Canada, 1884–1957
   Kevin Kee

45 The Churches and Social Order
   in Nineteenth- and Twentieth-
   Century Canada
   *Edited by Michael Gauvreau
   and Ollivier Hubert*

46 Political Ecumenism
   Catholics, Jews, and Protestants in
   De Gaulle's Free France, 1940–1945
   Geoffrey Adams

47 From Quaker to Upper Canadian
   Faith and Community among Yonge
   Street Friends, 1801–1850
   Robynne Rogers Healey

48 The Congrégation de Notre-Dame,
   Superiors, and the Paradox of Power,
   1693–1796
   Colleen Gray

49 Canadian Pentecostalism
   Transition and Transformation
   Edited by Michael Wilkinson

50 A War with a Silver Lining
   Canadian Protestant Churches
   and the South African War,
   1899–1902
   Gordon L. Heath

51 In the Aftermath of Catastrophe
   Founding Judaism, 70 to 640
   Jacob Neusner

52 Imagining Holiness
   Classic Hasidic Tales in Modern Times
   Justin Jaron Lewis

53 Shouting, Embracing, and
   Dancing with Ecstasy
   The Growth of Methodism in
   Newfoundland, 1774–1874
   Calvin Hollett

54 Into Deep Waters
   Evangelical Spirituality and
   Maritime Calvinist Baptist
   Ministers, 1790–1855
   Daniel C. Goodwin

55 Vanguard of the New Age
   The Toronto Theosophical
   Society, 1891–1945
   Gillian McCann

56 A Commerce of Taste
   Church Architecture in
   Canada, 1867–1914
   Barry Magrill

57 The Big Picture
   The Antigonish Movement
   of Eastern Nova Scotia
   Santo Dodaro and Leonard Pluta

58 My Heart's Best Wishes for You
   A Biography of Archbishop
   John Walsh
   John P. Comiskey

59 The Covenanters in Canada
   Reformed Presbyterianism
   from 1820 to 2012
   Eldon Hay

60 The Guardianship of Best Interests
   Institutional Care for the Children
   of the Poor in Halifax, 1850–1960
   Renée N. Lafferty

61 In Defence of the Faith
   Joaquim Marques de Araújo,
   a Brazilian Comissário in the
   Age of Inquisitional Decline
   James E. Wadsworth

62 Contesting the Moral High Ground
   Popular Moralists in
   Mid-Twentieth-Century Britain
   Paul T. Phillips

63 The Catholicisms of Coutances
   Varieties of Religion in Early
   Modern France, 1350–1789
   J. Michael Hayden

64 After Evangelicalism
   The Sixties and the United
   Church of Canada
   Kevin N. Flatt

65 The Return of Ancestral Gods
   Modern Ukrainian Paganism
   as an Alternative Vision
   for a Nation
   Mariya Lesiv

66 Transatlantic Methodists
   British Wesleyanism and
   the Formation of an Evangelical
   Culture in Nineteenth-Century
   Ontario and Quebec
   Todd Webb

67 A Church with the Soul of a Nation
   Making and Remaking the United
   Church of Canada
   Phyllis D. Airhart

68 Fighting over God
A Legal and Political History
of Religious Freedom in Canada
Janet Epp Buckingham

69 From India to Israel
Identity, Immigration, and the Struggle
for Religious Equality
Joseph Hodes

70 Becoming Holy in Early Canada
Timothy G. Pearson

71 The Cistercian Arts
From the 12th to the 21st Century
*Edited by Terryl N. Kinder
and Roberto Cassanelli*

72 The Canny Scot
Archbishop James Morrison
of Antigonish
Peter Ludlow

73 Religion and Greater Ireland
Christianity and Irish Global
Networks, 1750–1950
*Edited by Colin Barr and
Hilary M. Carey*

74 The Invisible Irish
Finding Protestants in the Nineteenth-
Century Migrations to America
Rankin Sherling

75 Beating against the Wind
Popular Opposition to Bishop Feild
and Tractarianism in Newfoundland
and Labrador, 1844–1876
Calvin Hollett

76 The Body or the Soul?
Religion and Culture in a Quebec
Parish, 1736–1901
Frank A. Abbott

77 Saving Germany
North American Protestants and
Christian Mission to West Germany,
1945–1974
James C. Enns

78 The Imperial Irish
Canada's Irish Catholics Fight
the Great War, 1914–1918
Mark G. McGowan

79 Into Silence and Servitude
How American Girls Became Nuns,
1945–1965
Brian Titley

80 Boundless Dominion
Providence, Politics, and the Early
Canadian Presbyterian Worldview
Denis McKim

81 Faithful Encounters
Authorities and American Missionaries
in the Ottoman Empire
Emrah Şahin

82 Beyond the Noise of Solemn Assemblies
The Protestant Ethic and the Quest
for Social Justice in Canada
Richard Allen

83 Not Quite Us
Anti-Catholic Thought in English
Canada since 1900
Kevin P. Anderson

84 Scandal in the Parish
Priests and Parishioners Behaving Badly
in Eighteenth-Century France
Karen E. Carter

85 Ordinary Saints
Women, Work, and Faith
in Newfoundland
Bonnie Morgan

86 Patriot and Priest
Jean-Baptiste Volfius and
the Constitutional Church in the
Côte-d'Or
Annette Chapman-Adisho

87 A.B. Simpson and the Making
of Modern Evangelicalism
Daryn Henry

88 The Uncomfortable Pew
Christianity and the New Left
in Toronto
Bruce Douville

The Uncomfortable Pew

Christianity and the New Left in Toronto

BRUCE DOUVILLE

McGill-Queen's University Press
Montreal & Kingston • London • Chicago

© McGill-Queen's University Press 2021

ISBN 978-0-2280-0635-0 (cloth)
ISBN 978-0-2280-0636-7 (paper)
ISBN 978-0-2280-0726-5 (ePDF)
ISBN 978-0-2280-0727-2 (ePUB)

Legal deposit second quarter 2021
Bibliothèque nationale du Québec

Printed in Canada on acid-free paper that is 100% ancient forest free (100% post-consumer recycled), processed chlorine free

This book has been published with the help of a grant from the Canadian Federation for the Humanities and Social Sciences, through the Awards to Scholarly Publications Program, using funds provided by the Social Sciences and Humanities Research Council of Canada.

Funded by the Government of Canada   Financé par le gouvernement du Canada   Canada   Canada Council for the Arts   Conseil des arts du Canada

We acknowledge the support of the Canada Council for the Arts.

Nous remercions le Conseil des arts du Canada de son soutien.

Library and Archives Canada Cataloguing in Publication

Title: The uncomfortable pew: Christianity and the new left in Toronto / Bruce Douville.

Names: Douville, Bruce, 1969– author.

Series: McGill-Queen's studies in the history of religion. Series two; 88.

Description: Series statement: McGill-Queen's studies in the history of religion. Series two; 88 | Includes bibliographical references and index.

Identifiers: Canadiana (print) 20210101679 | Canadiana (ebook) 20210101830 | ISBN 9780228006350 (cloth) | ISBN 9780228006367 (paper) | ISBN 9780228007265 (ePDF) | ISBN 9780228007272 (ePUB)

Subjects: LCSH: Christians—Political activity—Ontario—Toronto—History—20th century. | LCSH: Youth—Political activity—Ontario—Toronto—History—20th century. | LCSH: Radicalism—Ontario—Toronto—History—20th century. | LCSH: Right and left (Political science)—Ontario—Toronto—History—20th century. | LCSH: Social movements—Ontario—Toronto—History—20th century. | LCSH: Toronto (Ont.)—Church history—20th century.

Classification: LCC BR580.T67 D68 2021 | DDC 261/.109713541—dc23

This book was typeset by Marquis Interscript in 10.5 / 13 Sabon.

I dedicate this to all those who, in their journeys of faith, envision a world of love, peace, and justice, and work to make that vision a reality.

In particular, I dedicate The Uncomfortable Pew *to the memory of Richard Allen (1929–2019), for whom the connection between Christianity and social justice was both personal and academic. This was abundantly evident in his lifelong scholarly work on the social gospel in Canada, and his engagement in Ontario politics in the 1980s and 1990s.*

In 1995, while doing research for an undergraduate essay on the social gospel in Canada, I discovered Professor Allen's groundbreaking monograph The Social Passion. *This book was my introduction to the milieu of radical left-wing Christians in early twentieth-century Canada. From my own experience, I already knew that there was a strong connection between Christian spirituality and the struggle for social justice, but witnessing that connection in Canadian history inspired me on both a personal and an academic level. In writing* The Uncomfortable Pew, *about a later generation of Christian radicals in Canada, I hope that some of that inspiration shines through.*

Contents

Acknowledgments xiii

Abbreviations xvii

1 Introduction: English-Canadian Christianity and the New Left during the Long Sixties 3

2 The Twilight of Christendom: Canadian Christianity in Changing Times 22

3 Changing Times: Christianity and the Formation of Canada's New Left 44

4 Where the Action Is: Christianity and New Left Activism in Toronto, 1965–66 68

5 Descent of the Avatars: Christian Youth and the Late Sixties Youth Revolt 104

6 Engaging with the Avatars: Churches, Clergy, and the Late Sixties Youth Revolt 125

7 Liberation: English-Canadian Christianity and the New Left in the Early 1970s 149

8 Liberation, Part Two: Christianity, Gender, and Sexuality in the Early 1970s 171

9 Beyond the Long Sixties: Why Christian Engagement with the New Left Mattered 195

Notes 213

Bibliography 259

Index 281

Acknowledgments

This work had its genesis in my doctoral dissertation at York University. I owe a large debt of gratitude to my primary dissertation supervisor, William Westfall. His wisdom, wit, and willingness to go the extra mile meant a great deal to me. In addition, my two other supervisors, Marcel Martel and Paul Axelrod, provided prompt and insightful feedback. I could not have asked for a more wonderful supervisory team.

My interviewees deserve high praise. I was impressed not only by their generosity (sharing stories, archival documents, food, and, of course, their time), but also by the enthusiasm that many of them expressed for this project. It is both a great honour and an awesome responsibility to be entrusted with someone else's stories.

This work also entailed countless hours in archives, libraries, and special collections. I wish to thank archivists and librarians, particularly those at the Archives of the Roman Catholic Archdiocese of Toronto; the Clara Thomas Archives at York University, Toronto; the General Synod Archives of the Anglican Church of Canada, Toronto; the Thomas Fisher Rare Book Library at the University of Toronto; the United Church of Canada Archives, Toronto; the University of Toronto Archives; and the William Ready Archives at McMaster University in Hamilton.

In my research and writing, I have benefitted immeasurably from my interactions with other historians, particularly those that have written about Canada in the 1960s and 1970s, as well as historians of religion in Canada. More than a few answered my inquiries and offered helpful suggestions about potential interviewees or source material, and some even shared their work in progress. Others offered helpful feedback and much-needed encouragement at various stages of this project. Regarding feedback and encouragement, two important venues deserve special mention. First, I am especially thankful for the annual meetings of the Canadian Society of Church History. Second, I wish to single out the Algoma University History Writers' Group, which met between 2014 and 2018. It is impossible to name all the historians who have helped along the way, but a few names would include Katrina Ackerman, Phyllis Airhart, Sandra Beardsall, Marisha Caswell, Kelly Deluca, Stuart Henderson, Warren Johnston, Roberta Lexier, Ian Milligan, Stuart Macdonald, Roberto Perin, Sheila Redmond, Robynne Rogers Healey, Robert Rutherdale, Shannon Stettner, Shay Sweeney, and Jason Young.

In this book, I have incorporated material from some of my previously published works. I thank University of Toronto Press for permission to quote from "'In the Image and Likeness of God': Christianity and Public Opinion on Abortion in the Globe and Mail during the Sixties," by Shannon Stettner and Bruce Douville, published in *Journal of Canadian Studies* 50, no 1 (2016), 179–213; Between the Lines Press for permission to quote from my chapter "Project La Macaza: A Study of Two Canadian Peace Protests in the 1960s," which was published in *Worth Fighting For: Canada's Tradition of War Resistance from 1812 to the War on Terror*, edited by Lara Campbell, Michael Dawson, and Catherine Gidney (Toronto: Between the Lines, 2015); and University of British Columbia Press for permission to quote from "'Is Abortion Ever Right?': The United Church of Canada and the Debate over Abortion Law Reform, 1960–1980," by Katrina Ackerman, Bruce Douville, and Shannon Stettner, which was published in *No Place for the State: The Origins and Legacies of the 1969 Omnibus Bill*, edited by Christopher Dummitt and Christabelle Sethna (Vancouver: UBC Press, 2020). I also thank Special Rider Music for permission to reprint the first verse of "The Times They Are a-Changin'," written by Bob Dylan, copyright © 1963, 1964 by Warner Bros. Inc.; renewed 1991, 1992 by Special Rider Music (all rights reserved; international copyright secured).

It is an honour and a pleasure to publish with McGill-Queen's University Press. I cannot sufficiently express my gratitude for my wonderful editor, Kyla Madden. As I navigated the process of turning a manuscript into a book, she has been immensely helpful at every stage. Thanks as well to her editorial assistant Elli Stylianou, and also to Kate Merriman for careful copy-editing. I am appreciative, as well, for the thoughtful criticism of two anonymous readers. The revisions I made in response to their constructive input have made this a better book.

Between initial research and final publication, most scholarly projects benefit from funding, and this monograph is no exception. In the 2008–09 academic year, York University's School of Graduate Studies provided me with a Research Assistantship, which allowed me the time to explore archival sources and conduct interviews that were germane to this book. At the publication stage, I am grateful for two sources of funding. This book has been published with the help of a grant from the Federation for the Humanities and Social Sciences, through the Awards to Scholarly Publications Program, using funds provided by the Social Sciences and Humanities Research Council of Canada. The Jackman Foundation funds the McGill-Queen's Studies in the History of Religion Series, and I thank Donald Harman Akenson for choosing to include this work in the series.

Many friends and family alternately distracted me from my work and encouraged me to get it done. In my years of study at York University, I was especially thankful for my community of friends at Emmanuel Anglican Church in Richmond Hill, Ontario. Since returning to Sault Ste Marie, my friendship with Laura Strum has been a great source of emotional sustenance. Together, Laura and I have shared music, heartfelt conversations, plenty of tea, and even more laughter. And of course, there is not sufficient space to express how thankful I am for the love, support, and encouragement of my family. This includes my brothers and their spouses – Steven and Shirley Douville, and David and Linda Douville – and, most of all, my parents, Joseph and Helen Douville.

Finally, thanks to the Giver of Life and Grace. I have been blessed with an abundance of life and grace, and my continuing desire is to "pay it forward." Freely, we have received; freely, we give.

Abbreviations

AYM	Anglican Youth Movement
AYPA	Anglican Young People's Association
CALCAV	Clergy and Laity Concerned about Vietnam
CCC	Canadian Council of Churches
CCF	Cooperative Commonwealth Federation
CENSIT	Centre for the Study of Institutions and Theology
CFLC	Christian Faith-and-Life Community
CHAT	Community Homophile Association of Toronto
CUCND	Combined Universities Campaign for Nuclear Disarmament
CUS	Canadian Union of Students
CUT	Canadian Urban Training Program
CYC	Company of Young Canadians
ERAP	Economic Research and Action Project
E&SS	Board of Evangelism and Social Service (United Church of Canada)
FLQ	Front de libération du Québec
FOR	Fellowship of Reconciliation
ICCC	Inter-Church Committee on Chile
IVCF, VCF	Intervarsity Christian Fellowship, Varsity Christian Fellowship
LAWG	Latin American Working Group
LID	League for Industrial Democracy
NACLA	North American Congress on Latin America
NATO	North Atlantic Treaty Organization
NCC	National Council of Churches
NDP	New Democratic Party

NORAD	North American Air Defence
PWRDF	Primate's World Relief and Development Fund
SAC	Students' Administrative Council (University of Toronto)
SCM	Student Christian Movement
SDS	Students for a Democratic Society
SNCC	Student Nonviolent Coordinating Committee
SOS	Summer of Service
SUPA	Student Union for Peace Action
SVM	Student Volunteer Movement
TADP	Toronto Anti-Draft Programme
UGEC	Union générale des étudiants du Quebec
UAE	Union of American Exiles
ULAJE	Union of Latin American Evangelical Youth
UTHA	University of Toronto Homophile Association
WSCF	World Student Christian Federation
YPU	Young People's Union (United Church of Canada)
YMCA	Young Men's Christian Association
YWCA	Young Women's Christian Association

THE UNCOMFORTABLE PEW

1

Introduction

English-Canadian Christianity and the New Left during the Long Sixties

This book explores the relationship between Christianity and the New Left in English Canada throughout the long sixties, focusing primarily on Toronto. It examines both the impact that left-wing student radicalism had on institutional Christianity, and the role that Christianity, institutional and otherwise, played in what adherents to the New Left called "the movement" or "the revolution." The key players in this study include both the younger Christian radicals who identified with the church and the revolution, and the older church officials (from denominational leaders to rank-and-file clergy and laity) who attempted to engage with the radical youth, Christian or otherwise, and the issues that concerned them. I argue that Christian radicals played a role in shaping Canada's New Left (especially, but not exclusively, in its earliest stages), and conversely, that the New Left played a role in shaping Canada's largest denominations in the sixties.

As I began to formulate these arguments over a decade ago, and shared them with both academics and former sixties activists, a few expressed skepticism that there was any meaningful, important connection between Christianity and the New Left. Such skepticism reflects the widely held belief that the New Left was essentially atheistic, rooted in the secular ideologies of Marxist humanists and anarchists, and in the activism of "red diaper babies" (youth raised by Communist parents, many of whom were secular Jews). But these were not the only roots. As both American and Canadian scholars of sixties radicalism have observed, many young people in the New Left began their activist careers in student Christian organizations, such as the Young Men's Christian Association (YMCA), Young Women's Christian Association (YWCA), and the Student Christian Movement (SCM). This strong link between youth radicalism and faith-based student organizations does not square with widespread assumptions about the New Left (that it was atheistic), or about institutional Christianity (that it was an entirely reactionary force). As Ian McKay observes, many Canadian "left historians in both linguistic communities are uncomfortable, as secularists, when face-to-face with evidence suggesting the power of religion as a force for socialism. Yet many leftists in Canada have been believers, rooting resistance to capitalism in religious values."[1]

This strong link did not surprise me. Growing up in an evangelical Christian household, by my teenage years, I had come to see my faith as radical and countercultural. From reading the Bible, I learned that Jesus proclaimed a message of liberation for the oppressed, calling his followers to reject wealth accumulation and warmongering and to embrace the ways of love, peace, and equality. As my political opinions began to take shape on the left, it was troubling to observe that the most prominent spokespersons for evangelicalism in the 1980s were decidedly right of centre. By my early twenties, I had come to identify with the radical left, and had adopted a countercultural lifestyle in several respects. Nevertheless, I remained acutely aware of how Christian spirituality[2] had shaped – and continued to shape – both my political views and lifestyle choices.

What is significant about my journey is not its uniqueness but its commonness. Many present-day Christians in North America – liberal Protestants, evangelicals, and Roman Catholics – are convinced that their faith compels them to work for peace and for economic, racial, and environmental justice. Furthermore, faith-based activism for radical social change is not only a modern phenomenon. Historically, movements of protest against the dominant social, political, and economic order have often originated in periods of religious renewal. For example, the configuration of radical reform movements that emerged in the northeastern United States in the 1830s, 1840s, and 1850s (e.g., abolitionist anti-slavery, women's rights, Grahamism, non-resistance, and anarchism) all had their roots in the evangelical Christian revivalist fervour of that era.[3] Also, the twentieth-century Canadian left drew much of its energy and leadership from the Social Gospel movement, which, in turn, originated in late nineteenth-century

Methodist evangelicalism.[4] William G. McLoughlin calls these times of renewal "awakenings," which he defines as "periods of cultural revitalization that begin in a general crisis of beliefs and values and extend over a period of a generation or so, during which time a profound reorientation in beliefs and values takes place."[5] Most importantly, McLoughlin contends that these revolutionary periods of spiritual awakening lead to social transformation and fundamental secular reforms.

My own interest in the 1960s and early 1970s was rooted in the conviction that these years constituted just such an era. As well, the period appealed to my sense of vicarious nostalgia. From the vantage point of the 1990s – a decade of lowered expectations on the left, deficit-cutting, and ascendant neo-liberalism – the "long sixties"[6] appeared to be a golden age of unbridled optimism, when personal and political liberation seemed to be real possibilities. The sixties were years of profound cultural transformation, evident in both the religious and secular developments of the period.

But what was the precise relationship between the religious and the secular developments of this era? In their determination to overthrow oppressive social structures, young radicals in the sixties rejected the institutions, practices, and symbols of the dominant culture. How could Christianity play any role in the formation of such a movement, or even engage in a dialogue with it? And finally, what impact would dialogue with these dissident youth have on institutional Christianity itself?

These are important questions, especially for those of us who trace our political and cultural lineage to the sixties, who hold that the core values of the sixties youth are also the core values of Christianity, and who still believe that communities of faith can be vehicles for radical social criticism and progressive social change. These are also important questions for any community of faith that seeks to remain engaged with the issues and concerns of the wider secular culture (especially with the issues and concerns of youth, on whom the continuation of the faith community depends) and remain relevant in a pluralistic society, without compromising its distinctive principles. To begin answering them, it is necessary to speak briefly of the challenges that Canada's main Christian denominations faced in the long sixties because these challenges impelled Canadian Christians to pay attention to the New Left, and to reach out.

CANADIAN CHRISTIANITY IN THE LONG SIXTIES

For Roman Catholic and mainline Protestant churches across the Western world, the 1960s was a decade of crisis. One of the features of the "religious crisis of the 1960s," as Hugh McLeod calls it, was prolonged institutional soul-searching.[7] Canada was no exception; the leaders of Canada's major denominations engaged in a process of self-criticism. Furthermore, by the mid-1960s, it was becoming clear that the churches throughout the Western world were declining in numbers and in influence. McLeod contends that as "Christianity lost a large part of its privileged position, the options in matters of belief, life-path, or 'spirituality' were open to a degree that they had not been for centuries."[8] In short, Canada's largest churches faced a multifaceted crisis – of identity, membership, and public authority.

Leading Canadian clergy and lay members, both mainline Protestant and Catholic, came to believe that if their churches were to survive, they must address the needs and issues of a rapidly changing society. More importantly, church leaders perceived that the teenagers and young adults of the Baby Boom generation were at the core of this society. And among the most visible representatives of the youth generation were the radicals of the New Left. While they constituted only a minority within the student population, they seemed to articulate their generation's values, concerns, and rebellious mood.[9] In this climate of institutional soul-searching, declining social status, and youth insurgency, some prominent Canadian church leaders reached out to young people – especially disaffected youth, such as student radicals and hippies – to dialogue with them and address their issues and concerns.

The nature of this dialogue varied from one denomination to another, but in the major Protestant and Catholic churches, some familiar patterns emerged. Canadian denominational periodicals devoted more coverage to youth issues, and allotted space for young people to have their say. Church structures were modified to encourage greater youth participation. Many church leaders and publications adopted radical rhetoric. More importantly, some of these leaders began to speak out critically and unequivocally on social justice issues of concern to young people, particularly the Vietnam War. In doing so, the churches aimed to fulfill their "prophetic" role. Throughout the long sixties, each of the major Protestant and Catholic churches wrestled with the perennial question of whether the church is to be a "priestly (legitimating)" institution in society or a "prophetic (critical)" one. By the 1960s, Canada's major denominations had lost much of their priestly authority, but by adopting a more critical stance, many individuals and congregations in these denominations sought to take up the prophetic mantle.[10]

This prophetic, dissenting spirit was most evident in youth organizations associated with the various denominations (including Youth Corps, Kairos, and the Anglican Youth Movement) as well as nondenominational organizations supported by various churches (chiefly the Student Christian Movement, but also Summer of Service). Young people in these groups were most receptive to the new theology that called them to engage with the social and political issues of their day. Unlike older church leaders, they were impelled less by concern for the long-term well-being of the institutional churches than by the need to be where the action is. Many also belonged to secular New Left groups or, at the very least, collaborated with them on issues of shared concern. Throughout the sixties, Christian youth organizations were formed, reformed, or reoriented, as they adopted, in varying degrees, the rhetoric and activist strategies of the student radicals. The new directions of these groups caused anxiety among many older church members; nevertheless, these organizations enjoyed the support of progressive, reform-minded clergy and denominational officials, who hoped that their churches would follow the prophetic lead of the young radicals.

The interactions between institutional Christianity and the New Left were an important element in the transformation of Canada's main denominations in the long sixties. Undoubtedly, these denominations would have evolved substantially in the sixties regardless of the New Left, as there were many other factors at play (e.g., Vatican II among Roman Catholics, "secular theology" and "death of God" theology among mainline Protestants, and an increasingly secular Canadian society). Nevertheless, one must remember the context of these developments: that they occurred in churches that were engaging with radicalized and disaffected youth, and as this study shows, these developments both shaped and were shaped by that engagement. The churches' interaction with the New Left had an impact on Canadian Christianity that reverberates to the present day, especially in the United Church of Canada.

Moreover, the impact was mutual. While the roots of the New Left in North America were primarily secular, the movement drew on religious roots too: the Social Gospel, Christian existentialism, and social Catholicism. In the United States, students encountered these religious traditions in the peace movement and the non-communist left, in the YMCA/YWCA, and in the churches themselves. In Canada, the pattern was much the same, but the vehicle for the Social Gospel and Christian existentialism, at least on the university campuses of English Canada, was the SCM. The SCM played an important role in the formation of the early Canadian New Left. Throughout the long sixties, the organization continued to pursue a radical political and theological agenda, though it no longer held the prominent place on Canadian campuses that it had in the 1930s, 1940s, or early 1950s. By the 1960s, the key student protest groups in Canada were ostensibly secular; nevertheless, their leaders included some practising Christians, both Protestant and Catholic. This is true not only in the early sixties, when the movement was taking shape, but also in the late sixties, when the movement rocked campuses across Canada. The presence of young people whose activism was rooted in their faith demands further attention.

LITERATURE ON RELIGION AND YOUTH MOVEMENTS IN THE LONG SIXTIES

There is a growing body of literature on religion and cultural change in the long sixties. Most of these studies narrate the declining fortunes of institutional Christianity in those years, and thus focus on the relationship between the churches and the dominant culture.[11] Few satisfactorily address the role of youth in the challenges facing churches in this era. Furthermore, since the nineties, there has been a flood of historical writing on the New Left and the hip counterculture of the long sixties, and most has little to say about the role of Christianity, institutional or otherwise, in these youth-based movements.[12] In other words, there are narratives of church decline in the sixties, and narratives of the youth revolt in the long sixties, but few historians explore deeply the intersections between these two narrative categories.

Historians who have explored these intersections include Doug Rossinow, whose monograph *The Politics of Authenticity* highlighted the relationship between Christianity and the New Left in Austin, Texas.[13] Hugh McLeod's *The Religious Crisis of the 1960s* attempts to explain the decline of "Christendom" between 1955 and 1975 in several nations (chiefly the United Kingdom, but also other Western

European countries, the United States, Canada, Australia, and New Zealand). While McLeod argues that there is no single over-riding cause of religious decline, he devotes several chapters to the role of youth and youth-based movements in the unfolding religious crisis of the era. McLeod identifies four changes as central to the decline of Christendom, and young people were at the heart of three of these changes: the "wide-ranging effects of 'affluence,'" particularly their impact "on patterns of home and neighbourhood life"; the seismic shifts "in the areas of gender and sexuality"; and the impact (especially by the late 1960s) of movements and ideals championed by radical youth.[14]

Little has been published on the relationship between Christianity and the sixties youth movements in Canada. Several studies of the Canadian New Left allude to the role that Christianity played in student radicalism, but only in passing. For example, Bryan Palmer's *Canada's 1960s: The Ironies of Identity in a Rebellious Era* includes a thorough and insightful chapter on Canada's New Left, but he allots a total of three sentences to the role of religion in the formative years of the movement.[15] Palmer contends that the "irony of Canadian identity in the 1960s was that as the old attachment to British Canada was finally and decisively shed, it was replaced only with uncertainty,"[16] and he shows that the emergence of Canada's New Left was one important factor that helped Canada shed its traditional identity. However, he does not discuss the ways that Christianity was a central component of identity in English Canada until the 1960s, and the ways in which the social upheavals of the sixties led to an uncoupling of Christian identity and national identity.[17] In contrast, Peter Graham and Ian McKay's *Radical Ambition*, a history of the New Left in Toronto, furnishes the reader with many examples of Christian involvement in the New Left from the 1950s to the 1980s.[18]

In a similar manner, most works on Canadian religious history in the sixties touch only briefly on youth radicalism or ignore it entirely,[19] or subsume their discussion of radicalism in a broader discussion of "counterculture." Michael Gauvreau's *The Catholic Origins of Quebec's Quiet Revolution* gives considerable attention to the response of Quebec Catholics to "the spectacle of youth countercultures."[20] While his study offers valuable insights into the youth-centred cultural shift of the sixties, his broad use of the term "counterculture" to denote many manifestations of youth in revolt against the values of their parents' generation does not lend itself to an analysis of interactions specifically between Catholics and young radicals. The most thorough examination of the intersection between Christianity and the New Left in Canada can be found in Catherine Gidney's *A Long Eclipse*. Her study explores the declining public role of Protestant Christianity on English-Canadian campuses, with a particular focus on the SCM. Gidney shows that the SCM played an influential role in the New Left, and that the SCM, in turn, was influenced by the secular New Left throughout the 1960s.[21] However, she does not explore the influence of social Catholicism (since her study focuses primarily on Protestant student groups) or other intersections between institutional Christianity and the New Left in English Canada. Her study ends in 1970 and does not explore the continuing leftward drift of the SCM in the early 1970s, nor does it consider the long-term consequences of this intersection in present-day churches or on present-day campuses.

ARGUMENT AND METHOD

The Uncomfortable Pew explores the ways that Christians, both young and old, engaged with the New Left and the issues of concern to the New Left. By examining both the impact that student radicalism had on institutional Christianity and the role that Christianity played in shaping Canada's New Left, this study makes explicit the connections between the profound changes that occurred in Canadian Christianity and the concurrent developments in the Canadian New Left. My title, *The Uncomfortable Pew*, is an allusion to Pierre Berton's *The Comfortable Pew*.[22] Published in 1965, Berton's book portrayed Canadian mainline Protestant churches as complacent and oblivious to the social upheavals of the era. While there was some merit to Berton's critical assessment, he failed to acknowledge that many mainline Protestants and Catholics in Canada were eager to transform their denominations into institutions that would be relevant in what Berton called "the New Age." In the ten years that followed, Canadian Christians had many reasons to feel uncomfortable: the decline in church attendance and the churches' declining influence in society; the seismic shifts in youth culture (with the emergence of both the New Left and also the hip counterculture); and the engagement of some churches, denominational hierarchies, and Christian youth organizations with radical youth and their concerns. In an era of experimentation and innovation, the pew was no longer quite so comfortable.

I make a case for three broad theses. First, I contend that the "generation gap," evident in the New Left, played a role in shaping the churches' crisis of relevance, and hence in the churches' response to that crisis. Second, the Canadian New Left was not as divorced from Christianity as popular accounts would lead one to believe. On the contrary, Christian youth and Christian youth organizations (particularly the SCM) played key roles in both the formation and leadership of Canada's New Left. The impact was reciprocal; the New Left shaped Canada's Christian youth organizations, and it influenced the evolution of Canada's leading denominations in the sixties and beyond. Finally, radical Christianity flourished in the long sixties, with ironic results for mainline Canadian churches and religious youth organizations.

To develop these arguments, this study examines the efforts of Canadian denominations, Christian youth organizations, and urban churches to reach out to radical youth, listen to their concerns, and learn to speak their language. It also explores the extent to which these attempts at dialogue were reciprocated. It considers the ways in which student radicals appropriated Christian symbols, language, and ideas; also, conversely, the ways in which Canadian Christians appropriated the symbols, language, and ideas of the New Left; and how these appropriations resulted in radical manifestations of Christianity. Finally, it places these Canadian events in the broader North American social-cultural context (e.g., New Left student activism on American campuses), as well as the context of significant international developments in Christianity in the 1960s (e.g., Vatican II, "secular theology," and the radicalization of the World Student Christian Federation).

I have chosen Toronto as the principal site for this study because it was an active centre in the long sixties for radical student activity at the University of Toronto, and home to the national office of the Student Union for Peace Action (SUPA). It was also the home of the headquarters of several Protestant denominations and the seat of the largest Catholic archdiocese in English Canada. While the relationship between religion and student radicalism played out differently in other major Canadian cities, focusing on one city makes it possible to explore this relationship in greater detail. Although Toronto is the principal focus, this study also considers the broader regional, national, and international contexts.

This study commences in the late 1950s, with the nascence of the Canadian student protest movement. However, I have chosen to devote most attention to the years 1965 to 1975. Although an arbitrary starting point, 1965 is a reasonable one. In this year, American ground troops were deployed in Vietnam, marking the beginning of a lengthy and costly war of occupation. While student left organizations existed before 1965, the Vietnam War intensified the radical opposition to dominant social structures.[23] This year also marked the birth of the Student Union for Peace Action (SUPA), and the Canadian government's announcement, in its throne speech, that it would create a "Company of Young Canadians." Both SUPA and CYC would play an important role in Toronto's activist scene.[24] Likewise, 1975 is an arbitrary point to conclude this study, but is also a significant date. In that year, the United States ceased providing aid to South Vietnam, and Saigon fell to the People's Army of Vietnam, effectively ending the Vietnam War, which had been a *cause célèbre* for the North American New Left.

My examination of the New Left focuses primarily, though not exclusively, on the University of Toronto and the student protest groups on campus, especially SUPA. I also give attention to Rochdale College, an experiment in alternative education that combined elements of both the New Left and the counterculture. In my examination of Canadian Christianity, I focus on Canada's three largest denominations in the 1960s: Roman Catholic, Anglican, and the United Church of Canada. Finally, much of this study centres on organizations in which the New Left and Christianity intersect. Chief among these was the SCM, but I also consider others, including the Anglican Youth Movement, Kairos, the Latin American Working Group, and Summer of Service.

The parameters of this study are wide, by necessity. For example, I have identified the University of Toronto as one of the central sites in this study, and I have singled out the SCM, particularly its large, active University of Toronto chapter, for special attention. However, many of the Christian youth organizations in this study were not campus-based. As we shall see, young Christian radicals participated in a milieu that transcended the boundaries of the campus, as did the New Left itself.[25] Furthermore, not all the young Christian radicals in this study were University of Toronto undergraduate students. Some were university dropouts, some had already completed their studies (often from other universities, before they relocated to Toronto to become full-time activists), and some were graduate students. Furthermore, even when we consider the bona fide undergraduate students at the

University of Toronto, not all Christian student activists were directly associated with the SCM. In short, my exploration of the role of young Christian radicals, and their relationship with the New Left, requires broad parameters to do full justice to the narrative.

More importantly, I must emphasize that this study is not confined to the young Christian radicals. Their importance is undeniable, and they occupy the bulk of this study because they constituted a key link between the institutional churches and the secular New Left. But the young radicals aren't the only players. The roles of the denominational hierarchies and editors of their monthly news publications are important. The roles of activist-oriented, progressive clergy and supportive laity are especially important. The institutional churches and their older progressive members are an integral part of this narrative. The participants in the SCM, and other radical Christian youth, belonged to churches, church organizations, and church committees (and also interchurch committees, given the close association of some young activists with the Canadian Council of Churches) and they carried out much of their work as activists in conjunction with clergy and laity that were anywhere from five to fifty years older than them, including many former SCM members. These stories are too intertwined to separate. Consequently, while much of this study focuses on Christian youth (and their organizations) and their engagement with the broader New Left, there are many parts of this study in which the spotlight is not on the youth but on the institutional church – its leaders and clergy – and how they engaged with both the younger Christian radicals *and* young secular radicals, and the issues that concerned them.

This study relies on a broad spectrum of research materials. News sources have proven to be the most rewarding, especially denominational periodicals. Both denominational archives and university archives have been essential to my research, and I make extensive use of oral interviews. My twenty-nine interviewees include participants in the New Left and others who participated in the intersection between Christianity and the youth revolt in the long sixties. In conducting these interviews and incorporating them into my study, I am conscious of the problematic nature of this kind of source. Memory can be fallible, sometimes adjusted to align with the communal narrative of public memory.[26] At the same time, memories can also be uncannily accurate, and interviews often bring to light issues and perspectives that would otherwise be lost to history. In dealing with living history, it would be negligent to overlook such a source. I endeavour to use these sources critically, and in conjunction with contemporaneous news sources and primary sources found in archives and personal collections.

METANARRATIVES OF THE SIXTIES: THEORETICAL AND CONCEPTUAL CONSIDERATIONS

The sixties generated powerful metanarratives about both youth and religion. The pervasive narrative about the former was that the Baby Boom generation, en masse, rejected the values, practices, and institutions of their parents' generation, and that this youthful "Great Refusal"[27] was the driving force behind social change in the era. The pervasive narrative about the latter was that modern societies were intrinsically secular and, thus, the decline of religion (both in its social importance and number of adherents) was inevitable. As frameworks to explain social change, these narratives gained currency during the decade and beyond, in popular culture and in academic analysis. For the purposes of this study, it is important to address these theoretical frameworks and concepts here, not only because they are pervasive and problematic, but also because they are relevant to my core arguments.

In this study, I apply the term "youth" flexibly: predominantly to young people in their late teens and early twenties (the widely accepted definition),[28] but often including those in their mid to late twenties who remained active in student groups and self-consciously identified as youth. Age is not a clear-cut category of identity. "Youth" is not a concept with a fixed meaning that transcends history. Age-based identities – like those based on race, class, and gender – are negotiated in a particular historical social context, and they intersect with categories of race, class, and gender.[29] There cannot be a single, unitary youth culture or identity, nor can we make blanket assertions about a generation. Yet such assertions are at the heart of the grand narrative of youth rebellion in 1960s North America. In part, this reflects the obsession with youth that was so pervasive in the 1960s. While the cultural preoccupation with youth and youth culture took shape in the early twentieth century, the demographics of the Baby Boom ensured that the sixties would be a youth-centred decade, evident in advertising, news media, and society at large.[30]

It is not surprising, then, that the protest movements of the long sixties, such as the New Left, were perceived by observers and by participants themselves to be youth-oriented movements. In large measure, this perception is correct. While the most prominent New Leftist leaders were too old to classify as Baby Boomers (i.e., born between 1946 and 1962),[31] and more than a few were in their late twenties or even early thirties, the rank and file of the New Left in the late sixties fell into the widely accepted age bracket for youth: late teens to early twenties. As for the leaders, they thought of themselves as young, and as representatives of sixties-era youth. But were they representative of an entire generation? And was this really a generation at odds with the values and culture of their parents' generation?

The "generation gap" was a construct of youth identity in the 1960s, and it continues to be central to the metanarratives about student radicalism in that decade (paradoxically, both the left-wing and right-wing metanarratives). But these narratives about rebellious youth are problematic, particularly those narratives that tell the story of campus radicals as though their experience was normative for Baby Boomers in the sixties. The reality is that university students constituted only a small subset of North American youth in the long sixties. In Canada, approximately one in ten young people attended university in the mid-sixties, and still only one in six by the early seventies.[32] Of that subset, a significantly smaller number self-identified as radicals. Moreover, several scholars have challenged the notion of a "generation gap" or a single, unitary "youth culture."[33] For example, sociologist Michael Brake has argued against the contentions of earlier sociologists such as Talcott Parsons (who coined the term "youth culture") that youth created a unified, inclusive social order, with its own set of values. According to Brake, this view is "ahistorical and dislocated from any class analysis." Instead, there are multiple youth subcultures, largely reflecting race and class. Writing in the 1980s, he claimed that the radical student movements and the counterculture should be seen primarily as middle-class youth movements, with values that were modifications of their parents' values (hence, continuous, not discontinuous).[34]

More recent scholars, however, have argued that the youth revolt of the long sixties was pervasive across class and race divisions, though it manifested itself in different ways. As Ian Milligan argues persuasively in *Rebel Youth*, while New Leftist students predominantly from middle-class backgrounds revolted on university campuses in the long sixties, young blue-collar workers rebelled against company management and union leadership by launching wildcat strikes. He argues that middle-class and working-class youth "shared important commonalities of mass experience, anti-authoritarianism, a belief in democracy, and being commonly constructed as a part of a youth culture."[35] In other words, a substantial number of youth had embraced values and practices that were markedly discontinuous from those of their parents, and of their parents' generation. More importantly, the student radicals believed that they belonged to a special generation, set apart from their elders – a belief often reinforced by the pronouncements of news media and politicians – and that youth would be the agents of social and political revolution.[36] While perception and reality are not always the same thing, perception is nonetheless a powerful thing because it shapes the actions of historical agents. For these reasons, terms such as "generation gap" and "youth culture" are useful terms to help us understand and analyze the long sixties, though we must acknowledge that factors such as race, class, and gender led to divergent experiences among Canadian youth. And while the student radicals did not represent the entire Baby Boom generation, I argue that they constituted a visible and influential element, and it was these youth that church officials courted in their attempts to dialogue with the youth generation.

But what about the church officials that courted the New Left? The narrative of secularization in the sixties suggests that they were rapidly becoming irrelevant. The 1950s, we are told, was an age of faith, but the inevitable march of modernity led to secularization in the 1960s. Both Roman Catholic and mainline Protestant denominations had been unofficial "national churches" up to the 1950s, but they were subsequently marginalized in the public sphere. The growing public sector rendered many of their services unnecessary – in education, health, and charity. Furthermore, most Canadians no longer found Christian beliefs or practices to be relevant to the modern age, leading to a sharp decline in church attendance in the 1960s. People turned their attention to the problems of the secular world and sought secular solutions. Church officials had, at best, a marginal role in this discourse.

The basic assumption in this narrative is the "secularization thesis": the idea that modernity inevitably leads to a decline in religious faith and a marginalization of religious institutions. This was not a new theory in the sixties; since the late nineteenth century, social thinkers such as Durkheim, Marx, and Weber had "all believed that religion would gradually fade in importance and cease to be significant with the advent of industrial society."[37] But for sociologists of religion in the 1960s, such as Peter Berger and Bryan Wilson, the secularization thesis seemed particularly applicable to their day and age.[38] As they observed the decline of both religious observance and the social influence of major religious bodies throughout the Western world, the secularization thesis seemed to provide an explanatory framework. The modern world, it seemed, was intrinsically secular, and the church belonged to a world of the past.

Since the 1970s, the secularization thesis has come under intense scrutiny. The persistence of spirituality in the 1970s, often in new and unconventional forms, forced sociologists to reconsider this assertion, as did the rise of the Christian Right in 1980s America. Writing in the 1990s, José Casanova argued that religion had been "privatized" throughout the Western world in the 1960s (i.e., that religious faith did not disappear but became a personal, private matter, decoupled from the public sphere), but that subsequent decades witnessed "the deprivatization of religion."[39] More recently, the strength of Islam in advanced industrial nations, and the emergence of a new "Christendom" in the global south, led sociologists of religion such as Peter Berger to rethink their earlier assertions.[40]

Not only have critics questioned the extent of secularization; they have also questioned the meaning and nature of "secularization" – a problematic concept because of its multiple meanings. The past two decades have yielded several important explorations of the history and current trajectory of secularization in North America and Western Europe.[41] Of these, Charles Taylor's *A Secular Age* provides both useful definitions of secularity and a helpful explanatory framework for understanding religion in the 1960s. In the first sense of the word, secularity means that "public spaces ... have been allegedly emptied of God, or of any reference to ultimate reality." In the second sense of the word, "secularity consists in the falling off of religious belief and practice, in people turning away from God, and no longer going to Church." But Taylor is most concerned with secularity in a third sense, which "would focus on the conditions of belief. The shift to secularity in this sense consists, among other things, of a move from a society where belief in God is unchallenged and indeed, unproblematic, to one in which it is understood to be one option among others, and frequently not the easiest to embrace. In this meaning, as against sense 2, at least many milieux in the United States are secularized, and I would argue that the United States as a whole is." In other words, the most salient feature of a secular society is not necessarily that belief itself is eroded (though Taylor acknowledges that this will be true for a portion of the population), but that belief is optional, and that the modern believer is rarely without doubts.[42]

Taylor's explanation of secularization, and how it takes place, is remarkably consistent with McLeod's equally insightful *Religious Crisis of the 1960s*, with its exploration of long-term, medium-term, and short-term processes. While both McLeod and Taylor see the long sixties as an era of significant change, they regard that time period as marking not the beginning of secularization, but the culmination. Taylor traces the rise of secular thought from approximately 1500, beginning with the rise of Renaissance humanism. However, the move toward an individualistic, voluntary approach to religion takes place later, beginning approximately in the late seventeenth century. A further watershed occurs in the 1960s, which Taylor identifies as the beginning of "the age of authenticity." In this age of expressivist individualism, the "religious life or practice that I become part of must not only be my choice, but it must speak to me, it must make sense in terms of my spiritual development as I understand this."[43] In other words, beginning in the long sixties, for many in the Western world, spirituality becomes a subjective, private journey.

The result, Taylor argues, is a society in which people may continue to believe but do not see the need to participate regularly in a community of faith. Very often, the belief system that they retain can be described as "diffusive Christianity" – a term Taylor borrows from John Wolffe. Wolffe defines diffusive Christianity as "a vague non-doctrinal kind of belief: God exists; Christ was a good man and an example to be followed; people should lead decent lives on charitable terms with their neighbours." Even more important, the churches are looked upon "with apathy rather than hostility," and it is acknowledged that "their social activities made some contribution to the community."[44] Furthermore, even those who don't hold religious beliefs admire those who do, especially those who are motivated by their faith to perform some noble deed.

Thus, we see that secularity is characterized by a plurality of options, a feature that was intensified by the expressive individualism of the long sixties. People in an individualistic society can freely choose to be atheists or agnostics; indeed, since the 1960s, this has been an increasingly viable option throughout the Western world, including Canada.[45] But they may also choose to participate in a community of faith, or to chart their own spiritual path. In a secular age, institutional religion is undeniably threatened, but it still has a role to play, even if it is largely vicarious. Furthermore, personal spirituality still persists in modern societies. Finally, as sociologists of religion since the 1970s have noted, a decline in religion's public role is neither inevitable nor irreversible.

While recent scholars have offered us a more nuanced understanding of secularization, few deny that the long sixties were a time of crisis for institutional Christianity throughout Western nations. Most agree that churches in these countries – in particular, the largest denominations – entered a period of decline, both in numbers of adherents and in the social authority they wielded in the public sphere. As I explain further in chapter 2, Canada is no exception. Most historians of religion in postwar Canada agree that the sixties were a watershed decade for this country's churches. For example, Gary Miedema argues that "the long process of secularization in Canada from the Victorian period on" is characterized by "years of ebbs and flows," and that the visible decline of "Christendom" chiefly takes place in the postwar period, particularly the 1960s. It was then "that the historic privileging of Christianity in Canadian national public life began very visibly to crumble."[46] While the declining fortunes of institutional Christianity in Canada and elsewhere were not absolute, inevitable, or irreversible, they were nonetheless very real in the long sixties.

What is the significance of these frameworks of secularization for this study? Clearly, if declining religious adherence and influence were intrinsic to modern Canadian society in the sixties, then it would seem unlikely that any church leader could engage successfully with young student radicals, or that Christian youth organizations such as the SCM could play a formative role in shaping Canada's New Left. But if Charles Taylor's framework is correct, then churches and religious organizations still could play a role, even in a secular age. Older progressive church members and young Christian radicals could make common cause with secular radicals who, in turn, would welcome their faith-based activism. Often, this engagement would be facilitated by a common discourse of "diffusive Christianity," which would provide a shared framework for morality and ethics. I contend that Taylor's framework is correct and Christian engagement with – and in – Canada's New Left was substantial and consequential.

ORGANIZATION

The subsequent chapters are laid out chronologically, though in some instances it will be necessary to reach backward or forward in time to provide the context for the story. Chapters 2 and 3 set the stage for the events that follow in 1965 and beyond. The second chapter begins with an overview of institutional Christianity in Canada, and the challenges it faced in the long sixties. Chapter 2 also introduces the three major denominations in this study (Roman Catholic, United Church of Canada, and Anglican Church of Canada), and the SCM. Briefly, it explores their relevant histories to the end of 1964, including the social, political, and theological developments that provide a context for their engagement with the New Left. Chapter 3 begins in the late 1950s, focusing on the origins and early development of student activism in Toronto and the role that Christianity played in these formative years. Chief attention is given to participation of the SCM in the Combined Universities Campaign for Nuclear Disarmament (CUCND) and the Student Nonviolent Coordinating Committee (SNCC).

The next five chapters centre on the core period of this study. Chapter 4 covers the years 1965 and 1966 and centres on the formal establishment of the New Left in Canada. It also examines the response of Catholics and mainline Protestants to youth political radicalism and the context for their response: a new, outward-looking theology. Most of all, it explores the continuing, integral role of the SCM in the campus left (as well as the emergence of new, more politicized Christian youth organizations, such as Kairos and Summer of Service) and the identity crisis of the SCM in the mid sixties. Chapters 5 and 6 cover the most turbulent years in this study, 1967 to 1969, years in which the New Left flourished, as young people sought control of their universities and opposed the Vietnam War. Chapter 5 explores the evolving place of young radical Christians in the broader New Left, both at the organizational level and the individual level. Chapter 6 considers the way that older Christians – church hierarchies, progressive clergy, and active lay members – addressed issues of concern to young activists, especially the Vietnam War. Chapters 7 and 8 cover the years 1970 to 1975 through the lens of "liberation," exploring how Canadian churches and the SCM responded in the early seventies to the challenges of the New Left and movements spawned by the New Left. Chapter 7 focuses on third-world liberation, Canadian left nationalism, and the Vietnam War, while chapter 8 focuses on women's liberation and gay liberation.

The concluding chapter looks beyond 1975 to consider the long-term impact of the long sixties on Canadian Christianity. Canadian churches experienced considerable changes in the decades that followed the long sixties, and in some denominations the ecclesiastical overhaul has been nothing short of transformative. These changes cannot be attributed solely to the churches' interactions with youth in the long sixties. Nevertheless, I contend that because Canada's mainline Protestants, and some progressive Roman Catholics, engaged with the New Left, the young radicals left an imprint on mainstream Christianity, especially the United Church of Canada. Moreover, I argue that if we are to understand the changes that Canadian churches have undergone since the seventies, we need to look at the specific ways in which they engaged with radical youth and their concerns in the long sixties.

2

The Twilight of Christendom

Canadian Christianity in Changing Times

For most Canadian children growing up in the 1940s and 1950s, church attendance was a normative part of their experience. In *Fragmented Gods*, Reginald Bibby, born in 1943, paints a picture of the Sunday morning ritual, circa 1946: "My father and mother bundled the three of us preschoolers into their 1938 Chev, setting out for the First Nazarene Church." At the same time, their neighbouring families, sporting their "Sunday best," were leaving to attend Roman Catholic, Anglican, and United churches. As Bibby writes, "it seemed the natural thing to do," not only in his Edmonton neighbourhood but across the country.[1]

Two examples illustrate just how pervasive church could be for this generation of children and youth. The Canadian singer-songwriter Bruce Cockburn, born in 1945, recalls that he was raised in a "secular household," but his family still attended Southminster United Church in Ottawa "because that's what was expected of us. This was the fifties. There was a need to observe the social norms to keep people from calling you a Communist." Cockburn was baptized, and as a child, he attended Sunday School at Westboro United Church, for which he composed a "jazz liturgy" in his teen years with the encouragement of his music teacher, who was the church organist.[2] James Laxer, born in 1941, had a less conventional upbringing; he was raised in a Communist household, and his father, the son of an Orthodox Jewish rabbi, was an atheist. But Laxer's maternal grandfather had been a Methodist missionary to China, and consequently, Laxer periodically attended Deer Park United Church in Toronto with his grandparents, and for a time, he and his siblings attended Sunday School at a United church near his parents' house.[3] The stories of Cockburn and Laxer show that Christianity was ubiquitous in postwar Canada, even for children raised in ostensibly "secular" or explicitly atheist homes.

Thus, the generation that would come of age in the sixties grew up in an era of ascendant Christianity, with Canada's largest denominations functioning as an unofficial religious establishment. By the early sixties, how well equipped were these churches, and related youth organizations such as the SCM, to engage with this generation of youth? Were they prepared to engage with the social and political concerns of these young Canadians, particularly those who, like James Laxer, gravitated to the New Left? Furthermore, while the religious establishment still appeared robust in the early sixties, there were worrisome indicators that Canadian "Christendom" was no longer secure. Were Canada's leading churches and Christian youth organizations prepared to navigate the challenging social and political currents of the era?

This chapter attempts to answer these questions by assessing the state of Canadian Christianity up to 1964 – after the momentous changes of the era had begun, but shortly before they would make their greatest impact on Canadian schools, homes, churches, and society at large. My purpose is to provide sufficient historical context and "set the stage" for subsequent chapters, in which I explore the relationship between Christianity and the New Left in the long sixties. While historical context necessitates some discussion of the nineteenth and early twentieth centuries, most of the focus is on the postwar period from the mid-forties to the mid-sixties with special attention to the role and status of institutional Christianity in Canadian society, including the extent to which it functioned as priestly "establishment" or prophetic social critic. I begin with a general overview of twentieth-century Canadian Christianity, and its shifting social position in an increasingly secular age. I follow with a more detailed presentation of four Christian institutions up to 1964, in particular to their development in Toronto: the Roman Catholic Church, the Anglican Church of Canada, the United Church of Canada, and the SCM.

I contend that in the early 1960s, there were troubling signs for Canada's leading denominations, which began to lose their place of exclusive privilege in the public sphere and, in some cases, witnessed the onset of a decline in religious observance. Nevertheless, in many respects, Canadian Christianity still appeared relatively robust, both in numbers and influence, and Canada's churches and religious institutions seemed well positioned to engage with the issues and concerns of youth. The fortunes of Canadian Christianity would change significantly from the mid sixties onward. Whether they knew it or not, by 1964, Canadians were living in the twilight years of Christendom. The different ways that Canadian churches would navigate these changes helped to shape their response to the youth-based protest movements of the era.

CRACKS IN THE EDIFICE: CANADIAN CHRISTENDOM TO 1964

For several decades, historians of religion in Canada have debated the nature and timing of secularization. In the 1980s and 1990s, much of the debate centred on whether or not Canada's Protestant churches were declining in social significance in the late nineteenth and early twentieth centuries.[4] However, more recent works on the declining fortunes of Canadian Christianity focus on postwar developments, with special attention to the sixties.[5] Gary Miedema argues that "the long process of secularization in Canada from the Victorian period on" is characterized by "years of ebbs and flows," and that the visible decline of "Christendom" chiefly takes place in the postwar period, particularly the 1960s. It was then "that the historic privileging of Christianity in Canadian national public life began very visibly to crumble."[6] As noted in chapter 1, many scholars agree that the sixties were a watershed decade for Canada's churches. By the early 1960s, there were troubling indications that both Catholic and mainline Protestant churches were headed for a crisis of decline, in both membership and public authority, and after the mid-1960s, these indications would become difficult to ignore.

In the late 1940s and 1950s, Canada's Catholic and mainline Protestant churches appeared to be moving from strength to strength. Sunday School enrolments were booming, churches were expanding their facilities and building bigger sanctuaries, and membership was on the rise. Between 1946 and 1956, membership "in all mainline denominations" increased, Doug Owram notes, "both in absolute terms and as a percentage of the adult Canadian population." Both John Webster Grant and Doug Owram argue that this strength was somewhat illusory, and attributable to the Baby Boom and the conservative social climate of the 1950s.[7] Nevertheless, the growth was real. Between 1951 and 1961, reported membership in the United Church of Canada rose by 24.3 percent from 834,118 to 1,036,936, and reported Anglican membership similarly rose by 24 percent, from 1,095,875 to 1,358,459.[8] In the same ten-year period, Canada's Roman Catholic population increased by 37.5 percent, from 6,069,496 to 8,342,826, thanks in part to high birth rates among Catholic families and large-scale immigration.[9]

Statistics for the early sixties, however, suggest a mixed picture. While Canada's major Protestant churches continued to gain members until the mid-1960s (Anglicans and Presbyterians reached peak membership in 1964, while United Church membership peaked in 1965), attendance figures told another story.[10] According to Gallup polls, 45 percent of Canadian Protestants reported that they attended church at least once a week in the mid-1950s, but by the mid-1960s, that figure had dropped to less than 30 percent.[11] Attendance was substantially higher for Canada's Roman Catholics: 85 percent reported attending at least once a week in 1960, and 83 percent in 1965, but by 1970, reported weekly attendance had plummeted to 65 percent.[12] Furthermore, in each of Canada's "big three" Protestant churches (Anglican, United, Presbyterian), the early sixties witnessed a steady decrease in the number of parents choosing to have their children baptized or to enroll them in Sunday School. In all three denominations, the decline in baptisms and Sunday School enrolment began in or shortly after 1961 – a particularly troubling indicator that these churches would play a less significant role in the lives of Canadian children in the years to come.[13] Likewise, while it had been common in each of these Protestant churches for young people to make "professions of faith" (a rite of passage on the road to becoming adult members of their faith communities), in the 1960s, the numbers of young people making professions of faith were far fewer than expected.[14] For Canada's largest Protestant churches, the statistics would become decidedly more gloomy from the mid-1960s onward, and the same is true for Roman Catholics, but to a lesser extent. In short, Canada's postwar religious revival had reached its peak by the early sixties, to be followed by a reversal of fortunes that would only accelerate as the decade wore on.

In addition to these statistics, there was growing evidence in the late 1950s and early 1960s of the declining public role and perceived relevance of Canada's mainline churches. The most dramatic example of this was Quebec's Quiet Revolution, when the province took over responsibility for health and education from the Roman Catholic Church. At the same time, key institutions in Quebec society severed their connections with the Church – notably the Confédération des travailleurs Catholiques du Canada, which became the secularized Confédération des syndicats nationaux in 1960. Significantly, these transitions took place with the approval and cooperation of the Quebec hierarchy of the Church, undoubtedly for pragmatic, financial reasons, but also because of new philosophical developments within Catholicism.[15] In English Canada, the diminished public influence of mainstream Protestantism was evident in several ways: in the increasingly secular and pluralistic academic world; in the weakening of laws restricting Sunday activities; and, arguably, in the demise of public symbols of Canada's British Protestant heritage (particularly the replacement of the Red Ensign with a new Canadian flag, which was the subject of a protracted public debate in 1964).[16]

As Hugh McLeod has shown, these developments were not unique to Canada. Across the Western world, throughout the sixties Roman Catholics and mainline Protestants experienced a decline both in numbers and in the social authority of their institutions. The same factors that McLeod identifies for European Christendom were at work in Canada: long-term factors such as the gradual societal shift throughout the twentieth century from a traditional value system to a liberal, humanistic one; and interrelated medium-term factors such as postwar affluence and the leisure opportunities it offered, and new patterns of home and community life.[17] In Canada, as elsewhere, the structural causes of religious decline long pre-dated the sixties. Nonetheless, the suddenness of religious decline in that decade seemed remarkable and alarming to observers, particularly following on the heels of a triumphal era for Canada's largest Christian churches.

Thus, by 1964, the year that the youngest cohort of Baby Boomers came of age, Canadian Christendom was in trouble. Many of that cohort had childhood memories from the 1950s of newly constructed or newly renovated churches, where they sat in pews during well-attended services or learned Bible stories in their Sunday School classes. Church, like school, had been one of the pillars of the establishment, and a key part of childhood socialization. But since the early sixties, many from their generation chose to forego the expected religious rites of passage (i.e., confirmation or professions of faith), and in the years to come, many would disappear from church. They had witnessed the peak of postwar religiosity, and by 1964, as decreasing numbers of the final wave of Baby Boomers were baptized or enrolled in Sunday School, they were witnessing its decline. Their generation did not bear primary responsibility for the religious crisis of the 1960s, but they played a part in it. Even if these Baby Boomers had not gravitated to movements of political and social dissent, Canada's religious establishment would have still faced significant challenges. The youth rebellion of the sixties was simply one more challenge, albeit a substantial one, for Canadian Christendom in an era of momentous change.

From the vantage point of the twenty-first century, when scholars have confidently asserted that Canadian Christendom is "no longer a reality,"[18] the sixties might appear to be halcyon years for Canada's churches. Compared to the present day, Canada's churches in the early to mid-sixties were still relatively robust and well attended. Membership numbers (if not attendance numbers) reached their peak. When denominational leaders or prominent clergy spoke out on social issues, Canadian media paid attention. In public schools, religious instruction, often explicitly Christian in nature, was still commonplace.[19] Nevertheless, cracks were beginning to appear in the edifice of Canadian Christendom, and even more substantial challenges lay ahead. But the ways in which Canada's churches navigated these challenges would differ from one denomination to another. Each had its own organizational structure, its own history of interaction with the state and with the broader culture, and its own heritage of "priestly" or "prophetic" religion. In responding to the new challenges, each built on particular traditions of theology and social engagement. Their responses were also shaped by new developments within the religious institutions themselves.

THE ROMAN CATHOLIC CHURCH

The Roman Catholic Church is, and always has been, Canada's largest religious denomination. Historically, the Church was strongest in the province of Quebec, particularly in the city of Montreal, where the devotional revolution of the mid-to-late nineteenth century established a religious tone that lingered until the 1950s.[20] The Church was also relatively strong in parts of English Canada, particularly in Toronto. Formed as the Diocese of Toronto in 1841, Toronto's Catholic community grew rapidly, due to an influx of Irish immigrants. The community expanded again in the twentieth century, and became much less homogeneous, as successive waves of immigration brought a large number of Italians, as well as other continental Europeans, to Toronto.

Thus, in the 1960s, Toronto was the seat of the largest Catholic archdiocese in English Canada, with a diverse constituency.[21]

The priests and religious orders of the archdiocese ministered to this constituency not only in its churches but also in its elementary and secondary schools. According to one source, in the early 1950s (before the incorporation of the Metropolitan Separate School Board in 1953), "Catholic education was offered in fifty-five schools, six of which were high schools, with an enrolment of 18,322 pupils."[22] The Church also had a presence in post-secondary education: St Michael's College, operated by the Basilian Fathers. As a federated college of the University of Toronto, it offered undergraduates the opportunity to live and learn in a Catholic educational community (with faculty such as the sixties media guru and devout Catholic Marshall McLuhan) nestled within a larger, secular university. It also provided training for the priesthood and graduate-level studies in theology. Beyond the college, there was the Newman Club – located in a sprawling Victorian mansion on the University of Toronto campus – which served as a social and spiritual centre for Catholic students. Through these means, the Roman Catholic Church maintained a consistent presence in the lives of young people throughout Toronto.

The governance of the Roman Catholic Church has always been hierarchical, and strictly clerical. Until the 1960s, when one spoke of "the Church," one thought primarily of the pope (Christ's representative on earth), the cardinals, bishops, and archbishops (successors of the original apostles), and priests (conferred with divine authority to dispense the sacraments necessary for salvation). As the one true Church, it was the collective responsibility of these men to preserve and to teach spiritual truth. The laity were expected to be active and involved, and a plethora of Catholic organizations existed to channel the energies of the community. Nevertheless, these organizations always required the guidance, or at least the approval, of the religious hierarchy. In the eyes of many outside critics, and a growing number of inside critics, the Roman Catholic Church at the end of the 1950s appeared to be insular, inflexible, and insufficiently attuned to the challenges or needs of the modern world.

The restive critics within the Church were encouraged in 1959 when the new pope, John XXIII, called for a council of bishops to meet in Rome.[23] The Second Vatican Council, held between 1962 and 1965, was an opportunity for the Catholic hierarchy to re-examine fundamental assumptions about the nature of the Church and its relationship with the world, and to engage the Church in the process of *aggiornamento* ("bringing up to date"). Many Canadian bishops were strong advocates for reform at the Council. The proceedings of the Council and the issues that it raised also received ample coverage in Canadian Catholic periodicals, such as the *Canadian Register*, based in Toronto and Kingston.

The reforms that emerged out of Vatican II were significant for the Church in Canada and throughout the world. The Mass could now be celebrated with the priest facing the people, and in the vernacular rather than in Latin. Permission was granted for experimental forms of liturgy, and new music was incorporated into weekly Masses. These changes reflected a fundamental shift in understanding the Church as "the people of God." The new theology of Vatican II affirmed the importance of the laity, acknowledging their ministerial role within the Church. Vatican II also established a new, conciliatory tone toward Protestants and Orthodox Christians, and with the ultimate aim of Christian unity, the Church now called for "dialogue" with these "separated brethren." Indeed, "dialogue" was a word frequently employed by Catholics in the 1960s, as was "renewal." These two words encapsulate the spirit of Vatican II, and in the sixties, this spirit permeated the Church. In progressive Catholic journals and newspapers, such as *Maintenant* in Quebec and the *Canadian Register* in Ontario, vocal lay members and clergy expressed their desire for dialogue with the contemporary world, and radical renewal of the Church. As the Church entered the mid-1960s, it embarked on a period of rising expectations. As we shall see in subsequent chapters, young Canadian Catholics, especially those that gravitated to the political left, would share in the excitement and expectations sparked by Vatican II.

In their desire to engage with the modern world, Catholics in the 1960s would begin to pay greater attention to social justice issues. In doing so, Canadian Catholics built on a heritage of social Catholicism. In his 1891 encyclical, *Rerum Novarum*, Pope Leo XIII had condemned socialism because it attacked private property. However, he supported labour rights: to form unions, to receive a just wage, and to work in decent conditions. Leo believed that the common good took precedence over individual gain, and if necessary, the state should intervene to protect the common good. Writing forty years later in *Quadragesimo Anno*, Pope Pius XI elaborated on Leo's social teaching. He recognized that workers endured an unjust economic system, but like his predecessor, Pius rejected socialism and communism.

Instead, he called for a "corporatist" system in which the workers would share in both the profits and direction of industries.[24] Catholic social thought in the early twentieth century was also shaped by the new philosophy of "personalism," which emphasized the dignity and value of human persons and personal engagement. In Quebec, personalism was the philosophical underpinning for the various Catholic Action groups, and its tenets were consistent with the tenor of papal social teaching.[25] For Catholics on the left, the legacy of Catholic social thought cut two ways. On the one hand, it discouraged support for the radical left and discouraged strike actions. On the other hand, it placed the Church squarely on the side of the poor and criticized fundamental aspects of the capitalist system. And for Catholic youth of the 1960s, the personalist orientation of Catholic social thought would provide a link to the humanistic New Left.

In the Archdiocese of Toronto, social Catholicism had been manifest in several ways. In the 1930s, it had been evident in the work of Catherine de Hueck at Friendship House. Inspired by the left-leaning Catholic Worker movement, and by her personal contacts with Dorothy Day and Peter Maurin (the movement's American directors), de Hueck ran an outreach mission, and on one occasion led a demonstration against a prominent Catholic employer, protesting unfair wages. Like her mentor Dorothy Day, Catherine de Hueck also endured rumours that she was a communist.[26] Social Catholicism was also evident in the pages of the *Catholic Register* (later the *Canadian Register*). Under the editorship of Henry Somerville in the 1930s, readers were advised to give serious thought to the issues raised in the Regina Manifesto of the CCF, and Archbishop McGuigan was advised against condemning the CCF, notwithstanding papal opposition to socialist parties.[27] The paper retained its leftward slant into the 1960s, under the editorship of P.A.G. McKay.[28] Thus, as they entered the era of Vatican II, many within Toronto's Catholic community already embraced a socially critical, "prophetic" Christianity – a factor that predisposed some young Toronto Catholics to engage in left activism in the sixties.

One possible reason for the strength of "prophetic" Catholicism in Toronto was the subordinate social and cultural status of the Roman Catholic Church in Ontario. Numerically, Ontario's Catholics were by no means marginal. At the time of Confederation, they constituted 17 percent of the province's population, and by the 1960s, they were 30 percent. And Roman Catholic separate schools continued to be publicly funded up to grade ten, though not generously, in accordance with the federal constitution. Nevertheless, the dominant culture of Ontario, forged in the nineteenth century and continuing well into the twentieth, was broadly Protestant. Anti-catholic sentiment was implicit in the culture, and occasionally made explicit. Among social, cultural, and economic elites of English Canada, Protestants were over-represented, and Catholics under-represented. Consequently, although Catholicism might have been the most "priestly" religion in terms of its hierarchical structure, historically, it did not enjoy the same privileged position in English Canada as the Anglicans or the United Church of Canada.[29]

THE ANGLICAN CHURCH OF CANADA

From 1791 until 1854, the Church of England was the established, state-supported church in what is now Ontario. In many respects, however, the Anglican Church remained an unofficial "establishment" church in Ontario for a century thereafter, a status it shared with the Methodists, Presbyterians, and later the United Church of Canada. It did not always share this status willingly; in the tenacious view of many Anglicans, the church still remained *the* establishment, and the legitimate face of English-Canadian Christianity. Though it was not the largest Protestant denomination in the province (that distinction was held by the Methodists, and later by the United Church of Canada), it was the largest religious grouping in the city of Toronto until the Second World War, and it remained the church of choice for many in the province's political, legal, and business elites.[30] And even more than their Protestant rivals, Canadian Anglicans constructed an identity that was closely bound with the nation and empire. Anglican churches such as Toronto's St Paul's, Bloor Street, were replete with the symbols of English-Canadian nationalism and British imperialism.[31] In many ways, the Church saw itself not only as defender of the faith, but of Canada's British heritage as well.

The imperial ties were abundant. From its first general synod in 1893 until 1955, the denomination styled itself "the Church of England in Canada," even though the British church had no jurisdiction over it.[32] The Church retained the prayers for the reigning monarch and all his/her ministers of government. It also retained the Book of Common Prayer, and every Sunday at Morning Prayer, Holy Eucharist, or Evensong, Canadian Anglicans uttered the same prayers, in the same Elizabethan wording, that their British co-religionists had been praying since the time of Thomas Cranmer. Not only the prayers, but the hymns, choral music, vestments, and even the architecture itself, all reflected the Church in the "Mother Country." Other reminders of the imperial British legacy in the Canadian church were the structure of the denomination itself (i.e., dioceses containing many parishes), the Church's close connections with prominent private schools modeled on famous British "public" schools, and the presence of many immigrants from Britain and other Commonwealth countries.

The Diocese of Toronto held a central place in the denomination because a substantial portion of all Canadian Anglicans dwelled within its boundaries. Toronto Anglicans also had financial clout. As Robert Merrill Black notes, the Canadian Church gained independence from British Anglican funding agencies in the 1940s, largely because of Toronto's efforts. Toronto was, according to one observer, "the tail which wagged the dog of the Canadian Church."[33] While the diocese covered an area much wider than the boundaries of Toronto, including Midland in the northwest, Algonquin Park in the northeast, and Brighton in the southeast, the strength and wealth of the diocese were situated in the city. In the 1950s, the balance was beginning to shift to the new suburbs, where new parish churches were being erected and pre-existing churches were expanding.[34] However, the historic congregations in the heart of the city still remained influential. Among these was the Church of the Holy Trinity in Trinity Square, known for its commitment to social justice issues, notably under John Frank (rector from 1935 to 1962), a strong CCF supporter who established a Social Action Committee at the church, and his successor James Fisk (rector from 1962 to 1976). Under Fisk, the church welcomed "all who were outcasts in conventional Anglicanism," including "the skid row men, artists, the mentally disturbed and alienated, political radicals, and especially women and gays."[35]

The Church of the Holy Trinity is one example of a parish that aimed to be more "prophetic" than "priestly," and it cultivated connections with young New Left activists in the 1960s and early 1970s. But in the postwar years, Holy Trinity was a striking exception to the rule. It is true that some Anglicans vocally advocated a social-democratic political agenda, especially those in the Anglican Fellowship for Social Action.[36] It is also true that some Anglicans were experimenting with new forms of worship and outreach.[37] However, as Canada entered the 1960s, the radicals and experimentalists were not the dominant face of Anglicanism. Many Anglicans and their churches were cautious and conservative, and some still conformed to the image of hidebound Tory traditionalists, fighting a rearguard action in defence of a British, Christian Canada, and in defence of their "priestly" privileged status.

The tentative, gradual shift to a more prophetic Christianity was underway by the early 1960s. In part, this was a response to the declining fortunes of the denomination. For example, in the Diocese of Toronto, following 1962, numbers of adherents, which had reached a high of about 236,000, began to slip.[38] As Alan Hayes argues, with "an increase in non-Christian immigration to Canada and a secularization of the Canadian ethos, fewer Anglicans could conceive of their Church entirely according to the English model of Anglicanism as the spiritual bulwark of civil society ... In a post-Christian Canada, fewer saw the Church as the bulwark of society; more saw it as one special interest group among others. Politicians no longer identified themselves as Church members or the friends of Church interests. Bishops could no longer count on an audience with their provincial premier. Synods, when they gathered every year or two, might still vote impassioned resolutions on the issues of the day, but government ministers had ceased to tremble at their word."[39]

Anglicans were also challenged by developments in theology. In the nineteenth century, evangelical Anglicans (who believed in the necessity of conversion, a greater role for the laity, and interdenominational cooperation) fought a protracted, bitter war against "high church" Anglicans (who placed a greater emphasis on the sacraments, liturgy, and exclusive claims of the Church).[40] These battles left a legacy; Toronto boasted two colleges for educating Anglican clergy: Wycliffe College (evangelical) and Trinity College (high church). Both were affiliated with the University of Toronto (and faced each other across Hoskin Avenue on the University of Toronto campus), and in addition to ministerial training, Trinity also functioned as an undergraduate college. Furthermore, many of Toronto's churches still identified as resolutely evangelical and others as high church. Nevertheless, by the early twentieth century, the overt war between these parties had ceased.[41]

In its place, a new battle had emerged between theological conservatives and liberals. In the late nineteenth century, liberal Protestantism emerged partly in response to new scientific paradigms (notably Darwin's theory of evolution) and new textual critical approaches to the study of the Bible. Throughout Europe and North America, exponents of liberal theology embraced these new developments. While there is no single definition of liberal Protestantism, in general its adherents approach the Bible more critically and interpret it less literally. Consequently, they are more willing to question traditional beliefs. Furthermore, many liberal Protestants emphasize the social dimensions of the gospel, as opposed to the purely personal.[42] Conservative Protestants responded to the challenges of liberal theology by defending the traditional faith. In the early twentieth century, throughout the United States and Canada, exponents of "fundamentalism" argued vigorously for biblical inerrancy and strict adherence to Christian doctrines, understood literally.[43] The Anglican Church of Canada was not immune to these debates, and its clergy included prominent exponents of liberal, conservative, and even fundamentalist theology. More than a few found ways of reconciling a liberal understanding of the Bible with a continuing faith in the doctrines of the Anglican Church.[44] But in the 1960s, even the moderate liberal Anglicans were disturbed by the radical new "death of God" theology. The most famous expression of this new theology was the 1962 book *Honest to God*, written by the Church of England bishop John A.T. Robinson.[45]

Faced with social change, declining church membership and attendance, and the erosion of old religious certainties, Canada's Anglicans were forced to look critically at their own denomination, and to seek new ways of understanding the nature and role of the church in a pluralistic world. For a denomination that highly valued tradition and mistrusted change for its own sake, this was not a comfortable prospect. As we see in subsequent chapters, young Anglicans, such as those associated with the Anglican Young People's Association, were more comfortable with the prospect of change than many of their elders. Their efforts to nudge their church in a more "prophetic" direction challenged an institution that often seemed fiercely resistant to change.

THE UNITED CHURCH OF CANADA

Unlike the Anglicans, the United Church of Canada had a tradition of change and innovation. The Church began its life in 1925, created from a merger of Canadian Methodists and most Presbyterians. (A third of the Presbyterians refused to enter into the union, and formed the "continuing" Presbyterian Church in Canada.[46]) The union brought together two of the largest Protestant denominations in Canada, representing very different theological traditions: the Methodists who possessed an Arminian faith in the human capacity to accept or reject the grace of God; and the Calvinist Presbyterians, who believed in the sovereignty of God and the total depravity of humankind. The merger was facilitated by the liberal evangelicalism of the early twentieth century (as distinct from the fundamentalism embraced by some "continuing" Presbyterians), which de-emphasized doctrine and placed greater emphasis on ethical Christianity. It was facilitated also by the widespread conviction that the relatively young dominion of Canada required a Protestant united national church to rival the Roman Catholic Church. It was hoped that this new denomination would be the dominant vehicle of English-Canadian Protestantism, and that it would use its influence to help make Canada a truly Christian society.[47] Because only two-thirds of the Presbyterians entered into the new denomination, the Methodists were numerically dominant. Indeed, the Methodists carried into the union their faith in progress and social betterment. This Methodist heritage of progressivism, with its emphasis of social Christianity and "serving the present age," set the tone for the United Church.[48]

By the time of Church Union, progressivism was not the exclusive property of the Methodists. From the 1890s to the 1920s, advocates of the Social Gospel could be found in all of Canada's main Protestant denominations. The Social Gospel movement was strongest among Methodists, present among Presbyterians, and weak but still present among Anglicans. Building on a tradition of liberal evangelicalism, Social Gospel proponents de-emphasized the necessity of personal conversion and preached social conversion instead. In the new industrial age, they were particularly concerned with ameliorating the conditions of the urban working class. They spoke of building "the kingdom of God," that is, a society governed by Christian principles of social justice. To articulate these principles, and to propose concrete ways to put them into practice, church and labour groups allied in 1907 to create the Moral and Social Reform Council of Canada, later renamed the Social Service Council of Canada. The organization enjoyed the active support of Methodists, Presbyterians, and later the United Church of Canada.[49]

The Social Gospel was pervasive in the new denomination. Some of its most radical proponents were United Church clergy, notably the Rev. Salem Bland, who declared socialism to be "the new Christianity."[50] As well, during the 1930s, some activists within the Church (particularly those connected with the Fellowship for a Christian Social Order) endeavoured to commit the denomination to a socialist agenda.[51] Chiefly, however, the main vehicle for the Social Gospel within the United Church was the Department of Evangelism and Social Service. It is significant that the denomination grouped evangelism together with social service because it suggests that in the minds of the church's leaders, salvation of souls and social reform were of equal importance in the Church's attempt to create a truly Christian Canada.

Under the leadership of James R. Mutchmor from 1937 to 1963, the Department of Evangelism and Social Service worked to address both the personal spiritual and social components of its mission. It sponsored evangelistic crusades by Billy Graham and Charles Templeton.[52] But Mutchmor and his department also advocated national health insurance, better housing for poor Canadians, civil rights, and – without using the term itself – multiculturalism.[53] Unfortunately, Mutchmor became known to a greater extent for his attachment to moralistic causes: opposing Sunday shopping, gambling, working mothers, and, above all, the production, sale, and consumption of alcohol. While temperance and the suppression of social "vices" had been progressive causes for social reformers in the early twentieth century, by the 1940s and 1950s they seemed anachronistic and laughable rather than radical or cutting-edge. At first, his successor, J.R. Hord, appeared to carry on the moralistic legacy of the old Social Gospel, calling for restrictions on boxing and liquor advertising.[54] Within a few years, however, Hord would turn sharply from the moralistic tone of Mutchmor toward a politically radical and provocative expression of the Social Gospel.

In the early 1960s, the tone of the United Church was changing in other ways too. Following years of work, the Church began releasing its controversial new curriculum in 1962. These new materials, designed for Sunday School teaching, directly addressed the problems of biblical authority and authorship. While biblical criticism had been a staple in many theological colleges since the nineteenth century, most ministers carefully avoided raising such matters in the pulpit, for fear of offending more conservative laity. But now, "modern" theology was being introduced into curriculum for lay use. The New Curriculum was undeniably controversial, and it generated significant attention outside the denomination, signalling that the United Church was in step with the liberalism of the broader culture. However, the curriculum was released at a time of declining Sunday School enrolment, and it did nothing to reverse the trend. If anything, it may have contributed to the steep drop in enrolment after 1964, in part because of its controversial theological content but also because of the difficult level of the teaching materials.[55]

Nevertheless, by 1964, the United Church of Canada could look back on the postwar years with satisfaction. Church growth had been phenomenal, and it was secure in its status as Canada's largest Protestant denomination. It had cultivated strong youth organizations: by the mid-1950s, the church's Young People's Union claimed a membership of about 30,000 between eighteen and twenty-four years of age, and the recently created "Hi-C" attracted 20,000 teens.[56] The denomination's bi-monthly magazine, the *Observer*, had a wider circulation than any of its rivals: 335,000, well above the 283,000 copies of the *Canadian Churchman* (the Anglican monthly), and several times that of the *Canadian Register*.[57] The pronouncements of the United Church moderator, the secretary of the Board of Evangelism and Social Service, and even its prominent preachers were given ample coverage in secular newspapers such as the *Toronto Star* and the *Globe and Mail*. The denomination had a secure place in English Canada, particularly in Toronto, where the church had its headquarters on St Clair Avenue, and could boast a number of prominent congregations in the downtown core. The Church also had a secure place in post-secondary education in the city: Victoria University, federated with the University of Toronto, lay on the northeastern edge of the University of Toronto's main campus, and Victoria's theological school, Emmanuel College, trained United Church clergy to minister throughout Canada. Unlike the Anglican Church, the United Church's identity was firmly Canadian, and the prime minister himself, Lester Pearson, was a United churchman and the son of a Methodist minister. The denomination's unabashed embrace of liberal theology, its desire to be politically engaged and socially relevant, and its "tradition of untraditionalism"[58] left it well equipped to meet the challenges of the 1960s. Or so it seemed.

THE STUDENT CHRISTIAN MOVEMENT

Like the United Church of Canada, the Student Christian Movement also was characterized by liberal theology, political and social engagement, and an untraditional orientation. Nobody could accuse the

SCM of being anti-modern or otherworldly. Not a denomination but rather an ecumenical Christian student organization, the SCM drew most of its participants from Canada's mainline Protestant churches. It was established in 1921 when the student wings of the YMCA and YWCA broke away to form a new entity. Strongly influenced by the Social Gospel, these students felt that traditional religious institutions (including their parent organizations as well as the churches) were too theologically and politically conservative, and believed that a nationwide coeducational student movement would be a more effective vehicle for Christian social engagement. Their goal was to apply the teachings of Jesus to the economic and social problems of the time, and thus to build a new Christian order, or in Social Gospel terms, "the kingdom of God." Clearly, these goals were widely shared: over a thousand students and professors attended the national SCM conference in December 1922. Furthermore, within a decade, there were SCM chapters at most of Canada's major colleges and universities, and these groups enjoyed the active support of administrators from the 1920s to the 1950s. At the University of Toronto, the SCM gained increased visibility because of its ties with Hart House, where it maintained an office and where the general secretary of the University of Toronto SCM chapter often doubled as chaplain of the House.[59]

The SCM approach to Bible study – and to traditional Christian doctrine – differed markedly from that of its parent organizations. SCM members examined the Bible in an open, questioning manner, and did not shy away from the difficulties posed by modern biblical criticism.[60] The movement claimed to be "a fellowship of students based on the conviction that in Jesus Christ are found the supreme revelation of God and the means to a full realization of life." Nevertheless, it did not require that students assent to a doctrinal statement, and by the 1950s, it welcomed agnostics and non-Christians to participate fully. This openness also extended to more theologically conservative Christians, including "neo-orthodox" Protestants (influenced by the writings of theologians such as Reinhold Niebuhr) and "high church" Anglicans.[61] Students who embraced a more fundamentalist understanding of Christianity generally stayed away from the SCM, preferring instead its evangelical rival, Intervarsity Christian Fellowship (IVCF)[62] while Roman Catholics opted for the Newman clubs. In spite of the radically liberal theology of many SCM members – and in spite of their critical attitude toward the churches – for the most part, they belonged to mainline Protestant denominations and the SCM received financial support from such churches. Indeed, a significant number of these young people would go on to become clergy, and even leaders within their denominations. Archbishop Edward Scott, primate of the Anglican Church of Canada from 1971 to 1986, and Lois Wilson, the first female moderator of the United Church of Canada from 1980 to 1982, were both active in the SCM.

From its inception, Canada's SCM was part of a global network of national student Christian movements, all under the umbrella of the World Student Christian Federation (WSCF).[63] As such, the Canadian SCM was outward-looking, establishing connections with like-minded Christians in other countries through exchanges and international conferences, and nurturing a keen interest in religious, social, and political developments outside of Canada. Canada's SCM paralleled ecumenical student movements in other countries, which drew inspiration from many of the same writers and speakers and thus shared similar theological trends and social concerns.[64] This included the global movement's engagement with and, sometimes, involvement in, the radical left.

The radicalism of the Canadian movement, both theologically and politically, waxed and waned between the 1920s and the 1960s. One must remember that the movement had close (though complicated) ties with Canada's religious establishment, and that its participants included young men and women from financially comfortable, well-connected homes. These factors may have mitigated the SCM's tendencies to radicalism. Even in its more "moderate" phases, however, its members still remained keenly interested in the social application of Christianity, and to some observers, it still appeared to be an organization of "socialists at prayer." In its more radical phases, it appeared to be a subversive group, and one critic went so far as to claim that the SCM was "poisoning the student mind." (The movement responded by making "Poisoning the Student Mind" into its theme song.) The subversive potential of the group was such that the RCMP gathered intelligence on some SCM groups, SCM-sponsored events, and individuals associated with the SCM from the 1930s to the 1970s.[65] In the 1930s, for example, the SCM was one of the few venues for progressive political discourse on campus. Some feared that the organization had been infiltrated by Communists.[66] Such fears were not entirely groundless; Mendel Laxer, an active Communist Party member, took part in an SCM seminar on Christianity and politics held in Algonquin Park in the summer of 1936, where he met and fell in love with Edna

May Quentin, a missionary's daughter raised in affluence. Her political journey to the left was facilitated by the SCM, and sealed by her marriage to Laxer.[67]

However, for the most part, such "communism" as was practised within the group had its roots in Christian socialism rather than Marxism. It manifested itself in the SCM summer work camps, which began in the 1940s and continued into the 1970s.[68] Students would live together, engaging in study of the Bible, and of relevant social and political issues, from a Christian perspective. Each student would find a job, often in industry, but they would pool their wages, and money would be apportioned according to needs.[69] According to Ian Gentles, who participated in an SCM summer work camp held in Toronto in the early 1960s, the wage pool "was very radical, socialistic, but it was really based on the example of the apostles in Acts, chapter two, when they lived together and shared their possessions in common. So it wasn't Marxist, it was grounded in Christianity ... It was very egalitarian and communistic in a primitive Christian sense." He noted that the Toronto work camp shared its wage pool with another camp in which the participants were having difficulty finding summer jobs.[70] As another participant observed, it was "both early Christianity at work, and one of the few Canadian instances of successful application of the Marxist doctrine: 'From each according to his ability. To each according to his needs.'" He also noted that it was "one of the most tangible exercises in human caring [he had] ever witnessed, and it was accomplished by fairly naive university students."[71] The movement's Christian socialist impulse was also manifested in SCM communal houses, where the principles of the summer work camps (including shared goods and wages) were practised year round. One such commune was Howland House in Toronto, led by Rev. Robert Miller, study secretary for the national SCM.[72]

These examples of communal living point to another important function of the SCM: it was a close-knit fellowship, and for more than a few participants, it was a surrogate family. The organization's intellectual, theological, and political dimensions were undeniable, but the lifeblood of the SCM was its sense of community. At a local level on campuses across the country, members forged ties of friendship by studying together and living together in communal houses. Each local unit had secretaries, whose role was to assist the group, though they sometimes functioned as de facto leaders and, in the words of a former participant in the University of Toronto SCM, as surrogate parents.[73] Through SCM summer work camps and its annual conferences, these familial bonds were extended across the country. The conferences were occasions for serious study, discussion, and prayer, but also for laughter, pranks, parody musical performances, and lighthearted songs poking fun at the church, the university, or themselves. (It became customary to write a new verse each year for the SCM anthem "Poisoning the Student Mind.") The familial bonds were extended internationally when Canadians travelled abroad to WSCF conferences, and when visitors from WSCF-affiliated groups came to Canada. Furthermore, SCM members often dated each other and married, leading some to joke that SCM stood for "Society of Courtship and Marriage." Through these various means, the movement created a close-knit community, which helped to draw in and retain new members;[74] it also facilitated the social and political activism of SCM members in the long sixties.

The balance between theology and social activism shifted throughout the decades and varied from campus to campus. At the University of Toronto, the SCM branch tended to lean most heavily toward a political focus. (This was especially the case among its leadership, though not always quite so much among rank and file SCM members. Many of the latter saw the organization primarily as a venue for Bible study and intellectual discussion from a Christian perspective.)[75] While the political radicalism waxed and waned throughout the years, it began flourishing again in the late 1950s and into the 1960s. In these years, the SCM followed international theological trends, which were evident in mainline Protestant churches as well, and embraced the philosophy of Christian existentialism as articulated by Søren Kierkegaard, Dietrich Bonhoeffer, and Paul Tillich. Existentialism emphasized authenticity and commitment in an uncertain age, and provided a philosophical and spiritual basis for political action.[76]

In the late 1950s and early 1960s, it is fitting that the SCM embraced a philosophy designed to cope with an uncertain age. In these years, fundamental changes were occurring in Canadian higher education. As more students completed high school and sought postsecondary education, old universities were expanding rapidly and new ones were being created. The university environment was becoming more secular and pluralistic, and new student groups emerged dedicated to political concerns. Meanwhile, the SCM's evangelical competitor, IVCF, continued to grow. The break-up of "Christendom" posed the same challenges to the SCM on campus that it did to the churches in broader

Canadian society. The movement no longer enjoyed the privileged status that it once did, and its functions were being usurped by a plethora of other student organizations.[77] Even in 1963–64, the University of Toronto SCM could still claim an impressive number of participants (at least 1,000 according to one estimate), but it is doubtful that the organization was growing at the same pace as the university community itself.[78] By the end of 1964, both the national SCM and the University of Toronto SCM were facing a crisis of identity. Such were the challenges of living in an uncertain age.

CONCLUSION

Officially, Canada did not have an established national church between the 1860s and the beginning of the 1960s, but there was an unofficial religious establishment. It consisted of the Roman Catholic Church, as well as the largest mainline Protestant churches. Christianity was woven into the fabric of society. Clergy from mainline denominations had a privileged status, and the sermons or pronouncements of key preachers were reported in secular newspapers.[79] Young Canadians who came of age in the long sixties had grown up in the shadow of this establishment. As they began university – and as some of them became active in the radical left – they also witnessed the declining fortunes of this establishment.

Arguably, the very success of Christendom in the 1940s and 1950s contributed to its declining fortunes throughout the sixties. In postwar Canada, denominations rejoiced in their institutional strength. The youth of the sixties were undeniably familiar with institutional Christianity, but familiarity does not equal love. Charles Taylor called the 1960s "the age of authenticity," and other scholars, such as Doug Rossinow, interpret the long sixties in the same way.[80] The existential drive – to overcome "alienation" and lead more "authentic" lives – was anti-institutional by nature. And this drive was at the core of the new youth movements of the sixties, including the New Left. To reach out effectively to these dissenting young people, churches and religious organizations perceived that they needed to become less institutional, less "priestly," and more "prophetic." Such a move would be a gamble for the churches, but doing nothing would have been equally risky.

Some of Canada's religious institutions appeared better positioned than others to engage in this kind of outreach, particularly as it concerned young activists and the social and political issues that mattered to them. The Roman Catholic Church, which had begun to embark on a rapid process of modernization, seemed eager to engage with the world and more willing to listen to "prophetic" voices both from within its ranks and from outside. On the whole, Canadian Anglicans did not welcome change enthusiastically, but by the mid-sixties many clergy and active laity saw the need for their denomination to address the social and political challenges of the day. In contrast, the United Church prided itself on being a modern, untraditional church, with a history of social and political engagement. In addition, while all three of these churches had been part of the "priestly" postwar religious establishment, each harboured elements of prophetic social criticism. Sometimes, these "anti-establishment" strains were more evident at the level of the individual clergy member or congregation, but these strains facilitated connections between Canadian Christianity and the New Left. As for the SCM, it was better positioned than any single religious denomination to forge links between Canadian Christianity and the New Left. Its mandate to establish an ecumenical Christian presence on Canada's English-Canadian university campuses, and to engage with the modern world, meant that it occupied an important liminal space between Canada's religious establishment and the campus left. In the next chapter, I explore the ways that the SCM forged these strategic links between the early and mid-sixties – formative years for Canada's New Left.

3

Changing Times

Christianity and the Formation of Canada's New Left

Come gather 'round people
Wherever you roam
And admit that the waters
Around you have grown
And accept it that soon
You'll be drenched to the bone
If your time to you is worth savin'
Then you better start swimmin' or you'll sink like a stone
For the times, they are a-changin'
                        Bob Dylan, "The Times They Are a-Changin'"[1]

For many young people who came of age in the long sixties and embraced new left politics, Bob Dylan's "The Times They Are a-Changin'" could have been their anthem. In this three-minute song released on his 1964 album of the same name, Dylan employed prophetic imagery and biblical language (as he frequently did) to announce the dawn of a new dispensation. He declared that "the line it is drawn, the curse it is cast," and the old "order is rapidly fadin'." To the youth of the 1960s – and to many adult observers – there was no doubt that the line was drawn between the youth and an older generation. Whatever Dylan's intent, the words of the song, advising parents that their sons and daughters were beyond their control, and admonishing politicians not to obstruct the new currents of change, could hardly be interpreted any other way.[2]

For many parents, politicians, and pundits in the long sixties, the new political and cultural developments among youth were puzzling, disturbing, and apparently rapid. However, both the apparent disjuncture between generations and the apparent rapidity of social change obscure the gradual way in which the New Left developed, and its roots in older movements of social and political dissent. The New Left had its origins in the old democratic left, the civil rights movement, and the peace/anti-nuclear movement. Particularly significant is the contributory role that Christianity played in the origins of the New Left, especially evident in Canada where a substantial minority of participants in groups that eventually coalesced to become the Canadian New Left were members of the SCM.

This chapter explores the origins and development of the "new dispensation" up to the end of 1964 in order to set the stage for an examination of the relationship between Christianity and the New Left from 1965 to 1975. I begin with an overview of the origins and development of the New Left in the United States and Canada, with particular attention to student organizations such as Students for a Democratic Society in the United States, and Combined Universities Campaign for Nuclear Disarmament in Canada. The focus then shifts to the role of left-leaning Christians and Christian student organizations in helping to forge the New Left, with particular attention to Canada's Student Christian Movement. In the 1960s, there were many roads that led to the formation of one's identity as a radical and an activist; for many young people, the road led through the SCM. The sense of community that the SCM nurtured, combined with the political and theological currents of the era, made it fertile ground for producing young radicals. SCM participants would never constitute a majority in Canada's New Left, but in the late 1950s and early 1960s, as the movement took shape, their involvement was undeniably important. In essence, the SCM served as a midwife at the birth of Canada's New Left.

THE NEW LEFT TO 1964

In the late 1950s, the North American radical left was in a state of disarray. In both Canada and the United States, many Communists resigned from their national parties due to Khrushchev's revelations in 1956 of Stalin's atrocities and the Soviet Union's invasion of

Hungary in 1957.[3] The non-Communist left had also been weakened by McCarthy-era paranoia and was further hampered by sectarianism. Consequently, many radicals in North America and Britain expressed a desire to reinvent the left – to create a "new left."[4] In 1960, the American sociologist C. Wright Mills wrote an open letter to the British *New Left Review*, arguing that leftists in advanced capitalist countries should stop expecting "the working class" to serve as the agent of revolutionary change. Rather, in the New Left, he argued, the agents of change would be "the young intelligentsia."[5]

Mills was astute in his observations. When a new left began to coalesce in the United States at the beginning of the 1960s, many of its leaders, and the vast majority of its followers, were university students or recent university graduates. In the earliest stages of the New Left, young activists worked closely with the veterans of the Old Left. Indeed, many of the young radicals were red diaper babies, who had grown up in Communist households. However, they alienated themselves from the older generation, particularly by their unwillingness to adhere to the dogmatic party lines of the Old Left.[6] Very quickly, the New Left assumed a generational character, and the term "New Left" became virtually synonymous with the "student revolt" of the 1960s (or at least with the core groups that led that revolt).[7] Their revolt was not against the values of their politically liberal or radical parents; rather, they felt "their parents had not put those values to consistent or effective use."[8]

The key values they sought to put to consistent and effective use were democracy and equality. Much of the inspiration and impetus for the New Left in the United States and, to a lesser extent, Canada came from the struggles of young African-Americans for civil rights in the southern states. In February 1960, black students in Greensboro, North Carolina staged a sit-in at Woolworth's to protest segregation, and the movement quickly spread to other cities across the American south. Inspired by Martin Luther King, Jr, these students employed nonviolent civil disobedience to challenge unjust laws.[9] As an organizational vehicle for their activism, they established the Student Nonviolent Coordinating Committee (SNCC) in May 1960, and soon, white students from across the United States (and some from Canada) became involved. Many began their activist careers by taking part in voter registration drives and campaigns for integration in the southern states.[10] Young white activists formed chapters of Friends of SNCC on American campuses, to raise awareness, raise funds to support the work of SNCC, and enlist white volunteers to assist in southern voter registration campaigns.[11] Young white students active in the civil rights movement were appalled by the gap between American rhetoric of democracy and equality on the one hand, and the reality of southern black oppression and inequality on the other. At the same time, these young radicals recognized that these problems were not confined to the American south. The solution, as they saw it, was to be found in nurturing "participatory democracy." The latter meant that ordinary citizens, especially those in disadvantaged communities, should have the right to make decisions that affect their individual lives and communities.

Participatory democracy was at the heart of the New Left project. In 1962, Students for a Democratic Society (SDS, a small student organization that would grow to become the largest and most visible cohort in the New Left) gathered in Port Huron, Michigan to produce a manifesto for social change. One of the most important features of the *Port Huron Statement* was its call for participatory democracy: "As a *social system* we seek the establishment of a democracy of individual participation, governed by two central aims: that the individual share in those social decisions determining the quality and direction of his life; that society be organized to encourage independence in men and provide the media for their common participation."[12] The members of SDS attempted to practise participatory democracy within their own organization, an example of what Wini Breines calls "prefigurative politics."[13] They also established the Economic Research and Action Project (ERAP), in which students would work as community organizers in low-income neighbourhoods located in northern cities such as Chicago, Newark, Boston, and Cleveland. The aims were to build "an interracial movement of the poor," to eradicate poverty and racial inequality, and to extend participatory democracy.[14]

Another notable feature of the *Port Huron Statement* was its condemnation of the nuclear arms race, not only for the risks it posed to human survival but also because it demanded that Americans "sacrifice values and social programs to the alleged needs of military power."[15] While many students had entered the New Left via the civil rights movement, a significant contingent became left activists because of their involvement in campaigns for nuclear disarmament.[16] This was particularly true in Canada, where New Left student organizing was a direct outgrowth of the movement to ban the bomb. In 1959, the government of John Diefenbaker announced that Canada would obtain American Bomarc missiles, which would be armed with nuclear warheads. Later that year, Dimitri Roussopoulos, a graduate student at the London School of Economics who had returned to Montreal for a visit, suggested to his friends that they form a Canadian peace group modelled on the British organization Combined Universities Campaign for Nuclear Disarmament, with which Roussopoulos had been involved while studying overseas. Shortly thereafter, Roussopoulos and students from Sir George Williams University and McGill formed the Canadian Combined Universities Campaign for Nuclear Disarmament (CUCND).[17] On 25 December 1959, approximately eighty students gathered on Parliament Hill to protest. They left a petition opposing nuclear weapons on Canadian soil (signed by more than a thousand students and faculty) with Prime Minister Diefenbaker, and placed a wreath at the National War Memorial. Following this demonstration, a secretariat for the CUCND was established, and throughout 1960 and 1961, chapters of the organization were formed on campuses across Canada, including Toronto.[18] The CUCND had become Canada's first nationwide student peace organization.

The CUCND started its life as a single-issue pressure group rather than a movement for fundamental social change. Its proposed policies (unilateral nuclear disarmament and withdrawal from military alliances such as NATO and NORAD) would have required a substantial about-face for the government, but they would not have necessitated revolutionary change in the structures of government or society. Nevertheless, the positions that the CUCND advocated in its earliest years contained the seeds of a broader New Left critique.[19] The early CUCND also imbued the nascent Canadian New Left with its sense of urgency; as Michael Dufresne notes, the "crucible of the Canadian 60s student movement rested within the framework of an apocalyptic view of the future."[20] In its initial years, however, the CUCND was still politically liberal and reformist in its approach, and its diverse membership included some identifying as liberal, and others identifying with the radical left.

For many student activists, this distinction was an important one. While those who opposed youthful protest and activism used the term "radical" pejoratively, many in the New Left chose it willingly. It denoted a philosophical position: that one can create real change only by attacking the root of the problem. (The term *radical* is derived from the Latin word *radix*, which means "root" or "base.") Activists that identified as radicals distinguished themselves from liberals who sought gradual changes within a social and political system that they believed to be fundamentally sound. In contrast, radicals believed that there were fundamental flaws in the social and political fabric, and they were less patient with gradual change or compromise solutions. Consequently, they were willing to challenge the system in ways that often seemed imprudent to liberals, including confrontational protests and nonviolent civil disobedience. Many of the participants in the early New Left started out as liberals but were radicalized by their involvement in the peace movement, the civil rights movement, or both (personnel in these movements often overlapped).[21]

In the United States, student radicals were cautiously willing to work with American liberals, but that changed following the August 1964 Democratic National Convention in Atlantic City. At that convention, white northern radicals and southern black civil rights activists, many of whom had taken part in the Freedom Summer voter registration campaign in Mississippi in the face of brutal opposition, found that the Democrats were unwilling to risk losing southern white support. When the Democrats chose to seat the regular Mississippi delegation, rather than the Mississippi Freedom Democratic Party delegates, those in the New Left felt betrayed. Young peace activists also felt betrayed by the Democrats when, earlier the same month, President Johnson escalated American military involvement in Vietnam in response to the Gulf of Tonkin incident.[22] Previously, participants in the New Left had "tried to be fraternal critics of liberal institutions and organizations," avoiding "direct and personal confrontations in favor of arguments over issues." By the end of 1964, however, leading activists were moving toward the "position that the liberal establishment ... constitutes the most dangerous enemy we confront."[23]

A similar process of radicalization was occurring among Canadian student peace activists in 1963, chiefly as a result of political developments in that year. Although the Liberal opposition leader Lester Pearson had originally declared his opposition to nuclear arms on Canadian soil, he publicly reversed his position in January 1963, arguing that Canada should fulfill its international obligations and accept American nuclear warheads. The governing Conservatives were divided on the issue; Prime Minister Diefenbaker, after some vacillation, ultimately decided to reject nuclear warheads on Canadian soil in peacetime. While Diefenbaker's decision was strongly supported by Howard Green, minister of external affairs, it was not supported by his minister of defence, Doug Harkness, who resigned in protest. Pearson and the Liberals took advantage of Conservative disarray and precipitated an election in April.[24] During the election campaign, the Canadian Campaign for Nuclear Disarmament (a non-student peace group associated with CUCND) worked vigorously, distributing fact sheets on the nuclear issue, sponsoring meet-the-candidate evenings, and privately lobbying candidates.[25] Nevertheless, the Liberals won, and by January 1964, nuclear weapons were installed at bases in Ontario and Quebec.[26]

This turn of events had a profound effect on members of the CUCND.[27] They had been disillusioned by the parliamentary political process and could no longer believe in it as a means to effect progressive change. The system needed fundamental reform. Furthermore, they saw that peace and democracy were inextricably linked, that activists could not work for one without also working for the other, and they began to expand radically their understanding of both peace and democracy. Peace now meant not only opposition to nuclear weapons but also a complete commitment to the principles of nonviolence and faith in nonviolent civil disobedience as a strategy. And their understanding of democracy began to reflect the SDS concept of "participatory democracy." In the words of one historian of the CUCND, this meant "that all Canadians had a right and duty to make foreign policy decisions; they decided that questions of war and peace were too important to citizens to be left in the hands of government and so-called 'experts.'" The CUCND argued for "a fundamental reconstitution on the basis of the Canadian Confederation as a minimum and the changing of the constitution to allow people to have a more direct influence on these matters."[28] The CUCND also began to examine the economic structures that led communities to accept nuclear bases, and this led to a greater emphasis on the socio-economic dimensions of democracy. Thus, within the space of a year, the CUCND had transformed itself from a predominantly single-issue organization to a New Left student group similar to the SDS south of the border. Students in the CUCND were still committed to the primacy of peace but were aware that wholesale change was required to achieve it.

As noted above, radicalization meant embracing not only radical ideas but also radical strategies, and this was evident both in the United States and Canada. At the University of California, Berkeley, in the fall of 1964, attempts by the administration to prohibit political activism on campus (particularly by civil rights activists who had just returned from the Freedom Summer in Mississippi) resulted in the first large-scale campus revolt of the 1960s. The Free Speech Movement at Berkeley involved a series of protests, including prolonged sit-ins at the administration offices and rallies that drew thousands of students. By December the students had succeeded in their campaign, gaining the right to speak freely and engage in political action on campus. Their battle received ample media coverage, and student activists across the United States and Canada took note of their strategies and their successes. In the ensuing decade, confrontations between radical students and comparably conservative administrators or faculty (though they might have been ostensibly "liberal" administrators or faculty) became a frequent feature of North American campus life.[29] The New Left was beginning to take the form of a mass youth movement, and the public was taking notice.

CHRISTIANITY AND THE ORIGINS OF THE NEW LEFT

Most of the historians who have written about the origins of America's New Left focus on the role of red diaper babies; that is, the children of Communist, ex-Communist, or socialist parents, many of whom were Jewish.[30] The children of liberal parents (likewise, many of them Jewish) also figure prominently in these studies.[31] While the red diaper babies and the sons and daughters of Jewish liberals were important in shaping the movement in its early days, particularly in New York where the SDS had its headquarters until 1965, not enough attention has been paid to the role of Christianity in the origins of the New Left. The earlier non-Communist left, from which the New Left emerged, included some prominent and influential Christians. One of these was Norman Thomas, the pacifist minister who led the Socialist Party and who was widely respected by early New Leftists.[32] Another was A.J. Muste, a former Dutch Reformed minister who had served as executive director for the Fellowship of Reconciliation, a Christian pacifist organization. Though he repudiated pacifism in the 1930s when he became a Trotskyist, a mystical experience led him to return to his earlier faith and to Gandhian pacifism.[33] As one historian noted, Muste "always seemed a little too 'religious' for his political associates and too 'political' for his religious associates; too prone to mysticism for the taste of the practical minded and too prone to expedience for the taste of spiritual or political absolutists."[34] But according to Dimitri Roussopoulos (one of the founders of CUCND), his "philosophical and ideological and political impact on [the New Left] was legendary, enormous. He was an extraordinary influence."[35]

Religious influence extended beyond key individuals such as Thomas or Muste. Both the civil rights and peace movements, which provided much of the impetus for the New Left, had strong Christian roots. For the civil rights movement, these roots could be found in the spirituality of the black churches. It is no accident that young activists, both black and white, employed African-American spirituals as the anthems for their movement.[36] For the peace activists, those roots could be found in the historic peace churches (e.g., the Mennonites and the Society of Friends) and in twentieth-century faith-based social action groups such as the Fellowship of Reconciliation (FOR) or the Catholic Worker movement.[37] While the New Left was secular, in that its focus was very much on this world, it drew inspiration from spiritual traditions and values that transcended the wholly secular.

Furthermore, on many campuses across the United States, student Christian groups contributed significantly to the formation of the New Left in the early 1960s. In his study of the New Left in Austin, Texas, Doug Rossinow has shown how the Christian Faith-and-Life Community and the YMCA/YWCA served as breeding grounds for student activists. The Christian Faith-and-Life Community (CFLC) was a residential centre associated with the University of Texas, which Tom Hayden (one of the most prominent New Left activists of the early sixties) called "*the* liberated spot on the silent campus." [38] Students in CFLC were introduced to the writings of Paul Tillich and Dietrich Bonhoeffer, Christian existentialists whose theology provided a faith-based rationale for social activism. Their writings encouraged students to discover a meaningful, authentic faith that was not otherworldly but, rather, lived out in their relationships with each other and their work for social justice.[39] Students in the YMCA and YWCA were exposed to similar theological currents, but these Christian youth organizations also built on an older liberal Protestant tradition of social engagement.[40] Whether in the CFLC, YMCA, or YWCA, the path to student activism was more than an intellectual journey. Students made these journeys in the context of close-knit communities – studying together, praying together, and ultimately, working together for social change. Several of these activists ended up in Students for a Democratic Society.

In facilitating student activism, these campus Christian groups at the University of Texas were not unique. Across the United States, student Christian organizations encouraged young people to adopt an outward-looking faith, suited to respond to the needs of the world. By the early sixties, students in these groups, and many of their leaders, aligned themselves with secular, activist-oriented student associations, particularly on issues of shared concern such as civil rights and nuclear disarmament.[41] Similar dynamics were at work on campuses in Canada.

MAKING YOUNG ACTIVISTS AND SHAPING CUCND: THE ROLE OF THE STUDENT CHRISTIAN MOVEMENT

In keeping with the *zeitgeist* of the long 1960s, participants in Canada's SCM were also becoming more politically active and moving from political liberalism to radicalism. The SCM facilitated these journeys in several ways. It provided a nurturing, close-knit environment – in essence, a surrogate family. In this community setting, students were introduced to the intellectual and theological currents of the sixties, which challenged them to engage with the wider world and take action on pressing social issues. Furthermore, leading figures in the SCM maintained close ties with activist groups on Canadian campuses, particularly those involved in the African-American civil rights movement and the campaign for nuclear disarmament. While there were multiple routes to student activism, the fact remains that the SCM was a significant breeding ground for young activists. In the process, it laid the groundwork for the formation of Canada's New Left in the sixties.

In the late 1950s and early 1960s, an SCM participant's journey to the left, and to left activism, could take many forms; nevertheless, there were patterns. First, few, if any, of the SCM participants that I interviewed had parents who were active on the political left. Most described an apolitical upbringing, and some explicitly recalled that their parents' politics were anything but left-of-centre. Eilert Frerichs, who was born in Germany in 1939 and immigrated to Canada in 1956, described his mother as a "convinced Nazi" and his father as a "convinced anti-Semite."[42] His adoption of left politics was, at the very least, an implicit rejection of his parents' views. For John Alan Lee (born 1933, and active in the SCM from 1955 to 1964), the rejection of his foster parents' conservative politics was explicit. As a student at the University of Toronto in the mid-1950s, he joined the CCF (at the time Canada's largest democratic socialist party), and while he credited this decision in part to the influence of a friend, he also recalled it in his memoirs as an act of filial rebellion. "Socialism," he wrote, "provided a perfect outlet for my childhood rage, fuelling scorn for the false consciousness of a working-class 'father' who voted Conservative."[43]

Like many of their contemporaries, most of the SCM participants I interviewed grew up in Christian homes, affiliated with mainline Protestant churches. Several described their upbringing as exceptionally religious, and some could even claim impressive religious pedigrees. For example, George Hartwell (born in 1943) was the grandson of a Methodist missionary to western China, and Eilert Frerichs descended from a long line of Lutheran ministers dating back to the Reformation.[44] However, none of these interviewees credited a particular clergyman from their childhood or youth (in the 1940s and 1950s) as an influence in their political development. In general, it seems that there was little in either their home or religious upbringing to explicitly nudge them toward New Left activism.

What, then, drew them to the left and to social action? Solid answers remain elusive, even to my interviewees themselves. As Wolfe Erlichman (born in 1941) recalled, he inclined to the left even in high school, but he could not explain why.[45] Whether by nature or nurture, several of my interviewees had developed a penchant for questioning orthodoxy and challenging authority, characteristics that would render them well suited for activism. Even so, their entry into activism required a catalyst. The SCM was just such a catalyst.

University students gravitated to the SCM for many reasons. For most, it was a logical extension of their mainline Protestant upbringing. In more than a few instances, their parents had belonged a generation earlier, so joining the SCM was partly a matter of carrying on a family tradition. Even if this had not been the case, the SCM was the organization that embodied and represented mainline Protestant Christianity on Canada's campuses. They could have chosen the SCM's evangelical fundamentalist rival, IVCF, but those that opted for the SCM preferred its intellectual and theological openness. Richard Hyde (born in 1942) had been a conservative evangelical in his teenage years, and at the beginning of the sixties, in his first year at the University of Toronto, he attended Varsity Christian Fellowship. He shifted to the SCM because he found the intellectual environment preferable to VCF: "It wasn't quite as high school-y, you know, just sitting around, each reading a verse of the Bible, and each time, the leader says 'what is the Lord saying to us through this verse?'"[46] Eilert Frerichs, who began his studies at Queen's University in 1957, likewise found the SCM's intellectual environment appealing; members "were open to varieties of belief or lack thereof, and didn't have a prescribed 'statement of faith.'"[47] While the SCM included students who identified as "orthodox" (i.e., adhering to the core tenets of Christianity), it also included many students who still valued their Christian upbringing and identity but questioned basic Christian beliefs. The SCM was a safe environment to ask such questions.

The liberal theological and intellectual environment was only part of the appeal. The close-knit community that the Canadian SCM provided (similar to its counterparts in the United States and elsewhere) was of equal or greater importance in drawing and retaining students. For more than a few, the SCM functioned as a surrogate family. Eilert Frerichs, who had emigrated from Europe only a year before beginning university in 1957, appreciated the congenial intellectual setting of the SCM at Queen's University, but as a shy newcomer, he also appreciated the welcoming environment – "they were the ones that made me feel comfortable and at home."[48]

At the University of Toronto, the SCM secretaries – general secretary George Hopton and associate secretary Jane Blanchard – played an important role in fostering such a welcoming environment. Blanchard, in particular, made a strong impression due to her charismatic personality, her life experience, and her social and political engagement.[49] As a student in the early sixties, Wolfe Erlichman visited the SCM's office in Hart House with a friend. He had no intention of joining, but in the office, he encountered Blanchard (whom he described as "a character"), who engaged him in conversation and informed Erlichman that he'd be a good candidate to lead an SCM work camp. Erlichman was an agnostic Jew with little interest in Christianity, but he responded to Blanchard's welcome and soon was involved in the life of the SCM – its regular meetings, summer work camps, and annual conferences. As he recalled, he was impressed "by how receptive they were to my being there ... There certainly was a lot of Christianity and Bible study and that kind of thing. That was definitely there. But there was also the very strong social conscience thing. Jane Blanchard was very important in that aspect of it."[50] The warmth and openness of the SCM, fostered by influential figures such as Blanchard, could draw unlikely participants into the life of the community.

The warm familial nature of the SCM was particularly important to students who found their home lives comparatively lacking in warmth. John Alan Lee was raised by unaffectionate foster parents, with whom he frequently found himself in conflict. In the mid-1950s, through the socialist youth group that he led, Lee met members of Howland House (an SCM communal house in Toronto's Annex neighbourhood). This led him to take part in an SCM residential work camp at Bathurst Street United Church in the summer of 1955, where he was initiated "into the emotional warmth most children take for granted by growing up in a family." The SCM became his "family of choice," and soon he moved into Howland House, where the commune's leader, SCM study secretary Rev. Bob Miller, functioned as a father figure. Though Lee was already a socialist, it was in the Christian socialist milieu of SCM work camps and Howland House that he discovered the lived experience of socialism.[51]

Lee's experience was not unique. George Hartwell grew up in a household where intellect and rationality were valued (and modelled by his father, an expert in time-motion studies), but as Hartwell recalled, his home environment was insufficiently nurturing and did not leave ample room for expression of feelings. When Hartwell joined the University of Toronto SCM in the early sixties, he found a nurturing community, where the secretaries Hopton and Blanchard were like a surrogate mother and father "in terms of birthing me into this new place where I'm going to get to talk about ideas."[52] Hartwell's choice of words is revealing; it shows that communal and intellectual dimensions of the SCM were inextricably linked. Students discovered ideas in the context of small weekly seminars, summer work camps, communal houses, and conferences. Personal interaction was key; at the University of Toronto SCM, students learned predominantly through active participation in discussion rather than passively listening to lectures.[53] Human warmth and fellowship provided a context for intellectual growth, and consequently, political formation.

The intellectual program of the early sixties SCM, particularly in Toronto, is significant. Like their counterparts in Austin and elsewhere, students in Canada's SCM learned about existentialism. In small group seminars, students read the works of Christian existentialists including Søren Kierkegaard and Fyodor Dostoyevsky.[54] Richard Hyde, student president of the University of Toronto chapter in the early to mid sixties, recalled organizing a lecture series on existentialism, with notable speakers including Marshall McLuhan and Gregory Baum.[55]

As a philosophy that emphasized the need to create authentic meaning through action in the face of an alienating world and anxiety over one's finitude, existentialism provided a rationale for social and political engagement in the sixties. This was as true of young secular activists (who encountered existential philosophy from reading Sartre and Camus, among others) as it was of participants in the SCM (who encountered existentialism not only through secular writers but also Christian existentialists such as Kierkegaard and Tillich). Having grown up in Cold War Canada, with an omnipresent threat of nuclear annihilation, they understood anxiety over the finite nature of existence. They also understood the need to resist a culture that seemed to encourage conformity and complacency at the expense of authenticity and action.

A parody musical performed at the SCM annual banquet in 1963 provides a glimpse into the intellectual life of the SCM in the early sixties. In "My Fair Convert" (a spoof on "My Fair Lady"), the character of Liza debated whether she would be more at home in the SCM or its evangelical competitor, the VCF. She expressed her frustration with the SCM because "all they ever do about religion is sit around and talk about it. And about lots of other things too: all kinds of heathen philosophers like Sartre, Nietzsche, Bertrand Russell, and even Ayn Rand. And all kinds of weird organizations – WSCF, FROS, CUCND, WFDY, FOR, WFA, UFSC, and NDP."[56] What this parody musical reveals (aside from the SCM's longstanding fondness for self-mockery, acronyms, and self-mockery *about* acronyms) is that the intellectual content of SCM study in the 1960s was wide-ranging and, given the reference to groups such as the NDP and CUCND, that discussions frequently touched on politics and political activism.

It should come as no surprise that the SCM shifted to the left in the sixties, and that its members inclined toward political involvement and social activism. This was particularly true of the University of Toronto SCM, but the shift was perceptible across the country. One factor in this shift was the SCM's tradition of social engagement, which, in the 1920s and 1930s, had made it a congenial home for radical leftists. A more immediate factor was the role of influential figures such as Jane Blanchard, who helped shape the tone of the group and inspired younger members through her commitment to left-wing politics and social activism. Moreover, the broader student milieu – in Toronto and across North America – was a key factor. The SCM shared in the same participatory ethos that drove groups like

CUCND in Canada or SDS in the United States, and the social issues that engaged young people in these organizations also engaged participants in the Canadian SCM.

The Canadian SCM's growing engagement in political activism mirrored trends in the wider global network of student Christian movements,[57] especially the American movement. Students from across Canada took part in the quadrennial conference of the Student Volunteer Movement, held in Athens, Ohio at the end of December 1959. (The SVM was one of the groups that made up the National Student Christian Federation, which was the American counterpart to the Canadian SCM.) That event drew together more than four thousand students to hear keynote speaker Dr Martin Luther King, and in the words of one of the conference organizers, it "inspired a generation of students to become active Christians for social change." Many of the American conference participants would soon take part in lunch-time counter demonstrations across the southern United States, demonstrations that energized the civil rights movement and contributed to the formation of the New Left in both United States and Canada.[58] Significantly, participants in the Canadian SCM were motivated in their activism and radicalization by the same the issues that served as a catalyst for the wider student left in this time period, particularly the civil rights movement and nuclear disarmament.

Civil rights activism was a good fit for Christian students, both Canadian and American, who wished to work for social change. King's dream of racial equality and his commitment to nonviolence resonated with the Christian ideals of these young people. To assist in the civil rights struggle, members of the University of Toronto SCM endeavoured to establish a chapter of Friends of SNCC in late 1963 and early 1964. As with other Friends of SNCC chapters in universities across the United States, its purpose was to raise awareness by providing literature, and more importantly, to raise funds to support volunteers engaged in voter registration throughout the southern United States.[59] While supporting civil rights was not radical in itself, it was a frequently travelled route to radicalism for both Canadian and American students because it brought liberal students into association with students much further to the left and exposed them to new ideas.

Peace and disarmament activism were also a good fit for Christian students in Canada in the late fifties and early sixties. Their actions were not without precedent; a generation earlier, many Canadian

Christians, particularly those on the left, articulated a pacifist position, and more than a few were associated with the SCM.[60] Christian pacifists opposed militarism because they believed that war was inconsistent with the teachings of Jesus, who called his followers to be peacemakers. Recalling his involvement in the University of Toronto SCM and the Toronto CUCND in the early sixties, Ian Gentles explained how pacifism was the link between his Christian faith and political radicalism: "I was fairly orthodox theologically – I've become more orthodox theologically since then – but I was also very politically radical. And I was very much taken with the pacifist message of the New Testament. So I considered myself a Christian pacifist. The reason for my activity in the peace movement was because of my conviction that a Christian had to be working for peace in the world – it was a theological imperative. I'm not so sure of pacifism now, although I still have immense respect for it. But then I was utterly convinced that pacifism was the correct Christian position."[61]

SCM involvement in the postwar movement for nuclear disarmament, rooted in Christian pacifism, predated the formation of the CUCND. In November 1957, the University of Toronto SCM "passed a motion in favour of the banning of nuclear weapons for a period of three years." To follow up their words with action, and to respond to encouragement from the Indian SCM and the International Union of Students in Japan, the SCM then proceeded to invite eleven other university clubs to jointly sponsor a conference on disarmament and peace. The three-day conference, held in February 1958, drew four hundred participants and featured "addresses, panel discussions and films ... on scientific, religious, defensive and political aspects of the question."[62] Neither the initial resolution, nor the conference itself, could be described as "radical." Though the conference's organizer, twenty-four-year-old Howland House resident John Alan Lee, was a committed socialist, he went out of his way to ensure that the event was undeniably mainstream in all aspects. The conference was sufficiently mainstream to receive funding from the Students Administrative Council, to include the university vice-president Murray Ross as one of the panel chairs, and to be co-sponsored by campus Conservatives and Liberals. Significantly, the campus Communist club was not invited.[63] Nevertheless, both the resolution and the event show that the SCM was responding to international currents and was laying the groundwork for future participation with young secular peace activists, and for its own radicalization.

Interest in disarmament and peace led many SCM participants to work closely with the CUCND, almost from its inception. Eilert Frerichs, at the time a twenty-year-old student in the SCM at Queen's University, was one of the protesters in the first CUCND march on Parliament Hill on Christmas Day 1959. According to Frerichs, he became aware of the CUCND and the protest through his involvement with the SCM. (He left shortly after the Ottawa protest to attend the aforementioned conference in Athens, Ohio.)[64] This suggests that the CUCND was actively working to establish connections with like-minded groups at a very early stage. Such links were vital to the success of CUCND. CUCND co-founder Dimitri Roussopoulos recalls, "In 1959/1960/1961, the CUCND spread across this country like wildfire, from one campus to the other. I don't think there was a campus where there wasn't a CUCND chapter established, I mean, it was just incredible. One of the reasons why that happened so quickly was because of SCM on certain campuses and SCM [and] CCF groups on others. Those were very important sparks in establishing the CUCND as a national organization. There's no question about that."[65] On some campuses, there was substantial overlap in membership between CUCND and SCM local units, or at least close cooperation. Eilert Frerichs recalls significant overlap between the two groups at Queen's University, and claims that "for me, participating in the CUCND and in the SCM, they were more or less one and the same."[66] At the University of Saskatchewan, the SCM provided material support to the newly formed CUCND unit on campus. The campus SCM also formed a study group to read *Peacemaker or Powder-Monkey*, an influential book published in 1960 by Canadian journalist James Minifie, which argued that Canada should withdraw from NORAD and NATO and take no part in defence policies involving nuclear deterrence.[67]

Connections between the University of Toronto SCM and CUCND were established in February 1961. The CUCND had invited the SCM to declare its support for the group and to send two representatives to serve on the executive of CUCND. At a meeting on 22 February, the University of Toronto SCM responded affirmatively to this request. The resolution to support the CUCND also called on the Canadian government to work "for world-wide nuclear disarmament," to oppose "the spread of nuclear arms to nations not now possessing them," and to forbid "the possession and use of nuclear arms in Canada or by Canadian troops."[68] Two things are significant about the SCM local unit's decisions, embodied in this resolution. First, it marked the beginning of an ongoing relationship between the SCM and CUCND at the University of Toronto, and it appears to have strengthened the relationship between the national parent organizations. In the fall of 1963, for example, the University of Toronto SCM joined with the CUCND to present a lecture series on peace, and the national SCM sent "fraternal observers" to the CUCND conference in Montreal.[69] Second, the wording of the resolution was decidedly more categorical and less moderate than the peace resolution it passed three and a half years earlier, which merely called for a three-year moratorium on nuclear arms. Gradually, the SCM was moving toward a more radical position.

LA MACAZA

The best illustration of the SCM's integral involvement in CUCND is the protest held at La Macaza, Quebec in June 1964, and repeated again on Labour Day of that year.[70] The SCM's involvement also shows that its members participated fully in the radicalization of the peace movement, radicalization both in principles and strategies. Although Project La Macaza was not officially connected with any single peace organization, much of the leadership for the protests came from CUCND. The organizers of the initial action in June (known as "Operation St Jean Baptiste") were activists associated with the Montreal Peace Centre, including Dimitri Roussopoulos of CUCND. The target of their protests was Canadian Forces Base La Macaza, located in the Laurentian Mountains northwest of Montreal, which housed American nuclear-armed Bomarc missiles. As Roussopoulos explained, the purpose of the June protest was to "confront militarism" by employing "the best strategies of the radical pacifist tradition, of the civil rights tradition, and [blocking] La Macaza with our bodies as a form of protest. And that's what we did."[71]

The protesters employed the techniques of nonviolent civil disobedience, which they learned in a training session conducted by a black American civil rights activist. Their plan was to seek entry to the base with the intention of dismantling the Bomarc missiles, and if denied entry, to sit down on the road to block the entry to the base. The action in June 1964 began with a week-long vigil, and then on 21 June, seventeen participants (of the approximately one hundred young people who had gathered by the roadside) approached the entrance of the base, singing "We Shall Overcome," a spiritual that had become the key anthem of the civil rights movement south of the border, and proceeded to sit down. The following morning, military police began dragging students into the ditch, and the students promptly returned to block the road. This process was repeated, according to one source, at least thirty times.[72]

Organizers had hoped that Operation St Jean Baptiste would generate a popular movement of nonviolent civil disobedience at Canada's military bases. Consequently, in consultation with CUCND members in Toronto, they decided that a second, larger demonstration would take place at La Macaza at the beginning of September. The second protest followed the template of the first; it began with a vigil on 31 August and ended with a prolonged sit-in on the road in front of the base entrance. However, the September protest was significantly larger and longer; about 150 took part in the vigil, and over fifty protestors engaged in civil disobedience for forty-eight hours. As in June, the military police responded by dragging protesters off the road, though reports suggest that they were considerably rougher in their handling of demonstrators.[73]

Among the protesters at both demonstrations were young people from the SCM. While it is impossible to tally precise numbers, David Lewis Stein, who wrote a feature article about the June protest for *Maclean's*, reported that the first protesters to arrive were "twenty peaceniks and half a dozen others, members of the Student Christian Movement." More SCM students arrived on 20 June, as did "carloads of peaceniks from Montreal and Toronto."[74] It is certain that participants from the SCM work camps in Toronto and Montreal were present at both protests. The Toronto work camp was specifically a peace camp, directed by John Alan Lee. Since the focus of the camp's study and action was peace, it was appropriate that Lee and others from the Toronto work camp took part in the protests at La Macaza.[75] From the Montreal work camp came Wolfe Erlichman, and also Eilert Frerichs, by now a United Church minister, who would play a prominent role in the June protest.[76]

Frerichs was one of three SCM members that took part in civil disobedience at La Macaza in June 1964 (the other two were students from Toronto).[77] Dimitri Roussopoulos remembers Frerichs as "one of the most committed persons" at the demonstration; he "was there in full regalia with his black cloth and collar. Not that that impressed the military. They threw him into the ditch too."[78] At least one military policeman was impressed, but not favourably; as Stein reported it, this officer "looked at Bert Frerichs, whose clerical collar had been ripped from his shirt, and shouted into the minister's face, 'I'm United Church too, mister. But I'm switching. Right today, I'm switching.'"[79] By his presence as a clergyman (albeit in tattered and torn regalia), Frerichs made an explicit link between Christianity and the cause of peace.[80] But he "Christianized" the protest even further by concluding the demonstration with what Stein called "probably the strangest devotional meeting ever held at a Canadian military installation ... The peaceniks formed a semi-circle on one side of a barbed-wire fence; the airforce police lined the other side. Bert Frerichs, still wearing his torn clerical collar, read the Sermon on the Mount and led the peaceniks in the Lord's Prayer. Only one airman seemed to be praying along with the peaceniks. But when the group joined hands to sing, for the last time, *We Shall Overcome*, and Frerichs thrust his hand over the barbed wire, one of the airmen took it."[81]

Likewise, the Christian presence at the subsequent protest at La Macaza in September 1964 was substantial and visible. Several SCM members were among the group that committed civil disobedience at the September demonstration, including Ian Gentles (the secretary of the University of Toronto CUCND who had taken part in the June sit-in as well), John Alan Lee, and two Anglican priests from Toronto: Don Heap (a long-time SCM member and mentor to younger activists) and William Whitla (a professor of English at York University).[82] The latter led a communion service as part of the protest: "There was a question – I guess some of the students had asked if something could happen, if there could be a service ... And Don said, he had serious concerns about doing it, because ... it would be too ecumenical and that the legalities wouldn't be necessarily observed. And I didn't have those concerns. And so I celebrated on a huge rock that was outside the place where we had our tents up, and it was reasonably informal, and we sang some of the same songs that we had used during the protest. And it was tremendously moving because all sorts of people were there who were in various stages of belief or non-belief ... but it was a moment of ... spiritual solidarity that was very significant. It was a very significant gathering of hearts and minds."[83]

The performance of overtly Christian symbols at the protests – public prayer, singing, Bible reading, and communion – is significant for several reasons. First, it shows the willingness of young secular activists to make space for public expressions of faith. This was in spite of the fact that some of the "peaceniks" present, possibly even the majority, were not Christian.[84] One can only speculate about their motives in allowing religious symbols to assume such a prominent place in the demonstration, but two motives seem highly plausible. First, the demonstration was a performance, not only for the military base or the townspeople of La Macaza but ultimately for the Canadian public (via Stein's article in *Maclean's*). It was also a performance for themselves, to reinforce their own identity as activists.[85] By permitting overtly Christian acts in this performance, they were presenting an image of respectability and righteousness to the public. Thus, on one level, secular activists likely felt that religious symbols lent their protest an aura of legitimacy. On a less cynical level, however, these Christian elements reinforced both the Christian and non-Christian activists' sense of identification with the civil rights struggle in the south, which was permeated with the spirituality of the black churches. These elements also reflected the profound influence of American Christian pacifists such as A.J. Muste on Canadian activists.[86]

For SCM members at La Macaza, these public performances of Christian spirituality, and the fact that they participated as a Christian contingent in a secular political protest, reflected the liberal Protestant tradition of privileging action over doctrine. Twentieth-century liberal Protestantism was not merely a religion of intellectual assent; it was an embodied religion. More significantly, their public involvement in the La Macaza protests reflected dominant theological trends in student Christian movements throughout the world at the time. Historically, the World Student Christian Federation had supported foreign missions and evangelization, but by the late 1950s and early 1960s, many were deeply uncomfortable with the traditional model of missionary work. In a postcolonial world, foreign missionaries were often perceived as agents of imperialism. Consequently, leaders of the WSCF (including many from developing nations) were challenged to rethink the very concepts of "mission" and "evangelization," and ultimately to rethink the purpose of student Christian movements. Their response, drawing on the writings of Dietrich Bonhoeffer, was to embrace a more secular, less institutionally oriented understanding of Christian mission.[87] God was at work in the world, and the purpose of the Church in the world was to discern where God was acting, and then to take part, providing a witness to God's presence in secular human struggles.[88] As Risto Lehtonen explains, by 1964, terms such as "mission," "witness," and "evangelization" had been reinterpreted as "Christian presence."[89] For activism-oriented Christians, he writes, this interpretation was very appealing: "the idea of Christian presence

... was used to emphasize God's sovereign action in the world and consequently to describe the task of the Church as tracing signs of God's presence in secular events and political movements, and thus following their lead in its work. Perceiving and following Christ in the midst of peoples' struggles and movements was primary. The gathering of those who acknowledged Christ was secondary. Many of those who wanted to free the Church from its institutional heritage and develop a politically and socially relevant ministry welcomed this interpretation and saw in it the theological rationale for their contextual approaches."[90]

By participating in the protests at La Macaza, members of the SCM put the principle of "Christian presence" into practice. While they took part as Christians (or, at least, as members of a Christian student organization), they did not draw a sharp distinction between themselves and the non-Christian participants in the demonstrations. All, presumably, were doing God's work. As Don Heap wrote in the *Project La Macaza Bulletin* shortly after the September protest,

> La Macaza brought me for the first time into nonviolent resistance of evil. There was a glimpse of new ways of doing the Christian faith ... Christianity is about love, the giving of ourselves one to another. In this community, people did that, everyone, though many deny Christianity. People took care of each other's needs ... We gave ourselves for the peace of the world and have already some evidences of how others have responded. This is all as Jesus did. La Macaza showed me how Jesus' life grew from the truth of the nature of the world. I knew that theoretically, but now I trust it more practically. Of course, many of you are not Christians, as you tell me. That proves the basic truth of our community and our action all the more strongly ... You are my brothers.[91]

Heap's words, and Whitla's sense of "spiritual solidarity" in an open communion service, reflected the growing sense among left-leaning Christians that God's work and presence were to be determined by actions rather than beliefs, and that "the beloved community" might be found more readily among secular activists than in the institutional churches. The openness of the SCM was evident in other ways too: by 1964, several of its active members were doubting Christians, agnostics, or atheists. For example, Wolfe Erlichman was an agnostic, and John Alan Lee's connection with Christianity was tenuous, in spite of his leadership of the Peace Camp and his ability to conduct engaging Bible studies.[92] Thus, the protests at La Macaza only highlight the evolving nature of the SCM's complicated sense of identity as a Christian community.

Finally, Christians' participation in the demonstrations at La Macaza was important because it signalled their commitment to nonviolent civil disobedience, a principle and practice which, though it owed much to Gandhi, was consonant with the teachings of Christ. By participating in the protests at La Macaza, not only did members of the SCM (and, for that matter, Catholics, both lay and religious) make a link between Christianity and the cause of peace; they also made an explicit link between Christianity and civil disobedience. Within the Christian tradition, a tension exists between the mandate to "be subject to the governing authorities" because they "are appointed by God," and the mandate to disobey unjust laws in obedience to a higher law, for one "ought to obey God rather than men."[93] To use the terms employed in the first chapter, this is the tension between "priestly" religion and "prophetic religion," or between what H. Richard Niebuhr called "the Christ of culture" and "Christ against culture."[94] By engaging in civil disobedience, Gentles, Frerichs, Heap, and other members of the SCM at La Macaza came down firmly on the side of "prophetic" Christianity. In so doing, they chose a path that had radical implications, for rejecting the legitimacy of a "human" law in favour of "higher" law is a potentially revolutionary act, even an anarchic act.[95] In short, in Canada's nascent New Left, young Christian radicals were every bit as radical as their secular counterparts.

CONCLUSION

By late 1964, the New Left was a part of the Canadian student landscape, and participants in the SCM shared in this "new dispensation." More than that, they also helped to bring it about. Inspired by the activist *zeitgeist* of the sixties and by global theological currents, left-leaning Christians, many of them from Toronto, literally occupied the front lines of protest alongside their secular colleagues. The vitality that the SCM brought to both the peace movement (in the CUCND) and the civil rights movement (in Friends of SNCC) ultimately flowed into the formation of Canada's first nationwide New Left student organization, which I examine in the next chapter.

By the end of 1964, any urban Canadian who read the news, listened to popular radio, or watched the Beatles perform on the *Ed Sullivan Show* knew that Dylan was right: the times indeed were changing. However, it was still possible to underestimate the seismic shifts that were occurring in North American youth culture. The young radicals who protested at sit-ins were newsworthy, but to many observers, they were only a small contingent of the youth population. Even perceptive observers failed to read the signs of the times. They could not see that the stage had been set for youth movements such as the New Left to take the spotlight, that a new dispensation would follow the old, that the waters around them had grown, and that soon they would be drenched to the bone. The role of Christian radicals in this rising tide of youth radicalism, particularly in Toronto, and the response of Canadian churches and Christian organizations (largely based in Toronto) to the New Left, is the subject of the chapters that follow.

4

Where the Action Is

Christianity and New Left Activism in Toronto, 1965–66

By the beginning of 1965, Canada's New Left had emerged as a movement characterized by new ideas such as participatory democracy and new strategies such as nonviolent direct action. The movement found its expression in a new student-led organization – the Student Union for Peace Action (SUPA). These activists were committed to putting their ideas and strategies into practice; revolutionary social change required action, and students would be the agents of change. SUPA would have a relatively short lifespan as an organization, and it would never become a mass movement on the scale of SDS in the United States. Nonetheless, the establishment of SUPA marked a new phase for Canada's New Left, and it would lay the groundwork for a more expansive – and disruptive – Canadian campus left in the final years of the sixties.[1]

The most active years of SUPA, 1965 and 1966, were crucial years for Christian youth activism. Like their secular counterparts, radicals in Christian youth organizations also believed in the essential unity of thought and action. From its earliest days, one of the consistent features of the SCM was a marriage between theology and social involvement. By the mid-sixties, the SCM was particularly driven by a theology that demanded action in the secular political arena. To some critics within the organization, the marriage between theology and action was a troubled one, and the tensions between "religious" and "secular," between discussion and action, nearly stretched this relationship to its breaking point. Nevertheless, even troubled marriages can be fruitful ones, and throughout 1965 and 1966 the SCM was a visible part of the youth protest scene on English Canadian campuses, often working in close conjunction with SUPA and with a notable overlap in membership.

As well, in English Canada in the mid-sixties, the SCM was not the only haven for young radicals whose activism was rooted in a Christian understanding of social justice. They could be found in other Christian youth organizations, such as Kairos and Summer of Service, and in secular organizations such as SUPA and the Canadian Union of Students. They could also be found working in church-based agencies such as the Canadian Urban Training Centre. Furthermore, young activists who identified with the Christian community[2] received encouragement and support from older progressives in mainline denominations. These young people in the "Christian left" did not leave their stamp on the Canadian New Left to the same degree that the Social Gospel left its mark on the Canadian left in the early twentieth century; nevertheless, they constituted an important stream that flowed into the broader movement in the mid-sixties. In any case, they were not as concerned about leaving a distinctly Christian imprint on the movement as they were about being "where the action is" (an expression that had currency among socially conscious Christians in the sixties). In other words, they sought out sites of struggle, communities where they could identify injustices and work to rectify them, in solidarity with the oppressed. Thus, young Christian radicals were very similar to their non-Christian counterparts in the New Left.

They were also similar to older progressive Christians in their "theology of social involvement." In 1965 and 1966, Harvey Cox, Pierre Berton, and the "death of God" theologians had a profound influence on Canada's mainstream Protestant churches. Among Canada's Roman Catholics, Vatican II had an even more far-reaching impact, with its emphasis on ecumenism, social justice, the "lay apostolate," and "dialogue with the world." These theological developments helped to shape the response of leading clergy and laity toward the young radicals of the sixties, be they Christian or other.

The result, as one of the Christian radicals from the sixties recalls, was a "mélange."[3] In 1965 and 1966, a community of activism took shape in which Christians collaborated with atheists, the young collaborated with progressives of their parents' generation, individuals flowed from one organization into another, and everybody wanted to be where the action was. At times, the tensions and fault lines between "religious" and "secular" surfaced, but for most activists these concerns were of little importance in the face of pressing social issues, including institutionalized racism in the southern United States and the Vietnam War. These two issues, especially the latter, would prove to be a galvanizing force, drawing a greater number of students into the orbit of the New Left and facilitating participation between socially conscious clergy and young radicals. This chapter explores this mélange, with a focus on the role played by Toronto-based Christian activists within it. Attention is given to new social, political, and theological developments; to the emergence of Christian youth activist groups such as Kairos, the Latin American Working Group, Summer of Service, and the Youth Corps; to the relationship between SUPA and the "Christian left," particularly the SCM; and to the identity crisis that shook the national SCM in these years. That identity crisis reflected the widespread ethos that left-leaning Christians, both radical youth and older supportive progressives, shared in these years. It was an ethos that gave primacy to action in the secular sphere, even if it came at the expense of an institutional structure, or its distinctive Christian identity.

THE SOCIAL AND POLITICAL CONTEXT: SUPA, SELMA, AND THE VIETNAM WAR

Between 28 December 1964 and 1 January 1965, 150 students from eighteen Canadian universities assembled in a church basement in Regina. The occasion was the annual CUCND conference, and on the agenda was the dissolution of the CUCND. In its place, they would establish a New Left student organization dedicated to the transformation of society. By the conclusion of the conference, the Student Union for Peace Action had been born.[4] The metamorphosis of CUCND from a single-issue "ban the bomb" group into a radical movement for participatory democracy had been gradual, and the formation of SUPA simply recognized this transformation. As the name suggests, the new organization still retained a peace agenda, but it was part of a wider commitment "to the panoramic aim of working toward the fundamental changes in institutions and attitudes that would abolish war, racism, poverty, undemocratic political and technological procedures, and bellicose and belligerent values."[5] As the name also suggests, they believed that young people in general – and students in particular – would be the key agents of fundamental social change. In this respect, they agreed with their radical colleagues in SDS, SUPA's American counterpart. SUPA had close ties to the SDS, and in many ways mirrored the American group.[6] This included SUPA's adoption of the Quaker model of reaching decisions through consensus, which ensured that participatory democracy was not only preached but practised in the group.

SUPA was dedicated to action, and its first public action in Toronto was more visible and successful than its organizers anticipated. On 7 March 1965, nearly 600 African American activists began a trek from Selma, Alabama to the state capital, Montgomery, to protest for civil rights. As the demonstrators reached the Edmund Pettus Bridge in Selma, they were brutally attacked by state troopers wielding nightsticks and lobbing tear gas canisters. This violent assault on protesters drew national attention, and soon thousands of Americans joined in sympathy marches throughout the country.[7] In Toronto, SUPA organized a march from the University of Toronto campus to the United States consulate, to call for federal intervention on behalf of blacks in Alabama. Approximately 250 took part in the march on the first day, 10 March; about thirty of them staged a sit-in in the lobby of the American consulate, and they were forcibly removed by Toronto police. Thanks to front page news coverage in the *Globe and Mail*, their numbers swelled, and on 12 March, 2,000 protesters had converged on the consulate, not only student demonstrators but also several New Democrat MPPs, labour leaders, clergy, and an Anglican bishop.[8] The demonstration also helped to forge a closer relationship between student peace activists, who were largely associated with SUPA, and student civil rights activists, who were associated with Friends of SNCC. (It also strengthened ties between SUPA and the American SNCC.) Eventually, students in Friends of SNCC were drawn into the orbit of SUPA, which cemented its place as the chief organizational vehicle for Canadian student activism in the mid-sixties.[9]

The demonstration also radicalized some young people, who chose to follow the advice of a visiting SDS speaker to drop out of university and work for the movement, since students "were just in training for the system."[10] SUPA provided many opportunities to work for the movement, whether for young people who left school, or for students on summer holidays, or for those who had recently graduated, as was the case with many SUPA workers. Inspired by the example of the American SDS and its ERAP projects in Newark and Chicago, SUPA set up community organizing projects across Canada, among the poor in Kingston and Toronto, Doukhobors in British Columbia, First

Nations in Saskatchewan, and blacks in Nova Scotia. Young activists hoped to organize disadvantaged members in these communities, who in turn would adopt the principles and practices of participatory democracy and challenge unjust power structures.[11] These SUPA projects met with limited success, but in an interview several decades later, SUPA staff member Cathleen Kneen argued that "the process was critically important" because it "brought a bunch of nice middle-class kids into the gritty reality of the social injustice of Canada, and plunged them into bootstrap community organizing ... I have a feeling that those individuals who were engaged in that process were influential far beyond the specific projects they were engaged [in] ... That vision and the idea that you could actually be in solidarity and practical solidarity with people in struggle even though you came out of a nice middle-class background was revolutionary."[12]

SUPA's philosophy and practice of community organizing, drawn from SDS and ultimately from activists such as Saul Alinsky,[13] also influenced the shape of a new federal agency: the Company of Young Canadians (CYC). In its 1965 throne speech, the government announced its intention to create "a Company of Young Canadians, through which the energies and talents of youth can be enlisted in projects for economic and social development both in Canada and abroad."[14] The Pearson government initially envisioned an agency similar to the Peace Corps in the United States, but beyond that, it was not clear what form these "projects for economic and social development" would take.[15] A committee was set up to determine the direction of the new company, and Joan Newman, a twenty-two-year-old recent graduate from Carleton University, was hired to approach other Canadian organizations and gather ideas. When she met with Art Pape, who worked for the SUPA national office in Toronto, Pape informed her that youth in CYC "should be learning to change the world," and that CYC should set up community organizing projects "like the SDS ones in the States."[16] When the committee decided that community development would be a central feature of CYC, it turned to SUPA as its main model. The government agreed to fund five of SUPA's summer projects in 1965 in exchange for information on these projects.[17] The government also funded the SUPA Fall Institute held at the end of the summer of 1965 at a rural campsite near St Calixte de Kilkenny, northwest of Montreal, where workers from the SUPA summer projects gathered to "report and evaluate their activities, and to work out commonalities and a general analysis of society and a strategy for action."[18] They were joined at the conference by members of other youth organizations who were interested in working for social change, including some from the CYC.

The representatives from the CYC made a compelling sales pitch to the SUPA volunteers at St Calixte, and over the next two years, many SUPA members, and some entire SUPA projects, would be drawn into the orbit of the federally funded CYC. Since SUPA sought to be a radical, anti-institutional movement, working for democracy from the bottom up rather than the top down, it is not surprising that it had a troubled relationship with the CYC. Many within SUPA believed that the CYC was simply co-opting the New Left, and they resented the CYC for plundering the membership of SUPA, and thus weakening the solidarity of the radical New Left.[19] However, the CYC was not a competitor in every respect, for it could not duplicate all of SUPA's functions, such as its activism in opposition to the Vietnam War.

As early as 1950, the United States was committed to fighting the Vietminh in an effort to prevent the spread of Communism, even if it meant supporting France in its struggle to retain colonial power in Vietnam. By the mid 1950s, Vietnam had been partitioned into Communist-controlled North Vietnam and the non-Communist south, and the United States had replaced France as the "imperial" power in the region. Under Eisenhower and Kennedy, the Americans continued to prop up unstable and repressive regimes in the south, but attempted to limit American involvement.[20] This policy of limited involvement changed under Johnson in 1964. Faced with an imminent election and determined to outflank his more hawkish Republican opponent, Johnson used the pretext of a North Vietnamese attack on a US destroyer ship to demand that Congress pass the Tonkin Gulf resolution.[21] Although the resolution was not a formal declaration of war, it enabled the president "to take all necessary measures to repel any armed attack against the forces of the United States and to prevent further aggression," and "to take all necessary steps, including the use of armed force," to defend the "freedom" of Vietnam.[22] The US government embarked on a series of increasingly destructive aerial bombing campaigns over North Vietnam, and dramatically increased the number of American military personnel in the region. At the end of 1964, there were 23,300 American "advisers" stationed in Vietnam; by the end of 1966, that number had risen to 385,300.[23]

In both the United States and Canada, the New Left responded to the Vietnam War with vigorous protest. Young radicals made a clear connection between their own struggles against "the system" and the struggle of the Vietnamese people. Student activists perceived that in both cases, they fought for liberation from the same oppressive system, a system that must have seemed doubly oppressive since it forcibly conscripted young Americans to take part in a war of imperialist aggression. In the spring of 1965, twenty to twenty-five thousand protesters, mostly students, took part in a peace demonstration in Washington, and radical faculty and students organized well-attended "teach-ins" on the Vietnam War at several American universities.[24] In Canada, SUPA members assisted in organizing "Revolution and Response," a highly successful teach-in on Vietnam held at the University of Toronto in September 1965, which drew 4,000 students. In March 1966, SUPA held its own teach-in at the University of Ottawa, as well as a demonstration on Parliament Hill that led to the arrest of sixty-one SUPA activists on charges of obstruction. SUPA's most significant and long-lasting contribution to the struggle against the Vietnam War, however, was the establishment of the Toronto Anti-Draft Programme (TADP) to encourage and assist young Americans who chose to evade the draft by moving to Canada. TADP outlived SUPA, and its *Manual for Draft-Age Immigrants to Canada* sold in the tens of thousands.[25]

However, SUPA was not the only Canadian organization engaged in antiwar mobilization. For example, when Adlai Stevenson, the United States ambassador to the UN, came to the University of Toronto to receive an honorary degree in the spring of 1965, SUPA organized a silent vigil. At the same time, a more radical group, mostly Trotskyites, held a protest. Significantly, the latter protest consisted mostly of high school students.[26] It was a harbinger of the future direction of the New Left; as opposition to the Vietnam War intensified on English-Canadian campuses in the late 1960s, SUPA would no longer be its leader, nor would it retain the mantle of leadership in the English-Canadian New Left. As chapter 5 explains, the later New Left would be more radical, confrontational, and pervasively Marxist in its analysis. And unlike SUPA, its main site of struggle would be the university campus, not the broader community.

"WHERE THE ACTION IS":
THE CHURCHES' RESPONSE TO THE NEW LEFT

The emergent New Left did not escape the notice of church officials in Toronto, particularly clergy who were active on the left and supportive of younger radical Christians. By 1965, prominent clergy and laity in the Roman Catholic Church, the Anglican Church of Canada, and the United Church of Canada demonstrated an outward-looking attitude and a willingness to engage, in varying degrees, with the progressive politics of the young radicals. Their willingness to bestow blessings on the young radicals may have reflected a belief that these youth were representative of the burgeoning youth population as a whole. More importantly, their responses to youth activism reflected the new theological developments of the sixties. Impelled by theology that emphasized engagement and action, older clergy and sympathetic laity played a crucial role in supporting young Christian activists in the sixties. Youth may have been central, but older church officials, and the theology that shaped them, were essential to the development of Canada's Christian left in the sixties.

Among Canada's mainstream Protestants, this engagement was shaped by the same prevalent theological currents that shaped the Canadian SCM in the long sixties. These theological trends found their expression in two influential books, both published in 1965. The popularity and influence of these books was evidence of an identity crisis in churches throughout the Western world, as leading clergy and prominent laity engaged in a process of self-reflection over what a church should be and do. The first was *The Secular City* by Harvard theologian Harvey Cox. Cox argued that urbanization and secularization were two closely related phenomena, and that churches have been wrong to criticize them. Rather, the church should embrace the secular city, for God was present and active within it, and embrace social change. "Theology ... is concerned *first* of all with finding out where the action is," he wrote. "Only then can it begin the work of shaping a church which can get to the action. This is why the discussion of a theology of social change must precede a theology of the church."[27] The kind of church that Cox envisioned was radically different from the traditional model. His alternative model had little regard for denominational distinctiveness or traditional dogma, but very high regard for social action in the secular sphere. For many mainstream Protestants, *The Secular City* was their introduction to the radical secular theology of the sixties. Drawing from the ideas of Dietrich Bonhoeffer, theologians such as Paul Van Buren, Thomas Althizer, and William Hamilton argued that traditional Christian language about God, as well as the traditional understandings embodied in that language (e.g., God as "father"), were meaningless in a modern, secular world. While Cox did not boldly proclaim the "death of God," as other secular theologians did, he did emphasize that God was hidden and unknowable, and argued that Jesus was not the "revelation" of God, but was God's way of "teaching man to get along without Him, to become mature, freed from infantile dependencies, fully human."[28] Thus freed from metaphysical speculations, man (*sic*) could turn his attentions away from the next world and focus resolutely on this one.[29]

Even more influential for Canadian mainstream Protestants was Pierre Berton's *The Comfortable Pew*. The Anglican Church of Canada commissioned this work, because Anglicans wanted an outsider's view of their institution and its shortcomings. The result was an indictment, not merely of the Anglican Church, but of all mainline Protestant churches in Canada. Berton criticized the church for being out of touch with modern society and argued that it needed to become more up to date in both its medium and its message, more secular in its focus, less restrictive in its teachings on sexuality, and less concerned about literal belief in the supernatural. Moreover, he demanded that the churches take clear, unequivocal stands on current social issues. These changes were necessary, he contended, if the churches were to remain relevant in "the new age." Berton's book became a bestseller – 175,000 copies in Canada alone – and whether they agreed or disagreed, Canadian churches were compelled to take it seriously.[30] The *Observer* (United Church) carried an interview with Berton and a review of his book, while the *Canadian Churchman* (Anglican) printed no fewer than five reviews of the book in early 1965.[31] The churches also responded directly to *The Comfortable Pew* with books of their own, including *Why the Sea Is Boiling Hot* (a symposium published by the United Church's Board of Evangelism and Social Service), and *The Restless Church* (a collection of reflections on Berton's book and the issues it raised by an impressive array of authors, published by the Anglican Church).[32] In all of these reviews and responses, the writers fundamentally agreed with Berton's main contention: the churches needed to be attentive to the social and political issues of the day.

Consequently, Canada's mainline Protestant churches were moving from an understanding of theology as *dogma* towards theology as *action*. If one accepted the arguments of Berton and Cox, then it was the churches' duty to accept the challenge: to speak prophetically on secular issues and to engage with the wider world. On the whole, the Anglican Church responded cautiously to this challenge, but Anglicans who embraced a post-dogmatic, activist faith could be found in certain progressive parishes. In the Diocese of Toronto, the most notable of these was the Church of the Holy Trinity, whose parishioners included several contributors to *The Restless Church*, as well as politically active clergy connected to the SCM.[33]

The challenge to engage with the world was more readily accepted in the United Church, where some church officials spoke of a "new evangelism" as distinct from the evangelism of the fifties that concerned itself with securing conversions or increasing church attendance. In contrast, the new evangelism was hard to distinguish from social service or social activism.[34] This new paradigm was evident in the United Church's Board of World Mission, which oversaw the denomination's overseas missions. There was a clear shift away from proselytizing and toward missions of a much more secular nature, similar to the development work carried by organizations such as CUSO.[35] On the domestic front, the key proponents of the "new evangelism" were executives of the denomination's Board of Evangelism and Social Service.[36] The influence of *The Secular City* was particularly evident in the board, for when it published a book about churches that were carrying out innovative community outreach projects, its title, *Churches Where the Action Is*, was a clear reference to Cox's book.[37] The leaders of the Board of Evangelism and Social Service were more receptive than others in the United Church hierarchy to the New Left activists, a point further discussed in chapter 6.

The theology of action was also central to the Canadian Urban Training Program, an ecumenical ministry supported largely by the United Church. Beginning its operations at Toronto's Woodgreen United Church in 1966, under the direction of Rev. Edgar File, CUT trained clergy and some young laypeople in urban ministry. Its understanding of "urban ministry," however, closely resembled the confrontational type of community organizing advocated by Saul Alinsky and SUPA, which "attempted to give disenfranchised people a sense of collective identity and tangible methods of unbalancing and changing inequitable power structures."[38] In spite of the support it received from the United Church, CUT remained independent, reflecting the anti-institutional spirit of the times. As former staff member Nancy Hannum later recalled, CUT was a clear example of the churches' response to youth activism of the sixties.[39]

The Roman Catholic Church's response to youth activism was conditioned by a similar movement toward a theology of engagement.

For Catholics, this movement was driven by Vatican II, which concluded in 1965. In that year, several important documents were promulgated, including *Gaudium et Spes* (joy and hope). Its focus was "the Church in the modern world," and it addressed many of the same social justice issues that concerned the young radicals, such as poverty, war, and economic injustice as a root cause of war. This was nothing new; Catholic social teaching was familiar terrain to anybody that had read older papal encyclicals such as *Rerum Novarum* or *Quadragesimo Anno*. What was new, however, was the extent to which the document emphasized the dignity of all humankind and the importance of human freedom – in a manner consonant with the "Values" chapter in the *Port Huron Statement*.[40] The concept of "dialogue with the modern world" was also new. The Church hierarchy rejected a fortress mentality and invited both clergy and laity to engage in dialogue with non-Catholics, even to work with them on issues of common concern.[41] The role of laity in this new mission to the world was underscored in another document promulgated in the final year of Vatican II: *Apostolicam Actuositatem* (apostolic activity). This document put forward the idea of the "lay apostolate;" that is, the idea that laypeople had a sacred calling, just as clergy did. Consequently, they shared a role in the mission of the Church, a mission that included not only spiritual goals, but earthly goals as well.[42]

These two ideas – "dialogue with the world" and "the lay apostolate" – had a profound impact on Canadian Catholics. Undoubtedly, the impact was most pronounced on laity and clergy in Quebec, where the historical role of the Church was much more central to society and where progressive Catholics played an important role in the social and political developments of the Quiet Revolution.[43] But the impact was felt in English Canada, too, and readers of the *Canadian Register* in 1965 and 1966 regularly encountered the terms "dialogue" and "the apostolate of the laity."[44] These terms had radical implications; to engage in dialogue implied that truth could be found outside the Church, that perhaps the Church had something to learn from Protestants, Jews, or even young secular activists. Also, the idea that laypeople could have an apostolic ministry that derived its authority from Christ and not from the Church hierarchy was even more radical. If God could work directly through laity, and the Holy Spirit could speak directly to a person's conscience, then surely "the whole people of God" should have a say in determining Catholic teaching and practice. This rationale (essentially a Catholic version of "participatory democracy") would be central to the arguments of Catholics who wanted to liberalize the Church's position on contraception, a topic taken up again in chapter 6.

In the aftermath of Vatican II, some perceptive Catholics in the Archdiocese of Toronto realized that the challenge to engage with the modern world extended not only to lay adults but also to youth. The Catholic Youth Organization provided opportunities for recreation for young Catholics, but not for activism. So in 1966, while SUPA and the CYC sought to channel the idealism of youth into various social action projects, Father Tom McKillop created the Youth Corps to form "youth to become apostles in the world." The name "was chosen after Peace Corps or Job Corps to give the connotation of being a tightly knit group of young people who would be active," but did not include the label "Catholic" "so that the Youth Corps would be open to every young person with the realization that the vast majority have not made a personal commitment to the Catholic faith or to Christ." Its founders explained their goals as follows: "We decided to try to lead the young to be servants of the poor ... We did not want to fragment aspects of human life with spiritual as something separate, but to integrate the whole of action, reflection and friendship in Christ. We wanted to open up awareness of the young to themselves, to others, to Christ and then to the institutions in society. We so needed and need Christian leaders to be Christ-centred agents of social change, but at the same time to be contemplative and those who work together as friends."[45] While its professed goals were social and institutional change, most of the activities that the Youth Corps would carry out were benevolent and charitable rather than confrontational community organizing. But even though its actions were not as radical as its aims, the Youth Corps was a clear response by Toronto's Roman Catholics to the new ideas of Vatican II, and to the new youth activism of the sixties.

In summary, Canadian Christians who readily embraced the new theological trends of the sixties (whether Protestant or Catholic) played an important role in supporting youth activism. There were limits on how much radicalism and revolution Canada's major denominations could handle. Even so, it is important that Canadian churches made space for expressions of youthful idealism. Church-sponsored organizations such as the Youth Corps were more radical in rhetoric and intent than in practice, but they gave many young people their first taste of social activism. Several of these youth would go on to join groups more explicitly aligned with the goals, philosophy, and practices of the New Left.

THE CHRISTIAN LEFT

If groups such as the Youth Corps were not explicitly "New Left," then where could one find young people who identified with the Christian community and whose involvement in that community led them to embrace a New Left analysis of society? In Toronto, the largest and most established community of young radical Christians (politically, socially, and often theologically) was the Student Christian Movement at the University of Toronto. The SCM was many things: a place to study the Bible or discuss books; a forum to explore new political or theological ideas; and for many, a close-knit community that functioned as a surrogate family. In the mid-sixties, however, a number of its participants in Toronto saw the SCM as "an international cooperative movement for radical Christian thinking and acting in and through the university," whose "basis for participation [was] not individual belief, but willingness to cooperate towards achieving common goals."[46] These activists were likely a minority within the University of Toronto unit, but they included the unit's core leaders. For example, the student president of the unit during the 1964–65 school year was George Hartwell, who had been active in the Friends of SNCC chapter at the university, and who would later work full-time with the SUPA project in Halifax.[47]

These activists received support from SCM national office members such as Fred Caloren (1934–2016). Throughout his graduate studies in both political economy and theology (in the late fifties and early sixties), Caloren had maintained a lively interest in the relationship between Christianity and sociopolitical concerns. While he was pursuing doctoral studies in Strasbourg, France, his Québécois colleagues had introduced him to the emergent Quebec nationalism of the sixties.[48] As SCM study secretary from 1963 to 1966, Caloren travelled the country, providing literature and program ideas to local units. He also served as a spokesperson for the SCM, addressing secular student groups on current issues of concern such as Quebec nationalism. As a bilingual Canadian with a sympathetic understanding of Quebec nationalism, working in an organization that was very Anglo-Canadian and Protestant, Caloren became the SCM's expert on French-English relations and was responsible for the organization's brief to the Bilingualism and Biculturalism Commission. As Caloren recalled his role, "rather rapidly I was integrated into the politics and the social analysis of committed, politicized Canadian students. I remember hustling off to talk to a conference in the Maritimes ... It was in New Brunswick. It was French-speaking universities and colleges. And I was invited down there to go and talk about participatory democracy ... I had to do some quick reading up on this notion, and fashioning a few talks as a theme speaker in this conference on participatory democracy and how that would pertain in these institutions from New Brunswick (French-speaking). How they got a line on me –?"[49]

More importantly, young radicals in the University of Toronto's local unit also received support from longtime SCM alumni who maintained their involvement in the movement. This included Jane Blanchard, who had been active in the SCM in the 1950s and, as associate secretary of the University of Toronto local unit, would play a central role in establishing the political tone of the group. Perhaps the most influential SCM alumni were Dan Heap (1925–2014), an Anglican worker-priest associated with Church of the Holy Trinity, and his wife Alice Heap (1925–2012). Dan (also known as Don)[50] and Alice had met through their involvement in the postwar SCM, and together they were active in the labour movement, peace movement (including civil disobedience at La Macaza), and left politics. Their ongoing involvement in the SCM included directing SCM summer work camps and welcoming countless SCM participants into their home (which became an important hub of political activism) in Toronto's Kensington Market neighbourhood. As hosts, examples, and mentors for young Christian radicals in the 1950s, 1960s, and beyond, their impact was immense.[51]

Outside the SCM, young Christian activists also found a home in denominational youth organizations, particularly the new United Church association Kairos. The latter came into existence in 1965, specifically to meet the needs of young adults. It replaced the Young People's Union, which had encompassed both high school and post-high school youth.[52] The Greek word *kairos* signified "the opportune time – the moment of truth – time filled with meaning – the critical moment," which made it an appropriate name for a group of young adults who were conscious of the challenges of the sixties.[53] Unlike the old YPU, the leadership of Kairos was explicitly concerned with social and political issues and explored them from a left perspective.

In 1965, leaders of both Kairos and the Anglican Young People's Association (AYPA) met with officials from the Canadian Young Communist League. When somebody suggested that they were flirting with subversives, the Kairos official replied, "The Kairos movement is far too radical to be subverted by the sedate people of the Canadian Communist Party."[54] In August 1965, the National Council of Kairos and the National Conference of AYPA gathered in Saskatoon for Assembly '65, and the two groups "addressed themselves to the mission of the church in terms of war and peace, race prejudice, poverty, Canadian bi-nationalism, hunger, and morality." For a key speaker, they invited Dimitri Roussopoulos, a founder of SUPA and one of the most articulate spokespersons for the Canadian New Left.[55]

Kairos resembled the SCM in its desire to combine radical Christian theology with a radical critique of society. But political radicalism was not pervasive in Kairos, just as it was not pervasive in the SCM. Writing in the SUPA Newsletter following the 1966 Kairos Summer Event (during which participants studied Bonhoeffer, Tillich, and Cox and attended workshops on international affairs and nonviolence), Bronwyn Wallace acknowledged that unlike SUPA, "Kairos includes local groups which call themselves Kairos, but which may not be turned on to the outlook of the 'national movement' which is pitifully small. In fact most of the field workers' time this year will be devoted to interpreting Kairos to local groups as well as to communities and to the church institution which is as yet not fully aware of what the rumblings it hears from the basement are all about."[56] Thus, the more politicized members of Kairos made it their business to "turn on" adults and young people in the United Church to the outlook of the "national movement."

These politicized youth included John Foster (born 1942), national student president of Kairos. Foster had been raised in a United Church household, and in the early sixties served as national student president of the church's Young Peoples' Union. As an undergraduate at the University of Saskatchewan, Foster had attended meetings of the SCM, where he recalled discussing international politics from a left perspective, discussions he could not readily have in the United Church. As a leader of Kairos in the late sixties, Foster sought to bring a left perspective into the church by engaging with its youth. Foster spent the 1966–67 school year "driving ... from Victoria to St John's visiting youth organizations, visiting community projects and so on, trying to animate the United Church youth movement."[57] As well, Bronwyn

Wallace, a member of both Kairos and SUPA (and a worker in SUPA's Kingston Community Project), wrote a play entitled "Blowin' in the Wind" in 1965. Based on the Dylan song, the play was antiwar and concerned with social justice. True to its name, it spread from church to church. As Foster recalls, "it travelled on its own. It wasn't a program controlled from the centre. It was something that people heard about and they got it and they did it. So [it went] further than a lot of officially endorsed initiatives."[58] Foster and Wallace were not merely interpreting Kairos to United Church youth and adults, but interpreting the New Left to the church.

The intersection between Christianity and youth activism could also be found in ecumenical projects such as the Summer of Service (SOS). In 1966, its director was George Cram (1938–2018), a theology graduate, former president of the United Church Young People's Union, and a close associate of John Foster. Like Foster, Cram was eager to revolutionize Canada's churches via their young people. When Cram discovered that "the Canadian Council of Churches was planning an ecumenical conference as its centennial youth project," he responded critically. A "tame little conference" was not what Canada needed. As an alternative, he proposed that church youth "spend the Centennial summer doing community development." Furthermore, he was anxious to avoid trivial projects "like staffing charity bazaars ... Too many kids have their desire for service railroaded by adults into dull meaningless projects. That's because adults have too much vested interest in today's society to really want to change it." The council accepted Cram's idea, appointed him to spearhead it, and he began to meet with youth groups across the country.[59]

As an ecumenical Christian organization, SOS was supported by fifteen religious bodies, including the Roman Catholic Church, all of the largest Protestant denominations, and the SCM.[60] While many participants were associated with Protestant or Catholic youth groups (including six from Youth Corps[61]), participants were not expected to adhere to any particular creed, and none of the projects involved religious proselytizing.[62] The fact that Canada's churches were willing to support this venture reflects the theological frameworks of the sixties, which placed greater emphasis on action in the secular sphere and less emphasis on propagating particular religious teachings or preserving the institutional church. Liberal Protestants in particular had redefined "evangelism" to include social service of a secular nature, even if it tended toward radical social activism.

There were four pilot projects for SOS in 1966, and twenty-one projects across Canada in the centennial year. According to the philosophy of SOS, these were supposed to be community development projects, similar to the radical projects carried out by SUPA or the CYC. However, some of the projects more closely resembled traditional social service (providing assistance to a needy population) than social activism (community organizing to challenge unjust social structures). The final report on SOS '67 observed that "the volunteers were too prone to interpret their summer's experience in terms of the personal and the psychological. There was a tendency to neglect ... the importance of structural, economic, political, theological and other factors involved in questions of poverty and other forms of deprivation. There was a strong suspicion that this might be largely due to an overemphasis on sensitivity training."[63] Future training sessions should focus more on community development. At some point, the Canadian Urban Training Program, the ecumenical program described earlier in the chapter, began providing such training to SOS volunteers.[64]

The SOS program continued until at least 1970, by which point it had become more explicitly political and confrontational in its approach. In a newsletter published that year, an SOS worker noted that "our tendency in SOS is to not accept any project which doesn't have rather well defined tendencies toward social change" and asked, "what type of involvement is necessary to have people move from the servicy, stop-gap type of operation into more constructive development oriented movements?" In the same newsletter, another worker suggested that the acronym SOS should stand for "Screw Oppressive Systems."[65] However, even when volunteers found themselves engaged in a more traditional "social service" project, the nature of their work led them to question their middle-class assumptions about the poor. For example, in 1968, Linda Kealey (a student at St Michael's College who would soon become active in the New Left Caucus at the University of Toronto) travelled to Vancouver along with her husband Greg to take part in an SOS project aimed at transient youth. While her recollections of the experience were not entirely positive, she felt that social service projects of this kind were probably "a part of our evolution of ... a consciousness about oppression."[66] In this respect, the SOS projects were similar to those of SUPA, in that they had a more revolutionary effect on the project workers themselves than on the communities in which they worked.

Young radical Christians could also be found in more informal groupings, such as communal houses or study groups. A key example of the latter was a circle of young adults who met regularly for Bible study and discussion, known as the Christian Left group. It was begun in Toronto, in the mid-sixties, by Brewster and Cathleen Kneen, and included a cross-section of leading New Left activists. The group's leader, Brewster Kneen, was in his early thirties – approximately a decade older than most of the student radicals. Nonetheless, he was an omnipresent figure among younger activists, Christian or otherwise, in Toronto's New Left milieu from the mid to late sixties. Born in Ohio and raised in a nominally Presbyterian family, Kneen chose to study theology, first at Edinburgh and then Union Theological Seminary in New York, not because he wished to become a clergyman, but as he explained a half-century later, because of his "search for the big picture." During his undergraduate years at Cornell University, he was also drawn to progressive politics, and as a student at Union Theological Seminary, he had been active in the SDS and its parent organization LID. As a committed pacifist, he became student secretary for a faith-based peace group, the Fellowship of Reconciliation.[67] Through his peace activism in the early sixties, he came into contact with Dimitri Roussopoulos and other members of CUCND, one of whom (Cathleen Rosenberg) became his wife. In 1965, he and Cathleen moved to Toronto, where Cathleen worked in the national office of SUPA. In the late sixties, wherever Christianity intersected with radical social justice, Brewster and Cathleen were present: the two led the 1965 SCM Cuba work camp in Toronto; Brewster was a resource person at the 1966 Kairos Summer Event; both attended Holy Trinity; and both served on church social justice committees.[68] Brewster also acted as an older mentor to younger Christian activists in the Christian Left group.

A closer look at the younger participants in the Christian Left group reveals the extent to which Christians were imbricated in Toronto's New Left and how religion could be an impetus to activism. One of these participants was Doug Ward (born 1938). Initially, Ward had not been interested in social issues, and even in his early university years he "probably saw [himself] as a Tory." In part, Ward credited his United Church minister – Douglas Bradford of Lawrence Park Community Church – for shaping his social consciousness by exposing him to "the Old Testament prophetic tradition." He also credited Kenneth McNaught, a prominent left-wing professor of history at the University of Toronto, for awakening his political awareness: "I can remember his first lecture. It was about the end of the Second World War. And some soldiers were saying, if we can spend all this money on tanks and bombs, why can't we spend it on housing and health ... and it hit me between the eyes. I made sure that I had courses from McNaught in third and fourth year."[69] After graduating in 1961, Ward chose to study theology – first at Princeton, then at Emmanuel College – because of his interest in "the social gospel and the role of the church in social justice."[70] He also became active in campus politics, serving as president of the Students' Administrative Council at the University of Toronto in the 1963–64 school year, and was present at the founding of SUPA in Regina. Ward would go on to become president of the Canadian Union of Students and play a key role on the board of the CYC. In the sixties, he considered himself "a link between mainstream student life and the New Left – which is what they sort of saw me as too."[71]

Another member of the Christian Left group was Peter Warrian (born in 1943). He had become active in the left-leaning Catholic Worker movement as a teenager in Toronto and proceeded to study for the priesthood at a Paulist Seminary in Baltimore, Maryland. While in seminary, his political reading included Marx and the influential New Left theorists C. Wright Mills and Herbert Marcuse.[72] His political education in Maryland included practical lessons as well. While doing parish work, he was exposed to the challenges that African Americans faced, particularly in housing discrimination. In conjunction with the well-known Catholic activist Philip Berrigan, Warrian became engaged in civil rights activism, especially as it related to housing. His increasing involvement with these social issues proved to be too controversial for his superiors in the diocese, which led to his departure from seminary. He returned to Ontario, where he enrolled in St Jerome's College in Waterloo. Warrian became active in the SCM, and, in turn, in SUPA, where he would play a role in establishing the Toronto Anti-Draft Programme. Like Ward, Warrian would go on to become the president of the Canadian Union of Students, in its most radical phase.[73]

Then there was Nancy Hannum (born in 1942). Raised in the suburbs of Akron, Ohio, Hannum attended a Congregationalist church with her family, where a new minister, fresh out of Union Seminary, introduced his congregants to the ideas of Paul Tillich. While attending college in Ohio, Hannum belonged to a student group similar to the SCM, where she discovered the writings of Dietrich Bonhoeffer, which shaped her thinking about the relationship between faith and action. Hannum began attending Quaker meetings, and through her contacts in the Society of Friends, she learned of a summer program in Washington, DC run by the Friends Committee on National Legislation, which trained politically engaged youth in lobbying skills. While taking part in the program in 1964, one of her fellow participants was Peter Boothroyd, a Canadian activist in CUCND. Hannum indicated a willingness to leave the United States and see more of the world, and Boothroyd recommended that she consider Canada. She moved to Toronto in 1964, where she was one of four workers in the CUCND national office, and later, the SUPA national office. (One of her co-workers in the SUPA national office, Dennis McDermott, also belonged to the Christian Left group.) She went on to work for the interfaith Canadian Urban Training Program, led by United Church minister Edgar File, where her duties included training SOS volunteers in community development.[74]

Hannum's story closely resembles that of Judith Skinner (born in 1942), another member of the Christian Left group. Raised in Massachusetts, Skinner attended college in Colorado, where she joined the Student YWCA. Similar to the Canadian SCM, the group offered "an alternative way of thinking about issues and theology ... that made sense to me."[75] She appreciated the group's social and political awareness, and through the Student YWCA, Skinner engaged in civil rights activism. In the mid 1960s, she took part in a program in Pennsylvania sponsored by the American Friends' Service Committee, which trained young organizers for the peace and civil rights movement. Through the program, Skinner met Toronto-based SUPA activist Don Roebuck, and in 1966, she moved to Toronto. She lived in the same communal house as Kairos leader John Foster, who was also a member of the Christian Left group. Initially, Skinner worked with the Latin American Working Group, which ran out of Brewster and Cathleen Kneen's house, and later, would hold important positions in other New Left-inspired organizations.[76]

The Christian Left group was small and informal; it did not make resolutions or issue public statements. Instead, it was a circle of friends who met for worship and meals. As Foster recalls, "We marked both Christian and Jewish holidays, which meant we had lots of holidays to celebrate, because of Cathy ... And of course we ate, that was also important ... This was really Brewster's project and initiative. They were very much the mother and father of this group ... He would have different people there who were part of different movements, like Peter Warrian, and I think perhaps there was a certain idea that we'd somehow influence through this leadership group what was happening in different organizations."[77] If Foster's speculation is correct and Brewster Kneen had hoped to influence the wider movement, then the influence was, at best, subtle. As Nancy Hannum recollects, "Some may have thought that. [But] I don't think we did have any capital-I influence in that way. I have no memory of going to any group and saying, 'we're from the Christian Left group and here's our position on this or we think it should be this way.' I don't think anybody used that in any kind of argumentative way. Brewster maybe – as Brewster often does talk from a theological place – but I think he may be the only one of the Christian people who would have brought a theological position to the table." For the most part, though, the Christian Left group was a social and supportive group for radical Christians. As Hannum put it, "it was a study group who met and really enjoyed eating together."[78]

Thus, the milieu of Christian radicals was not confined to a single organization such as the SCM. Rather it included several groups, both formal and informal, and often with overlapping membership. Youth were central to the life of these groups, but older mentors played key roles too. Furthermore, the foci and functions of each group varied. What their politically and socially engaged members shared was a commitment to the values and principles of the New Left, and a certainty that the gospel demanded action for social change.

THEOLOGY OF THE NEW LEFT

These activists explained that their Christianity (or their involvement in Christian communities such as the SCM) was an important part of their political formation. For many, it was the central part, and it remained integral to their identity as political radicals throughout these years. But did they share a common theology of social involvement? In other words, could they articulate a shared rationale for action based on their faith? Without question, certain theologians were held in high esteem among Christian radicals in the sixties. Among these was Paul Tillich, whose left-wing politics and vocal opposition to Nazism prompted his dismissal from his professorship at the University of Frankfurt in 1933. He moved to the United States, where he taught theology at Union Theological Seminary and wrote several influential books that conveyed his theological ideas to a wide popular audience.[79] He died in 1965.

Tillich argued that love is the basis for morality, ethics, and justice. One could not rely on external laws as guides to moral action, or even legal principles that "had become ideologies used for the maintenance of decaying institutions and powers."[80] In a rapidly changing world, moral action must address the present situation, and for Tillich, only love could "transform itself according to the concrete demands of every individual and social situation without losing its eternity and dignity and unconventional validity."[81] Love, understood in the Christian sense, is "the highest work of the divine Spirit."[82] As "the ultimate principle of morality," love is unchanging, but "entering the unique situation, in the power of the Spirit, [it] is always different."[83] In his explanation of how love is put into action, Tillich turned to the concept of *kairos*. In Tillich's usage, *kairos* "is the historical moment when something new, eternally important, manifests itself in temporal forms, in the potentialities and tasks of a special period. It is the power of the prophetic spirit in all periods of history to pronounce the coming of such a *kairos*, to discover its meaning and express the criticism of what is given and the hope for what is to come."[84] At these special junctures in history, love could be embodied in action for justice, with the capacity to break through existing legal systems and institutions and to establish new legal and ethical systems.[85] For young radical Christians in the sixties, the political implications of Tillich's spirituality of love were undeniable. To respond to the prompting of the Spirit meant being attentive to the needs of a changing world and addressing these in a spirit of love, even if it put one at odds with existing power structures.

Even more influential were the prison writings of Dietrich Bonhoeffer, the German theologian imprisoned by Nazis in 1944 and hanged a year later because of his participation in a plot to assassinate Hitler. Bonhoeffer envisioned a new kind of "religionless" Christianity that suited a secular era when humankind had "come of age" and shed obsolete ideas about God.[86] The role of a Christian in such a society would be to serve humanity and "plunge himself into the life of a godless world, without attempting to gloss over its ungodliness with a veneer of religion or trying to transfigure it."[87] Bonhoeffer's writings formed a basis for the secular theology of the 1960s, especially *The Secular City* by Harvey Cox.

These three authors – Tillich, Bonhoeffer, and Cox – were widely read (and even more widely cited) by young Christian activists in the sixties in Canada, the United States, and beyond.[88] For example, Nancy Hannum cited the influence of both Tillich and Bonhoeffer, and at the Kairos Summer Event in 1966, Bronwyn Wallace described how participants studied Bonhoeffer, Tillich, and Cox in an attempt "to slay the Cosmic Bellhop for good and to become relevant at last."[89] Older progressive Christians read these sources too, and the themes of "religionless" Christianity were influential in the broader liberal Protestant milieu in the sixties. But it resonated particularly with younger Christians, many of whom were less inclined to identify with the institutional church than their parents' generation and more inclined to identify with the secular activist milieu. It resonated with their deep need for social commitment and action. The Christian existentialist dimensions of this theology reflected the prevalence of secular existentialism in the broader New Left. Both varieties of existentialism encouraged readers to find meaning and overcome alienation through social action.

But how central was theology to their activism? As Bronwyn Wallace asked concerning Kairos, "are we just a cheap imitation of SUPA gilded with the prose of Tillich and Bonhoeffer? ... Do we have a theology? Do we need one? Why?" If radical Christians shared the same political analysis as secular activists, and shared in the same strategies of protest, was a theological rationale important? For some participants in the Christian left, it was important because it provided a starting point for their activism. For other Christian participants, however, a precisely articulated theology was not as important, particularly if they did not have a background in theology or religious studies. Many students in the SCM who took part in its seminars and attended its sponsored lectures acquired "snippets" of Cox and other theologians, but did not acquire a deep understanding of their writings – much in the same way that student activists learned about community development through "snippets" of Saul Alinsky.[90] In interviews, even some of the more theologically oriented participants in the Christian left had difficulty recalling a clearly articulated, commonly held theology for social action, though they had no difficulty recalling their involvement in social action.[91] This suggests that for many Christian radicals, action and a general *ethic* were more important than specific theology. This is consistent with trends in mainline Protestantism throughout the sixties, which de-emphasized theology in favour of "ethical Christianity,"[92] and with the ideas of influential secular theologians such as Harvey Cox who privileged action over dogma. The paradox of secular theology was that, in essence, it argued that theology (as traditionally understood) did not matter. Arguably, this privileging of ethics over dogma was also in keeping with the nature of the Canadian New Left in the mid-sixties, which rejected the Old Left's adherence to ideological orthodoxy in favour of a general ethic of social action.[93]

For some, the theological underpinnings of their activism may have been rooted in their childhood faith, and thus not as conscious or as clearly articulated as something they might have learned in an SCM seminar or Kairos weekend. George Hartwell was president of the University of Toronto SCM and later a SUPA activist. In an interview over four decades later, he reflected on his own motivations: "From my point of view, I don't think I'm theologically articulate enough to be giving a rationale for what I'm doing. I'm growing up, trying different things, discovering who I am and engaging in action ... It takes some sense of your identity and who you are enough to be able to say 'I'm going to do something, I'm going to take action.' Right? So, there's something there rooted in me that's allowing me to act, do something, make some risky decisions, in the midst of still trying to figure out who I am and major questions of belief and whether I believe in God." Looking back, Hartwell contends that in spite of his uncertainty about God's existence in the mid-sixties, his activism was rooted in a "deep-core belief" instilled in his United Church upbringing: "to act, you need hope, and you need a belief that taking action is going to have an impact ... So it actually involves a theory of history, if you will. Exposure to biblical knowledge is exposure to a theory of history, because in a sense, you pick up, inadvertently, the fact that God is working through huge realms of time ... I'd been exposed to a radicalizing view of history through the Bible that says, 'action is meaningful, it has purpose.' ... And I think that [there was] a deep sense of theology within me that says, 'you can take risks, you can do things, you can try things.'" Hartwell believed that this unarticulated "deep sense of theology" was shared by students in SUPA who had Christian or Jewish backgrounds.[94]

Hartwell's theory is speculative, but it does raise an important question: what role did religious upbringing have in the formation of sixties activists? For in addition to those young radicals who specifically identified as Christian or who belonged to Christian groups like the SCM, there was an even larger number of youth in secular organizations like SUPA, CYC, and the Combined University Services Overseas (CUSO) who did not necessarily identify as Christian but had been brought up in Christian (typically mainline Protestant) households.[95] As explained in chapter 2, the generation of Canadians that would come of age in the 1960s spent their childhood years in Sunday schools and churches. According to Doug Owram, their parents enrolled them in Sunday School because they "were searching not so much for faith as for ethics for their children." Many of these children, possibly the majority, abandoned church when they became teenagers or young adults.[96] Nevertheless, one could argue, as Hartwell does, that on some level, they carried with them a residue of Christian ethics: work for peace, love your neighbour, love your enemies, turn the other cheek. It is impossible to measure the extent to which such an upbringing shaped the ideals of young activists. What is certain, however, is that in addition to the many activists in these secular organizations who were red diaper babies or who had been raised in liberal Jewish households, there were also many who had been raised in practising Christian homes. As Harvey Shepherd, a product of a liberal United Church household and a SUPA activist, explained it after the fact: "I remember having a feeling at the time, or having developed a strong suspicion, that religion or having a Christian background would have seemed to probably predispose some people toward getting involved in the New Left, although I think that by and large, the people in SUPA at the time ... would not have considered themselves [Christian]. I'm thinking particularly of Peggy Morton ... there seemed to be a number of people around with religion in their family backgrounds, who did not themselves seem to have any religious commitment now."[97]

The New Left students were not rebelling against the values of their elders but against the hypocrisy of their elders, who did not live up to the values they professed. This was true in SUPA as well. As one contributor to a 1966 SUPA newsletter was keen to point out, there was a disparity within a nation that celebrates "the Prince of Peace" yet participates in genocide in Vietnam.[98] While they may have had no interest in institutional religion or radical Christian theology, clearly there were young activists who were trying to live up to the values that their parents' generation professed but failed to put into practice. In this sense, the Christian "stream" that flowed into the New Left was not confined only to the self-identified Christian radicals.

This is not to suggest that a religious rationale or religious upbringing were the only factors in shaping New Left activists, not even for those who identified as Christian radicals. Other factors were important, such as class, education, and family. What is certain, however, is that they were key factors for several of my interviewees. Whether the religious influences were cultivated in childhood or acquired later through exposure to secular theology, they facilitated the entry of many young activists into the broader New Left.

THE MÉLANGE: SUPA, SCM, AND KAIROS

Since many participants in the SCM and Kairos shared a common political analysis with members of SUPA, it is not surprising that these groups – Christian and secular – collaborated. For example, when SUPA held its Selma demonstrations at the American consulate, they used the SCM office to train volunteers in nonviolent protest.[99] Speakers from SUPA addressed SCM or Kairos gatherings,[100] and several students in the SCM ended up working on SUPA projects. Members of these different groups believed that they were a part of a common struggle to enhance democracy and overthrow oppressive structures. SUPA identified both SCM and Kairos as part of the "left/liberal protest action on campus,"[101] and an SCM song sheet from this era includes "The SCM, NDP, SUPA, SNCC Song," a light-hearted piece about skipping class and failing courses because engaging in sit-ins and civil disobedience does not allow time for school.[102] As Joan Newman Kuyek recalled in a 2009 interview, "I think ... my perception was the SCM was almost the same as SUPA. It was the student movement within the church."[103] However, there were differences, as Cathleen Kneen noted in the same interview: "Our sense at the time was that the SCM were nicer than we were. Their rhetoric wasn't ... as colourful as ours."[104] (Or as Kuyek added, "they didn't say 'fuck' as much.")

There were two key gatherings that best illustrate the presence of the Christian left in this mélange of activism. The first was the SUPA Fall Training Institute, held in September 1965 at a campsite near St Calixte, Quebec, following the conclusion of the 1965 summer projects. For SUPA workers, the St Calixte conference served a dual purpose. On the one hand, it was an opportunity to assess the strengths and weaknesses of their summer projects and to plan for the future. On the other, it was an opportunity to generate interest in community activism and to recruit more workers for ongoing SUPA projects (e.g., Kingston, Halifax, Toronto). And it was an ideal recruiting ground, for the gathering included many young people, from SUPA and from other organizations, who had not participated in the projects but were interested in the kind of activism that SUPA was doing.

This included a number of young people from socially conscious Christian groups such as the SCM and others who had become activists because of their Christian faith. Among the 116 listed participants at the St Calixte conference from across Canada, I have identified fourteen to twenty such students.[105] There were at least six participants (and possibly ten or more) associated with the Canadian SCM, including George Hartwell, the recent student president of the University of Toronto SCM.[106] He had just returned from an SCM Peace Camp, and in his own words, was "primed" for activism. The St Calixte conference inspired him to quit school, hitchhike out east, and begin working full-time with the SUPA project in Halifax.[107] Also present were Brewster and Cathleen Kneen (who conducted a workshop on why Christians should be involved in social action) as well as other members of the Christian Left group.[108] George Cram was there from the Summer of Service, as was John Foster of Kairos. Foster attended as an observer and was favourably impressed by the revolutionary rhetoric, by the consensus model of decision-making, and the coed accommodations. (The latter, as he recalls, "was probably the most impressive element in terms of influence, in terms of loosening up a sort of uptight churchy kid.") Following the conference, Foster wrote a glowing review of SUPA, designed to explain SUPA to non-SUPA people in the churches.[109] Foster praised the "new ethical spirit" of nonviolence present in SUPA and argued that the organization was "a theological workshop": "There is a real quest for values, and a new and basic redefinition of what is found to be truly human in our Canadian situation, here and now. This is real practical theology, as far as I'm concerned. I am convinced that in many ways SUPA is prophetic. Its analysis of society is half-baked in many ways, but what it is saying youth are questioning is something which extends beyond Canadian boundaries, and which shouts the world of tomorrow (our world) will not be like the world of today."[110]

In keeping with the "movement" ethos of the sixties, neither the SCM nor SUPA had card-carrying, dues-paying members, and consequently, they did not keep membership lists.[111] For this reason, it is impossible to provide solid numbers on how many participants in the SCM were also SUPA members. Nevertheless, the list of attendees at the St Calixte Conference provides us with a snapshot of the New Left in English Canada in late 1965.[112] From this list, we see that 12 to 17 percent of the conference participants were people who drew a close connection between their faith and their social activism, or who were involved in activist-oriented Christian groups. Since my research has focused on Toronto, it is highly likely that participants from elsewhere in the country (e.g., British Columbia and the prairie provinces) had connections to the SCM, or otherwise identified as Christian radicals, but I have not yet confirmed this. Thus, 12 to 17 percent is a conservative estimate of the Christian left presence at the St Calixte conference. If this conference was representative, then we can extrapolate a conservative figure of about 15 percent that entered the English-Canadian New Left through the Christian left.

An even better illustration of the close connections between radical Christian activists and SUPA was the combined SCM-SUPA conference held in Saskatoon in late December 1965, which drew about three hundred participants from across Canada.[113] While the St Calixte conference was a SUPA event, the Saskatoon conference was principally an SCM event, though both groups shared in the planning. The chief organizer was Fred Caloren, the SCM study secretary, who was eager to move the SCM further in the direction of social engagement on national and global issues. As Nancy Hannum observed in the SUPA Newsletter prior to the conference, some "in the SCM see this conference as setting a role for the SCM as being 'with the revolution' or as acting in response to revolutionary change. They are also quite interested in what unique things Christianity might have to say in a student movement or in a revolutionary age."[114] Clearly, conference organizers attempted to include not only SCM and SUPA members but members of other progressive youth organizations such as CUS, AYPA, and Kairos.[115] Furthermore, Caloren actively canvassed to include French-Canadian participants from Union générale des étudiants du Quebec (UGEQ) and Jeunesse étudiantes catholiques, and to make the Saskatoon conference fully bilingual.[116] As Caloren recalls, "The key speaker for that conference was a French-speaking professor, a geographer from the University of Montreal: Robert Garry. He was an expert on Indo-China, and he talked about China at that conference. We chose specifically – and this was done in conjunction with the SUPA people – [that] the theme speaker was a French-speaker. We brought in, at tremendous cost, simultaneous translation services (for a conference in Saskatoon) and we translated all the documents. I think we had to employ these high-cost simultaneous translators-interpreters ... If we were going to be talking to and representing and seeking contact with the Quebec society, we had to do so on their terms."[117]

If the goal of the five-day conference was to bring together a diverse group of young adults to examine the issues of the day, and to explore jointly strategies for social change, the conference was a success. Robert Garry addressed students on global development and the conflicts in Southeast Asia, particularly Vietnam. The Czech theologian Milan Opocensky spoke about the role of Christianity in communist countries, while the Dutch theologian Albert Van Den Heuvel spoke about the courage to fail (a challenge familiar to student activists who protested against entrenched structural injustice). Robert Nelson, president of UGEQ, led a discussion on student activism in Quebec. Stewart Goodings held a meeting on the CYC and project organizing.[118] And on the concluding evening, students took part in a session hosted by SUPA on responding to the war in Vietnam, where they discussed holding a sit-in on Parliament Hill.[119] The Saskatoon conference provided a space for students in the SCM to meet with SUPA activists. For example, as a representative from the University of Waterloo SCM, Peter Warrian encountered SUPA for the first time at the conference and soon became an active member.[120] Kairos president John Foster left the conference satisfied with its achievements and feeling optimistic about the future of student activism: "the conference had, and to a great extent met, a great potential for opening a new fluidity among Canadian youth movements and creating new bases for unity and joint action. The chances of follow-up events in the next year or so on many local campuses involving a spectrum of youth groups look good and the potential for breaking down silly parochial walls and minor ideological gaps is there to be realized as perhaps never before."[121]

However, the tone of the conference was not as harmonious or as optimistic as Foster suggests. In an evaluation written shortly after the Saskatoon conference, Jim Harding noted that there were tensions within SUPA between campus activists and those involved in community-organizing projects, and the group was engaged in uncomfortable soul-searching over the value of community-organizing.[122] Nancy Hannum recalled the meeting as "fairly fractious": "I think what Jim is saying is that the organization was starting to dissipate even then, and it had a lot of agendas and a lot of different directions. And there was talk about elitism, and then there were people who were leaving because they were getting more interested in the CYC. So, there was an agenda that came out of it. We decided to do more summer projects and I think we planned that big Vietnam action in Ottawa at this conference. So there were things still happening, but it was a difficult conference ... The St Calixte Conference was really strong, and then this one was full of dissension."[123]

Furthermore, Hannum recalled that there were "some people in SUPA that felt we had no business meeting with the SCM."[124] Some members felt that the SCM was not sufficiently radical and that it placed too much emphasis on developing interpersonal relationships and community-building. Without question, relationships and community were a vital part of the SCM and, for many of its members, the SCM functioned as a surrogate family.[125] But as Cathleen Kneen argued in a SUPA newsletter prior to the Saskatoon conference, "an overemphasized concentration on interpersonal relations is neurotic. We feel that the nature of man is such that he expresses his being through action (social and political), and that strong friendship or love relations are incomplete if they do not provide the impetus and the security somewhere for social and political action ... Among the SCM branches and national staff there seems to be a basic attitude which is contrary to this: that is, that there can be a clear distinction between the personal and the political, and that what ought to be concentrated on is the quality of interpersonal relationships – and that this bears no obvious implications in the realm of politics."

At the same time, Kneen recognized that one could not make generalizations about the SCM since its membership was diverse: "some of them more radical than others, some committed to SUPA, some fundamentalist Christians (though not very many) who *to a certain extent* share assumptions about the nature of man and society." Kneen proposed that SUPA members attend the conference "as individuals, prepared to meet the people who will be there as individuals," in a spirit of sensitivity, willingness to learn, and love.[126] Ironically, by the conclusion of her article, Kneen was arguing that SUPA members must attend the conference aiming to build interpersonal relationships and create community. However, it seems likely that some of the conference attendees from SUPA were not convinced that the SCM was the best choice of partner in the struggle for social change, nor were they convinced that the SCM could become the revolutionary organization that many of its own radical members wanted it to be.

Such critics in SUPA had reason to doubt; while the SCM had an abundance of radical members, it was not designed to be a revolutionary organization. It allied itself with SUPA and supported its protest actions, but on its own, it did not organize demonstrations or sit-ins. Aside from its partnership with activist groups such as SUPA or Friends of SNCC, the primary political role of the SCM was as a forum for learning and discussion. But because the SCM was open to all participants regardless of their political views, its members did not all share a common social-political analysis. Eilert Frerichs, who had been active in the movement from the late 1950s until 1964, observed that "there was no thoroughgoing political, economic, and social analysis of society," and that the resolutions of the National Council were "pretty liberal sorts of statements simply because we didn't have any sort of tools of analysis."[127] Furthermore, while some SCM units (especially the University of Toronto) were more concerned with radical politics, others focused more on personal issues, such as the emotional and psychological well-being of students.[128] Thus, the SCM was home to many Christian activists who were drawn to the organization because of its radical tradition, but it was also home to other students who had no political orientation. Perhaps this was the reason that activists in the SCM (including Wolfe Erlichman, George Hartwell, and Peter Warrian) migrated to SUPA, which was explicitly committed to social transformation through direct action.

CRISIS IN THE SCM

By the time of the Saskatoon conference, the Canadian SCM was experiencing an identity crisis. Traditionally, the SCM had functioned as a gathering place for students interested in both social justice and Christian spirituality. But in the mid sixties, the balance was fraught. There were those who found the SCM insufficiently political and others who found it insufficiently Christian. At the same time, competing groups were usurping both the political and religious roles of the SCM. In the political domain, SUPA was as much a competitor as it was an ally. In the religious domain, throughout the 1950s and 1960s, the SCM faced growing competition not only from the evangelical IVCF but also from mainline chaplaincies and denominational clubs.[129] As Peter Paris stated in a 1965 report on the SCM, "The SCM by and large does not understand what it ought to be and in very few places does there seem to be any consensus of opinion about what they actually stand for or what their underlying philosophy is ... The SCM does not wish to duplicate what is already being done in the university by other groups, many of which are now sponsoring programmes in social concern and academic topics that not too long ago were the sole service of the SCM to the university. So many of the services formerly provided by the SCM have now been taken over by various organizations who can often do a better job because of a much narrower purpose."[130]

Ostensibly, the "underlying philosophy" of the SCM was articulated in its "Basis and Aim," which stated that the movement "is a fellowship of students based on the conviction that in Jesus Christ are found the supreme revelation of God and the means to a full realization of life," that it "seeks through study, prayer, and practice to know and follow Jesus Christ," and that it "desires to share with others the values discovered in Jesus Christ and to join with those of like mind ... in the creation of a world-wide order of society in harmony with the mind and purpose of God as revealed in Jesus Christ."[131] To many students in the SCM of the sixties, this statement was outdated and even embarrassing. The Basis and Aim was not exclusive, since it allowed for the participation of "those of like mind" who shared the *values* of Jesus, though not necessarily the dogma. However, the reality of the SCM in the sixties was that fewer and fewer of its participants adhered to core Christian beliefs. It was not uncommon for active SCM members to identify as agnostic or atheist. Agnostics and atheists were drawn to the SCM for the same reasons that Christian-identified students were; some were interested in Christian spirituality; others shared its vision of social justice; and most were drawn to the SCM because it was a mutually supportive, close-knit community that welcomed newcomers in an open, nonjudgmental way. Furthermore, in the mid sixties, the line between agnostics and Christians was not always very clear; some members who identified as Christian (even those in positions of leadership) still questioned basic tenets such as the existence of God.[132] As the minutes of a 1965 meeting on the Basis and Aim reveal: "Discussion of substance centered about the validity of 'C' in SCM and the validity of openness ... The trouble with the old statement seemed to be that at this time the lines are drawn elsewhere than it draws them; it envisages a mass of confessing Christians and a fringe of inquirers, whereas we have a comparatively small number of strong confessors and a majority of seekers. Moreover we tend to seek answers in other than a confessional form

– i.e., through involvement rather than words – or perhaps give up a sincere search for 'answers' altogether."[133]

Thus, the national movement was asking fundamental questions: how can the SCM serve a unique purpose on the university campus? How can the movement remain relevant to university students more interested in Vietnam than in theology? How can the movement accommodate the diverse interests of the various SCM units? And should the SCM continue to call itself "Christian"? In addition to these, the SCM faced an even more pressing question: how must the movement restructure itself to survive financially? Stan Jolly recalled that "mainstream churches didn't see the SCM as being Christian enough. The increasing social justice activities of the SCM and its attacks on the status quo within the Church, [and] its perceived radicalism ... were becoming troubling to the traditional donors."[134] In 1965, the SCM chose Jolly (an undergraduate in religious studies at McMaster) as its national president, to spearhead the process of clarifying its purpose and restructuring. A constitutional committee was formed to explore these matters, and it "split evenly over the theological issue." The "only report forthcoming was that produced by the more 'radical' element," which included Stan Jolly and the study secretary, Fred Caloren.[135]

This report, issued in 1966, was divided into two parts. The first was the most controversial because, essentially, it proposed a student movement that no longer identified as specifically Christian. The document began by asserting that the "world is in ferment," that "university students in Canada live in the midst of social and academic crisis," and that "their doubts and hesitations are deeply personal and existential." It asked what "distinctive contribution ... the SCM can make to persons seeking wholeness in the university and world 'come of age'"? The answer was that the movement could serve as "an agora, an open forum which will facilitate the *encounter of persons* in freedom and acceptance, and the forthright *exchange of ideas and questions*." The Agora (which the document implicitly proposed as the new name for the SCM) would aim "to enable men and women, in spite of the fragmentation and decadence which confronts them on every hand, to realize the richness and wholeness of a more fully integrated humanity." Unlike the old Basis and Aim, there was no reference to "knowing and following Jesus Christ." The document specified that "no particular approach to what is human shall be favoured a priori," and that students should be free to examine and test "whatever avenues of life and truth may commend themselves to participants." To accommodate the diversity of the SCM units (some of which remained more Christian in their orientation, with others being more interested in psychology or politics), it was acknowledged that "the structuring of the forum, and the orientations adopted from time to time and place to place will reflect the nature of the agora and the diversity of people and issues which meet there." The only "Christian" element in this document appeared at the end of the first section, perhaps added to reassure more traditional Christians in the SCM: "We are fully confident that the agora as described in terms of its *raison d'être* and its concern for persons will enjoy the presence of students who style themselves Christian, and will not be deprived of the self-authenticating presence of Jesus Christ."[136]

What is surprising about this document is not only its religious neutrality but also its political neutrality. If "no particular approach to what is human" was to be privileged a priori, and if students in each unit of the Agora could choose whatever focus they wished, then there was little chance that it would develop a nation-wide political character similar to SUPA. This is particularly surprising considering that Fred Caloren, a co-author of the document, was politically sympathetic to the New Left and wished to make the SCM more relevant in the politically charged student milieu of the sixties. Stan Jolly argued that the document was not apolitical but rather "profoundly political," since "it recommended a loosely structured forum where important issues could be freely and openly debated without the financial or ideological constraints imposed by organized religion or political bias."[137] In many ways, the document would have formalized what was already happening within the SCM; that is, that it would be a decentralized movement in which each local unit would serve as a forum for discussion, and that discussion topics would be determined by what the participants deemed to be important. But the nature and history of the SCM had ensured that much of that discussion would revolve around the nexus between spirituality and social justice. With the severing of the link between the movement and its historical roots in the Christian left, it was far from certain that the proposed Agora would continue to be a political force in the student protest scene on campuses. At the same time, officially severing its connection from Christianity most certainly would have led many mainline Protestant churches (the SCM's chief source of revenue) to cease funding the movement.

A special session of the SCM National Council was held in Aurora, Ontario in February 1966 to debate and vote on the report's proposals. The students rejected the first part of the document by a margin of three to one. Even the representatives from the University of Toronto (arguably the most "secular" of the SCM units) opposed the report, arguing that the Christian basis of the SCM provided a frame of reference and a "particular theological horizon" which "liberated us ... [to be] free to change and move with the time."[138] According to Richard Hyde, president of the University of Toronto SCM at the time, the document's proposals veered "a little too far towards no focus – too little discipline, too little anchor. I favoured going as far in that direction as you could with still a Jesus connection. But I can imagine it would have to be more tangible than 'the self-authenticating presence.' The Bible was always very important to me as an idea head-rack. The language, the linguistics were important. If we didn't have something a little more concrete to relate to ... we would just sort of fade, sort of melt down, there'd be no identity to talk about." In addition, Hyde acknowledged a more pragmatic concern: retaining the "C" in the SCM ensured the continuation of financial support from the churches.[139] However, the National Council did not propose any alternative to the Agora. The only solution to the SCM's identity crisis, it appears, was to live with the tension between religious and secular, between thought and action.

While the National Council rejected the Agora proposals, it was much more receptive to the second half of the document, which called for a significant reduction in the size of the national office. There was widespread agreement that this was a financial necessity, and as Caloren observes, it was also consistent with the student left's distrust for centralized national structures.[140] The national office was "stripped to the bone," and the general secretary, Tom Barnett, attempted to put a positive spin on it. "What has really happened," he asserted, "is that flexible structures have been thrown up and the members at all levels freed to get on with the job. The process has been drastic, but the results are already apparent – the Movement is moving again."[141] These results were not as apparent as Barnett suggested. The restructuring of the SCM allowed it to continue living, but it made it more difficult for the movement to carry out some traditional functions, which relied on national staff. For example, work camps, a regular feature of the SCM since 1945, ceased in 1967 and did not begin again until 1973.[142] And never again would there be a gathering to rival the Saskatoon conference. Furthermore, restructuring did nothing to halt the decline of the SCM. From the early to the mid-sixties, the SCM was sizeable and influential, and its contributory role to the formation of Canada's New Left was undeniable. By the late 1960s, however, far fewer students attended the SCM, and it no longer carried the same weight in the campus activist scene. As discussed in the next chapter, the increasingly secular nature of the late sixties New Left did not leave as much room for a visible Christian left in the mélange of student activism.

CONCLUSION

The years 1965 and 1966 were important for progressive and radical Christians within the mainline churches. Inspired by the challenge of the modern world, and by the new student radicalism, they were determined to engage with the wider world, to challenge unjust social structures, and to be "where the action is." While their achievements were not always as radical as their intentions, they were clearly responding to the new currents of the sixties, including the youth protest movement.

More importantly, these years mark a high point for young Christian-identified radicals and socially conscious Christian youth organizations within the Canadian New Left, particularly for the SCM, and particularly in centres of student activism such as Toronto. But at the same time, the SCM contained the seeds of its own disintegration. Tensions between religious and secular identity, and between thought and action, put a severe strain on the movement and its traditional revenue base. In the early sixties, the SCM had served as a "midwife" to the CUCND, and remained a useful ally when the latter organization transformed itself into SUPA.[143] But by the late 1960s, the midwife no longer had a central role in the New Left that she had helped bring into being. The Christian left was one of several streams that flowed into the Canadian New Left, but as the river of student radicalism would wind its way through the late sixties, it would move further and further from the Christian stream.

5

Descent of the Avatars

Christian Youth and the Late Sixties Youth Revolt

Throughout the sixties, North American adults were reminded of the demographic importance of the youth generation in popular songs, movies, academic studies, and news media. But by 1967, the reminders were pervasive and inescapable. In January of that year, *Time* nominated "Young Generation" – which it identified as all young people under twenty-five – for Man of the Year.[1] In Robert Ellwood's terminology, 1967 was the "year of the avatars." Ellwood defines an avatar as "the 'descent' of a deity to Earth and the world of men and women, wherein the god takes visible form," or more broadly, "the embodiment in concrete reality of an abstract idea." For Ellwood, "the new youth" were the "fresh avatars" that embodied the new dissenting ideas of the sixties.[2] In 1967, as the first wave of Baby Boomers reached the age of majority, youth took centre stage; the media spotlight shone brightest on the student protestors, and on their cultural counterpart, the hippies. These groups constituted only a fraction of the Baby Boom, but in the late sixties they were perceived to be the political and cultural vanguard of their generation. There was a measure of truth in this perception, for the issues and concerns of the New Left would capture a substantial segment of the North American student population. Furthermore, as the hippie counterculture became more politicized, and as many student radicals took on elements of hip identity, the two movements began to come together. Both the counterculture and the New Left opposed oppressive social structures (though they differed on what form that opposition should take), and more importantly, they coalesced in their opposition to the Vietnam War.

Most of the iconic events that we associate with the emerging oppositional youth culture of the sixties come from these three years, 1967–69 – for example, the March on the Pentagon to end the Vietnam War, the Paris uprising of May 1968, and the protests at the 1968 Democratic National Convention in Chicago. These were pivotal years for the New Left throughout North America, as it underwent metamorphoses in its ideology, composition, and location.

What was the role of radical Christian youth in an era of revolutionary avatars? On English-Canadian campuses, and in national student organizations, some Christian youth would take a leading role in the struggles for greater student control of the education process and against Canada's complicity in the Vietnam War. Young members of Toronto's Christian left would take the lead, also, in raising awareness of US imperialism in Latin America and the complicity of Canadians in this process. However, the place of the Christian left in the English-Canadian New Left in these years was no longer as prominent as it had been in the early to mid sixties. While Christian activists and their organizations continued to play important roles, they did so in a New Left milieu that was decidedly secular in its ideology, rhetoric, and primary organizations. In the late sixties, the secularity of the New Left even pervaded Christian youth organizations such as the SCM. This chapter focuses primarily on the engagement of young radical Christians, and the organizations with which they were associated, with the evolving New Left of the late sixties. The subsequent chapter explores the ways that older Canadian Christians and the largest denominations engaged with young radicals in the late sixties, Christian or otherwise. I begin by considering the context of the New Left of the late sixties.

A "SECOND NEW LEFT"?

The years 1967 and 1968 were pivotal for the New Left throughout North America. Many historical accounts agree that the movement, in Canada, the United States, and Western Europe, experienced significant transformation.[3] Between the mid-sixties and 1968, there were several dramatic shifts: from community organizing to campus organizing; from a focus on issues to a focus on analysis; and from relative ideological openness to various Marxist ideologies. Most importantly, the protest scene in the late sixties was characterized by two contradictory features: the radicalization of the core New Left and the mainstreaming of student activism, as growing numbers of students demonstrated for control of the universities and against the Vietnam War. This profound disjuncture between the early phase and the later phase led one of my interviewees to observe that there were "two New Lefts."[4]

In English Canada, this transition was marked by the end of the Student Union for Peace Action (SUPA) in late 1967. Several factors led to its demise, including competition from the government-funded Company of Young Canadians (CYC), which absorbed many of SUPA's community organizers, and most of the organization's Toronto-based leadership.[5] As CYC drew the community organizers, the Canadian Union of Students (CUS) drew the campus activists. Some activists in SUPA, chiefly younger members, were concerned that a great deal of attention was devoted to off-campus projects while not enough was being done to foster participatory democracy in the universities. Consequently, by 1968, three or four students from "the remnants of the SUPA campus group" had become staff members of CUS.[6] Furthermore, there were two significant sources of conflict in the final months of SUPA's existence: Marxism and feminism.

The early New Left was ideologically fluid, both in the United States and Canada. What united the early New Left was a common ethos (often summed up in the term "participatory democracy"), not a common analysis. However, as Bryan Palmer notes, when young activists faced the "limitations and frustrations of community organizing, as well as the problem of why America was in Vietnam," they concluded that the movement required "a more rigorous analytic praxis."[7] According to radicals within SUPA (and without), the organization failed "to develop a coherent analysis of the structure of modern capitalism and of its specific characteristics in Canada." Marxism, they argued, provided just such a coherent analysis.[8] Many in SUPA did not accept this interpretation of the organization's weaknesses, and consequently quit. By the fall of 1967, what remained of SUPA was a short-lived "New Left Committee" of twelve radicals, whose goal was to "engage in ideological communication and other activities designed to further the New Left in Canada."[9] The committee dissolved a few months later, in early 1968.[10] However, Marxist analysis, with its emphasis on the working class as agents of change, would continue to pervade the broader movement. The New Left's turn to Marxism did not provide a unified analysis; young leftists continued to debate about the precise relationship between students and workers.[11] Thus, in the place of SUPA, there arose on English-Canadian campuses a plethora of radical groups, each offering a competing interpretation of Marxism. On the University of Toronto campus in 1969, one could find the more "mainstream" New Left Caucus (which held to the prevalent view that students could be agents of change in conjunction with the working class), but also the Stalinists, Trotskyites, and Maoists.[12]

The campus was also an important site for women's liberationists to organize. One reason for this is that the women's liberation movement originated in New Left student organizations, both in Canada and the United States.[13] The challenge posed by feminism was the other key source of friction in the final months of SUPA's existence. By 1967, women in SUPA were expressing concern over their subordinate status not only in society but also in the radical community. Like other women in the New Left across North America, they became conscious of their own exploitation and oppression. Just as the exploitation of workers or oppression of racial minorities were systemic issues requiring radical social and political restructuring, women's inequality also required fundamental changes. These changes, they argued, must begin in the radical community itself, and they began to demand that "participatory democracy" and "liberation" be extended to include women.

Throughout 1968 and 1969, women's liberation groups, such as the Toronto Women's Liberation Movement, sprang up across the country.[14] Furthermore, New Left groups that formed in the wake of SUPA such as the New Left Caucus at the University of Toronto were more inclined to take seriously the demand for women's equality, and the importance of women's issues.[15] Women's liberationists distinguished themselves from reform-minded "liberal feminists" who sought equal opportunities for women in the current social system. The young feminists who emerged from the New Left believed that the political, social, and economic system was inherently oppressive to women, and that revolution was necessary. Women's liberationists were also more likely than liberal feminists to employ confrontational protest of a kind familiar to the New Left. Nevertheless, women's liberationists shared many of the same concerns as liberal feminists, and they often worked together. These concerns included equality in the workplace, affordable daycare, and women's reproductive rights, such as the right to contraception and safe, legal abortions.[16]

Debates over Marxist analysis and feminism were responsible for the splintering of the New Left, resulting in an array of campus groups. But while a contingent of the New Left became more fractious and dogmatic, there was a countervailing tendency: student protest became a growing reality on campus, drawing an increasing number of active students, and an even larger number of supporters. Following the disappearance of SUPA, the New Left found its most popular expression in student governments (such as the Students' Administrative Council at the University of Toronto), in the larger campus left groups (such as the Toronto Student Movement or its successor, the New Left Caucus), and in nationwide student organizations (particularly the Canadian Union of Students). In the late sixties, these entities were not marked by rigidity or exclusivity, but they were characterized by radical politics, fiery rhetoric, and confrontational dealings with the university administration.[17] These groups constituted the leadership, and their constituency was a more politicized student body, chiefly in the social sciences and humanities. In all likelihood, few of these students would have self-identified as "radical" (unlike the committed core of leading activists), but growing numbers of them took part in sit-ins and protests for more student control over the universities, and against Canadian complicity in the Vietnam War. The student left waxed and waned in the late sixties, and its strength varied from campus to campus; consequently, it is nearly impossible to describe its support in precise numbers.[18] What is certain, however, is that it constituted a sizeable and visible contingent on many Canadian campuses between 1967 and 1970 (most notably at Simon Fraser University and the University of Toronto), and it often garnered sufficient support to gain control of the student governments.[19]

The "mainstream" New Left of the late sixties also developed stronger links with the burgeoning hippie counterculture.[20] Across the continent, young people rejected what they believed to be the dominant cultural values of their parents' generation: material acquisitiveness, conformity, adherence to tradition. Rather than participate in a culture that treated people like machines, the hippies chose to be "free people." In practice, this meant dropping out of school, leaving home, and moving to hip neighbourhoods in large cities, such as Yorkville in Toronto, where they embraced a lifestyle of voluntary poverty and sought spiritual enlightenment. In these communities, they nurtured an oppositional youth culture characterized by colourful clothing, rock music, drug use, a permissive sexual ethic, and alternative spirituality.[21]

The New Left could not ignore the counterculture. In spite of the turn toward orthodox Marxism, many in the New Left still believed that youth in general, especially dissident youth, would be the agents of change. They understood that the "Great Refusal" that Marcuse wrote about was cultural as well as political; thus, the hippies were co-belligerents in the struggle.[22] Furthermore, the new counterculture was a form of rebellion that many youth found accessible and appealing. Consequently, student radicals reached out to the countercultural residents of Yorkville, Toronto's hippie neighbourhood.[23] Furthermore, as the counterculture began permeating the broader youth culture in the late sixties (a trend that would increase in the early seventies), it became more common to see university students sporting long hair, smoking marijuana, and adopting the musical, artistic, and sartorial styles of the hippies.[24] While "student radical" and "hippie" remained two distinct identities, the boundaries between these identities began to blur, especially in the minds of conservative critics.

In summary, the New Left of the late sixties looked significantly different from the earlier New Left. It was more ideologically driven (at least at its core), more radical in its rhetoric, more confrontational in its strategies, and more countercultural in its style. In contrast with SUPA and its focus on community projects, many young leftists in the late sixties chose the campus as the central site for their activism, and very often the issues that engaged them were campus issues. However, many remained equally engaged with struggles for justice in the broader community and the world. The later New Left was simultaneously more exclusive (among some of the fractious campus groups) and more mainstream (particularly notable in the mass protests against the Vietnam War). On the whole, this fresh crop of New Leftists were younger, largely Baby Boomers, and while the early New Left was unwavering in its commitment to peace and nonviolence, the new radicals were more open to the possible usefulness of violence, if not in their actions, then at least in their words. All these features shaped the way that young Christians engaged with the New Left, and, as the next chapter shows, the way that denominations and sympathetic clergy responded to it.

SECULARITY AND THE "SECOND NEW LEFT"

According to Peter Warrian, there was another significant feature of the later movement: it was "more secular."[25] Compared to Canada's New Left in the early to mid sixties, in which the SCM figured prominently and protests such as those at La Macaza included Bible reading and prayer, the New Left of 1967 and beyond was decidedly more secular. In part, this reflected a broader cultural trend among young Canadians: their growing disaffection with organized religion throughout the 1960s.[26] As discussed in chapter 2, even in the early sixties there was a decline in young Canadians making professions of faith (i.e., through rites such as confirmation). By the late sixties, the burgeoning counterculture provided further impetus for youth to reject religious values that they found obsolete.[27]

Furthermore, religion occupied an increasingly marginalized space on Canadian campuses throughout the sixties. Catherine Gidney has argued that by the sixties, at English Canada's leading universities, institutional goals and purposes were no longer rooted in a specifically Christian tradition, and the place of religion on campus was largely confined to chaplaincies or to departments devoted to the academic study of religion.[28] As well, she shows that by the sixties, in response to student resistance, university administrators had largely abandoned the principle of *in loco parentis* and ceased to enforce Christian moral codes regulating student behaviour.[29] While there is limited data on the religious evolution of Canadian students themselves in the sixties, at least one study has shown that a substantial minority of students who attended Toronto's Glendon College (affiliated with York University) between 1963 and 1967 reported a shift from Christianity to agnosticism or atheism in that time period. In interviews, students credited this shift to exposure to new knowledge (including but not limited to course learning) and to their interactions with colleagues and faculty.[30]

Beyond the broader context of youth disaffection and campus secularization, an important factor in the secularity of the late-sixties New Left was the growing adherence of young radicals to varieties of Marxism. In the late 1960s, Linda Kealey (born in 1947) was a student at St Michael's College at the University of Toronto. She had grown up in a Roman Catholic home in Rochester, New York, and in her early years as a university student was active in the Newman Centre on campus. But gradually, she and her husband Greg Kealey (also a student at St Michael's) became more involved in the campus left; they attended anti-Vietnam War protests and joined the New Left Caucus, and Linda also became active in the women's movement. By her third year of university, she fully identified as a campus radical, and in her recollection four decades later, she noted that "church just kind of faded into the background. I just didn't think it was so important anymore. I don't think I attended as much either."[31] Concurrent with this shift in involvement and identity (from primary involvement and identity with the Catholic community on campus to involvement and identity with the radical community), Kealey identified a shift in worldviews. As she explained, Marxism was "not exactly a friendly ideology" to spiritual worldviews:

> It's more about the material world and material relations ... It really doesn't allow for a spiritual dimension, if you're going to take that materialist approach. I felt that was totally different from any of the religious things or [any] belief or perspective that I'd had before. I saw materialism as a new way of looking at the world ... The spiritual side seems pretty irrelevant ... it's not the perspective that's going to move things forward. And it does seem very personal and selfish too. When you think about ... class struggle and all of that, it's about the wider world and it's not just about you. It's not about the individual so much ... The solutions were not found in individuals ... but rather that you need to change the way policy works and the way institutions work. So a lot of the focus was on change and changing those larger structures [rather] than talking about perhaps your inner concerns or your inner emotions or your spiritual side. I think spirituality kind of got kicked out.[32]

Not all of Kealey's radical contemporaries at the University of Toronto shared her perspective; many in the Christian left believed that Christianity and Marxism were compatible worldviews. Nonetheless, in the aforementioned study of Glendon graduates in 1967, the majority of students who identified with the radical left also identified as "no religion," agnostic, or atheist.[33]

In short, in the late sixties, it appears that Canada's New Left was more secular – in its rhetoric, in the organizations that dominated the scene, and in the worldviews of many of its adherents. This development can be attributed to the cumulative effect of general trends among youth more broadly and students in particular, and perhaps even more so, to the increasing influence of Marxist thought among New Leftists. How did this shift affect the relationship between Christianity and the New Left in this time period? In an increasingly secular environment, was there any place for progressive or radical Christianity in the student protest scene of the late sixties?

RADICAL CHRISTIANS IN THE LATE SIXTIES NEW LEFT SCENE

Indeed, there was still space in the movement for a Christian left, made manifest in groups such as Kairos, Anglican Youth Movement (AYM) and the SCM, and in key individuals such as Peter Warrian and Tom Faulkner. However, the impact of groups such as Kairos and AYM was confined largely to their own denominations. Furthermore, the SCM no longer enjoyed the visibility that it had in the early 1960s, and the secularity of the broader New Left appears to have made its mark on the SCM itself (much to the chagrin of older supporters). Finally, prominent leaders such as Warrian and Faulkner, while motivated by their faith, operated in a decidedly secular milieu.

As the national youth organization of the United Church of Canada in the late sixties, Kairos continued to serve as a base for youth activism. While some local units still functioned as traditional church youth groups, hosting Bible studies and social events, there was a concerted effort on the part of Kairos's leaders, such as president John Foster and field worker Wayne Barr, to move the organization toward radicalism. As Harvey Shepherd noted in an article on Kairos for the *Observer*, "if people like Mr Barr, a former Company of Young Canadians volunteer, have their way, Kairos people will be looking more closely at local social and economic structures in their areas. And not necessarily endearing themselves to the people involved in those structures."[34] Clearly, the model they had in mind was the project-based activism that had begun with SUPA and continued with the CYC. Their success in fostering radical action, however, was limited. Individual members worked to raise awareness on justice issues. Kairos youth also operated "church-related coffee houses and drop-in centres across the country," and there were "close relations, formal and informal, between Kairos and such volunteer-service programs as the United Church's Caravans and the ecumenical Summer of Service and Operation Beaver."[35] There were also ambitious projects – "a Winnipeg study of slum housing, a Montreal project on high school reform, and a national project to work with the handicapped" – which "were at least in talking stages."[36] But a careful read of Shepherd's article shows that Kairos was a weak, decentralized organization with a limited budget and shrinking numbers.[37] Nevertheless, Kairos was an attempt, at least on the part of leaders such as Foster, to bring the youth revolution into the United Church of Canada, and to bring United Church of Canada youth into the revolution.

The leaders of the AYM endeavoured to do the same within the Anglican Church of Canada. Created in 1967 to replace the old Anglican Young Peoples' Association, AYM had close connections with Kairos.[38] The group's leaders saw themselves as part of the global youth movement working for a new world. One such leader was Larry Sanders, a long-haired resident of Yorkville, employee of the CYC, and a member of AYM's executive, who penned an essay on "Internationalism and Youth," which led to a panel presentation on "Youth in a Changing World" at the 1969 General Synod.[39] Like Kairos, the leaders of AYM worked not only for a new world, but also for a "New Church." As Tim Agg, AYM's national co-ordinator, explained, "the church must free itself to be Christ's agent in the world ... We must all become ministers. Ministry will continue to be personal and person-oriented. It will also have social and political dimensions, injecting Christian presence heavily into social chaos and into the political arenas."[40] AYM practised what it preached. With funding from the Anglican Church of Canada, executive members of AYM worked with Kairos, Pollution Probe, and other groups to raise environmental awareness and launch "Survival Day" – Canada's first "Earth Day" – on 14 October 1970.[41] The leaders of AYM did not succeed in transforming an ossified church structure, but they did point a way forward for Anglican youth seeking new models of radical engagement.

Radical engagement was also central for the SCM in the late sixties. Following its period of soul-searching in the mid sixties, the SCM retained its Christian identity (though agnostics and atheists were welcome), but it also became more explicitly political. The general secretary, Don Wilson, spoke of "students quoting Amos and Isaiah and pilfering considerably from Marx."[42] In 1968 the National Council noted that a "developing radical perspective characterizes the main thrust of a growing number of SCMs in Canada" – a perspective that was political, but also had personal and spiritual dimensions.[43] Without question, many students in the SCM (though not all) continued to share the ideology and concerns of the broader New Left, just as they had in the mid sixties. The difference was that by the late sixties, the SCM was a smaller organization. While the combined SCM-SUPA conference in December 1965 drew about three hundred participants, only about seventy members took part in the SCM National Council meeting in September 1967.[44] In the fall of 1969, the University of Toronto SCM had a core group of only a dozen members, and nation-wide, there were "between 200 and 300 members on about half of Canada's university campuses."[45] With the rise of New Left groups on campus, the SCM lost its traditional place of prominence as a forum for progressive and radical youth.[46] While the SCM had been an acknowledged part of the protest scene on campuses in 1965 or 1966, it is telling that when Andy Wernick published a guide to the campus left in the *Varsity* in 1969, covering a plethora of University of Toronto student groups from the Maoists to the NDP, he never mentioned the SCM.[47] This shows that Christian groups such as Kairos, AYM, and SCM were still welcome to march in the parade of the New Left in the late sixties, as they had in earlier years, but they were no longer marching at the front of the procession, nor were they calling the tune of the marching band.

Furthermore, while the SCM had chosen in 1966 to retain its Christian identity, it also retained its policy of openness. Given the increasingly secular university milieu (and the secularity of the New Left, in particular), it is not surprising that many of the participants in the late 1960s SCM were non-Christians, and this even extended to the organization's leadership. In the fall of 1969, the *Globe and Mail* published an article on the SCM in which national student president Tom Murphy (described as "a long-haired 21-year-old") speculated that half of all SCM participants did not identify as Christian or subscribe to key tenets of Christianity. Murphy added that he was not "necessarily Christian in perspective." He was, however, committed to the political goals of the broader student movement, and to the SCM's place in that broader movement.[48] For the SCM's traditional financial supporters in Canada's largest churches, news of this kind was troubling. It may have been a factor in the United Church of Canada's decision to reduce its annual grant to the SCM in the early 1970s.[49] Clearly, the secularity of the New Left permeated even ostensibly Christian student organizations in the late sixties.

On an organizational level, the New Left of the late sixties was predominantly secular, but some individual Christians held prominent positions within the movement. For instance, in 1968–69, the president of the CUS was Peter Warrian, a devout Roman Catholic who had been active in both the SCM and SUPA.[50] As someone who first read Marx, Herbert Marcuse, and C. Wright Mills while studying for the priesthood in a Baltimore seminary, Warrian was comfortable "mixing a Marxian sociology and a Christian theology,"[51] and he moved easily between the secular New Left and the Christian left. Consider, for example, two speeches that he made in late 1968. In August, Warrian made front-page news for allegedly urging Canadian students to "sock it to the administration" and "burn down their buildings if need be" in their attempt to "gain control of our universities."[52] The following month, he spoke to the SCM National Council and informed them that the SCM's primary task was to develop a theology of social action for the broader student movement, noting that the organization was "about the only Canadian student movement from which we can expect this."[53] For Warrian, there was no contradiction between his Christian identity and his radical politics.

Likewise, there was no contradiction between faith and social engagement for Tom Faulkner (1945–2010), a theology student at Victoria College and president of the Students' Administrative Council (SAC) at the University of Toronto between 1966 and 1968. Faulkner may have seemed like unlikely material for a student radical. Growing up in a middle-class family of "genetic Liberals," Faulkner had been inspired by Lester B. Pearson's role in the creation of UN peacekeeping forces. Consequently, in his first year at university (1963–64), he signed up for the Royal Canadian Air Force. However, instead of being posted in a peacekeeping position, he ended up with NORAD. As he later recalled, his brief stint in the military deepened his commitment to the peace cause because it taught him how horrible war was. Consequently, even during his years of service (while off-duty and wearing civilian garb), he attended demonstrations against nuclear war and committed acts of civil disobedience around the issue of Canadian engagement with the American military.[54]

Even though his military experience confirmed his antiwar stance, he was hesitant to label himself a radical. In a 1967 feature article for the University of Toronto *Varsity*, Faulkner claimed to be intrigued by Marxism, but he stated that he was "still a long way from being a radical," classifying himself instead as a "pseudo-liberal."[55] As he recalled in an interview, "I remember when I first ran for office, making a speech in which I put my tongue in my cheek and described myself as a representative of the extreme middle ... I hoped for ways of reconciling and bringing people together and accomplishing something, but I didn't have a program as such."[56] Nevertheless, his involvement in student politics radicalized him, and by the time he finished his final year as president, he "had no trouble identifying ... as a member of the New Left," albeit a more pragmatic leftist than an ideologue.[57] Faulkner's shift to the left was also intrinsically connected to his faith. According to a 1967 article in the *Varsity*, he believed that Christianity is "not a retreat from the world; it's a command to get involved in the world."[58] Faulkner was also inspired by J.R. Hord, his close friend and former minister at Royal York Road United Church, and by the early sixties, secretary of the United Church's Board of Evangelism and Social Service. Hord's activism is discussed in chapter 6.

Under Faulkner's leadership as the first full-time SAC president, the council adopted several radical, controversial measures.[59] It made information about birth control available to single women at a time when that contravened the law.[60] Council also rejected an offer from the academic senate for student representation because "we wanted to have real numbers, not token numbers," and because council objected to the lack of openness in university government.[61] Furthermore, councillors nearly passed a measure that would have granted money to assist American war resistors. It did not pass (though Faulkner pushed hard for it), but they did publish the Toronto Anti-Draft Programme's *Manual for Draft-Age Immigrants* at the council's printing press.[62] Initially, at the time of the Gulf of Tonkin incident in 1964, Faulkner had defended American action in Vietnam, but as the war progressed, "it just seemed to me that they were making such a serious mistake in Vietnam that we simply had to oppose it."[63]

It was Faulkner's opposition to the war that led to his most provocative decision: voting to ban Dow Chemical Company from recruiting employees on campus through the University Placement Service. In one example of Canada's extensive industrial complicity in the Vietnam War, Dow's Canadian plant manufactured polystyrene, one of the ingredients that Dow's American parent firm used to make napalm.[64] Antiwar students and faculty members opposed Dow's presence on campus because they believed that universities "should not be a cog in a machine which is invading Vietnam." As Roberta Lexier argues, "this position was directly related to debates over the purpose of the university: rather than accepting the scientific, technological, and job-training functions of higher education that unproblematically allowed corporations access to the facilities on campus, these students and professors demanded that the university should morally oppose the Vietnam War."[65] Consequently, when Dow Chemical Company was scheduled to conduct interviews on campus in November 1967, about two hundred antiwar students and faculty staged a sit-in, blocking entrances to the University Placement Services. Their actions generated counter-protests by engineering students and the right-wing Edmund Burke Society. When Faulkner and the SAC took the side of the antiwar students and moved to ban industries producing war materials from recruiting on campus, many students were outraged (especially those in engineering and law) because they did not believe that student government should engage in moral or political issues. They circulated a petition, which attracted more than 1,600 signatures, and Faulkner decided to step down from the presidency and seek a fresh mandate.[66]

The election of December 1967, which pitted Faulkner against law student Bill Charlton, was essentially a referendum on whether SAC should weigh in on controversial moral and political issues. Charlton argued that student government should remain neutral and that the university "should facilitate debate and discussion among its members rather than dictating one official truth to which all must subscribe." In contrast, Faulkner argued that neutrality was not possible, that refusing "to take action on controversial issues" was "tantamount to accepting the status quo ... Student government must, therefore, initiate debate and action to challenge the inequalities and injustices in society."[67] Out of 16,000 eligible voters, more than 50 percent took part, and returned Faulkner to office, 5,084 votes to 4,281.[68] For Faulkner, it was a vindication for a morally engaged approach to student politics, an approach rooted in his Christian faith.

THE CHRISTIAN LEFT AND THE POLITICS OF ANTI-IMPERIALISM: THE LATIN AMERICAN WORKING GROUP

Faulkner's stand against the Dow Chemical Company was part of a much broader struggle among New Leftists in the late sixties against Canadian complicity with American imperialism. For radicals in the late sixties, both in Canada and the United States, the politics of anti-imperialism were central to their political analysis and activism. The flipside of their opposition to American empire was a commitment to solidarity with international revolutionary movements. This was nothing new. Many young radicals of the early sixties New Left had been inspired by the Castro's Cuba, "for here," as Todd Gitlin writes, "was the model of a revolution led by students." On visits to Cuba from 1959 to 1961, young radicals "mixed with Cuban students, identified with their esprit and their defiance of the Colossus of the North." Furthermore, the *Port Huron Statement* called on Americans to support anti-colonial revolutions, even if these new regimes tended toward "more or less authoritarian variants of socialism and collectivism."[69] As early as 1965, activist Paul Potter could report that, increasingly, "people whom I speak to not only oppose the American intervention in Vietnam, but actively identify with the National Liberation Front and the Viet Cong."[70] The tendency of New Leftists to romanticize Cuba and Vietnam as sites of grassroots resistance against American imperialism, however, intensified in the late sixties, especially as young activists embraced revolutionary Marxism. In Bryan Palmer's words, "Student radicals could see that the weak links of the global chain of oppression and exploitation were exposed in revolutionary struggles that might actually *defeat* capitalism in Third World movements of guerilla warfare or colonial liberation. The New Left began the process of congealing different strands of revolutionary thought, from Marx and Lenin, on the one hand, through Che Guevera, Regis Debray, Frantz Fanon, and Kwame Nkrumah on the other, into a mix in which Mao often percolated to the surface."[71] The appeal of Third World Marxism for young North American radicals manifested itself in many ways, such as the Venceremos Brigades, in which thousands of young activists volunteered to visit Cuba in 1969 and 1970, where they worked cutting sugarcane.[72] In Quebec, francophone radicals eagerly expressed solidarity with revolutionary liberation movements around the world because they believed that their province was a colony of both English Canada and the United States, in need of liberation.[73] For young radicals throughout North America, to oppose the United States' imperialistic foreign policy also meant supporting global resistance movements.

Young Christians who held a radical left perspective shared the New Left's broader concerns about American foreign policy, particularly in Latin America. Four Canadian delegates (Norm Laverty, Deanna Copeland, Hugh and Judi Miller) who travelled to Puerto Rico for a Congress of Latin American Christian youth in 1966 were confronted with the challenge to educate themselves on Latin America and involve themselves in the struggle for justice. These four, along with several participants in the "Summer Event '66" organized by Kairos, decided to form the Latin American Working Group.[74]

Throughout the late sixties and beyond, the Latin American Working Group (LAWG) functioned as a centre for research, education, and advocacy for social justice in Latin America. In its earliest years, the organizational core of LAWG consisted of the core members of Toronto's Christian Left group described in chapter 4: Brewster Kneen (whose home doubled as an office for LAWG), Judy Skinner, and John Foster. Others included Peter Warrian, Nancy Hannum (who worked in the head office of SUPA), and George Cram (former president of the United Church Young Peoples' Union, and founder of Summer of Service).[75]

The make-up of LAWG is significant for several reasons. First, though LAWG never required participants to adhere to any particular creed, most of its members were Christian, with a history of active involvement in Christian youth organizations. Clearly, LAWG was intentionally ecumenical, involving both Protestants and Catholics. Furthermore, LAWG members were well connected, not only to various church, inter-church, and ecumenical bodies, but also to secular, New Left-oriented student groups. Members of LAWG would cultivate these organizational connections to raise awareness of Latin American issues and to establish partnerships (e.g., with the Canadian Council of Churches, Kairos, SCM) that would enable LAWG to extend its influence well beyond the confines of a relatively small group.

LAWG members also cultivated connections beyond Canada's borders. Partnerships were formed with Mexico's student Christian movement (MEC), and also with ULAJE (the Union of Latin American Evangelical Youth).[76] The early meetings of LAWG often included Latin American clergy or students, especially Oscar Bolioli (a Uruguayan minister, who was secretary-general of ULAJE), and Ignacio de Posadas (also from Uruguay and, at the time, a novice with the Jesuits).[77] Actual involvement with Latin Americans was important for LAWG, for its members did not wish their expressions of solidarity to be merely abstract. The minutes of an LAWG meeting from October 1966 noted that "this committee could be a contact base for Latin Americans seeking Canadian support in Latin American projects and events, that we could react to events in a useful way in times of crisis."[78] LAWG also partnered with its American counterpart, NACLA (the North American Congress on Latin America).[79]

At the outset, the group's primary purpose was to raise awareness of the Latin American struggle for social justice and to encourage Canadian young people to act in solidarity. LAWG was "determined that youth shouldn't leave things to the experts" and thus, they sought "ways in which we could all be involved as individuals." The working group decided that it would be "as much a learning group as an action group." Because knowledge provided an informed basis for action, the working group encouraged members to educate themselves on Latin American "culture, politics, its poverty, its economic relations with the rest of the continent and world."[80]

In its earliest years, LAWG encouraged that learning process by sponsoring and supporting trips to Latin America, so that Canadian youth could learn by direct observation and participation. The best way to learn was from Latin Americans themselves. LAWG's first major travel project centred on the Dominican Republic, where the United States Marines had intervened in April 1965 to quell a leftist uprising and remained for upwards of a year (facilitating the installation of President Joaquín Balaguer, and thus inaugurating a period of oppression and human rights violations). The four Canadian delegates that had attended the ULAJE Congress in Puerto Rico in early 1966 had made close contacts with youth from the Dominican Republic, from whom the Canadian delegates had learned more about the evolving political situation. With the founding of LAWG later that year, a focus on the Dominican Republic seemed like a logical place to start. These Dominicans "invited Canadians to participate in a social action project which would also facilitate dialogue between the 'north' and 'south.'"[81] Simultaneously, the Mexican Student Christian Movement invited Canadians to take part in a work camp. Consequently, in July and August of 1967, three LAWG members travelled to the Dominican Republic, where they learned "about rural and urban dynamics of Dominican society, the barriers between rich and poor, and sat in on Dominican discussions of agricultural and educational problems." Two other Canadians went to Mexico to participate in the SCM work camp, where they helped construct a conference centre. In addition, LAWG financed student activist Peter Warrian's trip to Cuernavaca, Mexico, where he spent time studying with the priest and social critic Ivan Illich. The following year, LAWG provided support for Warrian's trip to Puerto Rico, and Toronto community organizer Sarah Spinks's visit to the Dominican Republic and Cuba. When they returned to Canada, several of these participants wrote reports, reflecting on their experiences and sharing what they learned.[82]

By the fall of 1967, LAWG was devoting most of its energy and resources to educating Canadians about Latin America, largely by serving as a resource for information and a centre for research. Over the next several years, church groups, students, and others interested in Latin America would turn to LAWG for information or assistance in their research. Judy Skinner began to publish a newsletter for LAWG, which included reprints of relevant articles. In various forms, the LAWG Newsletter would continue to run for several years. Because of the group's close connection with the United Church youth movement, Kairos, they were able to publish a special issue of TAMBO (Kairos's magazine) on Latin American issues. In 1968, LAWG began to assemble study packets for interested groups, the first study kits being "Primer on Revolution," "Tentacles of Economic Power," and "Involvement in Latin America." By 1969, members of the working group were carrying out their own research to extend their knowledge base and to refine their own political analyses of the challenges facing Latin America. According to a 1969 publication about the first three years of LAWG, "we moved to attack areas of our ignorance regarding Canadian aid, trade, investment and foreign policy in Latin America."[83] Another means to educate themselves, and the broader public, was through holding seminar-style conferences, which often brought together participants from both the secular New Left and church groups. They brought in well-known experts to conduct these seminars, such as Richard Shaull, a Princeton theologian and former missionary in Latin America.[84]

Not surprisingly, as a resource centre, LAWG was not a neutral information dispenser. Its purpose was to encourage Canadians to support left-wing movements of liberation in Central and South America and the Caribbean, movements that placed activists in opposition to American imperial power and to the brutal regimes that the United States propped up in its southern sphere of influence. Another purpose was to raise awareness among Canadians about the complicity of the Canadian government and Canadian corporations in the exploitation and oppression of Latin America. Furthermore, it encouraged Canadians to make connections between economic exploitation and underdevelopment in Latin America and economic exploitation and underdevelopment in Canada. One of the significant features of Canada's anti-imperialist New Left in the sixties was left nationalism. Inspired by the work of philosopher George Grant and economists Walter Gordon and Mel Watkins, young leftists like Jim Laxer argued that Canada was an economic colony of corporate America and needed to struggle for independence.[85] They employed the same analysis and rhetoric that leftists applied to Latin America. In this way, left nationalism was essentially compatible with international solidarity. This perspective was clearly evident in LAWG's publications. A newsletter from 1969, with the caption "IMPERIALISMO," featured an image of a menacing eagle, with a long claw outstretched, a dollar sign in its beak, and perched atop a shield with the American stars and stripes.[86] The message was unambiguous: American military power and American capitalism, inextricably bound together, were the enemies of justice.

This critical interest in Latin American affairs from a left-wing, anti-imperialist Canadian perspective was also evident in the SCM throughout the late sixties. This was to be expected, given the shared membership of LAWG and the Canadian SCM. At the SCM National Conference in 1967, members passed a motion that the Organization of American States was "a subservient tool of American foreign policy for the control of Latin America" and "that were Canada to join, it would be inevitably, increasingly implicated in the economic exploitation and political domination of Latin America by the USA."[87] At the same meeting, SCM members explored the possibility of establishing an "Inter-American Work-Action-Study Project" involving students from Canada, the United States, and Latin America, to "study in depth the power structures of society in order to discover the creative role of the revolutionary community in social change."[88]

Both LAWG and the SCM were influenced by the same theological developments of the sixties. First, there was the "secular theology" of the sixties, explored in detail in chapters 3 and 4. Then there was the aforementioned influential theologian of the New Left, Richard Shaull. Throughout the sixties and early seventies, Shaull played a leading role in the World Student Christian Federation (the global parent body of the SCM), and his experience as a former missionary in Colombia lent weight to his writings about American imperialism in Latin America.[89] Furthermore, by the end of the sixties, young Christian radicals in North America were beginning to be influenced by the liberation theology emerging out of Latin America.[90]

While theology was important, it is telling that in most of its publications, LAWG's rhetoric and analysis were essentially secular. Its study packets and newsletters centred on political and economic realities rather than theological underpinnings or allusions to scripture. In this respect, LAWG reflected the dominant trend of Canada's young Christian left in the late 1960s. While Christian groups were present in the English-Canadian New Left, and while certain Christian individuals played a prominent role, they functioned in an environment where the dominant discourse, shared by all, was a secular one. In the early twentieth century, many Canadian radicals employed Christian language and concepts to communicate the socialist message[91] because Christianity was a discourse shared by most Canadians, and it clothed their message in an aura of legitimacy. However, by the late sixties, Canada had entered an era that was increasingly pluralistic and post-Christendom. Christianity was no longer a hegemonic discourse in the broader society, nor did religious phraseology lend additional weight to one's arguments. This was certainly the case among the New Left. Consequently, radicals could express their left-wing convictions in Christian terms, but their arguments were evaluated (both by their peers in the New Left and by outsiders) on political, not religious, grounds. Even as late as 1964, Christian language and symbols featured prominently in the anti-nuclear protests at La Macaza, Quebec.[92] But by the late sixties, while clergy and Christian groups took part in protests, the overall tone of left protest was decidedly secular.

CONCLUSION

The late sixties brought significant changes to the New Left. As Baby Boomers came of age and became politically active, they brought a new, impatient, and more confrontational style to the movement. The site of confrontation shifted from the community to the schools and universities, where youth campaigned for a greater role in the governing of these institutions. Moreover, as a deeply unpopular war dragged on in Vietnam, young Canadian activists demanded that Canadian institutions free themselves from complicity in the war. The avatars – the embodiment of a new set of values – had come to earth.

Radical Christian youth identified with the generation of avatars in revolt. Even in the secular milieu of late sixties radicalism, there was room for individuals like Warrian and Faulkner to speak openly about their faith as it related to politics. As well, there was still room for youth organizations like SCM, Kairos, AYM, and LAWG to function as part of the New Left. Admittedly, in the late 1960s, the SCM did not retain the place of prominence it once enjoyed, and groups such as Kairos and AYM had little visibility outside their respective denominations. Nevertheless, these groups were important because they were a Christian expression of the New Left, even if their Christian identity was often complicated, as was the case for the SCM. Furthermore, these groups and individuals also provided a link, however tenuous, between the youth of the New Left and clergy of the established churches, some of whom were eager to reach out to the young people on the other side of the generation gap. The churches had good reason to reach out to the generation of avatars.

6

Engaging with the Avatars

Churches, Clergy, and the Late Sixties Youth Revolt

By the late 1960s, North American adults were reminded on an almost daily basis of the importance of the youth generation. Denominational leaders, facing the realities of declining church attendance, especially among young people, were keenly aware of the demographic importance of youth. However, their interest in youth, and issues of importance to young people, was not merely pragmatic. Whether Roman Catholic or mainline Protestant, church leaders were impelled by the theological trends of the sixties to "dialogue with the modern world" and be "where the action is." Furthermore, some progressive clergy (including some in positions of denominational leadership) were sympathetic and eager to establish linkages with the generation of revolutionary young avatars.

Consequently, both Catholic and mainline Protestant church leaders began to pay closer attention to the youth generation, especially that subset of youth in open revolt against oppression and war, but also the youth in their own churches and denominational youth organizations. Denominational publications devoted more coverage to the increasing unrest on Canadian campuses, and to young people in general. Some denominational leaders, as well as campus chaplains, sought to ally themselves with activist students on issues of social justice, particularly Vietnam. By adopting a clear position on the Vietnam War, these progressive clerics took on a "prophetic" instead of a "priestly" role. Furthermore, progressive Christians, both clergy and active laity, would play a key role in the initial years of Rochdale College, which began its life as an alternative educational institution founded on New Left principles but soon replaced Yorkville as the beacon of Toronto's countercultural community.

While the previous chapter focused primarily on young Christian radicals in the late sixties, this chapter is concerned with older progressive Christians in Canada's largest churches, and their engagement with the young radicals of the New Left – Christian or otherwise – and the issues that concerned them. The examples in this chapter are wide-ranging, but they are illustrative of common patterns of adult engagement. Older Christians played an important role in supporting and mentoring young Christian radicals, and at times worked in close collaboration with young leftists on matters of shared concern. Radical youth provided inspiration for older clergy and laity that wished to push their denominations to the left on social and political issues. Yet, Canadian churches in the late sixties provided repeated examples of institutional inertia – of unwillingness or inability to embrace meaningful change. In spite of numerous examples of older Christians who were eager to transform the comfortable pew into an uncomfortable one, radical youth were unlikely to find a congenial home within Canada's religious establishment.

PROTESTANT CHURCHES AND THE LATE SIXTIES NEW LEFT

Canada's mainline Protestant denominations had good reasons to reach out to young people. By the late sixties, the demographic realities of the Baby Boom were hard to ignore. And for leaders of the United and Anglican churches, it was also impossible to ignore the statistics about church membership. In June 1967, the *United Church Observer* reported that between 1965 and 1966, for the first time in the history of the denomination, membership declined. There was also a decline in the number of Sunday School members and ministerial candidates, as well as an increase in the number of "non-resident members."[1] Likewise, in October 1967, the *Canadian Churchman* reported that membership in the Anglican Church of Canada had decreased by nearly 67,000 members since 1965, as well as a decline in Sunday School attendance and in the number of students training in Anglican theological seminaries.[2] Canada's Roman Catholics were not immune either; their attendance figures began to slide in the late sixties.[3] Although smaller evangelical groups such as the Pentecostal Assemblies of Canada witnessed steady growth in the sixties,[4] mainline churches were clearly in trouble. These trends were not unique to Canada, or even to North America. According to Hugh McLeod, around 1967 "the statistics of religious practice took a dramatic downward plunge. Nearly every country in the Western world saw a major decline, and the same broad trends were seen both in the Protestant churches and in the Roman Catholic Church."[5]

One of the key reasons for this decline, particularly in liberal Protestant churches, was their inability to retain young people. This was not an entirely new problem; even in the late nineteenth century, Canadian clergy expressed dismay that young people (in particular, young males) stayed away from church, in favour of less respectable activities. Revivals were a means of drawing young men away from the taverns and into the churches.[6] However, the circumstances of the sixties, especially the declining fortunes of the churches overall, and the demographic importance of young people, made the absence of youth much more alarming. Writing about American churches, Benton Johnson notes that "the single most important source of the unprecedented decline in the membership of liberal Protestant denominations that began in the late 1960s was the failure of their young people to become affiliated."[7] In these years, Canadian Protestant church leaders were not oblivious to the absence of young people, and some made an explicit connection between the membership crisis and the defection of youth.[8] Consequently, they believed that it was necessary to open a dialogue with the Baby Boom generation to bridge the cultural and political divide and discern the issues that were important to them. While the crisis in Canada's churches was not the only reason for engagement with youth, and not necessarily even the main reason, it was undeniably an important factor. It does not seem coincidental that churches increased their focus on youth in the late sixties, or that the leading church periodicals (the *Observer*, *Canadian Churchman*, and *Canadian Register*) intensified their coverage of youth issues between 1967 and 1969.

At the same time, the Canadian churches' attempts to reach disaffected youth or at least understand them were not merely a self-serving ploy to bolster attendance. New theological trends in both Roman Catholic and mainline Protestant churches compelled them to address the pressing social and political issues of the day, issues of great importance to young activists. Furthermore, by the late sixties, denominational youth organizations such as Kairos and AYM had been politicized, and young people in the churches, impatient for change, demanded that their voices be heard. These developments transcended national borders, and were evident at the 1968 assembly of the World

Council of Churches, held in Uppsala, Sweden. By all accounts, the two most noteworthy features of this gathering were its focus on social and political issues such as racism and global poverty, and the presence of a large, vocal contingent of youth delegates.[9] The latter were not permitted to vote on resolutions; nevertheless, their influence on the assembly was undeniable, and their demands were reflected in council resolutions opposing the draft and calling for a cessation of bombing in North Vietnam.[10] Adult delegates in Uppsala, and adult church leaders in Canada, were also aware of current events – the Paris uprising of May 1968, and the Prague Spring in Czechoslovakia – and knew that youth were making history. In short, the youth revolt was international and pervasive, and the churches, for reasons both theological and pragmatic, were ready to hear what the young revolutionaries had to say.

In their attempts to appeal to youth, some churches and church publications adopted the rhetoric, art, music, and institutions of the counterculture with varying degrees of success, and they created spaces where young people could perform their hip identities, but in a religious context. While churches devoted substantial attention to the hippies (and, to a greater degree, to the multitude of youth who had taken on elements of countercultural identity), churches also engaged with the political concerns of the New Left students. The appeal to the New Left took several forms. First, some ministers and church leaders, as well as individual congregations, openly expressed solidarity with activist youth. There was a greater sympathy evinced for the concerns of the student left in mainline churches. Furthermore, churches, both mainline Protestant and Roman Catholic, began to adopt the rhetoric of the student activists. On the whole, however, the churches' embrace of the New Left was more style than substance. Denominational hierarchies were usually willing to make token gestures and concessions to radical style, to make space for some radical experimentation (within limits), and even to permit some clergy and laity to challenge openly the institutional church (also within limits). But with a few notable exceptions, they were not prepared to allow their institutions to be radically transformed. Consequently, their appeal to activist youth remained limited.

Most often, the churches' attempt to express solidarity and support for New Left activists took place at the ground level (e.g., individual ministers and congregations), rather than at the level of church hierarchy. Not surprisingly, some of the most supportive clergy were to be found in the university milieu, where they had frequent contact with radical students and faculty. At the University of Toronto, they included the United Church minister Eilert Frerichs, an alumnus of the SCM and the anti-nuclear protests at La Macaza. In 1967, when he was in his late twenties, Frerichs was appointed the United Church chaplain at the university. His continuing involvement with the University of Toronto SCM was aided by the fact that the student organization shared its offices with the United Church chaplaincy.[11] Another sympathetic adult was Ian Mackenzie, an Anglican priest and faculty member at Trinity College. Born in Toronto in 1934, Mackenzie had spent the early sixties in New York City, where he became heavily involved in the civil rights movement, taking part in picketing and demonstrations, and helped establish an organization to combat racism within the Episcopal Church (the American counterpart to the Anglican Church of Canada). Upon his return to Toronto, Mackenzie found that his years of activism in an African-American milieu had changed him and that the genteel environment of Trinity College ("going at four o'clock to the faculty lounge and drinking sherry and playing chess") was not meeting his needs to work for social change.[12] His education activism will be explored later in the chapter.

As for congregations, radicals young and old found a welcoming home in a handful of downtown churches with established histories as hubs of social justice activism. Chief among these was the Church of the Holy Trinity, an Anglican parish located in the shadow of Eaton's. The church had a reputation for social and political activism under John Frank (rector from 1935 to 1962) and under his successor, Jim Fisk (rector from 1962 to 1976). Its parishioners included an array of prominent activists, several of them discussed in earlier chapters: Edgar File (who directed the Canadian Urban Training Program discussed in chapter 4); Brewster and Cathleen Kneen (omnipresent in the Christian left); Don Heap (also known as Dan Heap, a worker priest and alumnus of the SCM) and his wife Alice; and Ted Mann (another SCM alumnus and a former Anglican priest, who taught sociology at York University and ran "his own hippie haven at home").[13]

But even at higher levels, mainline churches showed a measure of support for young activists. One such measure was the decision of General Synod in 1969 to provide funding for an environmental awareness project carried out by Anglican youth.[14] Another was the convening of "youth synods," such as the gathering of 300 youth held in the Diocese of Toronto in March 1968. Although this synod had no decision-making power, it was an opportunity for their voice to be heard in the church, as they discussed issues of importance to youth, "everything from peace, drugs and birth control to education, politics and science."[15] Such issues received greater attention in the *Canadian Churchman* when the left-leaning Hugh McCullum took over as editor in 1968. Indeed, youth radicalism received a great deal of attention in the Anglican, United, and Roman Catholic periodicals in the late sixties (less so in the *Canadian Churchman*, more so in the *Observer* and the *Canadian Register*). Some of this coverage was sympathetic, though even sympathetic analyses were not free of criticism.[16]

In the hierarchy of the United Church of Canada, the most supportive voices for the young activists were to be found in the Board of Evangelism and Social Service (E & S S), led in the late sixties by J.R. ("Ray") Hord, the secretary of the board until his premature death in March 1968. When Hord succeeded J.R. Mutchmor as secretary in 1963, his superiors might have expected that he would continue his predecessor's legacy of denouncing vice, such as alcohol consumption and gambling. Instead, he shifted the emphasis of E & S S to social structural issues. Hord refused to distinguish "between moral issues and social problems. Poor housing, unjust working conditions, international aggression – they all were moral issues to him."[17] He developed a reputation for speaking bluntly on issues of social justice, driven by "a real passion to apply his understanding of the social implications of the gospel," and "his instinctive sympathy for the under-dog – the Viet Nam peasant, the Canadian Indian, the urban poor, the homeless draft resister."[18]

Ray Hord and his associate secretaries, Gordon Stewart and Arch McCurdy, openly expressed their admiration for the New Left. For example, Arch McCurdy ended a favourable review of "Youth and the Protest Movement" with the assertion that protest "is positive. To protest evil is to proclaim good. For the church to engage in protest is to be consistent with its historic witness. In today's terminology, Jesus was a Radical and the disciples constituted the New Left."[19] And in an address on "Youth" published posthumously in the *Observer*, Ray Hord observed that although he was "discouraged by the large numbers of conformists among the young," he was "a little more optimistic about the 'hippies'" and "much more optimistic about the future ... when I see the student radicals on the New Left." Hord was critical of the radicals' lack of "personal discipline" and their disdain for political parties, but he believed that their "emphasis on individual worth discovered in meaningful community must be accepted."[20] Hord was eager to make connections with such activists and to understand the seismic cultural and political shifts taking place among Canada's youth. To this end, in 1966, he set up the Youth Committee on Christian Presence, a think-tank of about a dozen members, including Tom Faulkner, John Foster, Nancy Hannum, and Brewster Kneen. As Faulkner recalls, its purpose was "to advise Ray as to what the church might do to cope with this new thing that was appearing in the sixties – the whole youth culture thing, and the break-away from the church, really."[21] Under Hord's direction, E & S S took the most substantive measures, and the most successful ones, in reaching out to student activists.

The least substantive gesture to the New Left, but probably the most pervasive, was the way in which churches adopted the rhetoric of student activists. "Radicalism" and "revolution" entered the ecclesiastical lexicon. For example, the editor of the *Canadian Register* noted "the modern revolutionary spirit" that gripped the Roman Catholic Church.[22] Likewise, in a feature article for the *Canadian Churchman* on the Anglican Church's 1967 General Synod meeting, Hugh McCullum spoke of the "radical tone" of the gathering, evident "in the sense of frustration with establishment practices; a sense of urgency that God might get away from the institutionalized church and out into the world, leaving the Church well behind Him; a sense that youth must be not only heard but listened to; a sense of revolution within and without the Church." In total, McCullum used the term "radical" or "radicalism" thirteen times in the article, not counting the title. Considering that synod rejected a motion that Canada discontinue "the sale of war material to the United States," it is possible that McCullum overstated its revolutionary zeal.[23]

It even became commonplace for Anglican and Roman Catholic bishops to employ anti-institutional rhetoric. For example, at the 1967 General Synod, Anglican bishop Ralph Dean remarked in his address, "We must realize that the world and the Church all over the world are in a state of revolt. It is puzzling and I don't have the answers, but I do know there is nothing more exciting because God is out there in the world and we must get out there with Him, rather than sitting in these musty halls trying to preserve something that may not be worth preserving."[24] Likewise, in a 1966 address in Toronto, Archbishop Pocock of Toronto told his audience that any "Catholic organization that does not renew itself internally and that does not become apostolic is going to die," and that "in this age of renewal of the Church, there are going to be organizations that will die, other organizations that will be renewed, and there will be new structures and organizations that will grow up in the Church."[25]

Editors and church leaders adopted this rhetoric in good faith; by choice or by necessity, churches underwent significant changes in the sixties, and these changes undoubtedly *seemed* revolutionary to the participants. By taking up the mantle of radicalism, they were also identifying with the youthful, dissenting spirit of the times, and presenting their denominations as places where young radicals could feel at home. Even some conservative evangelicals appropriated the popular rhetoric of radicalism, though they stripped it of its political meaning, such as the Ontario Bible College student who told a *Varsity* reporter that "we are revolutionaries in that we tell people they must be regenerated."[26]

As the latter example shows, rhetoric is not the same as substance, especially if the words take on an entirely different meaning. When it came to substantial measures to address the concerns of young activists, measures that would have generated controversy, challenged the power structure of the denominations, or threatened their sources of funding, the churches proved unwilling to move. For example, while the Anglican Church made token gestures to youth representation, General Synod still failed to pass a motion ensuring that future synods would include at least four voting delegates under twenty-five.[27] This was in 1969, when half the population was under twenty-five years of age and when students were finally succeeding in their demands for greater representation in university government. Whatever the "radical" rhetoric of mainline churches, they often proved to be more reactionary than revolutionary. Stymied by institutional inertia and fear of controversy, church leaders could not transform their denominations from "priestly" establishments into "prophetic" communities. There is no better illustration of the churches' failure to assume the "prophetic" mantle than the controversy in the United Church of Canada over Ray Hord and the Vietnam War.

A PUPPY-DOG TALE: RAY HORD, THE UNITED CHURCH, AND THE VIETNAM WAR

The key issue that galvanized the American New Left in the late sixties was the Vietnam War. As the war escalated, so too did the antiwar movement. By 1967, hundreds of thousands would take part in protests, and by 1969, millions – people of all ages and all walks of life.[28] But youth protest was at the core of the antiwar movement, and its prominent leaders were young radicals from groups like Students for a Democratic Society. The war also galvanized the New Left in Canada for several reasons. First, for better or worse, the Canadian movement was heavily influenced by its American counterpart. The war also had particular resonance in Canada because of the presence of some 40,000 American draft dodgers.[29] And as was noted in the previous chapter, Canadian leftists in the late sixties began paying more attention to the impact of America's global imperialism not only on Vietnam but also on the "wealthiest colony": Canada.[30] Young left nationalists saw Pearson as a colonial governor, a regional puppet of America's "corporate liberalism." Consequently, when Toronto students protested against Dow recruiting on campus, or worked to assist American draft dodgers, they were not only opposing an immoral war. They were also fighting for Canadian sovereignty, for Canada could only be free of complicity in the American war machine when it achieved economic and political independence from the American empire.

This is the context for Ray Hord's remarks in a speech to the Ontario Welfare Council on 18 May 1967. Deviating from his prepared address, Hord commented on America's influence on Canadian foreign policy. Prime Minister Pearson, he said, "appeared to be a puppy-dog on LBJ's leash." According to the *Globe and Mail*, Hord told his audience that "Canadians should not support 'Americans who are bombing the hell out of those poor people.' He added that God is on the side of the hurt, the maimed and the defenseless and said consequently God must be on the side of the Vietnamese."[31]

There was precedent for Hord's criticism of America's military within the United Church. In 1965, the United Church of Canada's Committee on the Church and International Affairs had issued a statement on the Vietnam War. While it was couched in the language of anti-communism, the tenor of the statement was critical of American prosecution of the war. The committee called on Prime Minister Pearson to urge the Johnson administration to refrain from invading North Vietnam and to cease the bombing campaigns.[32] However, Hord's choice of words was much more provocative; he seemed to side with the North Vietnamese against the United States, and he took aim, as well, at the Pearson government's apparent complicity. Furthermore, because Hord's comments appeared the following morning in the *Globe and Mail*, they generated immediate public attention – and ire.

Hord's remarks upset senior church leaders, especially Wilfred Lockhart, the moderator of the United Church, and Ernest Long, secretary of the General Council. This was partly because Pearson was "a United Church hero and son of the manse."[33] There was another reason, too. As Kenneth Bagnell explained in a *United Church Observer* feature article on Hord, "There was apparent agreement between the moderator and Long that the comment hurt the church in Ottawa especially since a delegation from the church's International Affairs Committee was to visit Paul Martin the next week. Though some persons, especially political journalists, take a somewhat cynical view of how productive are the visits of church delegations to astute politicians, this was to be an official call."[34] Lockhart acted quickly, issuing a hasty apology on behalf of the United Church and dissociating it from Hord's "personal" remarks, which he called "unworthy and unjustified."[35] However, not everybody agreed with the moderator; many rushed to Hord's defence and wrote supportive letters. As one of his friends wrote, "I wonder who apologized for Amos and Elijah?"[36] The implication in the latter question is clear: Hord had taken up the mantle of a prophet and was calling his denomination to do likewise.

Hord's "puppy-dog" remark was probably not as controversial as his next move. At some point in 1967, he asked his assistant to make contact with Mark Satin of the Toronto Anti-Draft Program, which offered aid to American draft resisters in Canada. His assistant replied, "talked to Mark Satin as you requested. He was quite interested in what we were doing and obviously quite willing to co-ordinate any efforts."[37] Ultimately, this led to a decision in late September 1967 by E&SS to grant $1,000 to the Toronto Anti-Draft Program.[38] The sum was not large, but the symbolic value of the donation was greater than the monetary value. The board was taking a stand because it supported the right of young Americans to abstain from war, leading by example, and encouraging ordinary church members to support the cause.

Once again, Hord and his colleagues at E&SS had created a media event without the approval of General Council or of the moderator. Within days, Wilfred Lockhart had overturned the board's decision.[39] But Lockhart's quick action did little to quell the backlash from conservative church members. Hord received a flood of letters, many of them from irate laypeople, threatening to withdraw financial support for the Church. "The Church is meddling with the liquor laws," one writer complained, "and now this meddling with American draft dodgers is, as far as I am concerned, the last straw." "If even *one penny* of my miniscule contribution to the work of the Church is directed toward this project," wrote another, "I would be inclined to withdraw it entirely." Another letter-writer railed against the character and behaviour of the war resisters: "Have you discussed the behavior of these young men with any responsible young people in Canada? (Not the coffee-house, demonstrator type, but the reliable young people the church expects to be its backbone in the future.) Many young Canadians frown on the entry of these men to Canada. I have heard the following comments, 'They're cowards, these types.' And 'In Canada they just criticize Canadians. I wonder what kind of men they will grow up to be.'"[40]

These writers were not alone in their opposition to aiding war resisters. A poll taken of 2,400 United Church members in 1968 showed that most respondents disapproved of the war, and approximately 49.7 percent agreed that the United States "should immediately and unconditionally stop the bombing of North Viet Nam." But when asked if "Canadian churchmen are justified in extending support to refugees from the US Selective Service," the majority of respondents, over 51 percent, answered no.[41] When Larry Hoffman, a war resister living in Toronto, was invited to speak at Timothy Eaton Memorial United Church on a Sunday evening in late 1968, the audience of about four hundred listened politely to his appeal for material support for draft dodgers. But during the question and answer session that followed, an older man stood up and berated Hoffman "for causing Canada so much difficulty. He said the United States was the protector of the world's freedom, benevolently looks after the interests of Canada, protects her private property and industry and is saving the world from the international Red menace. According to him, I and my fellow draft dodgers were placing this relationship in serious jeopardy."[42] The man's statement elicited "a tremendous ovation." Clearly, not all United Church members agreed with Hord on American foreign policy, or on draft dodgers.

However, Hord also received a flood of supportive letters, many of them from ministers, peace activists, and well-known public figures, including June Callwood, Senator Keith Davey, and Stanley Knowles. Significantly, he received a strong letter of support from N. Bruce

McLeod, who would serve as moderator of the United Church from 1972 to 1974: "If 'powers that be' think that actions such as your board has recently taken alienate support for the Church – they are mistaken – there are far more people daily alienated by the *up-tight fearfulness of a Church that is afraid to stick its neck out*."[43]

Hord's controversial actions were important for two reasons. First, more than any other high-ranking Canadian church official, he won the admiration of the New Left students. The issue of Vietnam forged a real link between E&SS and the young activists. For example, University of Toronto SAC president Tom Faulkner has identified Hord (his former minister at Royal York Road United Church in the early sixties) as an inspiration and mentor, and when Faulkner supported the Dow protest in the fall of 1967, he was undoubtedly well aware of Hord's controversial actions earlier in the year. Second, Hord's actions galvanized the left in the United Church, and thus played an important role in the denomination's eventual shift to the left. As Sandra Beardsall argues, for the first forty years of its existence, "the United Church had functioned, like other liberal Protestant churches in North America, as a classic 'denomination' in a sociological sense": "'securing peace and harmony through location of the broadest, uncontentious common ground.' Only occasionally had its progressive views threatened that harmony in a serious way, and Hord represented such a threat. What truly seemed to discomfit the leadership was the challenge to their perception of the church's vocation as a broad, centrist Christian home for Protestant Canadians. With that vocation had come not only the financial and institutional stability that accrued to the nation's largest group of Protestants, but also the perks of public recognition: the ear of the Prime Minister, the attention of the press, and a place at the civic table."[44] Hord challenged the Church to assume a critical, prophetic role in Canadian society, even if it meant abandoning the stability and perks of its priestly role.

By the end of the sixties, Canada's churches were responding to Hord's challenge. Between 1969 and 1971, the United Church moved much more boldly on the issue of the Vietnam War, working in conjunction with the Canadian Council of Churches and the Toronto Anti-Draft Program to aid American war resisters in Canada.[45] Significantly, while the decision to assist draft dodgers in 1967 had generated a torrent of angry letters to Hord and the E&SS, there was comparatively little push-back in 1970. Perhaps this was a sign that attitudes within the Church had changed. Moreover, the Church developed a heightened awareness of global justice issues, not only in Vietnam but in other countries throughout the developing world,[46] and it became less hesitant to speak prophetically about such matters. The United Church's engagement with the New Left was one factor in the transformation of the United Church, which began in the 1960s and continued in subsequent decades.[47] Sadly, Hord did not live to see the transformation he helped to inspire; he died from a sudden heart attack in March 1968, and was hailed as a "prophet" by both the secular and religious press.[48]

However, some argue that the greatest misfortune in this story was the United Church's missed opportunity in 1967. Beardsall explains: "Hord had seen the disaffection of the young. While he saw some as hopelessly conformist, he also was a beacon for many of them. The church's leaders did not take them into account. The young disappeared, and the church declined further. When, in the 1970s and 80s, the United Church did take, collectively, more culturally radical stands, the church's place in the public sphere had already significantly diminished. In trying to muzzle Ray Hord, the church may have muzzled its last truly public prophet."[49] In other words, Beardsall implies that if the denominational leadership had taken a more radical stance on Vietnam and other social justice issues in the late sixties, it might have retained its young people. At best, this is a debatable assertion, for there were factors other than politics that drove young people from church (for example, the fact that most churches were not youth-oriented in their music or style of worship). Furthermore, even if the church hierarchy had expressed solidarity with the New Left radicals, it is unlikely that most rank-and-file United Church members would have followed suit. Nevertheless, for some left-oriented youth, both inside the church and out, when the denomination failed to oppose the war, it conveyed the message that young radicals were not welcome. For progressives who hoped to bridge the gap between the United Church and youth, the late sixties were a time of hope and disappointment.

THE CATHOLIC LEFT IN TORONTO AND THE LIMITS OF "RENEWAL"

For progressive Roman Catholics, the late sixties were also marked by hopefulness and disappointment. In the wake of Vatican II, and the pervasive rhetoric of "renewal," "dialogue," and "the apostolate of the laity," some hoped that the Church could be transformed into a more democratic community, one attuned to the demands of global justice. Significantly, the most progressive voices in the Archdiocese of Toronto were those clergy and laity who worked with youth. They saw more evidence that the Spirit was moving in the dissenting young people than in the hierarchy of the Church, and they hoped that Church leaders would listen to these dissenting voices. But when Pope Paul VI issued the encyclical *Humanae Vitae*, progressive Catholics discovered that there were limits to institutional renewal. Just as the Catholic left was taking shape throughout North and South America, this document signalled a shift to the right and a retreat from the openness of Vatican II. Furthermore, for some progressive Catholics and young activists, and undoubtedly for many youth raised Catholic, it only confirmed their perception that the Church as an institution had become irrelevant.

Social Catholicism was nothing new in the Archdiocese of Toronto. As early as the 1930s, it found its expression in the *Catholic Register* (later the *Canadian Register*), under the direction of Henry Somerville. However, reform-minded Catholicism flourished in the sixties, due in no small part to Vatican II and its call to engage with the modern world. As well, Toronto benefited from the leadership of a relatively liberal archbishop, Philip Pocock,[50] and the leftward slant of the *Canadian Register* under the direction of P.A.G. McKay. And the late sixties witnessed the advent of a militant Catholic left. In the United States, its most visible exponents were two priests, Daniel and Philip Berrigan, who were involved in civil rights and antiwar activism. In South America, Roman Catholic bishops declared that the Church must have "a preferential option for the poor," which many priests and nuns understood to be a mandate for Marxist revolution. Thus, liberation theology spread throughout Latin America.[51] For progressive and radical Catholics, these developments within the Church were exciting, but so too were the developments outside the Church. Some Canadian Catholics were eager to understand the social justice movements led by radical youth.[52] Reflecting on the decade, Ted Schmidt (a layman in Toronto who taught at a Catholic high school in the sixties and would later edit the left-leaning *Catholic New Times*) recalls the sixties as "the greatest generation ... and largely because from what was seen as a secular movement in the world, to me was a moment of revelation, that the God of the Bible was expressing God's Self in movements of radical inclusivity. Witness [the] peace movement, the civil rights movement, the burgeoning of the feminist consciousness, [the] gay and lesbian movement, and I don't think the Church and its priestly leadership really grasped the fact that the spirit that was moving through the culture was really the Holy Spirit ... There were terrible excesses to it as well, but anybody with a background could set apart the excesses and see [that] the movement towards the earth, the movement towards understanding of feminism, peace and justice was really of God. To me it was an extraordinary time of God's activity in the world."[53]

In Toronto, the most prominent clerical advocates for progressive Catholicism were to be found at St Michael's College, affiliated with the University of Toronto. These included theologians Gregory Baum, an influential adviser at the Second Vatican Council, and Stan Kutz, associate chaplain at the university's Newman Centre. In the sixties, St Michael's acquired an international reputation as a magnet for reform-minded Catholics. As Kutz recalls, "we quickly attracted priests, nuns, laypeople. It was part of the ferment of the times. People were looking not only to get a graduate education in theology, but one that would be more liberal than what was generally available certainly anywhere in Canada, possibly anywhere in North America at that time."[54] A community of progressive Catholics, both lay and religious, developed at the University of Toronto. Their bonds were strengthened by the fact that many of them (including Baum and Kutz) also belonged to Therafields, a close-knit psychotherapeutic community centred around Lea Hindley-Smith.[55]

Undergraduate students at St Michael's College, like faculty, were also moving to the left, though this probably owed as much to the student movement at the University of Toronto and across North America as it did to Vatican II. While some students from St Michael's became involved in radical campus groups (notably Greg and Linda Kealey, who were active in the New Left Caucus), they were the exception.[56] Peter Warrian argues that "notwithstanding Vatican II, the ghetto psychology in Catholicism [was] still fairly strong." Consequently, he argues that Catholics were rare in SUPA, and even "getting actively involved in the SCM would be something like marrying a Protestant."[57] Nevertheless, while few would have identified as radicals, some Catholic students were still animated by the same concerns that drove the campus left: a demand for greater democracy and opposition to war. In many ways, progressive faculty shared these concerns too.

The vehicle that brought progressive students and faculty together was the Newman Centre. Occupying a Victorian mansion at the corner of St George and Hoskin Avenue, the Newman Centre ministered to the spiritual needs of Catholics on campus, functioning as a de facto parish for young adults. The club thrived in the mid to late sixties; undergraduates, graduates, and faculty, as well as reform-minded Catholics from off-campus, were drawn by the innovative worship. The Newman Centre's liturgical experiments included Mass celebrations in English instead of the traditional Latin (at the time, a new phenomenon for Toronto Catholics in the post-Vatican II era, and not yet officially sanctioned in the archdiocese) and folk music accompanied by young guitarists. People were also drawn to the centre by the personal charisma of its chaplain from 1965 to 1967, Michael Quealey. In these years, Quealey was in his early thirties, and was not only a priest in the Basilian order but also a doctoral candidate and teaching assistant in Canadian history at the University of Toronto (and, in later years, a popular teacher in the Humanities at York University). As his assistant chaplain, Stan Kutz, recalled, Quealey was the "driving energy" behind the innovative liturgies, as well as a gifted speaker: "people said when Mike preaches a sermon, everybody gets a big hug. And he was very good at inviting people in and listening to them."[58] Both Kutz and Quealey were theological liberals, critical of the Catholic Church's power structure, which, as they perceived it, discouraged lay participation and stifled free expression. Their theological critique was also political (at least implicitly), and it infused the community that gathered at the Newman Centre in the late sixties.

In these years, the Newman Centre does not appear to have been as politicized as the SCM (essentially its mainline Protestant counterpart), though some participants would later become active in radical campus groups.[59] However, both clergy and lay participants at the centre were sufficiently politically engaged to draw the ire of more conservative Catholics in Toronto. An example of this was the Newman Centre's antiwar position and activism. As Quealey recalled in his memoir *My Basilian Priesthood*, the Newman Centre included young antiwar Americans who had chosen to study at St Michael's College as a way to avoid the draft, and both Quealey and Kutz (who had opposed the Vietnam War from its earliest stages) counselled and supported these students. Quealey and Kutz even participated in raising funds at the Newman Centre's weekly gatherings for a Vietnam humanitarian assistance project organized by the Quaker Medical Relief Fund. Some of these funds would be disbursed among the North Vietnamese and the Viet Cong.[60] Recalling Toronto's Newman Centre, Warrian agreed that there were social justice activists associated with the Newman Centre, at least on certain issues, but he contended that "you didn't have an organizational outreach like the SCM and with SUPA."[61] Even so, the Newman Centre retained an important connection with the politicized SCM through Michael Quealey. He had become involved in the University of Toronto SCM chapter in 1965, and the following year he was nominated to serve on the SCM's national executive – the first Roman Catholic priest to hold such a position.[62] Nevertheless, what made the Newman Centre most significant, in terms of political formation, was not the specific linkages to New Left-inspired groups such as the SCM, or even its engagement on issues such as the Vietnam War. Rather, its chief significance was that it provided an atmosphere where questioning and challenging dominant structures – particularly the Church – was welcome.

In challenging the Church, a key issue for progressive Canadian Catholics in the sixties was contraception. In his 1930 encyclical *Casti Connubii*, Pope Pius XI decreed that "any use whatsoever of matrimony exercised in such a way that the act is deliberately frustrated in its natural power to generate life is an offence against the law of God and of nature, and those who indulge in such are branded with the guilt of a grave sin."[63] In the wake of Vatican II, many hoped that the Church would find a way to change its position on this matter. In the decade of the "sexual revolution," when "the Pill" was legalized throughout the Western world, this issue had significance beyond the confines of the Catholic Church.[64] For women's liberation activists (and their supporters in the New Left), the issue was very real, for it involved control over their own bodies and over family planning. For progressive Catholics such as Gregory Baum and Stan Kutz, however, the question of contraception was also symbolic of a wider problem – a dogmatic, authoritarian approach to religion, in which truth was handed down to the laity by a clerical hierarchy.[65] Instead, as Kutz told an audience at the Catholic Information Centre in 1965, lay Catholics should listen to their conscience on matters such as birth control, even if it leads them to disagree with the pope. Because the Spirit of God indwells lay members, Kutz argued, the locus of authority must shift from the institution to the individual. As the *Toronto Star* reported, he hoped that "the ferment stirring the Church" would result in mature Christians "who will act with competence and confidence in facing the challenges that life poses," and "act from inner principles and convictions, not because a certain response has been impressed by a process of brainwashing."[66] Polls suggest that nearly half of lay Catholics agreed with Kutz and his colleagues.

Unfortunately, the Church hierarchy did not agree. In July 1968, Pope Paul VI issued *Humanae Vitae*, in which he condemned "any action which either before, at the moment of, or after sexual intercourse, is specifically intended to prevent procreation – whether as an end or as a means."[67] What was meant to be a definitive statement, however, did not quell dissent on this issue. A poll taken by the Canadian Institute of Public Opinion late in 1968 showed that 41 percent of Canadian Catholics disagreed with the ban on contraception.[68] Even the Canadian bishops issued an ambivalent pastoral letter, "urging submission to the Church's teaching" while maintaining "that the faithful who in conscience could not, should not be regarded as outcasts."[69] While the Canadian hierarchy sought to mitigate the harshness of the encyclical, and while many Catholics simply ignored it, *Humanae Vitae* had wider implications for progressive Catholics. For them, it signalled that there were limits to the spirit of renewal in the Catholic Church, that the hierarchy would not share its power with the laity, and that attempts to move in a progressive direction on other issues (e.g., opening the priesthood to married men and to women) would be met with intransigence. It is no accident that from the late sixties onward, many progressive clergy left the priesthood, including Gregory Baum, Stan Kutz, and Michael Quealey. Quealey left in late 1967, and Kutz decided to leave in January 1968, in both cases, prior to *Humanae Vitae*. As Kutz recalled,

> birth control was part of the issue in the sense that even though by that time I was talking much more openly about what conscience really meant, and how you had to discover and formulate your own conscience through your life experience, and that nobody else could do that for you, mainly, the feeling was still "yeah, but tell us that it's okay." As I think Mike Quealey put it one time, "wherever there's a parade, there will be a lot of dogs barking." We came to a point where we were no longer willing to lead the parade. Because I felt that at least the people I was dealing with there should have passed the point where they needed

somebody to tell [them] that it was okay to do what they damned well knew was okay in their conscience.[70]

For many young radical Catholics, or those activists who came from a Catholic background, the pope's views on these matters were irrelevant.[71] In an interview some forty years later, Linda Kealey did not recall being conscious of *Humanae Vitae*, and maintained that it would not have made a difference to her: "I think my political opinions as someone in the women's movement were probably more important by then." At most, *Humanae Vitae* confirmed that the Church hierarchy was decidedly out of touch with activist youth, with whom it supposedly wished to dialogue. As Joan Newman Kuyek explained, "an awful lot of Catholic women at that point said 'well, that's too bad,' and went underground. And that was basically the reaction. ('He can say what he likes, but this is not divine teaching.') And that probably led to a whole lot of other interesting movements in the Catholic Church, come to think of it. It was kind of an intimate and basic position. [It] didn't lead to change among my Catholic friends of their approach to abortion ... they weren't about to support Morgentaler ... But it certainly did lead to a change in their whole approach to the infallibility of the Catholic Church."[72]

Indeed, even before the encyclical was issued, some young radical Catholics felt that the Church required a wholesale revolution, and that the reforms proposed by progressive Catholics had "only served to make the old faults less idiotic," as one young columnist in the St Michael's College student paper observed. He advocated abolishing the priesthood and establishing "a democracy of the Holy Spirit," and argued that the "dogmas, the rules, the impositions and the set-up have to disappear before an inspirational church, based on exemplifying Christ, could emerge."[73] Whether most Catholic youth agreed with his radical assessment or not, it appears that fewer were attending church by the late sixties. Attendance at Canadian Catholic churches began to drop off sharply in the late sixties, and the failure of churches to retain their young people was a key factor in the crisis of declining attendance. The youth of the late sixties, nourished on the New Left ideals of participatory democracy and liberation, had little patience for what they perceived to be a hierarchical, undemocratic institution, an institution that employed the rhetoric of "renewal" and "dialogue," while showing limited willingness to do either.

ROCHDALE COLLEGE AND THE CHRISTIAN LEFT

Although Canada's churches demonstrated institutional resistance to reform, individual progressive clergy, and some active laypersons, found ways of participating in radical experiments aimed at transforming education and, ultimately, transforming society. While New Left activists worked to revolutionize undemocratic institutions, some of them also sought to create *counter-institutions* – that is, institutional alternatives that would embody the radical values and principles lacking in mainstream institutions. This was especially evident in the field of education; from the late sixties to the early seventies, "free schools" and "free universities" flourished across North America.[74] Young radicals had good reason to focus a great deal of attention on the education system. They had spent most of their lives in school and university; thus, their primary experience of the oppressive establishment (and conflict with that establishment) had taken place in educational settings. Their critique of education concerned both the medium and the message: schools were undemocratic, and the curriculum was irrelevant to the kind of society they hoped to build.[75] Toronto radicals articulated their critique in publications like *This Magazine Is about Schools*, which begin its life in 1966. In addition, they embodied their critique in the establishment of alternative schools, and most visibly in an alternative, student-run "college," which took its name from a nineteenth-century co-operative experiment: Rochdale.

Rochdale College emerged from the confluence of two groups: housing activists associated with Campus Co-operative Residences, who wished to create an affordable, co-operatively owned residence for students attending the University of Toronto; and education activists, who wished to begin an experiment in student-run learning as an alternative to the impersonal and often irrelevant education offered at the "multiversity." A key member of the latter group was the aforementioned Anglican priest and social activist Ian Mackenzie. In 1965, he joined the original planning committee for Rochdale: "We went through a very, very intensive process. Usually we'd start meeting at nine o'clock at night and end around three in the morning, hotly debating all sorts of issues in the context of Canadian society and the world situation and areas of social reform and so on. Out of that came the idea of making Rochdale a college and applying for a licence for Rochdale as a charitable and educational institution. The idea was to make Rochdale into a place where people could determine the form and content of their own education. And, as members of a cooperative, they would also be responsible for their own residential environment."[76] The result, by late 1968, was an eighteen-story concrete high-rise at the southwest corner of Bloor and Huron, financed by a multi-million dollar loan from the federal government. The educational program, which began in 1967, a year before the building opened, was central to the college's raison d'être. It was expected that most residents would be students at the nearby University of Toronto, while taking part in the educational life of the college, which was independent from the university. However, Rochdale was open to all, from high school dropouts to graduate students. Instead of professors, there were "resource people," and learning would take place in small seminars, which could be initiated by resource persons or residents. (With funding from the CYC, Ian Mackenzie was one of the two original resource persons.) Rochdale College also served as a base for a variety of grassroots creative ventures, one of the most successful being the Institute for Indian Studies, with which Ian Mackenzie was deeply involved.[77] As a gigantic commune and a free university – two counter-institutions rolled into one – Rochdale was participatory democracy in action.[78]

It is striking that a priest, albeit a progressive, social activist priest, should be one of the key figures in the foundation of a radically New Left institution, which would soon transform itself into Toronto's countercultural fortress. But in its initial years, several of Rochdale's resource persons were drawn from the Christian left. This included United Church minister Bob Miller, the former national study secretary of the SCM. Miller also managed the SCM Bookroom (which rented the ground floor space of Rochdale College) and in 1967–68, he offered a seminar on the relevance of religious dogma in the twentieth century. (That same year, Ian Mackenzie offered seminars on "Religion and Social Change" and "Radical Theology and Modern Man.")[79] Other resource people were Philip McKenna, a former Dominican priest who held the title of "chairman of the Philosophy Department" at Rochdale,[80] and Brewster Kneen, an omnipresent figure in Toronto's Christian Left.[81]

Brewster Kneen's main contribution to Rochdale was the creation of CENSIT – Centre for the Study of Institutions and Theology – which he established in the summer of 1968 along with Farrell Toombs (a professor of psychiatry at the University of Toronto, and an Orthodox Christian "with a mystical side").[82] The purpose of CENSIT was to examine social and economic structures from a radical Christian perspective and to explore the connection between personal faith and political action. As Kneen explained, participants in CENSIT asked themselves, "What was our own motivation? What was the motivation for political action? Well, injustice is unacceptable and ... our faith requires us to try and understand what's going on, and see beyond it [to] what could be done ... I would say that in a sense it was a yearning and a desire to find some meaningful political expression of conviction ... Why are we involved in this? Well, because we have certain religious convictions. And to try to articulate that in meaningful terms both for ourselves and for the public and for political groups, that was the challenge."[83] Like many ventures associated with Rochdale College, CENSIT was much less formal than its name implies. Its primary activity was, in Kneen's words, "a weekly ... free-floating seminar. I was usually responsible for initiating whatever conversation, but we'd meet for a couple of hours and then we'd go down to the Brunswick for beer, [and] spend another half a day."[84] While membership fluctuated, the initial group consisted of about a dozen men and women, many of them associated with the University of Toronto – among them, Eilert Frerichs, Ian Mackenzie, and Philip McKenna. In addition to its weekly meeting, CENSIT also offered eight courses to Rochdalians in 1968–69, including "Dialectics, Marxist and Biblical" and "Violence."[85]

While the core members of CENSIT were undoubtedly edified by their weekly gathering, it appears that they were not able to engage Rochdale's younger residents in an examination of the relationship between faith and political institutions. In part, this was because CENSIT was only loosely affiliated with Rochdale College, even though several of its members were active participants in the Rochdale community (e.g., Ian Mackenzie and Philip McKenna). In its initial stages, it was independent, and by 1970, it may have been independent again.[86] According to Eilert Frerichs, the group's weekly seminar never took place at Rochdale.[87] Thus, it was never an integrated part of the college, unlike the Institute for Indian Studies, with which Ian Mackenzie was heavily involved. Also unlike the institute, CENSIT was small, unstructured, and had little visibility either inside or outside Rochdale.[88]

Moreover, while Kneen and McKenna (under the aegis of CENSIT) offered courses at Rochdale, the educational aspect of Rochdale was an exercise in "disappointments and frustration."[89] This was particularly true for some of the college's early resource persons who, while critical of the multiversity and irrelevant curriculum, were still academics at heart and saw learning as an intellectually rigorous exercise. As Rochdale quickly and unexpectedly became a hippie haven, this understanding of education had little appeal for residents. As one of the college's original founders recalls, "We thought that reform meant a rediscovery of liberal education ... giving students and faculty the opportunities to challenge assumptions about their own lives and to question how institutions were organized. But many of the people who came in from Yorkville and from other parts of the city or the country weren't interested in rediscovering values. They were interested in checking out of most kinds of restraints, discovering themselves and learning from experience – whatever that meant. It was a very anti-intellectual type of life."[90] Thus, the new clientele had no desire to engage in the kind of analysis that was integral to CENSIT. There was room for a "Christian left" at Rochdale, just as there was room for an infinite variety of spiritual, political, artistic, or purely recreational ventures (not to mention some very lucrative but not legal economic ventures). But overall, contrary to what its founders had envisioned, Rochdale did not become an educational institution operating along New Left lines. Instead, Rochdale became a countercultural fortress, a place for doing one's own thing.[91]

CONCLUSION

In the late sixties, media coverage of the young radicals was frequent and pervasive. The new generation of avatars, embodying a new set of values, could not be ignored. Canadian church leaders and denominational periodicals responded by adopting the youthful rhetoric of "radical change" and "revolution." For some high-ranking church leaders, the rhetoric was undoubtedly genuine, as were their sympathies with radical youth and the causes they espoused. Many progressive clergy and active laity were convinced that the young radicals had the potential to effect positive change in society, and even to revolutionize the churches. With varying degrees of success, progressive clergy challenged the churches to engage with the issues that concerned youth, to move with the changing times, to be "prophetic" instead of "priestly." Furthermore, in an age of declining church membership and attendance, church leaders perceived that young people were critically important for the long-term health of their denominations.

These endeavours by progressive clergy and laity, including high-ranking officials, were hampered by the institutional inertia of Canada's largest denominations. Anglicans were reluctant to reform church structures to grant youth a role in church governance, or to condemn Canadian corporate complicity in the Vietnam War. The United Church of Canada hierarchy rebuked Ray Hord for his provocative words and actions concerning the Vietnam War and war resisters – words and actions that signalled his support for young radicals, and in the process, earned their respect. And by reasserting its condemnation of contraception, the Roman Catholic Church demonstrated that there were limits to "renewal" and "dialogue." Notwithstanding the Vatican II emphasis on the "priesthood of all believers," the Church was not about to embrace participatory democracy. Not surprisingly, Canadian churches in the late sixties did not succeed in attracting or retaining youth to their parishes.

In their response to the New Left and, more broadly, to youth in revolt, progressive clergy enjoyed limited success. Ray Hord was able to establish alliances with young activists such as John Foster and Tom Faulkner, and to earn their respect. Likewise, Ian Mackenzie was able to work closely with education activists to help establish Rochdale College and shape that counterinstitution in its early years. But in the short-term, reform-minded ministers such as these were unable to reform their denominations, nor were they able to make them into congenial places for young people impatient for change. Nevertheless, they had a long-term impact on Canada's mainline churches. The United Church of Canada would move sharply to the left in the seventies and eighties, and a substantial Christian left would form in Canada's Anglican and Catholic churches. Developments within the New Left in the early seventies, and in movements spawned by the New Left, would help propel these changes within Canada's churches.

7

Liberation

English-Canadian Christianity
and the New Left in the Early 1970s

In December 1972, students from around the globe, including several delegates from Canada's Student Christian Movement, gathered in Addis Ababa for the quadrennial conference of the World Student Christian Federation. The political radicalism of those in attendance was evident in the reports of the working groups. These groups were established at the conference to study issues of common concern, including a "Working Group on Various Forms of Liberation Struggle." While the report recognized that there were many dimensions to the "liberation struggle," such as "the struggle against sexism and racism," it suggested "that these are all interrelated in the common class struggle against capitalism and its psychological/cultural consequences." Student radicalism was evident, too, in the resolutions of the WSCF general assembly: condemning US actions in Vietnam and showing solidarity with Allende's government in Chile, with "freedom fighters in Vietnam," and with "the anti-imperialist struggle of the Palestinian freedom fighter" against "the Zionist state of Israel."[1]

Clearly, the WSCF in the early seventies shared the radical left's all-encompassing commitment to "liberation." In these years, liberation was a word with multiple meanings, a rallying cry for a multitude of political and cultural causes on the left. The New Left championed a host of liberationist causes, most of which took shape in the final years of the sixties and gained momentum as the new decade unfolded. While Canadian radicals continued to express solidarity with revolutionary movements abroad (in Latin America, Vietnam, and elsewhere), and to seek "Canadian liberation" at home, other movements spawned by the New Left began to attract media attention, particularly women's liberation and gay liberation. For activists in the latter two movements, liberation was both personal and political.

The responses of Canadian Christians were as wide-ranging as the causes themselves. This chapter and the next explore the ways that Canadian Christians, including young radicals and older denominational decision-makers, engaged with these liberationist causes between 1970 and 1975. The present chapter begins by exploring developments in the New Left in the early seventies – arguably the final years of the "long sixties." It follows with an overview of the Christian left in these years, both in the SCM and in Canada's largest churches. Then it examines the specific ways in which Christian groups such as SCM and LAWG, and Canada's churches, engaged with anti-imperialist political movements, both internationally (Latin America and Vietnam), and nationally ("Canadian liberation"). While these topics may seem divergent, a common pattern is unmistakable: young radical Christians identified fully with the New Left, as did many older progressives; however, Canada's churches could only go so far in endorsing the political causes of left-leaning youth. Although young left-leaning Christians in such groups as LAWG and the SCM were unequivocally supportive in their response to global revolutionary movements, the response of churches and clergy was mixed. Much as they had embraced the language of "revolution" in the sixties, some leading clergy were willing to embrace the rhetoric of "liberation" in the seventies, and, selectively, to endorse its principles. But the churches' engagement with issues such as the Vietnam War in these years demonstrated that even the most liberal denominations were cautious and, by the standards of radical activists, relatively conservative.

The subsequent chapter builds on the theme of liberation in the early seventies by focusing on Canadian Christian responses to two New Left-inspired movements that gained momentum in the early seventies: women's liberation and gay liberation. These differed from other New Left causes in that they were perceived to be both personal and political. Furthermore, the ways that Canadian Christians engaged or failed to engage with these issues differed somewhat from their patterns of engagement with the political causes under consideration in this present chapter.

THE CONTINUATION OF THE NEW LEFT: 1970–75

Many historians of the sixties present the seventies as a time when "the movement" comes apart. Often, these authors identify 1969 or

1970 as pivotal years – or even terminal years – in this narrative of declension. The early seventies are portrayed as a rapid "fade-out" following the glory days of the late sixties, or as a mere epilogue.[2] More recent literature, however, challenges the latter interpretation and makes a more convincing case for a counter-narrative: that the early seventies witnessed the growth of movements spawned by the New Left. While the radical left did not loom as large on North American campuses at it had in the sixties, its presence off-campus grew, evident in the proliferation of community groups advocating for a variety of political causes, local, national, and global.[3] The success of such groups was mixed; in Van Gosse's words, the early seventies was a period of "merging into the mainstream," of "winning and losing."[4] In the drama of the "long sixties," the seventies were not a mere epilogue but rather a continuation of the story.

Across North America, campus radicalism diminished in the seventies. The left retained a vocal and visible presence on university campuses, but a shift was evident. Between the spring and fall of 1970, polls showed a drop in the percentage of students who identified as "radical or far left" (from 11 percent to 7 percent), and a growing number of students who identified with the middle-of-the-road category (from 26 percent to 34 percent).[5] Studies of the student movement in Canada show that campus radicalism followed a similar trajectory across English Canada.[6] There are several possible explanations. First, students may have been disillusioned by the destruction and violence perpetrated by some of the more extreme New Left groups. In the United States, the Weatherman Underground (a breakaway faction of Students for a Democratic Society) sought to "bring the Vietnam War home," most notably by detonating bombs.[7] In Canada, in October 1970, a cell of the Front de libération du Québec kidnapped James Cross, a British trade official, while another FLQ cell kidnapped and killed Pierre Laporte, the Quebec minister of labour. The net effect of actions such as these was to undermine support for the radical left. Other possible factors in the decline of student radicalism included the Kent State shootings in May 1970 (when troops of the Ohio National Guard fired on protesting students, killing four), and Trudeau's invocation of the War Measures Act in October 1970 (leading to the arrest of nearly five hundred). Activist youth realized that governments would go to draconian lengths to quell opposition. While actions such as the Kent State massacre intensified student protest in the short term, they may have had a demoralizing effect on student radicals in the long term.[8]

Perhaps the most important factor in the contraction of campus radicalism, particularly by the mid-seventies, was America's withdrawal from Vietnam. Nixon assumed the presidency in 1969, with a mandate to end the war "honorably." For Nixon, however, an "honorable" peace meant leaving South Vietnam in a strong position and avoiding "even the slightest appearance of defeat" for the United States. Consequently, Nixon waged "a war for peace," intensifying the bombing campaigns and ultimately widening the war in Indo-China to include Cambodia.[9] These actions led to renewed antiwar protests (including the Kent State University protests), and in the spring of 1971, a rally in Washington drew half a million participants. Unlike the protests of the late sixties, however, mass demonstrations against Vietnam were "old news," and press coverage declined.[10] Nevertheless, public antiwar sentiment remained high, and by January 1973, the government reached a peace deal with North Vietnam. American forces withdrew by March, and by August, Congress cut off funding for any further air operations in Indo-China. Meanwhile, President Nixon became engulfed in the Watergate scandal, and facing impeachment, he resigned in August 1974. When North Vietnamese forces advanced through the south and ultimately took Saigon in April 1975, Gerald Ford, Nixon's successor as president, made it clear that the United States would not intervene.[11] With the conclusion of the war, and the removal of an unpopular Cold Warrior president, campus radicals in the mid-seventies and beyond, in both the United States and Canada, were deprived of a popular cause (and an easily identifiable target) in their fight against American imperialism.

However, in the early seventies, the New Left was still far from over, particularly in Toronto. As Ian Milligan has shown in *Rebel Youth*, for many New Leftists in the late sixties and early seventies, their chief site of struggle was not on campus but on picket lines, as they sought to build a broader coalition with labour unions.[12] Meanwhile, on campus, as a *Varsity* article from the fall of 1972 made clear, student radicals could choose from a plethora of political groups across the socialist spectrum. Since the late sixties, their options had only increased. Students who wished to liberate Canada from American imperialism could join the campus NDP (which aligned itself with the Waffle wing of the party) or the more radical Canadian Liberation Movement. Those who wanted to campaign for abortion rights could join the women's groups associated with the Young Socialists, a Trotskyite youth organization. And gay or lesbian activists could become involved in such groups as Toronto Gay Action.[13] Moreover, the proliferation of New Left-inspired groups was not only a campus-based phenomenon. Across Toronto and in communities across Canada, leftists could join radical organizations devoted to various liberationist causes.[14]

The issues raised in this *Varsity* article reflected several new developments in left politics. First, radicals focused more attention on liberation movements in developing nations, as these nations struggled to free themselves from the domination of the American empire (or from undemocratic regimes that were either installed or propped up by the US government), especially in Latin America. Hand in hand with that concern came a greater sense that Canada needed to free itself from American political, economic, and cultural domination. Yet another development was the women's liberation movement, which emerged from the New Left in the late sixties and burgeoned in the early seventies. Finally, there was the movement for gay liberation.

Many of these movements coalesced near the end of the sixties but gained traction in the early seventies as the causes gained acceptance in mainstream society, drawing in participants who otherwise would not have identified as political, much less as radical (this was particularly true of women's liberation and gay liberation). These were critically important years for these liberationist causes, characterized by growing public awareness (thanks in part to media coverage, which savvy young activists cultivated through press releases and organized spectacles), and burgeoning numbers of active supporters. For participants in the proliferation of nascent activist groups, it was an era characterized by an undeniable freshness and vitality.

THE CONTINUATION OF THE CHRISTIAN LEFT: 1970–75

Not surprisingly, young Christian radicals who identified with the New Left shared in the vitality of the era. They identified with the liberationist ethos and analytical framework of leftists in the early seventies, and their own organizations, such as the SCM and LAWG, served as vehicles for political discussion and action. What is more surprising is that by the early seventies, both young radicals and older progressives were moderately successful in advancing their causes within the institutional structures of their denominations. In part, this reflected the growing presence of left-leaning Christians, young and old, working within church structures.

The SCM remained a rallying point for students interested in the relationship between Christian spirituality and social justice. As with the broader New Left, it was smaller than it had been in the sixties, but it retained a foothold on campuses across Canada, including the University of Toronto. As in the past, it drew participants from liberal or left-leaning Christian homes; in some cases, they were the sons and daughters of SCM alumni. Such was the case for Betsy Anderson (born 1952), whose family lived in Howland House (the SCM communal house led by former SCM study secretary Bob Miller) and attended Bathurst Street United Church (a progressive congregation closely connected to the SCM). When she began her studies at the University of Toronto in 1971, she intended to avoid the SCM. However, when she visited it along with her friend Marion Endicott (grand-daughter of the noted political activist and SCM alumnus James Endicott), from the moment she set foot in the room, she "knew it fit."[15] As she recalled, the University of Toronto SCM had approximately a dozen core members, though she added that "there used to be SCM units in all of the [affiliated] colleges, and not just the U of T." The associational life of the movement that Anderson recalled would be recognizable to SCM alumni from both earlier and later years; a close-knit community was fostered at local, national, and international levels, through regular Bible studies, retreats at Hart House Farm, national council meetings and conferences, and participation in the broader WSCF.[16]

At the local level, an important figure in the University of Toronto SCM was the chaplain Eilert Frerichs. As a United Church minister, Frerichs provided a link to the institutional church, and as a veteran of the SCM with a history of political activism, he provided a sense of continuity with the earlier SCM, with its amalgam of liberal Christian spirituality and progressive politics. Frerichs was equally adept at leading Bible studies and speaking knowledgably about political issues.

At the national level, Alan Rimmer (1934–2019) helped to maintain the political tone of the movement in his capacity as SCM general secretary from 1972 to 1975 and editor of the SCM newspaper, the *Canadian Student*. Born in Lancashire County in northwestern England, Rimmer had immigrated to Toronto in his early teens, along with his mother (his father had died in the Second World War).

Rimmer's left-wing politics were shaped by his working-class upbringing and by his involvement in the SCM, which he first encountered during his undergraduate studies at the University of British Columbia in the late 1950s. (He served as SCM study secretary briefly in the early sixties.) His politics were reinforced and deepened by his direct engagement throughout the sixties and early seventies, which included co-founding Everdale Alternative School and the journal *This Magazine Is about Schools*, and involvement in the left wing of the NDP. Although Rimmer claimed in a 2012 interview that he never saw himself as a radical, the anti-capitalist, anti-imperialist political views he espoused and the causes he supported aligned well with the radical left of the early seventies.[17] It is no coincidence that the SCM shared a similar radical political orientation in the early seventies while Rimmer was general secretary. The fight against neo-colonialism at home and abroad would shape the activism of the SCM in the early seventies, as it worked in close conjunction with like-minded groups.

In these years, Rimmer was in his late thirties and early forties – significantly older than many of the young activists in this study. He serves as a reminder that in the long sixties, neither the radical Christian milieu nor the broader New Left was the sole province of the young. Nor, for that matter, was it the sole province of student organizations. By the early seventies, Canada's largest churches were more congenial spaces for those who wished to champion progressive political causes. Indeed, as young Christians who identified with the New Left throughout the 1960s grew older, some chose to work within the institutional structures of their denominations. Among others, this included John Foster of LAWG (and, formerly, director of the United Church's youth organization Kairos). By 1971, Foster was in his late twenties and employed by the United Church's Division of Mission, the successor to the Board of Evangelism and Social Service.[18] In the years that followed, Foster would serve as a bridge between the denominational establishment and social justice activists.

It was not only the presence of young activists that helped push Canada's churches to the left. Older progressives working within the denominations were equally important. In the 1960s, church officials such as Ray Hord had prepared the way for later progressives to speak out more boldly on social issues and to take practical measures to assist refugees and draft resisters. In the early seventies, some of these progressives held high-level positions in their denominations. This included Bruce McLeod, United Church moderator from 1972 to 1974, who had been supportive of Hord's vocal stance on Vietnam in 1967; and Edward ("Ted") Scott, primate of the Anglican Church of Canada from 1971 to 1986, who envisioned the church as an agent of social change.[19] Several church officials were alumni of the SCM and brought with them an SCM sensibility: liberal in theology and left-wing (or outright radical) in politics. More than a few were deeply involved in ecumenical bodies committed to social justice. Even Canada's Roman Catholic bishops articulated progressive political positions in the 1970s.

However, there were limits to how far Canada's churches could shift to the left. In Canada's Roman Catholic churches, ecclesiastical structure and papal pronouncements delineated which political and social viewpoints were permissible and which were out of bounds. In Canada's Anglican and United churches, the issue was not so much with the hierarchy (which, to a greater degree than before, leaned to the left), but the rank and file. The important decision-making bodies in these denominations included not only clergy but also active laity. As such, they reflected the views of a broad constituency, views that were often more conservative than those of church leadership in the seventies. As Alan Hayes writes, Canadian Anglicans "respected Scott as a person of Christian conscience, and those who knew him liked him, but fewer agreed with his vision for the Church in society."[20] Even in the supposedly left-of-centre United Church of Canada, a 1972 pre-election survey of *United Church Observer* readers revealed that a majority of decided lay respondents intended to vote Progressive Conservative.[21]

Consequently, while groups such as the SCM and LAWG unambiguously aligned themselves with the New Left, the position of Canada's churches was more complicated. On the whole, denominational leaders either leaned further to the left than they had in the sixties or they were more willing to speak candidly about social justice issues from a progressive perspective. They were supported by younger radicals who had taken positions in their church's administrative bodies. However, social and structural factors prevented the churches from fully embracing New Left positions or policies. For this reason, it is important to examine not only the responses of young Christian radicals to the New Left of the early seventies but also the complex ways that Canada's institutional churches responded to the liberation movements of the era, even though there was an undeniable gap between church policies and the world that the young radicals envisioned.

RADICAL CHRISTIANITY AND THE POLITICS OF LIBERATION (ABROAD AND AT HOME)

The world that young Canadian radicals envisioned was a world liberated from imperialism, especially American imperialism. The anti-imperialistic ethos of the late sixties became an even more prevalent feature of Canada's New Left in the early seventies. Canadian radicals continued to declare their solidarity with the Viet Cong, Cuba, and leftist liberation movements in developing countries. Many Canadian New Leftists embraced left nationalism; they expressed growing dismay over what they perceived to be Canada's colonial status in the American empire. Radical Christians, particularly those involved in LAWG and the SCM, shared these concerns for liberation abroad and at home. They increasingly drew inspiration from the liberation theology emanating from Latin America, and showed a keen interest in Latin America. Likewise, the SCM and its members participated actively in the movement for Canadian liberation from perceived American domination.

In the early seventies, LAWG and SCM continued to collaborate closely in their efforts to raise awareness of America's imperialistic foreign policy in Latin America and of the complicity of Canadians. The SCM funded LAWG's research into "the role of Canadian commercial, governmental and religious organizations in Latin America and their influence in the development of [Latin America]."[22] In addition, the *Canadian Student* (the newspaper of the Canadian SCM published between 1972 and 1975) included substantial coverage of political developments in Latin America.[23] The relationship between the SCM and LAWG was facilitated by overlapping personnel. For example, Judy Skinner, who had been central in the operation of LAWG in the late sixties, worked with the SCM national office and was co-secretary for the North American region of the WSCF, the international umbrella group which included the SCM.[24] It was facilitated, too, by common interests: Alan Rimmer, the SCM general secretary from 1972 to 1975, had taken part in an SCM-sponsored trip to Cuba in the early sixties and remained a "big booster for Cuba."[25]

Canadian SCM members organized similar trips to Cuba in the seventies. At least one of these trips involved both Canadian and American participants, who travelled as guests of the Cuban SCM.[26] According to Skinner, the purpose of such trips was to expose North American students, especially American students, to the realities of

Cuban life, and to broaden their understanding: "It's totally different now, of course, but in those days, there were American students who didn't understand what it meant to cross the border and come *here*. The provincialism [of] virtually everything was pretty profound." [27] Similar to working trips organized by the Venceremos Brigades, students worked for a week on a Cuban vegetable farm. Following this, as Judy Skinner explains, the North American guests, "with some Cubans, spent a week or so travelling the length of the island 'on the ground.' So we got to visit with people in three or four different local communities, who were connected to the church in those communities. So people would have pretty basic discussions about what they were doing, and pray together and discuss stuff together ... And there was lots of criticism about doing it, but I always felt that the experience that it gave the students who participated on both sides – you can criticize all you like, but if it gives people a broader view and a more profound understanding of what it's like, then it's great."[28]

While progressive and radical Christians in Canada remained interested in Cuba in the early seventies and beyond,[29] they were even more attentive to events in Chile. Following his election as president in 1970, Salvador Allende embarked on an ambitious program to put Chile on the path to socialism. His government's nationalization of foreign-owned corporations in 1972 put the Allende administration on a collision course with American political and business interests. Furthermore, a wave of strikes in late 1972 (likely supported by the CIA) triggered economic and political instability in the country throughout 1973.

These developments became a focal point for members of LAWG. In 1972, John Foster (a founding member and director of LAWG and also an employee of the United Church of Canada's Division of Mission in Canada) travelled to Santiago, Chile, to attend the United Nations Conference on Trade and Development. During his six-week trip, he visited with other LAWG members present in the country and witnessed firsthand the "Chilean way to socialism." He returned to Canada determined to generate support for Allende's Chile, particularly among Canada's churches.[30] A LAWG pamphlet from January 1973, entitled *Chile Versus the Corporations: A Call for Canadian Support*, opened with the assertion that Christ's position "was in no way ambiguous: his was an option for the poor and against anyone or any system that stood in the way of man's liberation. The present international economic system is a situation of sin, and as such it must be rejected." The pamphlet laid out the challenges facing Chile: "Chile attempts to reclaim her heritage of natural resources, in order to provide an economic basis for redistributing wealth among her people, and progressive social policies. She finds herself attacked in world markets by a US-based copper corporation, Kennecott. At home, her democracy is threatened by the manoeuvrings of another US based giant International Telephone and Telegraph. International credit support disappears and the prospects for an innovative and humane society in Chile are threatened. Chile seeks assistance, and awaits Canada's response on debt negotiations and future credits." The pamphlet also warned Canadian Christians that Canadian mission work in Chile was being undermined by the actions of Canada's corporations and federal government. The message was clear: that an effective Christian witness required Canadian churches to show solidarity with the Chilean "experiment in democratic socialism."[31]

This "experiment" came to an end in September 1973, when a military coup installed a right-wing junta led by General Augusto Pinochet (whose government both Canada and the United States were quick to recognize) and inaugurated a period of martial law. Civil rights were suspended, thousands of political dissenters were arrested, and many were tortured, killed, or "disappeared." In Canada, LAWG members responded to the coup by establishing a Chile-Canada Solidarity committee. In essence, its mission was similar to that of LAWG, to raise public awareness of human rights abuses in Chile and of Canadian complicity, and to support activist efforts across the country. One of its chief goals was to pressure the Canadian government to accept a larger proportion of Chilean refugees, who numbered in the thousands in the months following the coup.[32]

Perhaps even more importantly, John Foster and other LAWG members were instrumental in the creation of the Inter-Church Committee on Chile (ICCC). This ad hoc ecumenical committee, founded in the days following the coup, brought together Canadian Roman Catholic and mainline Protestant church officials to draw attention to human rights abuses committed by the new Chilean regime, to counter misinformation, and most of all, to pressure the Canadian government to accept refugees. Church leaders, including Floyd Honey (general secretary of the Canadian Council of Churches), Archbishop Ted Scott (primate of the Anglican Church of Canada), Bruce McLeod (moderator of the United Church of Canada), and Bishop William Power (president of the Canadian Conference of Catholic Bishops), raised their concerns when they met with External Affairs Minister Mitchell Sharp in the weeks following the coup.[33] While their efforts initially met with resistance, the pressure they exerted, along with their public information campaign, eventually persuaded the Canadian government to accept Chilean political prisoners in the months following the coup, and ultimately to take in thousands of Chilean refugees.[34]

The work of the ICCC was significant for several reasons. First, even in a secularizing era, the churches still retained a measure of social authority; consequently, as Foster has observed, church leaders had ready access to both Canadian media (including the CBC and the leading daily newspapers) and top-ranking cabinet ministers.[35] Second, the ICCC is an example of the connections between New Leftist activists, such as Foster and other LAWG members, and Canada's major churches. The aforementioned church leaders were not necessarily politically radical, but each had a reputation as a reformer and/or social justice advocate. While humanitarian concerns likely were paramount in facilitating the partnership between the churches and activist groups such as LAWG, the progressive nature of church leadership in the early seventies was undoubtedly a factor.

The churches' renewed interest in Latin American anti-imperialist struggles was facilitated, as well, by the spread of liberation theology. At the Medellin conference in 1968, the Roman Catholic bishops of Latin America declared that God had a "preferential option for the poor." Many Latin American theologians (such as Gustavo Gutiérrez, whose *Theología de la liberación* was published in 1971) and priests extended this idea further, arguing Christians have a duty to support revolutionary struggles to overthrow oppressive governments. Across Central and South America, liberation theology gained wide adherence throughout the 1970s and into the eighties, among both clergy and the rural poor (who, with clerical support, formed base ecclesial communities in which they explored the relationship between faith and social justice). In practice, this was the New Left principle of "participatory democracy," but it was rooted in a radical understanding of Catholic social teaching.[36]

Liberation theology had a profound effect on North American Christian radicals. It offered a theological framework for the Catholic left and a way for them to express their solidarity with "the people of God" throughout the world. In Toronto, left-leaning Catholics were involved in both the SCM and LAWG in the early 1970s, and thus moved in a milieu where liberation theology was influential.

Liberation theology appealed to Protestant radicals as well. The Canadian SCM was introduced to these ideas through Placide Bazoche, a French Roman Catholic priest who served as secretary of the North American region of the WSCF. Writing twenty years afterward, Betsy Anderson recalls, "[Bazoche] was an exotic and intriguing presence at Canadian SCM national conferences, bringing news of student movements in the US and [student Christian movements] around the world. His conviction that Christians could and should support armed struggles for liberation was a lightning bolt that reflected the theological and political challenges that the WSCF brought to the life of the SCM in Canada at that time."[37] Given the SCM's roots in the Social Gospel movement of the early twentieth century, it was not shocking to be told that God was on the side of the poor. Nevertheless, liberation theology was novel in several ways. First, it marked a decisive rejection of Gandhian principles of nonviolence, or at least strict adherence to nonviolence (a shift that many radicals in the New Left made in the late sixties, as they expressed their solidarity with liberation movements in the developing world). As well, Anderson observes that liberation theology was "not as linear as Social Gospel theology. I think social gospel theology is still about a modernist view that things are going to get better and you can be a part of making them better, and history evolves, and we can build the Kingdom with God. It's more Kingdom theology ... And I think liberation theology is more about where God is in the journey of God's people, and who God is with and how God accompanies that ... It wasn't discontinuous with Social Gospel theology, but it had other elements to it. And the place of the Eucharist and sacraments – it was much more sacramental and not as head-based, I would say."[38]

For progressive Christians in Canada, liberation theology was not only about faraway struggles. It was also a challenge to affluent Canadians, and especially to the government, to consider their role in global systems of oppression and in perpetuating inequity at home. This was the contention of a Labour Day message released by the Canadian Conference of Catholic Bishops. Entitled "Liberation in a Christian Perspective" and published in the *Canadian Register* in September 1970, the communiqué was surprisingly radical in its tone (evidence of the influence of liberation theology even among the Canadian episcopate).[39] The bishops reflected on poverty in Canada, including the challenges faced by "most Indians, Métis and Eskimos," noted that the world's poor, including here in Canada, would not be patient forever, and warned of a "harvest of violence" if "peoples' just aspirations are denied." Applying the language and principles of liberation theology to the Canadian situation, the bishops called on governments to "implement, as soon as practically possible, social structures and policies which will ensure an equitable sharing of riches and distribution of power among citizens."[40]

The need for "liberation" at home was a central theme of the Canadian left in the early seventies – liberation for Canadians living on marginal incomes, for members of Canada's First Nations, and for the largely francophone population of Quebec.[41] Many in the English-Canadian New Left, however, focused on the overall need for Canada's liberation from the economic imperialism of the United States. These concerns were nothing new. Indeed, anti-Americanism has deep roots in Canada, from the Loyalists to the National Policy of John A. Macdonald to the Reciprocity Election of 1911 and beyond.[42] However, anxiety over American domination was given a new lease on life with the publication of George Grant's *Lament for a Nation* in 1965, which inspired many young activists in the Canadian New Left. Among these was James Laxer, who claimed that *Lament* was "the most important book I ever read in my life."[43] In their critique of corporate capitalism and militarism, left nationalists in Canada began to focus on the American empire as their prime enemy. They argued that Canadian socialism was inextricably intertwined with Canadian independence – economic, military, and cultural.[44]

From 1968 to 1975, left nationalism manifested itself in a variety of ways. In the late sixties, Robin Mathews and James Steele led a vocal campaign to increase the proportion of Canadian academics at Canadian universities, particularly in the social sciences.[45] In the early 1970s, Canadian Maoists spearheaded the Canadian Liberation Movement, which campaigned for a quota of 85 percent Canadian faculty in Canadian universities and for independent Canadian unions.[46] The largest and most visible left nationalist group, however, was the Waffle contingent of the NDP.[47] The Waffle's goals, as spelled out in its 1969 manifesto, were "to build an independent socialist Canada" and to make the NDP "a truly socialist party." The manifesto declared that the survival of Canada was endangered by "American control of the Canadian economy ... through the formidable medium of the multinational corporation." It also singled out the "American empire ... characterized by militarism abroad and racism at home" and "held together through world-wide military alliances and by giant corporations." Canada was unable to play "an independent role in the world" because of its "membership in the American alliance system and the ownership of the Canadian economy by American corporations."[48] One of the most prominent voices in the Waffle was James Laxer, who co-authored the group's manifesto, and ran against David Lewis for leadership of the NDP in 1971, coming in a strong second. The Waffle attracted many young radicals from the campus left; by 1972, for example, the University of Toronto NDP club was essentially a Waffle group.[49]

Without question, Canadian independence was a key issue for the SCM in the early seventies. The report of the SCM National Council meeting, held in New Brunswick in May 1970, included a section on "the Canadian dilemma." Council members expressed concern over "the presence of a growing number of US citizens as students and faculty on Canadian campuses." Following discussion, the council made several recommendations: that "each region in planning activities keep in mind the necessity for dealing with Canadian issues in the Canadian context"; that "two or three draft resistors or deserters should participate" in summer projects "in order to help them learn about the Canadian situation"; and that the "SCM should be involved in confronting the draft resistor communities with discussion of Canadian content and context and the decision about their role and future in it."[50] It is unclear how much of an impact these recommendations had on local SCM units across the country, but in the summer that followed, two new staff began work at the York University SCM "on the American presence in Canadian education."[51] Furthermore, individual SCM members were active in the various groups campaigning for Canadian independence. Betsy Anderson, of the University of Toronto SCM, was involved in the Canadian Liberation Movement, while others were involved in the Waffle, such as Philip Murton (also of the University of Toronto SCM).[52] As an active NDP member, SCM General Secretary Alan Rimmer had been supportive of the Waffle as well.[53]

Concerns over Canadian independence also strained the Canadian SCM's relations with its American counterpart in the North American Region of the WSCF. In their discussions with Americans on the regional council, Canadian SCM members had to explain that their identity was distinct, and that the Canadian historical experience was different.[54] As Anderson writes, "The American students brought the issues of race to Canada and challenged us to explain why there were few students of color in our movements. The American students also brought a more developed analysis of patriarchy and commitment to feminism to our interactions. There were lively debates and much mutual discussion, but it was often difficult, because Canadians were constantly operating in a context where they were far more knowledgeable about the US than were American students about Canada. There was not as much attention given to the need for cultural sensitivities in the relationships of a Region that at first glance, and to the rest of the world, may have appeared relatively homogenous."[55]

In summary, Canadian Christian radicals shared the concerns of the wider Canadian New Left in the seventies: solidarity with liberation movements abroad, particularly in Latin America, and working for Canadian liberation at home. In the latter movement, Canada's Christian radicals were followers, not leaders. However, in the movement for Latin American solidarity, Christian radicals inspired by liberation theology played a central role in drawing attention to social justice issues in Central and South America. LAWG, and other faith-based solidarity groups, would continue to raise awareness of these issues in Canadian churches, and in broader Canadian society, throughout the seventies, eighties, and early nineties.

THE WAR AND AID TO WAR RESISTERS: THE CONSERVATISM OF LIBERAL CHRISTIANS

Political liberation movements drew the attention of Christian radicals, but these movements did not generate much discussion for most Canadian churches or church publications, at least not in the early seventies. The relative conservatism of most mainstream Protestants and Catholics (at least when compared to younger radical Christians in the SCM or LAWG) is evident in the response of Canadian churches to the Vietnam War and to the growing influx of American war resisters. With the exception of the United Church of Canada, Canada's denominational hierarchies did not overtly criticize America's prosecution of the war. Furthermore, Canadian churches were slow in offering assistance to young war resisters, newly arrived from the United States. Finally, when churches did offer assistance, they justified it primarily on humanitarian grounds rather than on grounds of opposing America's involvement in the war – and certainly not on grounds of solidarity with Vietnam's liberation struggle.

The United Church's Committee on the Church and International Affairs had criticized America's conduct in the Vietnam War as early as 1965. However, other than the United Church (whose official statement was by no means a radical one), Canadian church bodies offered no explicit condemnation or denunciation of America's role in Southeast Asia. Throughout the late sixties and early seventies, no such statement emerged from the General Synod of the Anglican Church of Canada, or from the Anglican bishops, or from Canada's Catholic bishops. In 1973, a writer to the *Catholic Register* commended Canada's Catholic bishops for their stand against abortion, but added, "I can only wish that their ... concern for human life had expressed itself as strongly in another area where Christian principles are being widely abused. As a Catholic and a pacifist ... I am deeply ashamed at the official silence of the Catholic Church in Canada in the matter of the savage bombing attacks unleashed on the cities and countryside of North Vietnam during the Christmas period."[56] Canadian Catholics were not alone in their "official silence." Even the relatively liberal United Church hierarchy shied away from unequivocal declarations concerning the war. As Ray Hord discovered in 1967, he did not speak for his denomination when he called Pearson a "puppy dog on LBJ's leash" and sided with the people of Vietnam in their liberation struggle.[57] Subsequent statements about Vietnam were *individual* statements, even those of prominent church leaders, such as Gordon Stewart, the associate secretary of the Board of Evangelism and Social Service.

"Peace marchers are not my bit," wrote Stewart in an opinion piece for the *Observer*, published in March 1970. "Like other demonstrations, they tend to suggest simple answers to complex questions. Nevertheless," he continued, "I shall take part in the next march for peace in Viet Nam at which I can be present." There were many factors for Stewart's decision, but in his words, "they reduce themselves to this: that I have become convinced that the role of the United States in Viet Nam has become allied to and symbolic of so much that is evil, that the necessity of ending that role outweighs all other considerations." Stewart pointed to the Mylai massacre as evidence of the "brutalization" of the American military in Vietnam, and argued that the Americans must leave the country not only for the sake of Vietnam but even more "for the sake and soul of the West. We need time to take stock of ourselves before brutality becomes a way of life. That, after all, is what we say of the other side."[58]

His arguments were progressive, but when compared to the position of younger Christian radicals (such as the delegates to the 1972 WSCF assembly, who not only condemned the American bombing but also stood "in solidarity with the heroic freedom fighters in Vietnam, not least the students of the Democratic Republic of Vietnam, the Provisional Revolutionary Government of South Vietnam"[59]), one is struck by the relative conservatism of Stewart's rhetoric and logic. First, he stated that he would march "without sharing in any way the philosophy or excusing the ruthlessness of the Viet Cong." His desire for peace was not motivated by solidarity with Third World Marxism but by a conviction that victory by the Viet Cong could not "be worse for the average Vietnamese than the indefinite continuation of the present war."[60] In Stewart's op-ed piece, we see that even the most vocal ecclesiastical critics of the Vietnam War were moderates, not radicals. Such moderates were far to the left of many lay United Church members.

When Canada's churches decided to engage with youth on the issue of the Vietnam War, it was in their aid to American war resisters. In 1967, when Ray Hord and the Board of Evangelism and Social Service (E&SS) allotted $1,000 to support groups such as the Toronto Anti-Draft Programme (TADP), it set off a flurry of debate – over the Vietnam War, the morality of "draft-dodging," and more broadly, the church's role in society. The controversy only intensified after the United Church moderator overturned the board's decision, and after Hord's unexpected death in March 1968. Assistance to war resisters was an issue that would not go away, partly because the cause now had a "martyr" in Ray Hord, but perhaps even more because war resisters continued to stream across the border. Church periodicals kept the issue alive; between 1968 and 1970, the Anglican, Catholic, and United church press ran sympathetic features on American draft-age immigrants to Canada.[61] These features drew attention to the plight of young draft-evaders and deserters in Canada: many of them struggled financially; and more importantly, many experienced great emotional stress because of their precarious legal situation, rejection by family, loneliness, uncertainty over the rightness or wrongness of their decision, and the knowledge that they could not return home.

These concerns, shared by American and Canadian clergy alike, led to a series of joint meetings of the Canadian Council of Churches (CCC) and its American counterpart, the National Council of Churches (NCC), between December 1969 and May 1970. The two bodies embarked on a program of assistance to draft age immigrants, working in conjunction with the TADP and about twenty-five other aid organizations across Canada.[62] The program was administered primarily by the CCC, but initially, the bulk of the financial support came from American sources, including the NCC and Clergy and Laity Concerned about Vietnam (CALCAV),[63] and when the CCC hired a coordinator for its ministry to draft age immigrants, it chose an American – Robert Gardner, formerly an Episcopal chaplain at Michigan State University.[64]

Even though this was an initiative of the CCC, Canada's mainline Protestant denominations were slow to offer their support. Anglicans, in particular, were cautious and tepid in their response. At a meeting of the National Executive Council of the Anglican Church of Canada in February 1970, the council members "officially noted" a letter from the CCC requesting financial and pastoral aid for draft age immigrants, but took no action. At that meeting, G.E. Hobson, an archdeacon in the diocese of Qu'Appelle, moved a resolution "not to contribute any funds of the Anglican Church to the CCC," particularly not to a fund for "aiding and abetting draft dodgers."[65] In November 1970, the council agreed to endorse a program of aid and support to war resisters, but its endorsement did not include a cheque. Instead, National Executive Council resolved to publicize the established fund (which, by November, was being administered by the WCC), so that individual Anglicans, or parishes, or dioceses could contribute directly.[66] Clearly, Anglicans were not of one mind on the issue of assisting draft age immigrants. In contrast, the United Church was slow to respond, but more substantive in its support. In 1971, the denomination's Committee on Overseas Relief and Inter-Church Aid donated $5,000 to the WCC fund to aid American draft resisters.[67] Significantly, there was far less opposition in 1971 than there had been in 1967; unlike the deluge of mail that Hord received from angry laypeople in 1967, the correspondence in 1971 was inquisitive rather than hostile.[68]

The supportive response of the United Church hierarchy and the tacit acceptance of that support by its laity are evidence that the United Church leadership was moving to the left by the early seventies, and that it was more willing to take controversial, activist positions. But when the United Church of Canada or the CCC chose to assist American draft age immigrants, were their actions tantamount to opposing the Vietnam War? In his essay on Canadian churches and their assistance to draft resisters, Donald Maxwell answers in the affirmative.[69] However, the reality is more complicated. It is certain that Ray Hord, Gordon Stewart, and other progressive clergy openly opposed the Vietnam War, and their efforts to support war resisters reflected their views on American involvement in Southeast Asia. However, the assistance program of the CCC, supported, in varying degrees, by the Anglican and United churches, was framed in humanitarian, not political, terms. Church leaders and officials of the CCC went out of their way to stress that it was a matter of Christian duty to help the needy, regardless of what one thought of their reasons for coming to Canada. In the words of E.E. Long, secretary of the United Church General Council, "We see it as a ministry to people in need, whether we agree with their action or not."[70] It is likely that many CCC officials and church leaders opposed the Vietnam War, and that their support for draft resisters reflected an antiwar stance. However, it is certain that these views were not universally held, especially not by church laity.[71] By framing assistance in humanitarian terms (arguably, apolitical terms), church leaders sought to attain the broadest possible base of support for the program. In other words, the United Church's actions were progressive, controversial, and activist, but they cannot be construed as *explicitly* antiwar.

Secular aid groups welcomed the Canadian churches' assistance in dealing with an overwhelming problem. (Around 1970, the TADP reportedly dealt with thirty-five to fifty clients each day.)[72] However, if a statement released by the TADP in 1970 is any indication, these aid groups were disappointed that both Canadian and American churches had waited so long to address the issue. The statement, likely written for a joint meeting of Canadian and American church officials in May 1970, at which aid groups were present, began as follows: "It is very satisfying to see clergymen from Canada and the US meeting together to discuss what they can do to aid and support those young Americans who had to leave their country because of the horrors of the war in Viet Nam. It is doubly gratifying when we think that the clergy and churches are only 300 years too late in grappling with the black-white relations in their country, but only three years late in coming to grips with this problem." The TADP statement continued by observing that both Canadian and American churches had a dismal record of responding to the needs of draft refugees, and contended that while the "harm done to the American refugees by this lack of support is great ... the harm done to the churches I feel is far more devastating."[73] Church support was greatly desired, but for the young activists who worked daily for three years to meet the needs of war resisters, the churches seemed to be playing the role of Johnny-Come-Lately, and they had come too late to gain much respect for institutional Christianity.

The TADP indictment of churches is valid as it applies to the denominational leadership, but individual churches, clergy, and active laity had helped throughout the late sixties. These included progressive churches, such as the Church of the Holy Trinity, which housed draft age immigrants in the church in 1968, as well as radical clergy who opened up their homes (e.g., Eilert Frerichs and Ian Mackenzie). Furthermore, in late 1968, Father Peter Sheehan of the University of Toronto's Newman Centre helped provide meeting space for the Union of American Exiles (UAE), a Toronto-based organization of war resisters.[74] Then there were the young antiwar activists who were also practising Christians: Peter Warrian, the student activist and practising Catholic, who was instrumental in the formation of TADP,[75] and Stan Pietlock, a Catholic draft-evader, who edited the UAE's newsletter the *American Exile in Canada* (later *Amex Magazine*).[76] Into the seventies, individuals and local churches continued to play a crucial role. This was particularly true of the Anglican Church of Canada, whose National Executive Council donated no money to aid draft refugees but encouraged individual Anglicans and local parishes to offer financial support and direct assistance. It was also true of Canada's Roman Catholics; the Catholic hierarchy never issued a formal statement on war resisters, but individual Catholics and parishes were supportive. For example, Catholics in Victoria, British Columbia provided aid to that city's Committee to Aid War Resisters.[77]

Nevertheless, at the institutional level, as distinct from the individual or congregational levels, Canadian churches had been slow to respond to the crisis of American draft evaders. In the case of the Anglican Church, their response was hampered by conservative opposition within the denomination. The assistance that Canadian churches ultimately provided to draft evaders in the early seventies through the coordinating efforts of the CCC was undeniably important. However, when that assistance was offered, it was framed in humanitarian terms; it was not an overt expression of left nationalism, of opposition to the Vietnam War (or, more broadly, to American imperialism), or of solidarity with the Vietnamese liberation forces. In general, Canadian churches were reticent on the Vietnam issue, and even when progressive church leaders spoke out, they articulated views that were far less radical than the young activists of the New

Left. The evidence shows that in the early seventies, Canadian church leaders were grappling with a key issue that concerned young radicals, that they worked with some of these young radicals to assist draft evaders, and that some church leaders attempted to speak prophetically. This was a significant change from their record in the late sixties. Even so, their attempts betrayed the institutional conservatism of presumably "liberal" denominations, and the relative conservatism of individual progressives. While Canadian church leaders (especially in the United Church) were moving to the left in the early seventies on issues such as Latin America and the Vietnam War, they never wholeheartedly endorsed radical movements of political liberation.

CONCLUSION

The early seventies were not a mere postscript to the long sixties. The movements that emerged from the New Left and flourished in these years, including Third-World solidarity and left nationalism, would have an impact on Canada's social and political landscape in the decades that followed. This shifting social and political landscape posed challenges for Canadian Christians. Moved by the new liberation theology emerging out of Latin America, young Christian radicals in the SCM and LAWG expressed their solidarity with liberation struggles in the developing world and also engaged with the struggle for Canadian liberation.

However, young Christian radicals were not representative of the mainstream of Canada's religious establishment, though they continued to work within and alongside the institutional structures of Canada's churches and exert whatever influence they could. Canadian church leaders and the governing bodies of Canadian denominations were, at best, selective in their support for left. Consequently, they were progressive yet relatively conservative in their responses to the challenges of the New Left in the early seventies. Canadian churches assisted Latin American refugees and American draft dodgers, but this was more on the grounds of humanitarian assistance rather than explicit approval of the radical left, or solidarity with global resistance movements. While there were noteworthy examples of engagement, through the CCC or groups such as LAWG, the fact remained that most Canadian churches could never be radical enough for young activists of the early seventies. Likewise, Canadian churches demonstrated their relative conservatism in the ways that they responded to the challenges of women's liberation and gay liberation.

8

Liberation, Part Two

Christianity, Gender, and Sexuality in the Early 1970s

Jan Griesinger was not raised to be a radical. Like many of her contemporaries in the postwar years, she grew up in the suburbs, as part of a conventional nuclear family, actively involved in the life of their mainstream Protestant congregation. When she left her home in the Chicago area to attend university in Indiana in 1960, she imagined that she would ultimately become a minister's wife. Instead, following her undergraduate studies (where she majored in religion), she married a schoolteacher and, by the mid-sixties, took a position as director of religious education at a United Church of Christ congregation in the suburbs of Cincinnati, Ohio.[1]

Through her church work – through meeting activist clergy and attending denominational conference meetings – Griesinger learned about the social and political issues of the sixties. Her political involvement intensified following her enrolment in seminary in 1967, where she joined the antiwar movement. She soon became co-chair of Cincinnati Action for Peace, and by the end of the year, was arrested at a draft resistance sit-in.[2] However, the real turning point in her life began in late 1969, when a friend brought her to a meeting of Dayton Women's Liberation. According to Griesinger, "the arrival of feminism ... captured my imagination and made me a convert. The feminist movement ... propelled me back into church-affiliated organizations to reach other women with the good news of liberation to the captives."[3] From 1971 to 1975, she was employed by the WSCF's North American regional division (which included the United States and Canada) as director of the Women's Project, a ministry in which she worked "nationally and internationally to bring the good news of women's liberation into the church and student Christian movements."[4] Indeed, at the WSCF's 1972 quadrennial conference in Addis Ababa – where, in the name of "liberation," delegates expressed their solidarity with anti-imperialistic revolutionary movements around the world – Griesinger addressed the delegates, comparing the oppression of women to colonial oppression.[5] Furthermore, in 1977, she came out as a lesbian and became active within her denomination as a spokesperson and organizer for gay, lesbian, bisexual, and transgender people.[6]

Griesinger's story is significant, but not because it is unusual. On the contrary, it follows the trajectory of many North American New Left activists from the late sixties to the early seventies. By the end of the sixties, young women on the left, accustomed to protesting the oppression of African Americans or the North Vietnamese, began to see themselves as oppressed people and to engage in the struggle for women's liberation, employing the analysis, rhetoric, and strategies of the New Left. Gay and lesbian activists followed suit and, by the early seventies, the movement for gay liberation was underway. Women's liberation and gay liberation movements shared much in common with the other liberation movements of the early seventies New Left. They were similar in ideology, rhetoric, and protest strategies; and often, those involved in the women's movement and gay liberation were actively engaged in other New Left causes. What made these movements different, however, is that they were more explicitly *personal* as well as political.

For Christians in Canada and elsewhere, these movements were different in another significant way. While one could make a convincing theological case for political liberation in Vietnam, Latin America, or Canada by appealing to scripture or church teaching, it was harder to make the same case for women's liberation or gay liberation. These movements emerged in the wake of the "sexual revolution" of the sixties, and in the public mind, they were the progeny of that revolution.[7] And sexual revolution did not square easily with centuries of Christian teaching and practice, which underpinned traditional social and legal frameworks pertaining to gender and sexuality. It was easier for theologically liberal Christians to challenge these social and legal frameworks than it was for conservative Christians, but even among professed liberals, pervasive attitudes about gender and sexuality were not easily abandoned, particularly when they involved contentious moral issues such as abortion or homosexuality. Furthermore, church officials who attempted to champion left-of-centre causes in Canada's largest Protestant denominations faced resistance and censure from more conservative lay members, while Roman Catholics risked similar censure from a conservative hierarchy.

Consequently, the responses of Canada's churches, clergy, and young Christian radicals to these developments were mixed. In some cases – especially the challenge of the women's movement – the churches responded, though not always in ways that younger activists might have hoped. In other cases, Canadian Christians either condemned or ignored these voices. Surprisingly, young radicals in Canada's SCM were not fully engaged in women's liberation in the early seventies and seemed to ignore gay liberation altogether. These varied responses to second-wave feminism and homosexuality demonstrated that even the most liberal denominations and student groups were cautious, and by the standards of radical activists, relatively conservative. The extent to which these movements found any foothold within Canada's churches often depended on individual feminists – and individual gays and lesbians – working within denominational structures. This chapter extends the previous chapter's exploration of Christian responses to New Left liberation movements in the early seventies by examining the ways in which Anglo-Canadian churches, and Christian groups such as the SCM, responded to two important movements: women's liberation and gay liberation.

CANADIAN CHRISTIANITY AND WOMEN'S LIBERATION

Canadian churches were well aware of the women's liberation movement. In the early seventies, denominational periodicals devoted editorials and features to women's liberation, and mainline churches hotly debated issues such as abortion and the ordination of women. Curiously, the SCM paid little heed to the movement, at least in Toronto. The SCM's marginal attention to women's issues is puzzling, since several participants in the Christian left were active in Toronto's women's liberation movement. The evidence suggests that with some exceptions, liberal or radical Christians were slow to embrace fully the women's movement.

The second wave of feminism that began in the 1960s did not originate with New Left radicals but with an older generation of women's activists, exemplified in individuals such as Betty Friedan and groups such as the National Organization for Women. However, groups that identified as "women's liberation" did originate in the New Left,[8] and second-wave feminism received much of its impetus from women who emerged from such New Left groups as SDS in the United States and SUPA in Canada. It was women's liberationists who popularized the phrase "the personal is political," most notably in a 1970 essay by American activist Carol Hanisch.[9] Through consciousness-raising group meetings in cities across the continent, these activists helped women to perceive their own everyday experiences of personal oppression as manifestations of a larger systemic problem that required social change. With radical rhetoric and confrontational strategies adopted from the New Left, women's liberationists set the tone for second-wave feminism in the late sixties and early seventies.

The feminist movement burgeoned in the seventies, as it broadened its base of support and as North American women campaigned for equal opportunities in the workplace, for publicly funded childcare, and for women's reproductive rights. The Canadian movement received a boost in 1970, when the federal government's Royal Commission on the Status of Women issued its final report, containing 167 recommendations for changes in government policy.[10] In the United States, second-wave feminism became a mainstream movement between 1969 and 1974, and achieved its greatest successes in those years. For example, in 1972, Congress passed a constitutional amendment that stated that equal rights under the law could not be denied on the basis of sex. (The Equal Rights Amendment was forwarded to the states for ratification, but ultimately, not enough states agreed to ratify it, and the amendment failed.) Furthermore, in the 1973 case of *Roe v. Wade*, the United States Supreme Court ruled that the constitutional right to privacy includes a woman's right to have an abortion. For most second-wave feminists, the *Roe v. Wade* decision was a significant victory; however, it also goaded religious conservatives into action, leading to the establishment of a broad-based anti-abortion movement.[11]

For Canadian feminists at the beginning of the seventies, the fight for fully legalized abortion took centre stage. From a women's liberationist perspective, to restrict access to abortion was to restrict a woman's control over her own body and over her own life. And in Canada, access to a legal abortion was restricted. In 1969, the Trudeau government liberalized Canada's abortion laws, but the new legislation included conditions. Abortions had to take place at accredited hospitals, and first, a woman had to seek the approval of a committee of four doctors, on the grounds that the abortion would be necessary for her health. Feminist critics argued that this process was both demeaning and time-consuming, and that it denied a woman's fundamental reproductive rights. Consequently, women's liberation advocates protested the law by launching a cross-country Abortion Caravan. Beginning in Vancouver in April 1970, the activists travelled east to Ottawa. Their protest, which received favourable coverage in the press, culminated the following month in a march on Parliament Hill and a carefully planned disruption in the House of Commons.[12]

Canadian feminists also waged a campaign for publicly funded childcare.[13] Women's liberation activists played a leading role in the formation of daycare co-operatives across Canada, including two on the St George campus of the University of Toronto: the Sussex Day Care and the Devonshire Co-Op. To secure funding and accommodations, the activists who started these co-operatives employed the strategies of the New Left: in the spring of 1970, they occupied the Senate Chamber in Simcoe Hall, pressuring the university administration to pay for needed renovations to the Sussex co-operative; and in 1972, activists occupied the old meteorological building for ten months, before the university granted it permission to operate a daycare on the site.[14] Like the Abortion Caravan protests, these were radical actions that reflected the roots of the women's liberation movement in the New Left. More importantly, they drew public attention to the rapidly growing movement.

Canadian churches were attentive to women's liberation, but their responses varied widely. Of the various denominational periodicals, the *United Church Observer* was most sympathetic in its coverage, beginning in May 1970 with a feature article by Barbara Bagnell entitled "The Feminists." Bagnell paid little attention to the New Left and its role in second-wave feminism, and other than a brief reference to "liberalizing abortion laws," had nothing to say about abortion.[15] She mentioned the role of the Toronto Women's Liberation "Front" in organizing a co-operative day care, but did not mention that these women occupied Simcoe Hall to secure funding for the facility.[16] On the whole, Bagnell presented an image of feminism that older, middle-of-the-road, liberal Protestants might find palatable. Rather than focusing on the confrontational radicals, who sought revolutionary changes in the structure of society, Bagnell featured middle-class mothers and wives (including practising Christians) who simply wanted "a free choice for women."[17] This was liberal feminism, rather than radical or socialist feminism, but from the perspective of many *Observer* readers, it must have seemed progressive and daring.

Indeed, the ideas of women's liberation were daring when applied to the church itself. As early as 1936, it was possible for women to be ordained in the United Church. Nevertheless, there were few women ministers, and often women were discouraged from seeking ordination by the male-dominated denominational hierarchy.[18] In a 1973 editorial column for the *Observer*, Patricia Clarke provided numerous examples of patriarchy within the United Church: inequality in pay and benefits; expectations that women working in the church would perform clerical duties rather than pursue leadership positions; the assumption that women would take minutes and serve coffee at church committee meetings; and traditional sex-role stereotypes in Sunday school materials for children.[19] "You've come a long way, baby," Clarke quipped, "but in the Church, there is still a long way to go."

Women had an even longer way to go in other denominations, in which only men could be ordained as clergy. The campaign for women's ordination in Anglican and Roman Catholic churches, as well as other denominations, did not originate with the women's liberation movement. Nevertheless, it was no coincidence that the debates over women's ordination intensified in the early seventies, just as second-wave feminism was gaining momentum in the broader culture. According to Wendy Fletcher-Marsh,

> The feminist critique of the marginal place of women in Canadian society was being heard in the church through feminist theologians. This critique was a part of the ferment generated by the 1960s push for social revolution and massive social change. Feminist theologians were few and far between in Canada between 1968 and 1976; however, feminist theological ideas did form part of the theatre within which the ordination debate was being acted out ... Secular feminism did not have a direct and immediate effect on the ordination debates ... However, changes in the sphere of women's involvement in society throughout the twentieth century influenced the perceptions of church members and leaders with regard to what women were competent to do.[20]

Whether it was through feminist theologians or the broader milieu of the secular women's movement, there is little doubt that feminism informed the debate over women's ordination. In the Anglican Church of Canada, this campaign bore fruit in 1975, when General Synod voted overwhelmingly in favour of women's ordination.[21] Two years later, Sister Rosemary Benwell became the first female Anglican priest to be ordained in the Diocese of Toronto.[22]

A parallel campaign was underway in the Roman Catholic Church. Encouraged by the spirit of renewal that followed the Second Vatican Council, progressive Catholics voiced their support for women's ordination in the *Canadian Register/Catholic Register* throughout the early seventies.[23] In 1971, Catholic women "representing various groups and personal positions" met at a two-day conference in Ottawa (called by the Canadian bishops) to discuss subjects of their own choosing. The result of their discussions: these women wanted the Church to declare "that women are full and equal members of the Church" and asked "that all discriminatory barriers against women be removed." Among their requests was a call "for the ordination of qualified women for the ministry." Overall, the bishops' response was tentative but encouraging. Cardinal Flahiff of Winnipeg declared that there was "no dogmatic objection to reconsidering" the ordination of women. In 1975, the Canadian Conference of Catholic Bishops recommended to the pope that non-ordained ministries such as lector and acolyte (which were often stepping stones toward ordination) be extended to include women.[24]

These actions on the part of the Canadian episcopacy raised the expectations of Catholic feminists and other progressive Catholics. However, they overestimated the Church's willingness to change – even at a glacial pace. As Hugh McLeod argues, the reforms of Vatican II "raised hopes very high – often for them to be dashed when it became clear that actual results would fall far short of what seemed to have been promised."[25] Such was the case with the issue of women's ordination. Many bishops and priests, in Canada and elsewhere, held deeply conservative views on women's role in the Church.[26] Such views were shared by decision-makers in Rome. In 1976, Pope Paul VI approved a Declaration by the Sacred Congregation for the Doctrine of the Faith that closed the door on the possibility of women's ordination.[27] As with the issue of birth control, the all-male hierarchy made a decision on behalf of Catholic women without widely consulting them, a decision that reinforced a rigid view of gender roles that was anathema to second-wave feminists.

The Roman Catholic Church's unbending stance on abortion was also anathema to most second-wave feminists, who called for "abortion on demand." The issue of abortion was a flashpoint; while it was a matter of fundamental reproductive rights for second-wave feminists, it posed ethical challenges for Protestants and Catholics alike. It required them to ask questions such as does the biblical commandment "you shall not kill" apply to the fetus? If so, at what point would terminating the life of the fetus be murder? Throughout history, most Christians opposed abortion. While some, such as St Thomas Aquinas, regarded it as "murder" only after the fetus was formed and acquired a soul (which medieval thinkers believed to occur approximately forty days after conception for a male, and ninety days for a female), many others believed that any attempt to procure abortion after conception was the equivalent of murder. Nevertheless, there was wide agreement that abortion at any stage of pregnancy was sinful, regardless of whether or not it was murder.[28] By the 1960s and 1970s, however, the Christian consensus on abortion had fractured, especially among liberal Protestants who argued that abortion, while regrettable, could be morally permissible in certain circumstances. As feminists made the case for women's reproductive rights, and as the Canadian government liberalized its abortion laws (too little for women's liberation activists, and too much for social conservatives), churches grappled with both the morality and legality of abortion.[29] While the abortion debates in Canada's churches were internal, they reflected wider social debates over the morality and legality of abortion.[30] The actions of women's liberation activists were part of the broader social context in which these debates took place.

The Roman Catholic Church allowed no room for debate on this matter. As with birth control and women's ordination, the matter was decided by Rome. In 1869, Pope Pius IX decreed that abortion, at any stage of pregnancy, was a mortal sin, which would result in automatic excommunication. Subsequent statements by his successors, including Pope Paul VI in his 1968 encyclical *Humanae Vitae*, reinforced the position that all abortion is forbidden.[31] Even the Canadian episcopate (which, in a roundabout way, took exception to *Humanae Vitae*'s condemnation of birth control) was unequivocal in its denunciation of abortion. In 1968, when the federal government proposed changes to Canada's abortion laws, the Canadian bishops issued a pastoral statement opposing these changes.[32] They reiterated the Church's position, which "condemns the direct taking of foetal life, but not treatments needed to save a mother's life even if they sometimes result in the unwanted and unsought death of the foetus."[33] Furthermore, the anti-abortion views of the Catholic hierarchy were widely shared by Canada's lay Catholics, not only conservative lay members (who would fill the ranks of the pro-life movement in Toronto, and would chastise their bishops for not being sufficiently arduous in their opposition to abortion),[34] but many progressive Catholics as well, such as Bob McKay, editor of the *Canadian Register*. In a 1969 editorial entitled "No Deadlier Sin," McKay explained that opposing abortion was part and parcel of a Catholic reverence for human life, which also included opposition to the Vietnam War.[35] Clearly, in their campaign for abortion on demand, Canadian feminists would not find support in the mainstream of the Roman Catholic Church.

Within Canada's largest Protestant denominations, abortion activists found qualified support. As early as 1967, the Anglican Church of Canada advocated more liberal laws on abortion. The Primate's Committee, established to study the issue of abortion and make recommendations to the federal government, rejected both "abortion on demand" and "the absolute prohibition of all abortion." In typical Anglican fashion, it proposed an equivocal *via media*. On the one hand, the Church asserted "the general inviolability of the foetus" and claimed to "defend, as a first principle, its right to live and develop." On the other, it contended "that there are cases in which, granted the right of the foetus to live and develop, this right may be superseded by another right with greater claim to recognition," such as the mother's health. And "health," it insisted, must "be understood in its broadest sense. Termination of pregnancy on grounds of health must be based on an understanding of the relationship of the expectant mother to her total environment and her ability to cope with the problems within it."[36]

The Trudeau government's changes to the law in 1969 were in line with the Anglican Church's recommendations, but many Anglicans were troubled by the results. Some were concerned with the rise in reported abortions, which suggested that abortion was being used as a substitute for contraception, especially among the young. These statistics led some to question "whether our sense of responsibility for sexual behaviour and for unborn life is being undermined." Others were concerned "about the adequacy and fairness of the existing law," pointing to "the refusal or inability of many hospitals even to have committees" and "regional disparity and unequal access to abortion."[37] In light of these concerns, in 1971, General Synod recommended that a committee be formed to reconsider the abortion issue.

The ensuing report of the Task Force on Human Life, *Abortion: An Issue for Conscience*, contained recommendations that many feminists could applaud.[38] Women's liberation advocates would have been unsatisfied with the task force's rejection of "abortion on demand." Members of the task force were divided on "the adequacy of the existing Criminal Code provisions." Some recommended removing abortion from the Criminal Code, while others recommended the continuation of therapeutic abortion committees. Yet the tenor of the report was that the decision-making process should be collaborative, including "the mother and the medical personnel involved. If possible the husband or the father of the unborn should share in the decision."[39] Advocates of women's reproductive rights would have found the last suggestion problematic. However, they would have been encouraged by the task force's recommendations that the "church must work to reduce the necessity for abortion" through "action for social and economic measures to ensure support for mothers in economic need, availability of housing, day-care centres and fair employment opportunities." They would have been heartened, as well, by the recommendation "that effective means of contraception ought to be universally available," along with community facilities that could provide family planning resources.[40] In short, this report was as feminist a document as one could expect in the Anglican Church of Canada (now under the liberal leadership of Archbishop Edward Scott), and it reflected an uneasy consensus on a divisive issue.

As the United Church of Canada discovered in these years, abortion was indeed a divisive issue.[41] It appears that individual United Church congregations supported the feminists' demands, or at least supported their right to be heard, since the Abortion Caravan participants boarded at United churches on their journey to Ottawa.[42] But achieving agreement across the denomination proved to be elusive. In October 1970, the church's Board of Evangelism and Social Service and its Board of Women appointed a Joint Committee on Abortion. Its task "was to prepare a Statement and Resolutions, to be put before the 24th General Council of the United Church, on the present Canadian abortion law, with recommendations for change."[43] Significantly, two-thirds of the Joint Committee's members were women, and its chair was Ruth Evans, an abortion rights activist.[44] The statement that ultimately passed at the 1971 meeting of General Council, on the recommendations of the Joint Committee, was resolutely pro-choice. While it recognized the "value of the foetus," it also recognized the "right of the child to be wanted," and affirmed "that abortion is morally justifiable in certain medical, social and economic circumstances." The council also resolved "that an abortion should be a private matter between a woman and her doctor, without prejudice to the need for consulting her male partner." It called on the federal government "to remove from the present Criminal Code all sections relating to abortion."[45]

In an unusual move, the editors of the *United Church Observer* criticized General Council's decision. In an editorial published one year after the 1971 resolution, A.C. Forrest and Patricia Clarke rejected the notion that abortion is "a private matter." They grounded their criticism in two general principles: first, "that each person is responsible for his actions, and for their consequences," and second, "that life, unintelligent or unwanted though it may be, is sacred, and is not to be sacrificed because its continuance could be an embarrassment, a nuisance, or a great burden." The editors concluded that "the 1971 resolution should be rejected, and a new statement made at the August 1972 Council."[46] Forrest and Clarke's piece elicited a flood of telephone calls and letters to the editor; almost all of these supported the editors in their opposition to General Council's pro-choice stance.[47] Furthermore, across the country, presbyteries and conferences (respectively, local and regional divisions of the United Church of Canada) called on General Council to re-examine the issue.[48]

At the 1972 General Council meeting in Saskatoon, the debate over abortion was "heated and bitter," and marked by "widely divergent views," but ultimately, the council approved a new set of resolutions by a vote of about 380 to fifty.[49] Once again, the United Church urged the federal government to remove abortion from the Criminal Code. Yet it qualified its earlier position that abortion was "a personal matter between a woman and her doctor." The new statement read, "We do not support 'abortion on demand.' We believe that prior to twelve weeks of gestation ... abortion should be a personal matter between a woman and her doctor. After that period of time, abortion should only be performed following consultation with a second doctor. We further believe that her male partner and/or other supportive people have a responsibility to both the woman and the foetus and should be involved in the decision wherever possible."[50] Other parts of the resolution encouraged greater use of birth control, so that abortion would eventually be rendered unnecessary, or at least rare.

On the surface, the new statement endorsed by the 1972 General Council appeared to be a compromise. With its rejection of "abortion on demand," the denomination distanced itself from the rhetoric of women's liberationists. However, the 1972 statement reiterated the key positions of the 1971 statement: the assertion that abortion is a personal matter for a mother to decide (at least until twelve weeks of gestation), and a call for both the decriminalization of abortion and greater access to birth control. Throughout the early seventies, members of the church hierarchy defended the denomination's official pro-choice position. Chief among these was Harriet Christie (1912–1975), deputy secretary of the church's Division of Mission in Canada and an alumnus of the SCM.[51] Although she was in her early sixties, Christie shared many of the concerns of young second-wave feminists, including access to abortion. Joan Wyatt writes that Christie, as the former "secretary of the Board of Women and the sole female at the national level of the United Church at the time," believed that issues of importance to Canadian women's rights activists should be important to her denomination, and she "lamented that the church was lagging behind secular feminist movements in Canada."[52] The church's 1972 reaffirmation of its pro-choice stance – and Christie's vocal defence of that stance – signalled to younger secular feminists that the United Church was eager to catch up.

Nevertheless, the United Church leadership could not speak for all of its members, many of whom held considerably more conservative views on abortion. General Council's 1972 statement failed to appease dedicated opponents of abortion, and anti-abortion delegates registered their dissent from the resolutions of General Council.[53] A vocal contingent of United Church clergy and laity continued to express their opposition, and some began to rally to the burgeoning pro-life movement.[54] If Canada's most liberal mainline denomination could not achieve consensus on abortion (and a modified statement at that), it was not likely that women's liberation advocates would find unqualified support for their agenda in Canada's churches.

WOMEN'S LIBERATION AND THE STUDENT CHRISTIAN MOVEMENT

If Canada's Christian mainstream was unwilling to fully embrace women's liberation, what about the Christian radicals? How did the SCM respond to the challenge of feminism? In the early seventies, with few exceptions, the SCM did not engage with women's liberation on an organizational level. This is puzzling because by this time, many on the New Left had embraced feminism,[55] and the SCM was attentive to most other developments in the radical left. It is even more puzzling when one considers that on an *individual* level, Toronto's Christian left was well represented in the women's movement. John Foster of Kairos and LAWG was an active supporter of women's liberation, which he described as "an attempt to bring Marxist analysis and rhetoric into some practical actions," and his essay on the Sussex Daycare was included in the Canadian feminist anthology *Women Unite!*[56] Judy Skinner of SCM and LAWG participated in the Toronto Women's Liberation Movement and was heavily involved in the Canadian Women's Educational Press.[57] Others on the Christian left involved in the women's movement included Bonnie Ward of the Centre for the Study of Institutions and Theology, who belonged to the Canadian Women's Educational Press collective, and Heather Campbell (at the time, the wife of University of Toronto chaplain and SCM alumnus Eilert Frerichs).[58]

However, Canada's SCM paid little heed to the women's movement before the mid-seventies. There were some exceptions; for example, the London Women's Liberation Movement, which began in 1970, had origins in "the left, the student movement of the university, specifically out of a concern among some people in the SCM over the kinds of roles which women and men are forced to play."[59] And at least one local unit held Bible studies centred on the issue of women's liberation.[60] But in the national SCM records for these years, there is little mention of women's liberation – certainly no mention of specific issues, such as birth control, abortion, daycare, job equity, or even women's ordination. Betsy Anderson notes that her American counterparts in the WSCF were more attuned to these issues than Canadians, that they "brought a more developed analysis of patriarchy and commitment to feminism to our interactions." She cites the influence of Jan Griesinger, whose "experience as an American campus minister and involvement in the American feminist movement allowed her to sow seeds that bore fruit in the Canadian SCM some years later in the context of the Canadian feminist movement, which re-emerged in the mid-to-late 1970's."[61]

While the SCM would take up the cause at a later stage, the question still remains: why did the SCM of the early 1970s engage with so many liberation causes, both national and foreign, yet not engage with *women's* liberation? The most plausible answer is that consciously or unconsciously, core participants in the SCM did not place women's oppression on the same level as class- or race-based oppression. Unlike others in the New Left, they had not yet expanded their critique of capitalism to include gender and sexuality. And unlike their American counterparts in the WSCF, they had not yet developed a theology of women's liberation. As Anderson recalls, these developments occurred later for the Canadian SCM: "The SCM did a whole study kit on women's liberation ... and it had a lot of some of the earlier feminist theologians ... [but] I certainly didn't identify as a feminist until later on ... A feminist analysis of the discrimination against women and systemic discrimination and economic discrimination against women and all those things – that for me came later, like in the mid to late seventies. And I think that that kit had some of that stuff in it too."[62]

The late seventies and eighties would be key years for feminists in Canada's churches and mainline Christian organizations – not only in the SCM, but also in the United, Anglican, and Roman Catholic churches. While their initial response to the women's movement was slow and tentative, they could not help but be affected by the cumulative impact of feminist theology, the increased presence of women in full-time ministry, and the changing role of women in broader Canadian society. There are striking parallels between the churches' slow response to the challenge of feminism and their reaction to another manifestation of the New Left in the early seventies: the gay liberation movement.

CANADIAN CHRISTIANITY AND GAY LIBERATION

Being gay or lesbian was not easy at the onset of the long sixties, either in Canada or in the United States. Same-sex activity, even between consenting adults and in private, was a criminal offence throughout Canada and in all but two American states.[63] The RCMP and military believed that homosexuals were a security risk, which led to many gays and lesbians being purged from the civil service and military in the fifties and sixties. Such gay establishments as existed were subject to police surveillance and harassment.[64] Even among liberal Canadians, homosexuals generally were regarded as mentally ill or as objects of pity.[65] With few exceptions, most gays and lesbians chose to keep their sexual orientation a secret to protect their jobs and their social status.[66]

Slowly, the picture was changing. Influenced by the British *Wolfenden Report* (released in 1957, it recommended the legalization of homosexual acts between consenting adults), Canadian lawyers, clergy, and academics called for legal reforms. So did Canadian "homophile" groups such as the Association for Social Knowledge, founded in 1964. Modelled after their American counterparts such as the Mattachine Society, these groups advocated for the civil rights of homosexuals. Accordingly, in 1969, the Trudeau government legalized same-sex activity between consenting adults. In many respects, the new law was inadequate: it did not stop police surveillance of gay bars or "cruising" sites; it did not rectify the discrimination that gays and lesbians faced in public sector employment or immigration; and the age of consent for homosexual acts was set at twenty-one, which penalized gay youth. Nevertheless, it was a step forward, and undoubtedly a source of encouragement for Canada's gay rights activists.[67]

These activists took even more encouragement from the events that took place in New York City, beginning on 27 June 1969. In response to a routine police raid on Stonewall (an unlicensed gay bar in Greenwich Village), the gay community fought back. As clients of the tavern were loaded into paddy wagons, a crowd (which eventually reached 2,000) began throwing bottles and rocks at the police, who retreated into the tavern to take shelter. This grassroots revolt lasted for several days and sparked the beginnings of the gay liberation movement. One month after Stonewall, a group of gay and lesbian activists with ties to the New Left formed the Gay Liberation Front. Their objective was to "make a place for ourselves in the revolutionary movement," connecting gay liberation to other radical causes such as Third World revolution and Black Power. In the months and years that followed, similar groups were founded across the United States. Most of these groups focused exclusively on gay and lesbian rights, rather than debating "over left-wing theory, the nature of capitalism, or solidarity with the Panthers." Nevertheless, they employed the militant strategies and rhetorical style of the New Left.[68] In the same way that women's liberation gave new impetus to second-wave feminism, gay liberation galvanized the movement for homosexual rights.

In Canada, gay activists began organizing within months after Stonewall. The University of Toronto Homophile Association (UTHA) was formed in the fall of 1969, followed a year later by the Community Homophile Association of Toronto (CHAT), and homophile groups in other Canadian cities over the next few years.[69] Across the country, more militant groups also emerged espousing a gay liberation agenda, including Toronto Gay Action, which grew out of CHAT's political action committee. On 28 August 1971, Toronto Gay Action organized a protest in Ottawa involving 200 activists who called for "full human rights for lesbians and gay men, spousal and family benefits, the right to adopt children as lesbian and gay couples, age-of-consent-law reform ... the repeal of the offence of 'gross indecency,' and the right to be gay or lesbian and serve in the Armed Forces."[70] The fall of 1971 witnessed the birth of the *Body Politic*, a gay liberation magazine published in Toronto by a collective of writers associated with Toronto Gay Action.[71] A visible gay community developed in Toronto throughout the seventies (as it did in other major cities throughout North America), with the establishment of gay organizations, autonomous lesbian groups, the *Body Politic*, Glad Day Bookshop, and other gay and lesbian institutions.[72]

Some of these institutions were religious. The first of these in Toronto was an association of Unitarian-Universalist gays. In January 1971, Toronto's Unitarian congregation, which had been discussing the issue of homosexuality since the 1960s, established a "Sub-Committee on Homophiles."[73] Two years later, the Metropolitan Community Church of Toronto was formed. MCC-Toronto was affiliated with the Universal Fellowship of Metropolitan Community Churches, a denomination founded in 1968 by Troy Perry, a gay American minister. By June 1974, the Toronto congregation drew about seventy women and men regularly to its weekly services.[74] Also in these years, gay Anglicans in Toronto established Canada's first branch of Integrity (an international network of gays and lesbians in Anglican and Episcopal churches), and Toronto's gay Catholics formed a chapter of Dignity (a similar group for Roman Catholics).[75] For gays and lesbians who wished to affirm both their Christian faith and their sexuality, these networks were important because it was difficult to find such affirmation in most churches. As the *Body Politic* explained in its notice of MCC-Toronto's opening, it was "a church for gay people who, with good reason, have felt alienated, excluded and condemned by mainline christian groups."[76]

Gays and lesbians felt alienated from most Christian churches because of the traditional Christian position on homosexuality (shared by conservative and orthodox Jews): that it is an "abomination" to God.[77] Nevertheless, from the mid to late sixties, there was broad agreement among both Catholics and Protestants in Canada that even if same-sex activity is immoral, it should not be illegal.[78] This agreement was not unanimous. For example, a pseudonymous writer for *People's Magazine*, published by the fundamentalist People's Church of Toronto, argued that the "remedy" for homosexuality was execution: "That was God's remedy. He destroyed Sodom and Gomorrah because of the homosexuals. He exterminated the Canaanites for the same reason. Aside from the Gospel there is no cure. The death penalty is the only solution." However, the magazine editor subsequently told the *Globe and Mail* that this was "a mistake," and shortly thereafter, the pastor of People's Church publicly called for the decriminalization of homosexual acts between consenting adults, even though "homosexuality is a sin in the sight of God meriting spiritual death."[79]

Throughout the sixties and seventies, many progressive Christians disputed the traditional view of homosexuality as "a sin ... meriting spiritual death," and chose instead to affirm gay and lesbian identities. Among Anglicans in the Diocese of Toronto, the progressive parish of Holy Trinity Church (home to Christian left activists such as Dan Heap and Brewster Kneen) showed its support for the gay and lesbian community by hosting CHAT's first public meeting in February 1971, as well as its earliest dances.[80] Holy Trinity also allowed MCC-Toronto to hold evening services in its sanctuary in the early 1970s.[81] Some Toronto-based progressive Roman Catholics signalled their affirmation as well. For example, in 1974, Father Gregory Baum, a theologian at St Michael's College, addressed a gay audience in Toronto on "Homosexuality and Human Dignity," telling them, in essence, that they were fulfilling God's calling by being gay.[82] That same year, United Church moderator Bruce McLeod told the *Toronto Star* that "Christians and others had better not judge [homosexuals] too quickly ... We have been too ready to condemn in the past. We have to become more open to different forms of sexual relationships today."[83] McLeod's choice of words is problematic; to refrain from judging "too quickly" and to be "open" is not the same as unqualified affirmation. Nevertheless, McLeod's statement was surprisingly positive – and significant coming from the head of Canada's largest Protestant denomination.

McLeod's statements to the *Toronto Star* were consistent with the increasingly liberal trajectory of the United Church on matters of sexuality (and, as we have seen, related moral issues such as abortion) throughout the long sixties and beyond. As Philip Gardner argues, the United Church of the 1960s experienced a tension between a traditional sexual ethic "based on revealed law" and "what came to be called 'the New Morality.'" The latter was an ethical framework that "called for a more flexible approach to ethical issues (including sex and gender)," and "paid more attention to context and less to the enforcement of divinely ordained behavioural rules through shaming and social sanctions."[84] Not surprisingly, the younger generation, including young Christian radicals, more readily embraced this relativistic framework than did older church members. However, by the late sixties, United Church officials were increasingly receptive to the New Morality.

This is evident in a draft handbook produced by the Committee on Sex and Morality. The committee was established by the United Church's Board of Evangelism and Social Service in 1966 "to discuss the new morality as it pertains to the sexual revolution." One of the committee members was Nancy Hannum, who, in her mid-twenties, was the only committee member under thirty years of age. As a young Christian radical active in Toronto's New Left, Hannum expressed skepticism that a church committee whose members were mostly older males had anything relevant to say to young people about sexuality, and she rejected the fundamental premise that sex was a matter that could be subjected to religious rules. In her chapter, which she titled "I Prefer the Beatles," she wrote, "We cannot stand around judging whether or not people love each other enough to be making love. To do so is to proclaim a very narrow view of people and, in fact, to be 'hung-up on sex.' If kids are hung-up about 'sexual morality' it is partly because the older people, to whom they look for help, moralize and write books about 'sexual morality.' ... I'm serious when I say I'd rather listen to the Beatles because I think it is the artists and poets who are best expressing this 'turning-over' of some of our deepest social values."[85] While Hannum might have intended to set herself apart from other contributors to the project, the fact is that most of the other members of the committee shared her disdain for a rigid, rule-based approach to sexuality. This included Mervyn Dickinson, who, in 1965, had also written an article for the *United Church Observer* espousing a liberal view of homosexuality (calling for the decriminalization of homosexual acts and proposing that the church grant its blessing to same-sex unions).[86] Thus, some United Church officials and clergy held views about homosexuality (and sexual morality in general) that hewed more closely to the views of young radicals in the late sixties and early seventies.

But the United Church of Canada was not a monolith, and although McLeod and others espoused progressive views on homosexuality, other prominent voices in the denomination articulated a more conservative position. For example, a 1971 editorial in the *United Church Observer* noted that churchmen "are being subjected to a powerful, sustained drive from homosexuals who have organized themselves into 'gay' groups demanding acceptance of themselves as persons, and approval of their sexual activity as good." The editor observed that gays were "right in demanding acceptance as persons including full rights of church membership," and also approved of the legal reforms that decriminalized same-sex activity between consenting adults. At the same time, the writer argued that while homosexual acts were no longer criminal, they should not be considered good: "there are homosexual relationships marked by integrity, fidelity, mutual forbearance and love," but this was not sufficient justification for their goodness, since there "are also beautiful adulterous relationships, and common law marriages which are superior in many ways to many 'normal' Christian marriages." To be "a homosexual is tragic," the editor argued, and the duty of the Christian community was to help homosexuals to "sublimate" their desires, and "no Christian minister should perform or bless a homosexual 'marriage.'"[87] Undoubtedly, this editorial reflected the viewpoint of many conservative Christians. However, neither the editor of the *Observer* nor the United Church moderator spoke for the church as a whole. At no point in the early seventies did General Council endorse a resolution for or against gay liberation.

Nor, for that matter, did other churches. Most denominations were silent on the issue, and aside from the above-mentioned editorial in the *Observer*, there was little or no discussion of gay liberation in any of the major church periodicals. In late 1975, the Sacred Congregation for the Doctrine of Faith reiterated the Roman Catholic Church's longstanding condemnation of homosexual practice, but otherwise, neither the *Catholic Register* nor the Canadian Catholic hierarchy went out of its way to address gay liberation in the early seventies.[88] Such silence should not be construed as approval. Quite the opposite; it simply was unnecessary for Canadian Catholics to issue a statement on something that long-established church teaching or the Bible (as interpreted by conservative Christians) so clearly condemned. Thus, in the early seventies, the patterns of church response to gay liberation seemed to be vocal affirmation, vocal condemnation, or default condemnation by silence.

SILENT AFFIRMATION?
THE SCM AND GAY LIBERATION

While one can easily interpret the silence of the Roman Catholic Church in response to the gay liberation movement (in the light of longstanding church teaching), it is not nearly as easy to understand the silence of the SCM in the early seventies. The SCM's silence is surprising for two reasons: homosexuality and homosexual rights *were* a topic of discussion in the SCM in the mid sixties; and several participants in the SCM throughout the 1960s were gay, though not always openly identified as such.

One of the consistent characteristics of the SCM, acknowledged by many of my interviewees, was its openness, both to people and to ideas. In its associational life, the movement welcomed outsiders and provided a supportive, familial environment. In its intellectual life, questioning received religious orthodoxies was not merely permissible; it was encouraged. Consequently, the SCM community in Toronto and elsewhere often provided a relatively welcoming space for homosexuals, whether open or closeted, and an equally congenial environment for challenging prevalent orthodoxies about sexuality.

Homosexuality was a topic of discussion at some SCM work camps, including the 1965 work camp in Edmonton focused on "Sex and Society."[89] In the mid-sixties, it was also the central issue for an unusual group that met at the University of Toronto SCM's coffeehouse, the Inn of the Unmuzzled Ox. Occupying the ground floor of a house along St George Avenue, the Ox was a venue for poets, artists, folk-singers, and "a floating poker game in the basement."[90] Ian Young, a young gay male and peace activist, helped to run the Ox, and he decided to start a gay discussion group modelled on campus-based groups in the United States, groups which "were more militant and open than the old homophile groups that had been around since the early 50's. They had a new, younger leadership with an unapologetic attitude about being gay and an insistence on complete legal and social equality."[91] While Young's group was short-lived ("with very few exceptions, gays and lesbians were too timid to risk even showing up for a talk"), his effort was significant because the group he endeavoured to establish anticipated the gay liberationist ethos of later groups and it happened under the auspices of the SCM.[92]

By raising the issue of gay rights in both formal and informal settings, the Canadian SCM of the mid-sixties challenged heterosexual participants in the movement to question the religious and legal frameworks that oppressed homosexuals. In some cases, it also made it possible for participants to put a human face on an otherwise abstract issue. Wolfe Erlichman recalled "a big discussion about gay rights, which was pretty political and ahead of its time" at the annual Bala conference in the early sixties. Following the conference, Erlichman boarded an SCM participant from Nova Scotia, Tony Metie (1944–1986), at his home in north Toronto. Erlichman recalls that he and Metie were having a late-night discussion about homosexuals, and their rights: "it was about midnight and I was kind of falling asleep. And suddenly, [Metie] said, 'you know,' he said, 'I'm a homosexual.' ... And I woke up! And, 'oh ... ok.' That was my introduction to meeting somebody who was gay."[93]

Tony Metie (later an activist in Toronto Gay Action and a writer for *Body Politic*) was not unique in the SCM; there were several gay participants in the movement throughout the sixties.[94] Some of them were openly gay or in the process of coming out, such as John Lee (who came out while he was director of the 1964 SCM Peace Camp in Toronto) and Tony Metie. For others, their sexuality was widely known but little discussed; such was the case for Rev. Bob Miller (influential study secretary and manager of the SCM Book Room) and his partner Paul Warner. Others would come out at a later date, such as the Rev. Eilert Frerichs.[95] Some, such as Lee and Frerichs, had initially met and married women through the SCM (in its function as "Society of Courtship and Marriage"), before coming to terms with their sexuality.

For these reasons, the silence of the SCM in the early 1970s – just as the gay liberation movement was taking shape – is striking. There are no records clearly indicating that gay liberation was a topic of consideration. The report of the 1973–74 National Programme notes that one or more of the local SCMs hosted studies on "alternate lifestyles," a vague term that could refer to homosexuality, though it could also refer to communal living.[96] Furthermore, none of my interviewees who were active in the SCM of the early 1970s could recall any discussion of the matter.[97] Ian Young, who had formed the gay discussion group in the mid 1960s under the auspices of the University of Toronto SCM coffeehouse, and later was active in UTHA, recalls no connection between the campus gay club and the campus SCM.[98] It appears that the SCM's solidarity with liberation struggles did not extend this far. While the SCM's silence in the early seventies cannot be construed as condemnation (as in the case of conservative religious denominations), it cannot be construed as political affirmation either. In all likelihood, it reflected a laissez-faire attitude of "live and let live," of tolerance and disinterest.

The SCM's lack of interest in gay liberation in the early seventies, similar to its lack of interest in women's liberation, reflected its circumscribed understanding of politics. As Anderson explains, "we didn't think that much about sexual politics. I didn't anyway, and it didn't seem to come up very much in what we were doing. We were all into, you know, *politics* politics."[99] If SCM members in these years failed to perceive the political dimensions of sexuality and gender, they were not alone. While individual members of Toronto's radical left became involved in gay liberation, overall, radical left groups were not quick to embrace gay liberation. Gay liberationists were accused of being "petit bourgeois lifestylists." In essence, some saw gay liberation as a form of false consciousness, a diversion from the "real" struggle.[100] In contrast, the SCM of the mid-sixties had concerned itself with both "the personal" and "the political." In 1965, a critic of the SCM complained that the organization failed to make "a clear distinction between the personal and the political," and that it was too concerned with "the quality of interpersonal relationships," which bears "no obvious implications in the realm of politics."[101] The SCM's shift from "personal/political" in the sixties to "narrowly political" in the seventies may appear ironic, since the overall trajectory of the New Left went in the opposite direction.[102] But on closer inspection, the SCM was not out of step with elements of the radical left of its day. As with women's liberation, it would be some time before the SCM embraced the gay rights movement and developed a theology of gay liberation.[103]

Canadian Christians in the early seventies responded to gay liberation either by affirming it, condemning it, or ignoring it. The SCM, it seems, opted to ignore it. It would appear that neither Canada's largest churches nor the SCM were prepared to fully engage with the gay liberation movement; indeed, most would not engage at all in these years. It was not until the eighties and beyond that homosexuality became a matter of heated debate among Canadian Christians, when one's beliefs about sexuality became a litmus test determining whether one belonged on one side of the culture war or the other.

CONCLUSION

The women's movement and the movement for gay and lesbian rights, both inspired and energized by the New Left, demonstrated that in the early seventies, "liberation" was a political concept with multiple meanings and the potential for broad application. As with other New Left-inspired movements, they would have a profound impact on Canada's social and political landscape, continuing into subsequent decades. And as with other movements of the early seventies that employed the rhetoric of "liberation," they posed challenges for Canadian Christians. Clergy and active laity debated the difficult questions that these movements posed to their denominations: how can women participate fully and equally in the life and ministry of the church? What stance should the church take on the legality or morality of abortion? Are homosexual relationships consistent with Christian sexual ethics, and should Christians be advocating for gays and lesbians, as they would for other oppressed peoples?

The response of both Canadian churches and young Christian radicals to these movements was mixed. In relative terms, the United Church of Canada was the most receptive of Canada's main denominations to both women's liberation and gay liberation. Nevertheless, this was only relative to more conservative denominations. On the abortion issue, no denomination favoured "abortion on demand," and when the United Church called upon the government to further liberalize abortion laws, it encountered significant pushback from its membership. Furthermore, with a few notable exceptions, Canadian Christians were not prepared to engage with the gay liberation movement.

These responses demonstrate that for some young Christian radicals, a circumscribed understanding of politics led them to show solidarity with some liberation movements, but not with others. As for older Christians, for the clergy and active laity in Canada's largest denominations, their patterns of engagement (or lack thereof) reinforce our observation from the previous chapter: that most Canadian churches could never be radical enough for young activists of the early seventies. More broadly, Canadian churches' attempts to engage with the political and social issues that concerned young people – from the antiwar movement to changing values regarding gender and sexuality – highlight the "generation gap" of the era. In the early seventies, Catholics and mainline Protestants were eager to bridge that gap. Their efforts yielded limited success, at best. In particular, the United Church continued to bemoan the absence of youth in its services and to engage its young adherents in a discussion of how the Church could reverse this trend.[104]

Nevertheless, the engagement of Canada's mainline churches and Christian groups (such as LAWG and the SCM) with young New Leftists was a fruitful one. Churches did not succeed in retaining their young members, nor were churches transformed into politically radical institutions. Even so, in the decades that followed, the churches did change, often in ways that they might not have anticipated in the late sixties or early seventies. In the next chapter, I explore, briefly, the trajectory of Canadian Christianity since the long sixties, and how the churches of the twenty-first century, both Catholic and Protestant, owe a debt to the youth-based protest movements of the long sixties.

9

Beyond the Long Sixties

Why Christian Engagement with the New Left Mattered

Christians in English Canada (and Toronto in particular) interacted with radical youth who challenged the dominant social-political structures throughout the long sixties. They engaged with the New Left for a variety of reasons. Young radical Christians engaged because they were a part of the same activist milieu and shared the same concerns; consequently, they played a formative role in the earliest stages of the Canadian New Left. Older church leaders, both Roman Catholics and mainstream Protestants, reached out to the youth in revolt because theological trends of the sixties compelled them to be "prophetic," to "dialogue with the modern world," and to go "where the action is." They were also aware of the demographic importance of youth, and the fact that retaining young people was essential to the long-term health of their denominations.

This story of Canadian Christian interaction with the New Left is significant for several reasons. First, it forms a piece of a much larger international story. Hugh McLeod shows that the long sixties were years of crisis for institutional Christianity throughout the Western world, and the youth-oriented leftist movements of the era were an important factor in how this crisis unfolded.[1] Clearly, Canada was not exceptional in this regard. More importantly, the political engagement of Canadian Christians, both young and old, in the long sixties mattered because these interactions with the New Left had a lasting impact on Canada's churches, and on the trajectory of Canada's "Christian left" (whether in churches or ecumenical social justice groups).

This concluding chapter considers the legacies of these interactions for Canadian Christianity. Legacies are complex, and many factors have contributed to shaping present-day Canadian Christianity. Just as no single factor was responsible for initiating the religious crisis of the 1960s, no single factor determined the religious developments of the past four decades. Nonetheless, when we explore these developments, we see the legacies of sixties-era Christian engagement with the New Left: in the issues and concerns that engage the attention of Canadian Christians, and in the individuals who continued to play a role in the aftermath of the sixties. I give special attention to the ongoing impact of women's liberation and gay liberation on Canada's churches. I also consider a possible unintended legacy: the ways in which Christian engagement with the left may have contributed to decline in Canada's largest denominations. The chapter then concludes with some final observations on the significance of the relationship between Canadian Christianity and the New Left in the long sixties.

ROMAN CATHOLICS, MAINLINE PROTESTANTS, AND THE LEGACY OF NEW LEFT ENGAGEMENT

Social Catholicism and the Protestant social gospel are more than a century old, and they have enjoyed a continuous presence in Catholic, Anglican, and United churches. Nevertheless, it is particularly since the sixties and seventies that we see Canadian church bodies and faith-based NGOs speaking out "prophetically" on a wide range of social justice issues such as poverty, corporate responsibility, nuclear energy, native rights, refugees, and Canada's role in the developing world.[2] In part, we can credit this "prophetic" shift to Christian engagement with the radical youth of the sixties, and with the issues of concern to them.

Since the 1970s, the United Church of Canada has been the most consistent religious voice for a left-of-centre social justice agenda. When Ray Hord (secretary of the Board of Evangelism and Social Service until his death in 1968) unequivocally denounced the Vietnam War and Canadian complicity in it, he set an example that inspired subsequent United Church leaders. Hord, in turn, drew his inspiration from the radical youth of the New Left, and his contacts included young Christian radicals such as Tom Faulkner, John Foster, and Nancy Hannum. The Church he envisioned would be a place in which such radicals could work effectively.[3] Owing in part to his example, the United Church gradually became such a place, and the activists of the long sixties were a part of it. Tom Faulkner (former students' council president at the University of Toronto) became a professor of theology, taught at United Church colleges (including St Andrew's College at the University of Saskatchewan), and maintained a lifelong focus on global social justice issues until his death in July 2010.[4] From 1971, John Foster (of Kairos and LAWG) worked with the United Church's Division of Mission, focusing on issues of trade and development.[5] And in the 1980s, Nancy Hannum worked with Joan Newman Kuyek (both formerly of SUPA) on the United Church's "Church and Economic Crisis Project." Kuyek, who was the project's national animator between 1986 and 1989, recalled that she "worked all over the country with some of the most progressive people I've met – many were engaged in enormous fights that had been going on for twenty, thirty years with the same people in the church."[6]

Thus, the leftward shift of the United Church in the 1970s and 1980s owed much to the presence of clergy and laity who were inspired by Ray Hord's example, including those whose politics had been forged in the youth activism of the long sixties. One cannot overestimate the importance of left-leaning youth of the sixties who chose to remain in the United Church. Several of these, including alumni of the sixties-era SCM and related groups, became clergy, theology professors, or at the very least, active lay members. In the process, they served as progressive voices in the United Church over the past half-century.

Progressive voices became more prominent in the Anglican and Roman Catholic churches in these years too, though they often had to contend with conservative opposition. In the 1970s and 1980s, Canadian Anglicans found a champion in the progressive Archbishop Ted Scott, primate of the Anglican Church of Canada from 1971 to 1986 and a former member of the SCM. According to Alan Hayes, some "who knew him well said that, at heart, he remained an SCM secretary all his life, happiest in dialog and teaching and always ready to question received orthodoxies, plot social action, or catch a vision for creative ministry." For Scott, the "Church was there to have a dialog with the world and turn it toward justice. The problem was that government and business no longer needed to pay attention to what churches were trying to say to them. Publicity and confrontation would therefore be necessary." Though he was primate of the Church, his political views were at odds with many laity in the Church, which has long been the spiritual home of English Canadian business executives and conservative political elites.[7] Like Hord in the United Church, Scott helped to create a space for left-leaning youth (including SCM alumni) who wished to remain a part of the institutional church and who hoped to reform it from within. Some would go on to become clergy and active laity.

The contingent in the Church who shared Scott's left politics found social leadership in the Church's Public Social Responsibility Unit, formed in 1974 to address a broad range of social issues.[8] The Primate's World Relief and Development Fund (PWRDF) has been another voice for Anglican social justice concerns, and the PWRDF's affiliated Youth Movement is a gathering point for activist-minded Anglican youth. Furthermore, individual Anglicans who were activists in the sixties continued their activism in subsequent decades (such as Father Ian Mackenzie and his involvement in native rights issues),[9] and progressive congregations from the sixties (such as Holy Trinity parish in Toronto) continue to serve as spiritual homes for radicals in today's Anglican Church. Thus, left-leaning Anglicans have maintained a presence within the denomination and, within limits, managed to influence the decision-making process on select issues. And as with the United Church of Canada, it was the political engagement of progressive Anglicans with the youthful left of the long sixties that paved the way for these developments.

A similar process of engagement occurred among Roman Catholics, which involved not only young radical Catholics but also older reform-minded priests and laity. While the Catholic left predated the sixties, it gained new impetus in these years, due to Vatican II and the advent of liberation theology. In the sixties and early seventies, Toronto's progressive Catholics were active in secular New Left groups such as SUPA and the New Left Caucus, broader Christian groups such as the SCM and LAWG, and specifically Catholic organizations such as Youth Corps and the University of Toronto's Newman Centre. Some of these reform-minded Catholics would drift away from the Church and identify instead with the secular New Left. Others, however, would remain active in the Catholic community, working for justice in the structure of the Church as well as the wider world.

For the latter group, the seventies and eighties were a period of disappointment. Under Pope Paul VI and his successor, Pope John Paul II, the Church spoke with a more conservative voice, and the hopes of reformers (e.g., to extend the priesthood to women and married men) were dashed once again. Vatican II had signalled (or so reformers believed) that the Church was moving toward a more collegial model of governance, that it would be more willing to listen to critical voices, or at least tolerate them. But under Pope John Paul II, the Church moved decisively in a conservative direction, especially with Cardinal Joseph Ratzinger as prefect of the Congregation for the Doctrine of the Faith. In these years, the Church clarified its disapproval of birth control and homosexuality, leaving no room for doubts. It silenced or excommunicated Catholic theologians who articulated unorthodox viewpoints. Liberation theology – the distinctively Latin American blend of Catholicism and Third World Marxism – was denounced in no uncertain terms.[10] Likewise, with Larry Henderson as editor of the *Catholic Register* (1974–86) and Gerald Emmett Carter as archbishop (1978–90), the leading voices of Catholicism in the Archdiocese of Toronto now spoke in a more conservative tone as well.

Shocked by the rightward shift, and determined to defend their vision (inspired by Vatican II) of a people's Church, a handful of Toronto Catholics established *Catholic New Times* in 1976. The paper served as a social justice-oriented alternative voice for Canadian Catholics, and its editorial board included progressives such as Janet Somerville, Sister Mary Jo Leddy (a social activist and Baby Boomer who came of age in the years of Vatican II), Father Tom McKillop (who had founded Youth Corps in the Archdiocese of Toronto in 1966), and Ted Schmidt (a teacher and activist who had formerly written a youth column for the *Catholic Register*). Catholics who challenged the hierarchy on issues such as women's ordination, who continued to be inspired by Vatican II and the liberation theology emerging from Latin America, found encouragement in the *Catholic New Times*, until it ceased publication in 2006.[11]

For both progressive Catholics and mainline Protestants, including those that had engaged in the radical Christian left in the long sixties such as John Foster, ecumenical, interchurch groups have played a key role in social justice advocacy since the 1970s. Among these were GATT-Fly (an NGO focused on trade and international development issues, formed in 1972), the Taskforce on the Churches and Corporate Responsibility (1973), Project North (founded in 1975 by Anglican, Roman Catholic, and United churches, as a voice on native issues in northern Canada), Project Ploughshares (challenging the Canadian government's military spending and Canadian arms exports), and the

Inter-Church Committee on Human Rights in Latin America (formed in the wake of the 1973 coup in Chile).[12] Such groups brought together progressive Christians of different denominations to make common cause on issues of concern. Organizations such as these contributed to the creation of the ecumenical social justice advocacy and research group KAIROS in 2001.[13] Furthermore, New Left-inspired ecumenical Christian groups that were active in the sixties and had drawn the participation of radical Christian youth would continue to operate well beyond the time period of this study. LAWG remained active into the 1990s,[14] and the Canadian SCM continues to this day.

The SCM has occupied a central place in this study because it was an important incubator for young Christian left activists and because it played a crucial role in the formation of the New Left in English Canada. As an ecumenical Christian youth organization with a social justice focus, the Canadian SCM lives on, but it is no longer the mass movement it once was. The movement entered a period of decline in the sixties. The life trajectory of former SCM participants suggests that for some, the movement's particular combination of left politics and Christianity lost its appeal (even though, in interviews, they looked back fondly on the experience of close-knit community in the SCM of the sixties). For example, some participants from the sixties were drawn to the secular left and distanced themselves from the Christian community. This was particularly true of SCM participants who never fully identified with Christianity, such as John Lee (a resident of Howland House active in the peace movement of the early sixties). Others would remain committed Christians, but distance themselves from the left. This would include George Hartwell, a former student president of the University of Toronto SCM, and an activist in SUPA. By the mid-seventies, he had become a charismatic evangelical Christian.[15] Then there is the example of Ian Gentles, an SCM member who had played a central role in the Toronto chapter of CUCND and taken part in the civil disobedience protests at La Macaza in 1964. By the seventies, Gentles had been drawn to the pro-life movement, which he viewed as a logical extension of his earlier peace activism because he was "against destruction, particularly the destruction of innocent human beings." As he reflected in an interview, "most of my friends and colleagues in the peace movement disagreed with me on that, so we kind of parted ways. So I guess you could say I evolved into a conservative, though I still have some pretty radical views."[16]

Clearly, for some of the former participants in Canada's Christian left, the Christian-left nexus was a centre that could not hold.

For others, however, it did hold – and still does – and the movement has had a lasting impact both on Canada's churches and on the Canadian left. Older mentors in the SCM of the sixties, such as the late Anglican worker-priest Dan Heap, would remain politically active and continue to inspire and mentor young left-leaning Christians. Heap, for example, served as a Toronto city councillor in the seventies and an NDP member of parliament in the eighties, and also mentored Olivia Chow, a young Christian activist who would eventually play a prominent role in both municipal and federal politics.[17] Also, many of the young SCM participants from the sixties and beyond would go on to become clergy (such as United Church minister and former University of Toronto chaplain Eilert Frerichs) or active laity, and in this way, they contributed to the radical presence in their own denominations. Furthermore, SCM's members have worked closely with other faith-based organizations such as PWRDF and KAIROS, and on campuses, local units have made connections with the broader campus left (much as the SCM did in the sixties with SUPA and other activist groups).

The radicalism of the SCM has persisted well beyond the sixties. For me, this was most evident in May 2009, when I attended the week-long national conference of the SCM, held in Toronto. The approximately forty attendees at this gathering were diverse in their religious identities – Catholic, liberal Protestant, evangelical, pagan, agnostic, and atheist – but all shared an interest in the connections between spirituality and social justice. Furthermore, many of the participants self-identified as radicals or, at the very least, as left-of-centre social activists. And due in part to the theme of the conference ("Shine: Radiating a Dream of Liberation and Inclusion"), most of the participants were gay, lesbian, bisexual, or transgendered.

For those who knew little about the more recent incarnation of the SCM, the conference was a helpful introduction. It became clear that the SCM sought to combine an open, inclusive Christian spirituality with many of the concerns of the twenty-first century radical left. Conference attendees took part in anti-oppression training and worked throughout the week to maintain a "safe space" environment, and to avoid language or actions that excluded or demeaned anybody for reasons of ability, gender, race, or sexuality. Employing a consensus model of decision-making, they discussed SCM policy and drafted resolutions on "Gender Identity and Sexuality" and "Indigenous Rights." They held a variety of workshops: Christianity and anarchy; the spirituality of social activism; Jesus and queer identity; and SCM history. One of the unique events of the weekend was an adult immersion baptism, held on Toronto Island, in which one of the SCM student leaders (a theology student planning to become a United Church minister) baptized another student leader (also aspiring to become a United Church minister) in the frigid waters of Lake Ontario. His unusual baptism signified not only a personal spiritual commitment but also a commitment to a life of social justice and solidarity with the oppressed.

I took part in this conference while I was in the midst of my research for what would, ultimately, become this book. While the SCM of 2009 was not necessarily the SCM of 1969, the gathering reinforced my belief that it followed the same template confirmed in the sixties: that the movement would identify simultaneously with the message of Jesus and with the revolutionary agenda of young leftists because participants in the movement believed that these two things were one and the same. Since the sixties, SCM participants and young Christian radicals from like-minded groups, as well as older progressives who inspired and were inspired by the young radicals, also endeavoured to bring this same synthesis into Canada's churches The evidence provided in this section suggests that their efforts have met with some success over the past half-century.

GENDER, SEXUALITY, AND THE CHRISTIAN LEFT SINCE THE SIXTIES

Surprisingly, some of the Christian left's greatest successes in Canada's mainline Protestant churches have pertained to gender and sexuality. In particular, the United Church of Canada has embraced feminism and been unequivocal in its affirmation of gay, lesbian, bisexual, and transgendered peoples. At first glance, this might seem strange, for as we have seen in chapter 8, issues of gender and sexuality were, at most, secondary concerns for Christian left activists in this period. Nevertheless, by the early seventies, both women's liberation and gay liberation were strong, visible social movements, rooted in New Left philosophy and practice. Gradually, they made their presence known in Canada's churches and the SCM, and often, the leading advocates for these causes within the churches emerged from the Christian left. While the SCM may have been slower than its American counterparts in embracing women's liberation and gay liberation, the evidence suggests that by the late seventies, members of the Christian left had more fully embraced the concerns of these movements. In part, this reflected the strength of these broader social movements. More importantly, it likely reflected a growing awareness among women, gays, and lesbians active in the Christian left of their own oppression and of inequality in their faith communities.

On women's issues, the primary impetus for change within the United Church was the second-wave feminist movement of the early seventies, as many women within the denomination embraced the cause. In 1974, the Church's General Council responded to the concerns of feminists by setting up a Task Force on Women and Partnership between Men and Women in Church and Society.[18] Furthermore, feminist theology made inroads in the seventies and eighties, at a time when more women were entering ministry and holding key positions in the denomination, including Harriet Christie as head of the Division of Mission in the early seventies, and Lois Wilson as moderator in the early 1980s. (Both were SCM alumni, and Wilson would go on to serve as chair of the WSCF.) Through the work of the Task Force and the Division of Mission, feminism made its way into local congregations with the introduction of "inclusive language" – discouraging the exclusive use of masculine language and imagery when speaking of God (e.g., Father, King) or of God's people (e.g., sons of God, men of God).[19] The move was not without controversy and met resistance throughout the eighties and nineties. Inclusive language became harder for churches to ignore with the introduction of the new denominational hymnal *Voices United* in 1996. Only about sixteen hymns portray God as "Father," and some of the hymns envision God using female imagery.[20]

Even more controversial was the United Church's full acceptance of the LGBT+ communities, including ordination, blessing same-sex unions, and supporting equal marriage rights for gays and lesbians. Throughout the 1980s, the debate over same-sex relationships, and more specifically, over the ordination of gay and lesbian clergy, had a polarizing effect on theological liberals and conservatives in the United Church. The decision of General Council in 1988 to permit the ordination of homosexuals precipitated a mass exodus of conservative evangelical Christians from the United Church of Canada (though some continue to remain in the denomination).[21] It seems that the majority of remaining members accept the liberal position on these issues: when a motion was put forward at General Council in 2003 calling on the federal government to legalize same-sex marriage, it was passed after only forty-five minutes of debate.[22]

Many historical factors were responsible for this shift from a position of "tolerance" (i.e., "love the sinner but hate the sin") to one of full acceptance. First, there was the United Church's legacy of progressivism, evident in the social gospel movement of the late nineteenth and early twentieth century.[23] In addition, in the postwar years, a general trend of liberalization was afoot in the United Church, and more broadly in the Western world.[24] Also, these developments in the United Church occurred concurrently with significant legal advances for gays and lesbians in Canada. For example, between 1986 and 1999, federal and provincial human rights laws were amended to prohibit discrimination on the basis of sexual orientation. Furthermore, throughout the 1990s and early 2000s, a series of court victories resulted in federal and provincial recognition of same-sex relationships.[25] Nevertheless, these factors alone are insufficient to account for what happened in the United Church of Canada. Rather, developments in the denomination, and in broader Canadian society, were hastened by the activism that emerged from the gay liberation movement in the early seventies.

More specifically, the shift in the United Church was due in part to the activism of gays and lesbians within the denomination. "Affirm" was formed in 1982 "to affirm gay and lesbian people within the United Church of Canada ... and speak to the church in a united fashion encouraging it to act prophetically and pastorally both within and beyond the church structure."[26] One of the more vocal participants in Affirm was Rev. Eilert Frerichs, an SCM alumnus and chaplain at the University of Toronto. Frerichs (who would write on occasion for the *Body Politic,* Toronto's gay liberation newspaper) credits the SCM for helping him to accept himself: it "helped me to change from questioning all the time what God had given me, and instead to ask what should I be doing with these gifts – my life, my sexuality, and my other capacities."[27]

Thus, the legacy of the long sixties (of the gay liberation movement, and of the SCM) could be found in denominational groups such as Affirm, as well as Dignity for Roman Catholics and Integrity for Anglicans. Dignity and Integrity made their presence known in their respective denominations, and since the early 2000s, the Anglican Church of Canada has wrestled with the issue of blessing same-sex unions. Just as the debates over homosexuality led to a rupture in the United Church in the 1980s, recent debates over sexuality within the Anglican Church have threatened to rupture the denomination, and also to cause tension between the liberal Canadian church and its more conservative Anglican counterparts (many of them situated in the global south). Within the Anglican Church of Canada, conservative priests, parishes, and even some bishops have chosen to sever their connection with the denomination.[28]

CHRISTIAN ENGAGEMENT WITH THE NEW LEFT AND RELIGIOUS DECLINE: AN UNINTENDED LEGACY?

These crises over sexuality are one part of the broader ongoing institutional crisis facing Canadian Christianity. Figures from Statistics Canada show that between 1971 and 2011, both the Anglican and United churches saw a substantial drop in self-identified adherents: from 2,543,180 to 1,631,845 for Anglicans; from 3,768,800 to 2,007,615 for the United Church.[29] Roman Catholics increased in numbers between 1971 and 2011 (9,974,895 to 12,728,885), due in part to immigration, but as a percentage of the total Canadian population, they dropped from 46.2 percent to 38.7 percent.[30] Furthermore, among Canada's Roman Catholics, weekly attendance at religious services dropped dramatically: from 65 percent in 1970 to 36 percent in 1998 according to Gallup Poll data.[31] The same polls show that Protestant attendance appears to have risen modestly in the same time period; however, had these polls not included conservative Protestants, the figures would have shown an unmistakable decline in attendance.[32] Finally, the statistics show that youth were the least religious. In 2001, the median age of self-identified Protestants was forty-two, five years higher than the median age of the general population in Canada.[33] Furthermore, young people disproportionately identified as having no religion.[34] And in spite of apparently healthy numbers of adherents, Roman Catholics have seen a sizeable drop in the number of young men entering the priesthood, evidence not only that the priesthood is in crisis but that the Roman Catholic Church (as with its mainline Protestant counterparts) is not connecting successfully with its young people. Thus, the decline in Canadian churches that began in the long sixties continued to the beginning of the twenty-first century, and it appears that mainstream Canadian churches continue to fail or perform poorly in their attempts to secure youth participation and attendance.[35]

There is no single explanation for this situation, but what is certain is that for the Anglican, United, and Roman Catholic churches, the institutional crisis began in the long sixties. It is also certain that one important factor in this crisis is the churches' failure to connect with youth. Liberal Protestants in particular had engaged with the New Left, motivated by a secular theology that de-emphasized the institutional church and emphasized the importance of being "where the action is." It was not a theology that favoured institutional growth; church leaders neither intended nor expected that their dialogues with radical youth would turn them into church members. However, by addressing the issues and concerns of young activists, they did hope to retain their own young people. As the statistics suggest, this did not happen in mainline Protestant churches. After all, if secular theologians were right, and God was at work in the world outside the institutional church, then young people lacked a compelling reason to stay in their churches. Engagement with the issues and concerns of the New Left did not help the churches retain their young people, but it did move Canada's mainline Protestants churches to the left. In the United Church, the effect was nothing short of transformational. But transformation is not always welcomed, and being "prophetic" rather than "priestly" always comes with a cost. Since the late eighties, many longtime United Church members have deserted a denomination that no longer resembles the church of their youth. A similar process is currently underway in the Anglican Church of Canada. The situation in the Roman Catholic Church is more complex, but the evidence suggests that the changes ushered in by Vatican II (changes that included attempts to make Catholicism more youth-friendly and more politically engaged) may have alienated older Catholics, and simultaneously failed to secure the continued participation of Catholic youth.[36]

Conversely, a much greater proportion of Canadian youth in conservative evangelical churches remained active in their faith communities into adulthood. Furthermore, evangelical churches continued to attract youth from more mainline churches – and adults too. At first glance, it might seem puzzling that these denominations thrived in the sixties and seventies, even though they often opposed the social and political ideals of many youth in the long sixties.[37] Ultimately, however, the social and political conservatism of North American evangelicals may have contributed to their success in the decades following the sixties. Unlike the purveyors of secular theology in the 1960s, evangelicals maintained a clearly delineated worldview that set them apart from "the world." Youth in conservative evangelical denominations (unlike those in many Anglican or United churches) were provided with a compelling reason to remain active church members; to do so was to remain special and distinct, to be engaged with "the world" but ideologically separate – "in the world" but not "of it."[38]

In the introduction, I observed that the long sixties generated powerful metanarratives. Among these, there was the grand narrative that religion was a relic of the past, incompatible with the modern world and doomed to irrelevancy. If one were to accept such a framework as axiomatic (as many social commentators did in the long sixties), then it would follow that the youth of the Baby Boom generation were destined to be irreligious and that Christian attempts to engage with radical youth would be doomed to fail. But this was not the case. Even in a secular age, older progressive clergy and young Christian radicals could, and did, engage successfully with young secular radicals on issues of shared concern.

But in doing so, did these left-leaning Christians hasten the process of decline in Canada's largest churches? Many conservative Christians, both Protestant and Catholic, contend that the answer is yes. They argue that the mainline Protestant churches and the post-Vatican II Roman Catholic Church were agents of their own marginalization, hastening the secularization process not by being out of step with modern world but by embracing it. For reasons I have explained above, there may be some merit to their contentions. But as Hugh McLeod has argued, no monocausal theory – no "master factor" – can account for religious decline since the sixties. If Canada's largest churches since the sixties had eschewed the politics of the left and had remained socially and theologically conservative, it is far from certain that current statistics on adherence and attendance would be any better. (And in any event, counterfactual "choose your own adventure" history is, at best, a speculative exercise.) More importantly, when we consider the efforts of Canadian Christians who have sought to transform their churches into prophetic communities committed to social justice and inclusion, we must recognize that they have not been motivated primarily by the desire to fill pews or maintain names on church membership rolls (though clearly, they were conscious of the fact that many youth were becoming disenchanted with established religion). Rather, they have been motivated by what they believed to be moral imperatives.

CONCLUDING OBSERVATIONS: PROTEUS

For many Canadian Christians in the long sixties, the institutional church was no longer a comfortable place. Pierre Berton notwithstanding, one could not characterize the pew, or the pulpit, as comfortable. Canadian Christians were shaken out of their complacency by theology, by current events, and by disturbing evidence of their own declining fortunes. Consequently, they reached out to those young radicals who were challenging unjust social and political structures. In doing so, Canadian churches absorbed the oppositional and sometimes revolutionary mentality of these youth, or at least they adopted the rhetoric. In some cases, Canadian churches were building on pre-existing oppositional strains in their own faith traditions (i.e., for the United Church, the heritage of the Social Gospel). We have observed throughout this study that they engaged in different ways, and with varying degrees of success. For the United Church of Canada, in particular, the changes that have occurred over the past forty years have been nothing short of transformational, and one factor in its transformation was its interactions with the New Left during the long sixties.

What lessons can we draw from this study? Among others, the long sixties was an era of ironies. We see irony in the fact that the most liberal, politically progressive churches shared the values and concerns of the rebellious youth, but in spite of this (and perhaps, in part, because of this), their denominations entered a prolonged period of decline in the sixties and seventies. Likewise, radical Christians in organizations like the SCM were instrumental in the formation of the early New Left in English Canada and played a continuing role in the milieu of student radicalism throughout the long sixties, but by the end of this period, the SCM had become, at best, a marginal presence on the activist scene. The SCM and similar groups such as Kairos were eager to support secular radical groups such as SUPA, but in lighting the torch of the broader movement, they may have extinguished their own. Such were the ironies of an era marked by discrepancies between expected outcome and actual outcome.

Furthermore, because the long sixties were known for secularization, we need a more nuanced understanding of what secularization is, and what it is not. Without question, Canada's churches were in trouble throughout the long sixties; they were losing their privileged position in society, losing clergy, losing money, and most importantly, losing bodies to fill their pews. In spite of this, Canadian churches remained both visible and viable throughout this era, and involved themselves in the public discourse on many issues. Approximately half a century later, institutional Christianity is less visible in Canada's public sphere, but it has not vanished from the public sphere, nor should we expect that it will. The prevalent argument in recent studies of secularization, whether in Canada or the broader Western world, is that secularization is complicated. It is not a linear process ending in the absolute demise of religious life. The evidence provided in this study supports this argument.

Finally, this study shows that any grand narrative of Canada's rebellious youth in the long sixties that fails to include religion or spirituality (or simply relegates these factors to a passing nod) is incomplete. Historians of the counterculture have always been keenly aware of its deeply spiritual nature, and recent historians have done excellent work on the interaction between church organizations and hip youth. However, with a few exceptions, historians have not adequately explored the connections between churches or student Christian groups and the secular New Left, nor have they examined the role that faith played in the formation of leading activists.

This is a serious omission for two reasons. First, by leaving religion or spirituality out of the narrative, these historians fail to capture the richness and diversity of the radical youth scenes in the long sixties. Such an omission excludes or misrepresents the voices of those activists who were motivated by their faith. It leads us to forget that "The Movement" was not monolithic, either in its origins or in its composition. Second, many present-day activists in Canada are faith-based activists, motivated by personal spirituality or involvement in religious NGOs such as the SCM, KAIROS, and PWRDF.[39] Many of today's activists look back to the sixties as a source of inspiration, but where is the inspiration for faith-based activists, when they look back to the standard historical accounts of Canada's New Left, only to find "red diaper babies," Marxist materialist analysis, and a few sentences about the SCM? A more complete history will resonate more fully with those who struggle for justice and peace today. In this day and age, when the "culture wars" have nurtured a dichotomy between the secular left and the religious right, and when Christianity is often automatically assumed to be homophobic, pro-militaristic, and reactionary, it is especially important that faith-based activists know that there is another strain in their religious heritage, which manifested itself throughout history – including the long sixties.

There is yet another reason why our histories of activism in the long sixties must include religion and spirituality: because the children of the sixties were a generation of seekers. Living in a postmodern age, they rejected the metanarratives of earlier generations, but they sought to replace them with new grand narratives. Peter Turner (president of Rochdale's governing council in 1971) recognized this in his book on Rochdale College, *There Can Be No Light without Shadow*. Turner employed the Greek myth of Proteus (the sea-god who could transform himself to take on a variety of physical forms) to explain the youthful rebellion as a search for identity. He argued that like Proteus, young people would try out a variety of identities: the committed campus revolutionary ("To the cause of revolution everyone must subordinate themselves ... The Revolution Is Eternal"); the apostle ("Follow Christ, the Lamb of God ... He is Eternal Truth and Light"); the acid-head mystic ("Live one with All in the eternal cosmos ... Trip through the cosmos with LSD"); and the Buddhist ("Follow the Buddha/the Buddha is the Way ... the Way is the Truth/the light is eternal"). "Each of these and the many other roles have certain things in common," Turner observed. "They explain everything and have complete cosmologies. They outline and delineate the total life role of the individual and how he fits within the whole. They offer him a chance to identify with an 'eternal tangible' and meaningfulness and thus avoid being condemned to futility and absurdity." In short, these are total identities; the young person "is searching for the heirloom which his family and society failed to bequeath him."[40]

This Protean search for an all-encompassing narrative, for an identity to imbue life with ultimate meaning and connect with an "eternal tangible" was a spiritual search. For many of the New Leftists of the sixties, their concept of the "ultimate" may have been the Revolution rather than a transcendent God. For Christians active in the New Left, the "ultimate" may have been both God and the Revolution; for God was present in the struggle for justice. Whichever it was, it became the centrepiece in their identities, which they negotiated and performed with a fervour and earnestness we associate with religion. While many of my Generation X contemporaries find this sort of earnestness to be foreign and off-putting, it is noteworthy that the new generation of young activists, in secondary schools and universities across the world, have embraced it. Given the magnitude of the challenges that global citizens face in the present day – a worldwide economy of haves and have-nots, nations mired in war, the ongoing marginalization and exploitation of Indigenous peoples, and our ongoing destruction of the natural environment – the time has come to rediscover the fervour and earnestness of the sixties. If it is the children and youth that will lead us in this regard, then we have reason to remain hopeful about the future.

Notes

CHAPTER ONE

1 McKay, *Rebels, Red, Radicals*, 43.
2 I use the terms "spiritual" and "spirituality" to denote belief systems that, in Todd Maugans's words, focus "on intangible elements that impart vitality and meaning to life's events." I focus specifically on Christian spirituality, as it is understood and practised in both Roman Catholic and mainline Protestant communities. Christian spirituality is not contingent on membership in a religious denomination; nevertheless, most of the key subjects of this study belonged to religious denominations or Christian organizations that provided a framework for their spiritual lives. Consequently, while "spiritual" may not be synonymous with "religious," for the purposes of this study, these terms are inextricably linked. Maugans, "The SPIRITual History," 11.
3 See, for example, Abzug, *Cosmos Crumbling*; Perry, *Radical Abolitionism*; and Thomas, "Romantic Reform in America, 1815–1865."
4 On the Methodist roots of the Social Gospel, see Airhart, *Serving the Present Age*; on the role of the Social Gospel in the early Canadian left, the best sources are Allen, *The Social Passion*; and McKay, *Rebels, Reds, Radicals*, especially 213–78. For studies of three important figures to emerge from the Social Gospel movement in Canada, see Allen, *The View from Murney Tower*; McLeod and McLeod, *Tommy Douglas*; and Mills, *Fool for Christ*.
5 McLoughlin, *Revivals, Awakenings, and Reform*, xiii. McLoughlin adapts his model for awakenings from anthropologist Anthony F.C. Wallace. See Wallace, "Revitalization Movements."

6 Arthur Marwick identifies the "long sixties" as an era stretching from 1958 to 1974. While some might quibble with Marwick's precise delineation, many scholars have embraced the concept of a "long sixties" beginning in the late fifties and extending into the early seventies because it is more useful analytically than a strictly decadal approach. (For reasons that I will explain later, I have chosen a termination date of 1975.) Marwick, *The Sixties*, 7.
7 McLeod, *Religious Crisis of the 1960s*.
8 Ibid., 265. This international phenomenon is explored and interrogated further in Christie and Gauvreau, eds, *The Sixties and Beyond*.
9 Owram, *Born at the Right Time*, 216–47; and Milligan, *Rebel Youth*.
10 I have adapted these terms from Hans Mol. For him, the "priestly" and "prophetic" functions of religion are not dichotomous but complementary. I have chosen to use the terms in a more dichotomous sense. Mol, *Faith and Fragility*, 247, 260–4.
11 Some key works on Canadian Christianity during the long sixties include Airhart, *Church with the Soul of a Nation*; Beardsall, "'And Whether Pigs Have Wings'"; Clarke and Macdonald, *Leaving Christianity*; Flatt, *After Evangelicalism*; Gauvreau, *Catholic Origins*; Gidney, *Long Eclipse*; Miedema, *For Canada's Sake*; and Noll, "What Happened to Christian Canada?"
12 Recent articles and monographs that address the radical left and/or the hippie counterculture in Canada's 1960s include Graham and McKay, *Radical Ambition*; Henderson, *Making the Scene*; Martel, "'They smell bad, have diseases and are lazy'"; Milligan, *Rebel Youth*; Mills, *The Empire Within*; and Palmer, *Canada's 1960s*. Two collections of scholarly essays addressing these movements in Canada are Campbell, Clément, and Kealey, eds, *Debating Dissent*; and Palaeologu, ed., *The Sixties in Canada*. While not exclusively focused on Canada, there are several contributions about Canadian protest movements in Dubinsky et al., eds, *New World Coming*.
13 Rossinow, *The Politics of Authenticity*, 23–155. Other scholars who have explored these intersections in a specifically American context include McLoughlin, *Revivals, Awakenings, and Reform*. See also Ellwood, *The Sixties Spiritual Awakening*, 326–36; Oppenheimer, *Knocking on Heaven's Door*, 1–28, 212–28.
14 McLeod, *Religious Crisis of the 1960s*, 259–60.
15 Palmer, *Canada's 1960s*, 257. See also McKay, *Rebels, Reds, Radicals*, 184; Milligan, *Rebel Youth*, 29–30; and Owram, *Born at the Right Time*, 219, 360.

16 Palmer, *Canada's 1960s*, 5.
17 Airhart explores these themes extensively in *Church with the Soul of a Nation*, especially 196–224.
18 See, for example, Graham and McKay, *Radical Ambition*, 321–2.
19 See, for example, Flatt, *After Evangelicalism*, 198.
20 Gauvreau, *Catholic Origins*, 138–74. The specific quote is from p. 138.
21 Gidney, *Long Eclipse*, xiii–xv, 107–10.
22 Berton, *Comfortable Pew*.
23 Herring, *America's Longest War*, 155–61, 204–13.
24 David Churchill makes a convincing case for the central importance of 1965 for Canada's student left in "SUPA, Selma, and Stevenson."
25 Much of the recent literature about Canada's New Left – especially Ian Milligan's *Rebel Youth* – makes it clear that radicals felt it important to take their activism off campus, particularly from the late sixties onward.
26 In *Social Memory*, James Fentress and Chris Wickham argue that memory cannot be treated as an "oral text," particularly because it is shaped by collective memory and the needs of the present. In contrast, Alessandro Portelli recognizes the problematic nature of memory but argues that oral history offers valuable insights into the meaning of historical events from the perspective of the participants. See Portelli, *The Death of Luigi Trastulli*.
27 Herbert Marcuse coined the term "great refusal," which he advocated as a collective response to technocratic systems of social control. Marcuse, *One-Dimensional Man*, xiii–xiv, 63.
28 For example, the United Nations has defined "youth" as being between 15 and 24. United Nations Department of Economic and Social Affairs, *World Youth Report 2007*, vi.
29 Mintz, "Reflections on Age."
30 On youth identity and culture between the 1920s and the Second World War, see Cynthia Comacchio, *The Dominion of Youth*; and Gauvreau, "The Protracted Birth." On youth culture in postwar Canada, see Owram, *Born at the Right Time*, 136–84.
31 Owram, *Born at the Right Time*, xiii–xiv.
32 Ibid., 180–1.
33 For a survey of the debate over the nature of the generation gap, see Bengston, "The Generation Gap."
34 Brake, *Comparative Youth Culture*, 39–43, 83–115.
35 Milligan, *Rebel Youth*, 36. On wildcat strikes, also see Palmer, *Canada's 1960s*, 211–41; and McInnis, "'Hothead Troubles.'"
36 In *Born at the Right Time*, Owram's central argument is that the youth of the sixties had been conditioned from childhood (through parenting

practices, schooling, and marketing) to believe that they were a special, separate generation.
37 Norris and Inglehart, *Sacred and Secular*, 1.
38 For a more complete sociological exposition of the secularization thesis, see Berger, *The Sacred Canopy*, 105–17; and Wilson, *Religion in Secular Society*.
39 Casanova, *Public Religions*, 3–6.
40 Berger, Davie, and Fokas, *Religious America, Secular Europe?*, 1–7.
41 Brown, *The Death of Christian Britain*; McLeod, *Religious Crisis of the 1960s*; Taylor, *A Secular Age*; Clarke and Macdonald, *Leaving Christianity*. See also Nancy Christie and Michael Gauvreau, "'Even the hippies were only very slowly going secular,'" in Christie and Gauvreau, *The Sixties and Beyond*, 3–26.
42 Taylor, *A Secular Age*, 2–3, 10.
43 Ibid., 486–7.
44 Cited in ibid., 519.
45 McLeod, *Religious Crisis of the 1960s*, 212–13, 245–6; Clarke and Macdonald, *Leaving Christianity*, 163–4.
46 Miedema, *For Canada's Sake*, 4.

CHAPTER TWO

1 Bibby, *Fragmented Gods*, 11.
2 Cockburn and King, *Rumours of Glory*, 17–18, 36–8.
3 Laxer, *Red Diaper Baby*, 51–66, 81–7.
4 See, for example, Cook, *The Regenerators*; Gauvreau, *The Evangelical Century*; Marshall, *Secularizing the Faith*; and Christie and Gauvreau, *A Full-Orbed Christianity*.
5 See chapter 1, n10.
6 Miedema, *For Canada's Sake*, 4.
7 Grant, *Church in the Canadian Era*, 160–83; Owram, *Born at the Right Time*, 103–10, 337. Much of this apparent growth can also be attributed to the flight to the suburbs, where much of the new church construction took place.
8 Clarke and Macdonald, *Leaving Christianity*, 56.
9 Ibid., 124–5.
10 Ibid., 43–4.
11 Bibby, *Fragmented Gods*, 12–13. For a more nuanced consideration of polling data on Canadian church attendance, see Clarke and Macdonald, *Leaving Christianity*, 110–19.

12 Reginald Bibby notes that the drop-off was far more precipitous among Quebec Catholics than among Catholics outside Quebec. Bibby, *Fragmented Gods*, 16–21; Clarke and Macdonald, *Leaving Christianity*, 138.
13 Clarke and Macdonald, *Leaving Christianity*, 45–52.
14 Ibid., 52–3.
15 While earlier historiography paints a picture of a reactionary Roman Catholic Church in Quebec that fell victim to the secularizing forces of the Quiet Revolution, more recent examinations show that Catholicism contributed to the Quiet Revolution. Some of these recent examinations include Seljak, "Catholicism's 'Quiet Revolution'"; Fay, *History of Canadian Catholics*, 278–302; Meunier and Warren, *Sortir de la "Grande Noirceur"*; and Gauvreau, *Catholic Origins*. The latter two are particularly valuable, especially Gauvreau's iconoclastic and controversial study.
16 Gidney, *Long Eclipse*; Miedema, *For Canada's Sake*, 42–4, 47–9.
17 McLeod, *Religious Crisis of the 1960s*, 102–23, 231–4.
18 Clarke and Macdonald, *Leaving Christianity*, 234.
19 Gidney and Millar, "The Christian Recessional in Ontario's Public Schools."
20 Fay, *History of Canadian Catholics*, 73–81.
21 On Irish immigration and the shaping of Irish-Catholic identity in the Toronto archdiocese, see Clarke, *Piety and Nationalism*. On Toronto's Italian immigrants, including the role of Catholicism within the community, see Iacovetta, *Such Hardworking People*.
22 With the effects of the Baby Boom and immigration, and with increased government funding, Catholic education in Toronto would expand in the 1960s. See Dixon, *We Remember, We Believe*, 26, 65.
23 This account of Vatican II is based on Fay, *History of Canadian Catholics*, 278–302; and Livingston, *Modern Christian Thought*, 491–7.
24 Fay, *History of Canadian Catholics*, 203.
25 Gauvreau, *Catholic Origins*, 22–7. At the very least, personalist philosophy is implicit in *Quadragesimo Anno*. One of the reasons that Pius XI opposes socialism so unequivocally is because he believes that it is inconsistent with human freedom and human dignity. See Pius XI, *Quadragesimo Anno*, paragraph 119.
26 Fay, *History of Canadian Catholics*, 212–15. On the Catholic Worker Movement, see Miller, *A Harsh and Dreadful Love*.
27 Ultimately, McGuigan and other Canadian bishops accepted Somerville's advice. See Fay, *History of Canadian Catholics*, 209–11; Sinasac, *Fateful Passages*; and Baum, *Catholics and Canadian Socialism*, 119–34.

28 P.A.G. McKay, "Parting is such sweet ...," *Canadian Register*, 4 October 1969.
29 On the statistics, see Grant, *Church in the Canadian Era*, 223. On separate school funding, see Gidney, *From Hope to Harris*, 16–19. The shaping of Ontario's Protestant cultural consensus is the subject of William Westfall's *Two Worlds*. J.S. Moir, in "Toronto's Protestants," argues that anti-Catholicism was a waning force in Ontario. William J. Smyth contests this interpretation in *Toronto, the Belfast of Canada*. On the position of Catholics and Protestants in Canada's elites, see, for example, Porter, *The Vertical Mosaic*, 287–90.
30 See the provincial census figures in Airhart, "Ordering a New Nation," 103. On the city of Toronto, see Black, "Inwardly Renewed," 102. On Anglicans in the business elite, for example, see Porter, *The Vertical Mosaic*, 288–90.
31 Westfall, "Constructing Public Religions."
32 Following the Privy Council's 1863 decision on *Long v. Gray*, the Anglican dioceses in all self-governing colonies were no longer under any British jurisdiction. Hayes, *Anglicans in Canada*, 92–6.
33 Black, "Inwardly Renewed," 100.
34 Ibid., 106–7.
35 Whitla, *Church of the Holy Trinity*, 7–11.
36 Pulker, *We Stand on Their Shoulders*, 161–70. It is also worth noting that M.J. Coldwell, the second leader of the CCF, had been strongly influenced by Christian socialism within the Church of England. Grant, *Church in the Canadian Era*, 141–2.
37 Black, "Inwardly Renewed," 107.
38 The church population in the diocese dropped by a thousand the following year, from 235,861 to 234,843, and dropped by a further 3,449 in 1964 (to 231,394). The decline continued steadily over subsequent decades. By 1987, the Diocese of Toronto reported a church population of 116,236. At its peak, exactly twenty-five years earlier, the figure had been more than double that. See table 1 in the appendix of Hayes, *By Grace Co-Workers*, 302–3.
39 Hayes, *Anglicans in Canada*, 74.
40 The most thorough study of this controversy can be found in Turner, "The Evangelical Movement."
41 On the trajectory of evangelical Anglicanism in the twentieth century, see Katerberg, "Redefining Evangelicalism."
42 For an introduction to liberal Protestantism through the lens of three influential theologians, see Livingston, *Modern Christian Thought*, 245–70.

43 Marsden, *Fundamentalism and American Culture*.
44 Hayes, *Anglicans in Canada*, 145–51.
45 Black, "Inwardly Renewed," 118.
46 Airhart, *Church with the Soul of a Nation*, 30–64.
47 On the church union (its rationale and process), see Airhart, *Church with the Soul of a Nation*, 3–29; and C.T. McIntire, "Unity among Many." Also, on liberal evangelicalism, see Hayes, *Anglicans in Canada*, 146–8.
48 On the roots of progressive, social Christianity in nineteenth-century Methodist revivalism, perfectionism, and post-millennialism, see Airhart, *Serving the Present Age*, and Van Die, *An Evangelical Mind*, 143–77.
49 Allen, *The Social Passion*, xxiii–xxv, 3–34; see also Christie and Gauvreau, *A Full-Orbed Christianity*, especially 3–36.
50 Bland, *The New Christianity*; see also Allen, *The View from Murney Tower*.
51 Stebner, "The 1930s," 118–19.
52 Mutchmor, *Mutchmor*, 107–19.
53 Ibid., 151–62.
54 "4 Days in Coma, Moore Dies of Ring Injury," *Toronto Star*, 25 March 1963; "Churchmen Back Liquor Ad Curbs," *Toronto Star*, 14 March 1963.
55 For two perspectives on the New Curriculum and the decline of Sunday School enrolment, see Flatt, *After Evangelicalism*, 74–143, and Airhart, *Church with the Soul of a Nation*, 170–1, and 264–7.
56 Airhart, *Church with the Soul of a Nation*, 168.
57 E.L. Homewood, "About Ourselves," *Observer*, 15 November 1964, 12–15, 36.
58 Grant, *Church in the Canadian Era*, 186.
59 Gidney, *Long Eclipse*, 49–51; Allen, *The Social Passion*, 222–3; and Axelrod, *Making a Middle Class*, 129–30.
60 Gidney, *Long Eclipse*, 56–7; Beattie, *A Brief History*, 75–7.
61 Beattie, *A Brief History*, 97–111.
62 Gidney, *Long Eclipse*, 97–103.
63 On the history of the WSCF, see Lehtonen, *Story of a Storm*; and Selles, *The World Student Christian Federation, 1895-1925*.
64 For example, there are striking parallels between the development of Canada's SCM and the Australian SCM. See Howe, *A Century of Influence*.
65 Hewitt, *Spying* 101, 85, 89, 120, 161, 182; Lee, "Family of Choice," in *Love's Gay Fool*, paragraph 2; Beattie, *A Brief History*, 134; and Gidney, "Poisoning the Student Mind?" 150.
66 Gidney, *Long Eclipse*, 64–5; Hewitt, *Spying* 101, 85, 96.
67 Laxer, *Red Diaper Baby*, 69–70, 77–9.

68 On the work camps, see Anderson, "The Place Where 'Men' Earn Their Bread."
69 Ibid., 137–9.
70 Ian Gentles, interview by author, 1 February 2009.
71 Lee, "Family of Choice," paragraph 38.
72 Ibid., paragraph 3.
73 George Hartwell, interview by author, 21 August 2009.
74 In other national SCMs, fellowship was also central, and the dynamics of their associational life closely paralleled that of the Canadian SCM. On the importance of fellowship in the Australian SCM, see Howe, *A Century of Influence*, 224–7.
75 Ian Gentles, who was involved in the SCM in the early 1960s, stated, "I think for a lot of us, it was a place where you could do some serious Bible study, or reading Christian literature – for example, in one group, I think they read Dostoyevsky's *Crime and Punishment*. So there were a number of these study groups that people attended." In his view, the left-wing, political orientation of the SCM, "challenging the status quo and stirring up trouble, dismay among the churches … I think that was a minor part of it, although it grew to become more prominent." (Gentles, interview). However, it is worth noting that Gentles was not part of the core group of leaders, and that the decentralized structure of the SCM at the University of Toronto, where study groups were the primary unit, made it possible to be relatively unaware of some of the SCM chapter's more political activities.
76 Gidney, *Long Eclipse*, 60–1.
77 Ibid., 97–111.
78 G.A.D. Scott, "The Student Christian Movement in the University of Toronto – President's Report 1963–1964," B79-0059/015, University of Toronto Archives. In view of the information I have for the following two years, I find this estimate surprising. Involvement, however, could include people who came out to a single activity (e.g., a movie night or a special speaker). Scott also claims a mailing list of 700, but once again, being on a mailing list isn't necessarily evidence of active participation.
79 Hayes, *Anglicans in Canada*, 68–9.
80 Taylor, *A Secular Age*, 473–504; Rossinow, *Politics of Authenticity*, 1–8.

CHAPTER THREE

1 Bob Dylan, "The Times They Are a-Changin'." Reprinted here with permission from Special Rider Music.

2 Dylan soon denied that it was a song about the generation gap: "It happened that maybe those were the only words I could find to separate aliveness from deadness. It had nothing to do with age [1964]." He also said, "I can't really say that adults don't understand young people any more than you can say big fishes don't understand little fishes. I didn't mean it as a statement ... It's a feeling [1965]." Heylin, *Bob Dylan*, 126.
3 Laxer, *Red Diaper Baby*, 163–74.
4 See Isserman, *If I Had a Hammer*, especially 173–219.
5 Mills, "The New Left," 256, 257.
6 The most notable example is the split between the SDS and its parent organization, the LID, because the SDS was not sufficiently anti-Communist. Isserman, *If I Had a Hammer*, 202–19.
7 Scholars are not unanimous in their application of the term "New Left." Van Gosse uses the term to encompass the entire configuration of social movements, from the 1950s to about 1975, committed "to a radical form of democracy" and redefining "the meaning of democracy in America." For Gosse, this includes the civil rights movement in the South, as well as the antiwar movement, Black Power, Women's Liberation, and Gay Liberation. In contrast to Gosse's broad application, Wini Breines defines the New Left as "the largely student and racially white social movement that emerged in the United States in the late 1950s and early 1960s and which called itself the New left." She agrees with Richard Flacks that the New Left was not "simply another name for campus revolt, antiwar protest, or other youth-based insurgency," but rather was "a *particular* segment of young activists who were self-consciously radical ideologically ... and who self-consciously sought to provide political direction, theoretical coherence and organizational continuity to the student movement." While I acknowledge the inter-relatedness and broad shared objectives of the movements of the long sixties (particularly the crucial role of the civil rights movement in shaping the New Left), my use of the term hews closest to Breines. However, I would contend that the "youth-based insurgency" was also a manifestation of the New Left, to the extent that these young protesters shared the goals and aims of their "self-consciously radical" leaders. Without the campus revolt or the antiwar protests, the New Left would be largely an intellectual exercise, rather than a significant social movement. Gosse, *Rethinking the New Left*, 2–6; Breines, *Community and Organization*, 8–9.
8 Isserman and Kazin, *America Divided*, 175.
9 Chafe, *Civilities and Civil Rights*, 71–101.
10 Anderson, *The Movement and the Sixties*, 43–86.

11 Hayden, "Onto Open Ground," 49–52.
12 Hayden, *Port Huron Statement*, 53.
13 Breines, *Community and Organization*, 56–66.
14 Frost, "*An Interracial Movement of the Poor*," 1.
15 Hayden, *Port Huron Statement*, 106.
16 Levin, *Cold War University*, 50–7.
17 On Diefenbaker's decision, and the subsequent establishment of CUCND, see Moffatt, *History of the Canadian Peace Movement*, 146–9; Wittner, *Resisting the Bomb*, 196–203; and Dufresne, "'Let's Not Be Cremated Equal,'" 19–20.
18 According to Ian Gentles (interview by author), the student peace group at the University of Toronto began in the fall of 1959 or the winter of 1960 with a meeting of interested students in Howard Adelman's living room. That may have been the initial gathering, but the chapter had its first official meeting as the Student Peace Union in February 1960 at University College. It was chaired by Norm Johnson, a mathematics student and Quaker. The Toronto group didn't formally change its name to CUCND until October 1960. See Douglas K. Campbell, "A History of the Ban-the-Bomb Movement, Toronto, 1959–61," 2, 5, File "CUCND Toronto Office 1960–1961 Correspondence and Miscellaneous Material," Box 1, CUCND/SUPA Fonds, William Ready Archives. For a more comprehensive overview of the origins of the New Left in Toronto, and the key role of the peace movement, see Graham and McKay, *Radical Ambition*, 25–57.
19 Dufresne, "'Let's Not Be Cremated Equal,'" 22–3.
20 Ibid., 24.
21 The distinction between radicals and liberals is standard in most literature on the New Left, but the journey from liberal to radical, and the growing tensions between the two, is best explored in Todd Gitlin's *The Sixties*, 81–192.
22 Ibid., 151–66.
23 Ibid., 166.
24 On the Diefenbaker government's evolving nuclear policy, see McMahon, *Essence of Indecision*; and Ghent, "Did He Fall or Was He Pushed?"
25 Dufresne, "'Let's not Be Cremated Equal,'" 29.
26 Wittner, *Resisting the Bomb*, 200–2.
27 The description of CUCND's transformation that follows, unless otherwise stated, is drawn from Dufresne, "'Let's Not Be Cremated Equal,'" 28–38.
28 Ibid., 33.
29 Anderson, *The Movement and the Sixties*, 87–111; Gosse, *Rethinking the New Left*, 71–2.

30 See, for example, Breines, *Community and Organization*, 14–15.
31 This is certainly true of Todd Gitlin's *The Sixties*, which is, in part, an autobiographical tale of a young man from a liberal Jewish family in New York who becomes radicalized through his involvement in the peace movement.
32 Gosse, *Rethinking the New Left*, 25; and Isserman, *If I Had a Hammer*, 205. In *The Sixties*, Gitlin refers to Thomas as one of SDS's "erstwhile defenders" in its parent organization, the LID (182).
33 Danielson, "'It Is a Day of Judgment,'" 216–20.
34 Isserman, *If I Had a Hammer*, 175.
35 Dimitri Roussopoulos, interview by author, 11 February 2009.
36 For an understanding of the integral role of ministerial leadership and biblical rhetoric in the civil rights movement, see Garrows, *Bearing the Cross*. For a closer look at the importance of spirituality to the participants in the 1964 Freedom Summer, see Marsh, *God's Long Summer*.
37 Danielson, "'It Is a Day of Judgment,'" 215–36; Isserman, *If I Had a Hammer*, 127–69. On Catholic peace activism and the Catholic Worker movement, see McNeal, *Harder than War*; and Miller, *Harsh and Dreadful Love*, 171–84, 302–26.
38 Rossinow, *Politics of Authenticity*, 54.
39 Ibid., 60–80. For a further exploration of the ideas of Tillich and Bonhoeffer, see chapter 4.
40 Ibid., 85–114.
41 Matthew Levin identifies a pattern of Christian student involvement in peace and civil rights activism in Madison, Wisconsin, similar to what was happening in Austin and elsewhere. See Levin, *Cold War University*, 56.
42 Eilert Frerichs, interview by author, 18 June 2009.
43 Lee, "University Life," in *Love's Gay Fool*, paragraphs 6–8.
44 George Hartwell, interview by author, 21 August 2009; Frerichs, interview.
45 Wolfe Erlichman, phone interview by author, 2 April 2009.
46 Richard Hyde, phone interview by author, 2 June 2009.
47 Frerichs, interview.
48 Ibid.
49 "Before she signed up as associate secretary of the Toronto SCM, she had been working in Sheffield, England ... Seemed like a 'big girl' to us ... older, a person with a lot of relevant experience, because she was right in there with the workers, the workers' movement and she knew all these great songs like 'On Ilkla Moor Baht' at.' She was very committed, she was interested in Cuba, and all the progressive movements." Hyde, interview.

50 Erlichman, interview.
51 Lee, "Family of Choice" and "Howland House," in *Love's Gay Fool*.
52 Hartwell, interview.
53 Ibid.
54 Gentles, interview.
55 Hyde, interview.
56 "My Fair Convert," from the SCM Annual Banquet, 1 March 1963, File "SCM of Canada, Special Conferences," B1979-0059/68, University of Toronto Archives.
57 Lehtonen, *Story of a Storm*, 21-58.
58 Ruth Harris, "Ruth Harris," in Evans, ed., *Journeys That Opened Up the World*, 15-17.
59 The University of Toronto SCM also sponsored a speech by an American activist who had been indicted for advocating that blacks in the southern United States should defend themselves with arms if necessary. Student Christian Movement newsletters for 6 November 1963, 20 November 1963, 13 January 1964, and 11 February 1964, File "SCM of Canada, Special Conferences," B1979-0059/68, University of Toronto Archives.
60 Allen, *The Social Passion*, 313-30; Socknat, *Witness against War*, 147-52.
61 Gentles, interview.
62 University of Toronto SCM Mid-Term Newsletter, January 1958, File "1957-1958 Student Christian Movement," Hart House Records, A1973-0050/071, University of Toronto Archives; Student Christian Movement Newsletter Number 8, 13 February 1958, and Student Christian Movement Spring Term Newsletter, March-April 1958, File "FROS – post-1959," B1979-0059/7, University of Toronto Archives.
63 Lee, "Marriage and Career," in *Love's Gay Fool: Autobiography of John Alan Lee*, paragraphs 6-8. Lee erroneously places this event in February 1957.
64 Frerichs, interview.
65 Roussopoulos, interview.
66 Frerichs, interview.
67 Letter from Lorna Mackenzie to Howard Adelman, 25 October 1960, File "CUCND Toronto Office 1960-1961 Correspondence and Miscellaneous Material," Box 1, CUCND/SUPA Fonds, William Ready Archives. On *Peacemaker or Powder-Monkey* and its importance to the Canadian disarmament movement, see Moffatt, *History of the Canadian Peace Movement*, 81-6.
68 File "University of Toronto 1960s," SCM, B84-65, United Church of Canada Archives, Toronto, Ontario.

69 Student Christian Movement newsletters for 1 October 1963 and 1 November 1963, File "SCM of Canada, Special Conferences," B1979–0059/68, University of Toronto Archives.
70 Douville, "Project La Macaza," 161–71.
71 Roussopoulos, interview. See also "For Freedom and Peace: Operation St Jean Baptiste," *Sanity*, June 1964; and the letter sent out by Dan Daniels, André Cardinal, and Dimitrios Roussopoulos to multiple recipients, 28 March 1964, File 6, Box 10, CUCND/SUPA Fonds, William Ready Archives.
72 *Project La Macaza Bulletin* 1, no. 1 (18 June 1964): 1, and *Project La Macaza Bulletin* 1, no. 2 (6 July 1964): 3–5, File 6, Box 10, CUCND/SUPA Fonds, William Ready Archives. See also "A Breakthrough at La Macaza," *Sanity*, July 1964.
73 *Project La Macaza Bulletin* 1, no. 2 (6 July 1964): 1, and *Project La Macaza Bulletin* 1, no. 3 (September 1964): 2–4, in File 6, Box 10, CUCND/SUPA Fonds, William Ready Archives; "La Macaza," *Sanity*, October 1964.
74 "A Breakthrough at La Macaza," *Sanity*, July 1964; David Lewis Stein, "The Peaceniks Go to La Macaza," *Maclean's*, 8 August 1964, 13, 36. Stein has also written a fictionalized account of the protest at La Macaza in his novel *Scratch One Dreamer*.
75 John Alan Lee, interview by author, 24 February 2009.
76 Frerichs, interview.
77 *Project La Macaza Bulletin* 1, no. 2 (6 July 1964): 2.
78 Roussopoulos, interview.
79 Stein, "The Peaceniks," 36.
80 Frerichs was not the only protester with a religious vocation. In our interview, he recalled that Catholics were involved in the protest, including nuns.
81 Stein, "The Peaceniks," 37.
82 *Project La Macaza Bulletin* 1, no. 3 (September 1964): 4.
83 William Whitla, phone interview with author, 17 February 2011.
84 *Project La Macaza Bulletin* 1, no. 3 (September 1964): 9.
85 According to performativity theory, identities are constructed and reinforced by symbolic performances. These performances are interpreted by the gaze of the "audience" (in this case, the military and the Canadian public via the news media), and by the "actors" themselves (i.e., the protesters). Not surprisingly, the "actor" is often very conscious of his/her audience, and the meaning that the audience constructs of the performance. In this manner, identities are negotiated. My application of performativity theory is informed primarily by Stuart Henderson's *Making the Scene*, a study of hip identity performance in 1960s Yorkville.

86 For example, in 1959, Muste took part in a similar protest action at Mead missile base in Omaha, Nebraska. The protest began with a one-week vigil. This was followed by a service of silent worship, punctuated by a sermon in which Muste quoted the prophet Isaiah and called on the United States government to disarm. Then, as Danielson describes, "Muste, along with two others, committed civil disobedience by climbing over the gate, where they were promptly arrested for trespassing." Disarmament protests such as this were not unique in the late 1950s and early 1960s throughout the United States and Great Britain, and they provided a template for Canadian activists at La Macaza. Danielson, "'It Is a Day of Judgment,'" 215.

87 Lehtonen, *Story of a Storm*, 21–7.
88 Ibid., 30–6.
89 Ibid., 30.
90 Ibid., 31.
91 *Project La Macaza Bulletin* 1, no. 3 (September 1964): 9.
92 Erlichman, interview; Lee, interview; and Lee, "Straight to Gay," in *Love's Gay Fool*.
93 Romans 13:1, Acts 5:29, New King James Version.
94 Niebuhr, *Christ and Culture*.
95 Historically, many activists who followed the doctrine of "higher law" to its logical extreme ended up embracing anarchy, in some cases, nonviolent anarchy. This was particularly true of nineteenth-century antislavery activists such as William Lloyd Garrison. See Perry, *Radical Abolitionism*. On anarchist thought among present-day Christian radicals, see Claiborne and Haw, *Jesus for President*.

CHAPTER FOUR

1 Graham and McKay, *Radical Ambition*, 59–94.
2 In this category – those who "identified with the Christian community" – I include not only believing Christians but also those students who were agnostic or atheist but chose to be involved in explicitly Christian groups such as SCM or Kairos. This matter will be explored in greater detail later in the chapter.
3 John W. Foster, interview by author, 9 February 2009.
4 Kostash, *Long Way from Home*, 3; Dufresne, "'Let's Not Be Cremated Equal,'" 41–6; Doug Ward, interview by author, Ottawa, Ontario, 10 February 2009. The choice of Regina for the conference was no accident; it was intended to evoke memories of the founding of the CCF

and the Regina Manifesto. Nancy Hannum, phone interview by author, 4 June 2009.
5 Kostash, *Long Way from Home*, 5–6. In my interview with Dimitri Roussopoulos, he stated that peace was the *primary* objective of SUPA. However, Michael Dufresne argues that there was tension within SUPA over placing primary emphasis on peace or on participatory democracy. Dufresne does acknowledge, though, that all leading activists in SUPA saw the two goals as inextricably connected. Dufresne, "'Let's Not Be Cremated Equal,'" 46–50.
6 Palmer, *Canada's 1960s*, 269.
7 On the Selma protests and their national impact, see Anderson, *The Movement and the Sixties*, 113–20.
8 Kenneth Drushka, "U of T Protesters Bed Down for Night," *Globe and Mail*, 11 March 1965; "2,000 Student Pickets to March on Ottawa," *Globe and Mail*, 13 March 1965.
9 Moffatt, *History of the Canadian Peace Movement*, 160–4; Kostash, *Long Way from Home*, 9–12; Palmer, *Canada's 1960s*, 269. Several interviewees identified peace activism and civil rights activism as two separate streams that flowed into SUPA, though they recognized that there was some overlap. For example, *Varsity* editor Harvey Shepherd first became involved in Friends of SNCC as a result of the Selma protest, and later became editor of the SUPA newsletter (Harvey Shepherd, interview by author, 11 February 2009). For a more thorough exploration of the Selma protests at the American consulate, and their significance, see David Churchill, "SUPA, Selma, and Stevenson," 32–69.
10 Kostash, *Long Way from Home*, 11.
11 Ibid., 14. See also Palmer, *Canada's 1960s*, 260–8. On the Economic Research and Action Project of the SDS, see Frost, *"An Interracial Movement."*
12 Cathleen Kneen, interview by author, 9 February 2009.
13 Alinsky, *Reveille for Radicals*.
14 Senate, *Speech from the Throne*, 5 April 1965.
15 Brushett, "Making Shit Disturbers," 247–8.
16 Joan Newman Kuyek, interview by author, 9 February 2009. On Newman's instrumental role in the development of CYC, see also Daly, *The Revolution Game*, 15–25.
17 Dickenson and Campbell, "Strange Bedfellows."
18 John W. Foster, "you gotta do when the spirit says do…" (Toronto, 1965), 3. I am thankful to John Foster for providing me with a copy of this unpublished paper. On the St Calixte meeting, see Peter Gzowski, "The

Righteous Crusaders of the New Left," *Macleans*, 15 November 1965, 18–19, 38–42. On the St Calixte meeting's funding, and, in general, the relationship between SUPA and CYC, see Moffatt, *History of the Canadian Peace Movement*, 166–8.

19 Kostash, *Long Way from Home*, 20–1; Palmer, *Canada's 1960s*, 274–7.
20 Herring, *America's Longest War*, 3–129.
21 Ibid., 135–47.
22 US Congress, *Gulf of Tonkin Resolution*, 88th Cong., 2nd sess., 7 August 1964.
23 Herring, *America's Longest War*, 171–223, especially 182.
24 Gitlin, *The Sixties*, 177–88.
25 Churchill, "American Expatriates"; Kostash, *Long Way from Home*, 45–9, 60–1; Palmer, *Canada's 1960s*, 271–2; and Squires, *Building Sanctuary*, 32–8.
26 Moffatt, *History of the Canadian Peace Movement*, 164–6.
27 Cox, *The Secular City*, 109.
28 Ibid., 226. On radical secular theology and the "death of God," see Livingston, *Modern Christian Thought*, 479–84.
29 In his attempt to turn theology from a metaphysical exercise into a practical one, Cox still employs theistic language throughout *The Secular City*, speaking of God and God's work. Yet at the end of the book (232–5), Cox muses that in the future, Christians may have to abandon the word "God" itself.
30 On the success of *The Comfortable Pew*, see McKillop, *Pierre Berton: A Biography*, 427–34.
31 A.C. Forrest, "What Berton Would Say Differently if Writing for the United Church," 31–3. The *Canadian Churchman* published four reviews in February 1965, by Michael Barkway, Bishop H.R. Hunt, Reginald Stackhouse, and Ruth Taylor; and one in March 1965 by Arnold Edinborough.
32 Berton et al., *Why the Sea Is Boiling Hot*; and Kilbourn, ed., *The Restless Church*.
33 Contributors to *The Restless Church* associated with Holy Trinity included William and Elizabeth Kilbourn, Michael Creal, and the controversial priest Ernest Harrison, whose 1967 book *A Church without God* denied the existence of the supernatural. (See "Can There Be a Church without God?," *Canadian Churchman*, March 1967.) Politically active clergy at Holy Trinity associated with the SCM included Ted Mann and Dan Heap.
34 Flatt, *After Evangelicalism*, 200–5.

35 Brouwer, "When Missions Became Development."
36 Kenneth Bagnell, "What's All This So-Called New Evangelism?," *Observer*, 15 April 1966, 16–19, 40.
37 Crysdale, *Churches Where the Action Is*.
38 Reeve, "Walking the Talk," 23.
39 Hannum, interview.
40 This should not be too surprising, since the "Values" chapter incorporated language from a papal encyclical. Hayden, *The Port Huron Statement*, 36.
41 Second Vatican Council, *Gaudium et Spes*. See especially chapter 1 on "The Dignity of the Human Person" and chapter 4 on "The Role of the Church in the Modern World."
42 Second Vatican Council, *Apostolicam Actuositatem*.
43 Seljak, "Catholicism's 'Quiet Revolution'"; Fay, *History of Canadian Catholics*, 278–302; Meunier and Warren, *Sortir de la "Grande Noirceur"*; and Gauvreau, *Catholic Origins*.
44 See, for example, Gregory Baum's guest editorial, "The Church Today: Dialogue Is Vital," *Canadian Register*, 3 April 1965; and "Renew or Die, Societies Told," *Canadian Register*, 22 January 1966.
45 "Youth Corps" (n.d.), Office Files, Youth Corps, Accession 2005–075, Archives of the Roman Catholic Archdiocese of Toronto, Toronto, Ontario.
46 Written on back of "Suggestions for Fall Programme 1965," File "SCM – U of T. Cabinet minutes, 1964–5," B1979–0059/15, University of Toronto Archives.
47 Student Christian Movement Newsletter for 13 January 1964; and Newsletter #4, 6 December 1965, File "SCM of Canada, Special Conferences," B1979–0059/68, University of Toronto Archives.
48 Fred Caloren, interview with author, 31 March 2009.
49 Fred Caloren, interview with author, 9 April 2009.
50 Heap's friends addressed him as "Don," which was his preference. However, in public life, he was known as Dan.
51 Several of my interview subjects mentioned Dan Heap as an important participant in the SCM. See also "Heap Family."
52 United Church of Canada, *Year Book – Volume II* (1965), 103.
53 United Church of Canada, *Year Book – Volume II* (1966), 106.
54 Kenneth Bagnell, "The End of the Beat Generation," *Observer*, July 1965, 11.
55 United Church of Canada, *Year Book – Volume II* (1966), 106; *Canadian Churchman*, July-August 1965. At the time, the AYPA was also beginning the process of restructuring, for the same reasons that Kairos superseded

the old YPU in the United Church. See Anglican Church of Canada, *General Synod, Twenty-Second Session*, 78–9.
56 SUPA Newsletter, 5 October 1966, File "SUPA Newsletter, Volume Two," CUCND/SUPA Fonds, Box 21, William Ready Archives.
57 Foster, interview.
58 Ibid.
59 Tom Alderman, "The Committed Kids," *Canadian* (21 May 1966), 5.
60 Harvey Shepherd, *Summer of Service '67* (File 8, Box 21, CUCND/SUPA Fonds, William Ready Archives, McMaster University). Some evangelical churches supported SOS, including the Salvation Army and the Mennonites (churches with a tradition of social engagement).
61 Thomas McKillop and Sister M. Chabanel, "The First Year" (n.d.), Events and Office Files, Youth Corps, Accession 2005–075, Archives of the Roman Catholic Archdiocese of Toronto.
62 In the application forms for the 1966 pilot projects, one of the questions was, "Many views are expressed today both for and against Christianity and the Church. How do you feel about this debate?" The form stressed, "We are not looking for any 'right' answers ... and would appreciate your honest comments." "Summer of Service and Christian Youth Assembly 1967: Pilot Project – Summer 1966," File "Summer of Service and Christian Youth Assembly 1967," Box 5, CUCND/SUPA Fonds, William Ready Archives.
63 Shepherd, *Summer of Service '67*.
64 Hannum, interview.
65 File "Summer of Service – Volunteer Action for Social Change, SCM, B84–27, United Church of Canada Archives.
66 Linda Kealey, phone interview by author, 30 July 2009. Greg Kealey had also been involved in an SOS project held the previous year in the north end of Winnipeg.
67 In addition, it was Kneen who had inspired Father Philip Berrigan to become a civil rights and antiwar activist. Philip and his brother, Father Daniel Berrigan, would later achieve notoriety as anti-Vietnam activists. Interview with Brewster Kneen, 9 February 2009; Berrigan and Wilcox, *Fighting the Lamb's War*, 35–6.
68 As Cathleen recalls, "we called ourselves *Los Muchos Sombreros* at one point, because we had a lot of different hats within the church. And we kept popping up in different committees. Like, [laughing] 'oh my God, here they are again! We can't get rid of them! We make a different committee and there they are again!'" Cathleen Kneen, interview.
69 Ward, interview.

70 Ibid.
71 Ibid.
72 Volkmar Richter and Graham Fraser, "These Men Lead Our Student Rebels," *Toronto Star*, 14 September 1968.
73 Peter Warrian, phone interview by author, 4 February 2009.
74 Hannum, interview.
75 Judy Skinner, interview with author, 12 May 2010.
76 I explore the Latin American Working Group in greater detail in chapter 5.
77 Foster, interview.
78 Hannum, interview; Hannum, email message to author, 16 March 2011.
79 Livingston, *Modern Christian Thought*, 356–7.
80 Tillich, *Morality and Beyond*, 88–9.
81 Ibid., 89.
82 Ibid., 40.
83 Ibid., 43.
84 Ibid., 89.
85 Ibid., 94.
86 Bonhoeffer, *Letters and Papers from Prison*, 162–227.
87 Ibid., 222.
88 For the influence of Tillich and Bonhoeffer on a community of young Christians in Austin, Texas, and for a more thorough exploration of the ideas of these theologians and their social and political implications, see Rossinow, *Politics of Authenticity*, 53–84. Beyond North America, the New Left student leader in Germany, Rudi Dutschke, "was in the early years of the movement a believing Protestant, and among the strongest influences on his thinking were Dietrich Bonhoeffer, [and] Paul Tillich" (McLeod, *Religious Crisis of the 1960s*, 148). Also, Harvey Cox specifically wrote *The Secular City* "to serve as a study resource for a series of conferences planned for 1965 by the National Student Christian Federation," which was the American sister organization of the Canadian SCM. Consequently, it is not surprising that the book was enthusiastically received by students in the SCM. Cox, *The Secular City*, xi; University of Toronto SCM Spring Newsletter, April 1965, File "1965–66," B1979–0059/68, University of Toronto Archives.
89 Hannum, interview; SUPA Newsletter, 5 October 1966 (File "SUPA Newsletter, Volume 2," CUCND/SUPA Files, William Ready Archives). Also, on the influence of Bonhoeffer on young activists, see Bagnell, "End of the Beat Generation," 11.
90 Hartwell, interview.
91 Brewster Kneen, interview by author, 9 February 2009. Also Foster, interview; Ward, interview; Warrian, interview.

92 MacLeod, "Transformation of the United Church," 226.
93 The privileging of ethics and action over ideology and analysis was both a strength and a weakness of the earlier New Left. In my interview with Brewster Kneen, he argued that the student left has always suffered from intellectual laziness, and this quality is reflected in the lack of a clearly articulated theology among Christian radicals. James Harding called the Canadian New Left in the mid-sixties "an ethical movement in search of an analysis." See his essay "An Ethical Movement."
94 Hartwell, interview. It is significant that Hartwell includes students who were brought up in Judaism, for Jewish participation in the New Left was extensive. The influence of Judaism on the Canadian New Left is outside the scope of this study, but it is certainly worthy of future research.
95 By the sixties, many youth who had grown up in mainline Protestant churches, and otherwise would have chosen to work overseas in denominational missions, opted instead to serve with CUSO. Brouwer, "When Missions Became Development," 662, 684–5.
96 Owram, *Born at the Right Time*, 103–9, especially 106.
97 Shepherd, interview. For an example of what Shepherd is describing, consider Bob Davis, an activist in SUPA and CYC, who co-founded and edited *This Magazine Is about Schools*. His father was an Anglican priest (and by 1958, a bishop), and for a time, Davis intended to follow in his father's footsteps and enter the priesthood. Bob Davis, "Before Browndale," 229–31.
98 SUPA Newsletter, 12 February 1966, File "SUPA Newsletter Vol. 2," CUCND/SUPA Fonds, William Ready Archives.
99 Kostash, *Long Way from Home*, 10.
100 Roussopoulos addressed Anglican and United Church youth at Assembly '65. In the SCM, Art Pape (Toronto's leading SUPA activist) took part in a panel discussion on social issues at the SCM Bala conference in August 1965, and James Laxer addressed an SCM Peace Camp in Toronto in the summer of 1965. Stan Jolly, interview by author, 10 August 2009; Hartwell, interview.
101 SUPA Newsletter, 12 August 1966, File "SUPA Newsletter Vol. 2," CUCND/SUPA Fonds, William Ready Archives.
102 The song ends with the line, "See you in Don Jail." File "Archives B1," B1979–0059/68, University of Toronto Archives.
103 Kuyek, interview.
104 Cathleen Kneen, interview. In the mid-sixties, Cathleen Kneen perceived more fundamental differences between SUPA and SCM than rhetorical style.

105 Five of these were mentioned or identified by individual interviewees but not corroborated by others interviewees or by documentary evidence. Another appeared on an SCM mailing list from the mid-sixties. For the remaining fourteen, there is evidence from multiple sources that they were associated with SCM, Kairos, SOS, or the Christian Left group. However, this is a conservative number, making no allowance for uncorroborated identifications. Furthermore, my research focused largely on Toronto. Consequently, there might have been students from SCM units in western Canada, Quebec, or the Maritimes. See "Fall Training Institute Participants," File No. 2, Box 22, CUCND/SUPA Fonds, William Ready Archives.

106 There were also two members of the Cuban SCM, who had likely just taken part in the SCM work camp on Cuba led by Brewster and Cathleen Kneen.

107 Hartwell, interview.

108 Foster, interview.

109 Ibid. Though his intended audience was the churches, Foster's essay appears to have had some currency within SUPA itself.

110 Foster, "you gotta do when the spirit says do...," 10.

111 I have located a "Names for Mailing List" for the University of Toronto SCM (undated, but likely 1964 or 1965). However, it is unclear how many on this list were actually participants in the SCM. For example, although Nancy Hannum's name appears on the list, she was not involved in the SCM. But through her work with the SUPA National Office, she had close contact with the SCM (Box 15, B79–0059, University of Toronto Archives). For SUPA, there is a "Members of the Worklist" (undated, but likely 1965 or 1966), but the thirty-three names on the list appear to be representatives to National Council, Box 22, CUCND/SUPA Fonds, William Ready Archives.

112 Most of the participants at St Calixte were English-Canadian. As Dimitri Roussopoulos explains, this was "because there was only one summer project in Montreal, and also because there was a much stronger francophone community organising movement in the city." Roussopoulos, email to author, 1 February 2011.

113 "SCM Has $9,000 'Conscience Crisis,'" *Varsity* (University of Toronto), 3 January 1966.

114 The front page of this newsletter carried a reprint of Art Young's famous cartoon of Jesus as a revolutionary: "Wanted – for sedition, criminal anarchy – vagrancy, and conspiring to overthrow the established government." Perhaps this was the editor's way of recognizing the SCM as

co-belligerents in the revolutionary struggle. SUPA Newsletter, 21 December 1965, File "SUPA 1965–66," B1979–0047, University of Toronto Archives.

115 John W. Foster, "Momentary Thoughts on the Significance of the SCM Christmas Conference" (January 1966). I am grateful to Stan Jolly for providing me with a copy of this unpublished paper, along with many other documents.

116 Caloren, interview, 9 April 2009.

117 Ibid.

118 Stan Jolly provided "SCM Christmas Conference: Notes on the Daily Programme" and English texts of conference speeches by Robert Garry and Albert Van Den Heuvel .

119 "SUPA Considering an Ottawa Sit-in," *Varsity*, 3 January 1966. This protest would take place in March of 1966, with SCM involvement.

120 Warrian, interview.

121 Foster, "Momentary Thoughts on the Significance of the SCM Christmas Conference."

122 Jim Harding, "SUPA at Saskatoon: An Evaluation," SUPA Newsletter 2, no. 1 (27 January 1966), in File 5, Box 21, CUCND/SUPA Fonds, William Ready Archives.

123 Hannum, interview.

124 Ibid.

125 Hartwell, interview.

126 Cathleen Kneen, "Self-Fulfilling Prophecy, or How to Approach the Saskatoon Meetings," SUPA Newsletter, 21 December 1965, "SUPA 1965–1966," B1979–0047, University of Toronto Archives).

127 Cited in Beattie, *A Brief History*, 111.

128 On the disparate nature of SCM local units, see the accounts of the various SCM chapters in Peter Paris, *Report on SCM of Canada, Part One* (Toronto: Student Christian Movement, 1965), in Box 84-35, SCM, United Church of Canada Archives.

129 Gidney, *Long Eclipse*, 98–104.

130 Paris, *Report on SCM of Canada, Part One*, 7.

131 Beattie, *A Brief History*, 9.

132 Agnostics, atheists, or those who identified as Christian but doubted or denied core tenets included Fred Caloren (national study secretary), Wolfe Erlichman (work camp director), George Hartwell (University of Toronto unit president), Richard Hyde (national president), Stan Jolly (national president), and John Alan Lee (work camp director).

133 Cited in Beattie, *A Brief History*, 111–12.

134 Jolly, interview.
135 Fred Caloren, "To Be or Not to Be: Christian Presence and the SCM of Canada" (1966?), manuscript provided by Stan Jolly.
136 Student Christian Movement of Canada Constitutional Committee, "Preliminary Report and Proposals for the Restructuring of the SCM of Canada" (1966), in File One, Box 143, 82–001 C, United Church of Canada Archives. The document reflects the influence of George Grant on Stan Jolly (Grant was Jolly's teacher in the religious studies program at McMaster University), particularly in its reliance on the ideas of Jacques Ellul, and its overall pessimistic tone about the crises facing Canadian society in the sixties.
137 Jolly, interview.
138 Beattie, *A Brief History*, 115–17.
139 Hyde, interview.
140 Jolly, interview; Caloren, interview, 31 March 2009.
141 *Student Christian Movement of Canada Newsletter*, 23 September 1966, in File One, Box 143, 82–001 C, United Church of Canada Archives.
142 Beattie, *A Brief History*, 11.
143 Constitutional Committee, "Preliminary Report and Proposals."

CHAPTER FIVE

1 "Man of the Year: The Inheritor," *Time*, 7 January 1967.
2 Ellwood, *Sixties Spiritual Awakening*, 176–7.
3 For English Canada, see Levitt, *Children of Privilege*, 45–53 and Palmer, *Canada's 1960s*, 274–309. The year 1968 was pivotal for activists in French Canada as well: see Mills, *The Empire Within*; and Belliveau, "Tradition, libéralisme et communautarisme," 266–382. For the United States, see Gitlin, *The Sixties*, 285–408; and Matusow, *The Unraveling of America*, 325–44. For an exploration of 1968 and its significance, including events outside North America, see McLeod, *Religious Crisis of the 1960s*, 141–60.
4 Warrian, interview. Warrian was active in both periods.
5 Palmer, *Canada's 1960s*, 275; and Kostash, *Long Way from Home*, 28.
6 Warrian, interview. Warrian served as president of the CUS from 1968 to 1969.
7 Palmer, *Canada's 1960s*, 278–9.
8 New Left Committee, "The Revolutionary Process," 107. See also Graham and McKay, *Radical Ambition*, 88–9.
9 Kostash, *Long Way from Home*, 25.

10 Dufresne, "'Let's not Be Cremated Equal,'" 86; Graham and McKay, *Radical Ambition*, 92–3.
11 Levitt, *Children of Privilege*, 167–84. See also Milligan, *Rebel Youth*, 65–90.
12 Andy Wernick, "A Guide to the Student Left," *Varsity*, 24 September 1969.
13 On the New Left origins of the women's liberation movement in the United States, see Evans, *Personal Politics*; Gitlin, *The Sixties*, 362–76; and Gosse, *Rethinking the New Left*, 153–70. On the origins of the movement in Canada, see Adamson, "Feminists, Libbers, Lefties, and Radicals"; Graham and McKay, *Radical Ambition*, 89–92; Kostash, *Long Way from Home*, 166–87; Mills, *The Empire Within*, 119–37; and Palmer, *Canada's 1960s*, 297–304.
14 Adamson, "Feminists, Libbers, Lefties, and Radicals," 254–5.
15 Owram, *Born at the Right Time*, 296.
16 On the distinctions between liberal, radical, and socialist feminism, see Adamson, Briskin, and McPhail, *Feminist Organizing for Change*, 9–12, 28–9, 37–53.
17 For an administrator's view of student radicals and the student power movement, see Bissell, *Halfway Up Parnassus*.
18 The best quantitative study is contained in Sutherland, *Patterns of Belief and Action*. It focuses on the University of Alberta between 1968 and 1970 (when the student power movement was at its peak on campus). This study shows that "active radicals" constituted a very small segment of the student body, but also that a larger body of students were "passive radicals" who supported their aims. However, this is only one campus, and generalizing to the overall Canadian scene is problematic at best. Other quantitative studies of the Canadian New Left are limited in their usefulness because they date from the early seventies, when the movement had entered a different phase. See Simpson and Phillips, "Understanding Student Protest in Canada"; and Trenton, "Left-Wing Radicalism."
19 Lexier, "The Canadian Student." See also Graham and McKay, *Radical Ambition*, 95–108.
20 On the connections between the New Left and hippie counterculture in the United States (with a particular focus on Austin, Texas), see Rossinow, "The New Left in the Counterculture."
21 On the philosophy and practices of the hippie counterculture, see Miller, *The Hippies and American Values*; Roszak, *Making of a Counter Culture*; and Yablonsky, *The Hippie Trip*. On hippie neighbourhoods, see Didion, "Slouching towards Bethlehem"; Henderson, *Making the Scene*; and Perry, *Haight-Ashbury: A History*.

22 See Roussopoulos, "Towards a Revolutionary Youth Movement"; and Daniels, "The Cultural Revolution."
23 On the problematic relationship between Toronto's New Left and the Yorkville hippies, see Henderson, *Making the Scene*, 150–7.
24 Braunstein and Doyle, "Historicizing the American Counterculture."
25 Warrian, interview.
26 Clarke and Macdonald, *Leaving Christianity*, 197–231.
27 Ibid., 225–6.
28 Gidney, *A Long Eclipse*, 142.
29 Ibid., 97–124.
30 Grayson, "'Remember Now Thy Creator.'"
31 Kealey, interview.
32 Ibid.
33 Grayson, "'Remember Now Thy Creator,'" 107.
34 Harvey Shepherd, "Is There Room for You in Kairos?," *Observer*, 1 March 1969, 27.
35 Ibid.
36 Ibid. It is not known whether they progressed any further than the "talking stages."
37 "If you ask how many members Kairos might have, you'll probably be answered with an almost metaphysical definition of constituency. (The Board of Christian Education says Kairos mailings go to about 700 groups and 1,000 individuals.)" Ibid., 26.
38 AYM's national co-ordinator, Tim Agg, was also on the national executive of Kairos. Given the ecumenical trend of the sixties, and the protracted negotiations – ultimately unsuccessful – to merge the two denominations, it is not surprising that there should be close connections between Kairos and AYM. Ibid., 27.
39 As one account observed, "There could be no better place in Canada to provide a graphic setting for the need of change in our society." See the account of the Survival Day Project (the memoir is untitled, and neither the author nor date are indicated), in "AYM," Box One, GS 76–11, General Synod Archives, Anglican Church of Canada. Also "'Waste,' 'Put-on' Angers Observers," *Canadian Churchman*, September 1969; Jerry Hames, "Council's Future, Key Issue," *Canadian Churchman*, November 1969.
40 Tim Agg, "'It Was Amazing to See a Drama Unfold,'" *Canadian Churchman*, October 1970.
41 See the aforementioned account of the Survival Day Project. Also Francie Miller, "There's Just No Place Left to Go," *Canadian Churchman*, May 1970; and Agg, "'It Was Amazing to See a Drama Unfold.'"

42 Don Wilson "to SCMers and Friends of the Movement" (September 1968), in File One, Box 143, 82–001 C, United Church of Canada Archives.
43 Ibid.
44 "List of Members at National Council – 1967," File #25 "SCM Council, September 1967 Inter-American Project," Box 2004/16/001, in Latin American Working Group (LAWG) Fonds, Clara Thomas Archives, York University.
45 Linda Bohnen, "Second Half-Century Ahead: SCM Looks to the Non-Student," *Globe and Mail*, 27 September 1969. This is only an estimate of core members. The number of occasional participants, or attendees at various events might have been larger. Since SCM prided itself in being unstructured, it did not have formal membership. Therefore, it is impossible to obtain solid statistics on membership.
46 At least the SCM survived the 1960s. That is more than can be said for its American counterpart, the University Christian Movement (UCM), which dissolved itself in 1969 (though some regional UCM groups continued to operate). According to one critic, the UCM "reflected an anti-institutional and anti-authoritarian sentiment, directed against the structures of churches, traditional ecumenicity, and higher education, and maintained an uncritical faith in spontaneity and a participatory style" (Risto Lehtonen, cited in Hugh McLeod, *Religious Crisis of the 1960s*, 157). See also Bass, "Revolutions, Quiet and Otherwise."
47 Wernick, "Guide to the Student Left." It could also be that the local chapter of the University of Toronto SCM was not deemed sufficiently radical or politically engaged to make the cut. According to Bohnen's feature on the SCM in the *Globe and Mail* (27 September 1969), the University of Toronto SCM "was not especially radical," while the "York branch is more radical."
48 Bohnen, "Second Half-Century Ahead."
49 See the following correspondence: J. Scott Leith to E.E. Long (30 September 1969); E.E. Long to J. Scott Leith (2 October 1969); Roy De Marsh to J. Scott Leith (9 October 1969); Donald Wilson to E.E. Long (4 June 1970); and E.E. Long to Donald Wilson (6 November 1970), in File Two, Box 143, 82–001 C, United Church of Canada Archives.
50 Warrian also belonged to Brewster Kneen's Christian Left group in Toronto, which included Doug Ward, who was president of CUS in 1966–67, and Judy Skinner, who was associate secretary (international) of CUS in 1968–69.
51 Volkmar Richter and Graham Fraser, "These Men Lead Our Student Rebels," *Toronto Star*, 14 September 1968.

52 Donna Mason, "Burn! Sock It to 'Em! Canadian Students Told," *Toronto Star*, 29 August 1968. Warrian later claimed that he was misquoted by the "bourgeois press." See Richter and Fraser, "These Men Lead Our Student Rebels"; and "'Bourgeois Press' Hacks CUS Quote," *Ubyssey*, 17 September 1968.
53 Don Wilson "to SCMers and Friends of the Movement" (September 1968), in File One, Box 143, 82–001 C, United Church of Canada Archives.
54 Tom Faulkner, Skype interview by author, 11 May 2010.
55 Ian Harrison, "Tom Faulkner: Theolog Turned Businessman," *Varsity*, 17 March 1967.
56 Faulkner, interview.
57 "At the time, we generally tended to divide each other into 'wheelies' and 'feelies,' and I was very much a 'wheelie.'" Ibid.
58 Harrison, "Tom Faulkner," *Varsity*, 17 March 1967.
59 Harvey Shepherd, "Then Why Does He Have to Upset Everybody?," *Observer*, 1 May 1968, 10.
60 "I was persuaded by the head of the health service ... that this really was a moral issue, a justice issue, and that it needed to be done ... I had visions of young women going into back alleys and scraping themselves out with a rusty coat-hanger. The choice between that and jail for me was quite clear." Faulkner, interview. See also Sethna, "University of Toronto Health Service."
61 Faulkner, interview.
62 "We published the basic instrument that made it possible for draft-dodgers to leave the States and come to Canada ... It wouldn't have got off the ground if we hadn't provided the printing press for it." Ibid.
63 Ibid.
64 On Canada's military, diplomatic, and industrial role in the Vietnam War, see Levant, *Quiet Complicity*.
65 Lexier, "The Canadian Student," 296.
66 On the Dow controversy, including protests, counter-protests, Faulkner, the SAC, and the election of December 1967, see ibid., 292–302.
67 Ibid., 301–2.
68 Shepherd, "Then Why Does He Have to Upset Everybody?," 11.
69 Gitlin, *The Sixties*, 122.
70 Ibid., 188.
71 Palmer, *Canada's 1960s*, 279.
72 Gosse, *Rethinking the New Left*, 195.
73 Mills, *The Empire Within*, 62–85.
74 "The Latin American Working Group Background to September 1969," File #2 "1967 Minutes," Box 2004/16/001, in Latin American Working

Group (LAWG) Fonds, Clara Thomas Archives, York University. See also the "Interview with Norman Laverty," "LAWG: Hay Camino History Project."

75 Membership information drawn from minutes, conference records, and other archival records found in Box 2004/16/001, in LAWG Fonds. Also, interviews with John Foster and Brewster Kneen.
76 "The Latin American Working Group Background to September 1969."
77 "Meeting of the Working Committee on International Affairs," 9 October 1966; and "Notes on a Meeting of the Working Group on Latin America with Oscar Bolioli," 10 November 1966. Both documents can be found in File #12 "Notes/Activities – Formation of LAWG, 1966–1968," Box 2004/16/001, in LAWG Fonds.
78 "Meeting of the Working Committee on International Affairs," 9 October 1966.
79 "Notes from the International Working Group (Latin America)," 1 December 1966, File #12 "Notes/Activities – Formation of LAWG, 1966–1968," Box 2004/16/001, in LAWG Fonds.
80 "A Programme to Further Diakonia in the Americas," File #10 "Programme to Further Diakonia in the Americas (1966)," Box 2004/16/001, in LAWG Fonds.
81 "Latin American Working Group Background to September 1969."
82 Ibid.
83 Ibid.
84 File #5 "LAWG Conference, May 1967," Box 2004/16/001, in LAWG Fonds.
85 Azzi, "Nationalist Moment in English Canada"; Churchill, "Draft Resisters, Left Nationalism"; and Palmer, *Canada's 1960s*, 289–97.
86 "IMPERIALISMO, caderno especial," 30 August 1969, File #2 "1967 Minutes," Box 2004/16/001, in LAWG Fonds.
87 OAC Resolution, File #25 "SCM Council, September 1967 Inter-American Project," Box 2004/16/001, in LAWG Fonds.
88 "Suggestions for an Inter-American Work-Action-Study Project," File #25 "SCM Council, September 1967 Inter-American Project," Box 2004/16/001, in LAWG Fonds.
89 On Shaull, see Lehtonen, *Story of a Storm*. Shaull's relevant writings include *Containment and Change*, a critique of American foreign policy that he co-authored with Students for a Democratic Society activist Carl Oglesby.
90 I explore liberation theology in greater detail in chapter 6.
91 Allen, *The Social Passion*; McKay, *Reasoning Otherwise*, especially 213–78.
92 See chapter 3.

CHAPTER SIX

1 "Disappointment," *Observer*, 1 June 1967, 11; Clarke and Macdonald, *Leaving Christianity*, 43.
2 "Big Drop in Church Membership," *Canadian Churchman*, October 1967.
3 Bibby, *Fragmented Gods*, 11–23. On the declining membership and attendance figures (and related data) for Canada's largest Protestant churches in the sixties and beyond, see Clarke and Macdonald, *Leaving Christianity*, 27–71, 110–19.
4 Clarke and Macdonald, *Leaving Christianity*, 84–5.
5 McLeod, *Religious Crisis of the 1960s*, 188. See also 196–202.
6 Marks, *Revivals and Roller Rinks*, 81–106, 189–207.
7 Johnson, "Religion and Politics in America," 308.
8 Ernest E. Long, "The Truth about the 'Crisis' in the Church," *Observer*, 15 November 1967, 12–15, 30. Also, N. Bruce McLeod, "Are 18-Year-Olds Turned Off by What We Do?," *Observer*, 15 June 1968; and N. Bruce McLeod, "Why Won't They Go to Church?," *Observer*, 1 November 1969, 20–2, 40.
9 For largely favourable accounts in the Canadian denominational press, see R.F. Aldwinkle, "Impressions of Uppsala," *Canadian Baptist*, 15 September 1968, 15, 18–19; Patricia Clarke, "They Turned the Churches Inside Out," *Observer*, 15 September 1968, 26–8, 40; Hugh McCullum, "Problems of World Faced by Churches," *Canadian Churchman*, September 1968, 1, 18; Robert A. Wallace, "Disturbing," *Observer*, 15 September 1968, 11, 45; and "World Council Fourth Assembly Meets," *Presbyterian Record*, September 1968, 14–19. See also Lehtonen, *Story of a Storm*, 65–78.
10 Clarke, "They Turned the Churches Inside Out," 28.
11 Frerichs, interview.
12 Ian Mackenzie, phone interview with author, 19 October 2009.
13 Jeanne Wayling, "The Swingingest Church in Town," *Observer*, 1 June 1969, 18–20.
14 This was Survival Day, discussed in the previous chapter.
15 Frances Healy, "We're in! A Synod for Youth," *Canadian Churchman*, May 1968. See also "Youth Ask Greater Say," *The Anglican*, April 1968; and Peggy Carson, "More Youth Synod," the *Anglican*, May 1968.
16 For an example of sympathetic coverage, see J.R. Hord, "Youth," *Observer*, 1 April 1968, 11. For a decidedly unsympathetic analysis of student radicalism, see Wilson Woodside, "What's behind Student Riots," *Observer*, 1 July 1968, 24–5.

17 Clarke, "Ray Hord," 13–14. The differences between Mutchmor and Hord were not "night and day." Mutchmor was a progressive, and under his direction, the board addressed socio-economic issues as well. But his most famous battles were over issues such as liquor and gambling. See Beardsall, "Ray Hord: 'Prophet Evangelist,'" 52–3.
18 Clarke, "Ray Hord," 14.
19 *Twenty-Third General Council: Record of Proceedings* (United Church of Canada, 1968), 388.
20 J.R. Hord, "Youth," *Observer*, 1 April 1968, 11.
21 Faulkner, interview.
22 "Revolution Offers Choice to Be Victim or Shaper," *Canadian Register*, 11 May 1968.
23 McCullum, "Synod Hears Radical Talk," *Canadian Churchman*, October 1967.
24 Ibid.
25 "Renew or Die, Societies Told," *Canadian Churchman*, 22 January 1966.
26 Jim Struthers, "Ontario Bible College," *Varsity*, 12 November 1969.
27 "It's still 'No' to Youth at Synod," *Canadian Churchman*, September 1969.
28 For an overview of the American antiwar movement and its relationship with the New Left, see Gosse, *Rethinking the New Left*, 85–109.
29 The precise number of draft-age American males who immigrated to Canada during the Vietnam War is impossible to determine. According to David Churchill, estimates "vary between 30,000 and 100,000, but [a] figure of 40,000 seems closest to an accurate accounting." Churchill, "An Ambiguous Welcome," 4.
30 Palmer, *Canada's 1960s*, 289–97.
31 Kenneth Bagnell, "The View from the Firing Line," *Observer*, 1 September 1967, 13; "PM a Puppy Led by US, Hord Says," *Globe and Mail*, 19 May 1967.
32 Wilson Woodside, "Should the Yanks Go Home?," *Observer*, 1 June 1965, 22–3.
33 Clarke, "Ray Hord," 14.
34 Bagnell, "The View from the Firing Line," 13.
35 "Church Apologizes to PM over Hord's 'Puppy' Remark," *Toronto Star*, 19 May 1967.
36 Letter, Rev. C.B. Hickman to Ray Hord, 21 June 1967, File 316, Box 62, Board of Evangelism and Social Service Fonds, United Church of Canada Archives.
37 Memo, Tim Smith to Ray Hord, undated, File 1, Box 44, Board of Evangelism and Social Service Fonds, United Church of Canada Archives.

38 "Church Aid for Draft Dodgers," *Toronto Star*, 26 September 1967.
39 Allen Spraggett, "Church Killed Draft-Dodger Aid, Feared Collections Would Drop – Official," *Toronto Star*, 30 September 1967.
40 Letters from John Townson, R.C. Patterson, and Mrs B.E. Conquergood, all addressed to Hord, all dated 27 September 1967, File 1, Box 43, Board of Evangelism and Social Service Fonds, United Church of Canada Archives.
41 "How You Vote on Vietnam," *Observer*, 15 March 1968, 16–18, 46.
42 Larry Hoffman, "A Draft Dodger Goes to Church," *The American Exile in Canada* 1, no. 8 (29 December 1968): 6.
43 Letter, N. Bruce McLeod to Ray Hord, 4 October 1967, File 3, Box 43, Board of Evangelism and Social Service Fonds, United Church of Canada Archives.
44 Beardsall, "Ray Hord: 'Prophet Evangelist,'" 57–8, citing O'Toole et al., "The United Church in Crisis," 153.
45 See chapter 7.
46 Clarke, "Ray Hord," 15.
47 On the substantial shift in the United Church of Canada beginning in the sixties, see Flatt's *After Evangelicalism*.
48 Beardsall, "Ray Hord: 'Prophet Evangelist,'" 56–7.
49 Ibid., 58.
50 Pocock was coadjutor archbishop from 1961 to 1971, and archbishop from 1971 to 1978. Technically James McGuigan was the archbishop of Toronto from 1934 to 1971, but due to his failing health (including a stroke he suffered while attending the Second Vatican Council), his duties largely fell to Pocock.
51 Gosse, *Rethinking the New Left*, 97–8. See also Meconis, *With Clumsy Grace*.
52 One of the classic texts on Canada's student movement in the late sixties, *Student Protest*, was edited by a Basilian priest and educator at the University of British Columbia, Father Gerald McGuigan.
53 Ted Schmidt, interview by author, 27 April 2009.
54 Stan Kutz, interview by author, 4 February 2009.
55 Smith was a Welsh immigrant with no training in therapy, but she had a charismatic presence and clearly inspired sufficient confidence to form a therapeutic community which, by the seventies, would include a network of houses and farm property. A substantial contingent of participants were Catholics (including laity and approximately fifty nuns and priests who became laity), but it was not a religious community. On Therafields, see Goodbrand, *Therafields*; and Marchand, "Lea and Me."

56 Kealey, interview.
57 Warrian, interview.
58 Kutz, interview; Jim Martin, "Our Man on St George," *Mike*, 11 March 1966, 1–2; and Quealey, *My Basilian Priesthood*.
59 Greg and Linda Kealey had been active in the Newman Centre before they became involved in the New Left Caucus. While she acknowledges that the Newman Centre may have played a minor role in the development of her political consciousness, it was not as important as "being involved in the anti-Vietnam War protests ... the student movement on campus, the New Left Caucus, I think those secular things were more important at the time anyway." Kealey, interview.
60 Quealey, *My Basilian Priesthood*, 93–6.
61 Warrian, interview.
62 Quealey, *My Basilian Priesthood*, 87–9.
63 Pope Pius XI, *Casti Connubii*, par. 56.
64 Owram, *Born at the Right Time*, 248–79; Sethna, "University of Toronto Health Service," 265–92.
65 Both Baum and Kutz contributed to a volume criticizing the Church's position on birth control, entitled *Contraception and Holiness*.
66 "Priest Tells Roman Catholics, Obey Conscience on Birth Control," *Toronto Star*, 15 February 1965. Kutz's controversial remarks – or rather, the fact that they were broadcast in a Toronto daily – nearly led to his removal from the archdiocese: "Thank God – thank Gregory Baum. He went to the bishop and sort of talked him down. Otherwise, I'd have been on my way to Houston or some other Basilian faculty of theology to do penance and learn not to say things so bluntly." Kutz, interview.
67 Pope Paul VI, *Humanae Vitae*, par. 14.
68 Cited in Sethna, "University of Toronto Health Service," 286. On the debates over contraception in the sixties, see Stettner and Douville, "'In the Image and Likeness of God,'" 193–6.
69 Five years later, the bishops issued a decidedly more conservative statement, arguing that the decisive authority lay with Church teaching, not private conscience. See Perin, "Das englischsprachige Kanada."
70 Kutz, interview.
71 Kealey, interview.
72 Kuyek, interview.
73 Richard Smith, "From the Hairy Limits," *Mike*, 30 September 1966, 5.
74 On the context and philosophical underpinning of the free school movement that flourished between 1967 and 1972, see Miller, *Free Schools, Free People*.

75 Jasen, "'In Pursuit of Human Values."
76 Ian Mackenzie, cited in Mietkiewicz and Mackowycz, *Dream Tower*, 16.
77 On Ian Mackenzie's involvement in Indigenous issues, on his role in the initial years of Rochdale College, and on the creation of the Institute for Indian Studies, see Treat, *Around the Sacred Fire*, 83–113.
78 On the creation of Rochdale College, see Mietkiewicz and Mackowycz, *Dream Tower*, 7–23.
79 "Rochdale College Calendar 1967–1968," in "Publications and Misc. Essays," Box 5, T-10 00013, Thomas Fisher Rare Book Library (University of Toronto).
80 Philip McKenna, interview by author, 3 September 2009.
81 Another part-time resource person who should be mentioned was the conservative (and deeply Christian) hero of the New Left, George Grant. Grant's daughter, Rachel, had been a resident of Rochdale, but even after she left, Grant continued to take part in seminars at Rochdale. Christian, *George Grant: A Biography*, 272.
82 Brewster Kneen, interview.
83 Ibid.
84 Ibid.
85 CENSIT brochure, 1968, File "SUPA: Various Publications," Box 21, CUCND/SUPA Fonds, William Ready Archives.
86 In my interview with Brewster Kneen, he claimed CENSIT was initially independent, and a booklet published by CENSIT in the spring of 1970 describes the centre as "an independent study and action group." Kneen, *The Right Hand and the Left*.
87 Frerichs does not even recall an association between Rochdale and CENSIT. Frerichs, interview.
88 According to Kneen, "CENSIT was the first, and nearly only, organized voice to publicly condemn the War Measures Act." All members of CENSIT put their names to the document opposing Trudeau's invocation of the act. Brewster Kneen, email message to author, 17 March 2011.
89 Mietkiewicz and Mackowycz, *Dream Tower*, 35.
90 Jack Dimond, cited in Mietkiewicz and Mackowycz, *Dream Tower*, 22–3.
91 Henderson, "Off the Streets and into the Fortress."

CHAPTER SEVEN

1 Lehtonen, *Story of a Storm*, 306–10; "The World Scene," *Canadian Student*, Spring 1973, in File #40 "SCM Correspondence 1972–1977," Box 2004-016/007, in LAWG Fonds.

2 See Gitlin, *The Sixties*, 377–438; Kostash, *Long Way from Home*, 265–76; and Owram, *Born at the Right Time*, 280–307.
3 In *Radical Ambition*, Graham and McKay show that Toronto's New Left continued to thrive well beyond the sixties, evident in the plethora of groups devoted to various causes.
4 Gosse, *Rethinking the New Left*, 187–210.
5 Gitlin, *The Sixties*, 417.
6 Simpson and Phillips, "Understanding Student Protest in Canada," 59–67; and Lexier, "Canadian Student Movement," 308–16.
7 Gitlin, *The Sixties*, 381–403.
8 This is Todd Gitlin's contention (Gitlin, *The Sixties*, 409–11.) For a critical look at Trudeau's decision to turn Canada into a police state (albeit temporarily), and the effects of that decision, see Haggart and Golden, *Rumours of War*, 69–85; and Mills, *The Empire Within*, 175–186.
9 Herring, *America's Longest War*, 271–96.
10 Gitlin, *The Sixties*, 411.
11 Herring, *America's Longest War*, 323–40.
12 Milligan, *Rebel Youth*.
13 "A Student's Garden of Politics: Left, Right and Centre," *Varsity*, 18 September 1972.
14 Graham and McKay, *Radical Ambition*.
15 Betsy Anderson, interview by author, 26 May 2010.
16 Ibid.
17 Alan Rimmer, interview by author, 7 August 2012.
18 Foster, interview.
19 On McLeod, see chapter 6; on Scott, see Hayes, *Anglicans in Canada*, 75–6.
20 Hayes, *Anglicans in Canada*, 76.
21 "The United Church Votes Conservative," *Observer*, July 1972, 20–1.
22 "National Council 1970," Box 84–35, Student Christian Movement, United Church of Canada Archives.
23 I have located one extant copy of *The Canadian Student* (Spring 1973) in File #40 "SCM Correspondence 1972–1977," Box 2004-016/007, LAWG Fonds, Clara Thomas Archives, York University. It included features on Chile, a planned SCM educational trip to Cuba, and left-wing insurgency in the Dominican Republic.
24 Judy Skinner, interview by author, 12 May 2010; Anderson, interview by author. As well, Anderson was active in both LAWG and the University of Toronto chapter of SCM. See Anderson, interview with unspecified interviewer, Toronto, Ontario, 2014, available at the LAWG Hay Camino History Project.

25 Rimmer, interview.
26 One such trip was planned for August 1973, though it is not clear from the archival records whether these plans came to fruition. An SCM-sponsored trip did take place in late 1974, and the records indicate that a follow-up trip was planned. In my interview with Skinner, she indicated that she participated in two Cuba trips. See "Student Christian Movement of Canada," letter to SCM supporters from Brian Ruttan, Alan Rimmer, and Liz Brown, March 1973, in "Mrs Mary Rowell Jackman – SCM Correspondence, 1969–1975," Box 84-27, Student Christian Movement of Canada, United Church of Canada Archives; "Canadians to Go to Cuba," *Canadian Student*, Spring 1973, in File #40 "SCM Correspondence 1972–1977," Box 2004–016/007, in LAWG Fonds; and SCM National Council Minutes (Pigeon Lake, Alberta, 1975), 10, 12. I am thankful to Alan Rimmer for sharing the latter document with me.
27 Skinner, interview.
28 Ibid.
29 Sheinin, "Cuba's Long Shadow."
30 "Interview with John W. Foster, interview with unspecified interviewer, Ottawa, Ontario, February 2016, available at the LAWG Hay Camino History Project.
31 *Chile Versus the Corporations: A Call for Canadian Support* (January 1973), File #35 "Pamphlets and Newsletters, [197-]," Box 2004–016/001, LAWG Fonds.
32 *Chile Canada Solidarity Newsletter*, no. 6 (29 October 1972), in File #35 "Pamphlets and Newsletters, [197-]," Box 2004–016/001, LAWG Fonds.
33 Dan Mothersill, "Delay Recognition of Chile Regime, Churches Urge," *Catholic Register*, 29 September 1973, 1–2; and Terrence Belford, "Churches Criticize Canada's Policy on Chile," *Globe and Mail*, 4 October 1973, 4.
34 John W. Foster, "Canadians and the Coup," speech delivered at the Casa Salvador Allende 40th Anniversary Remembrance in Toronto, Ontario, September 2013, available at the LAWG Hay Camino History Project; George Cram, "The Political Prisoner Program," speech delivered at the Casa Salvador Allende 40th Anniversary Remembrance in Toronto, Ontario, 7 September 2013, available at the LAWG Hay Camino History Project. See also Sheinin and Lamble, "Discovering Dictatorship."
35 Foster, "Canadians and the Coup."
36 Rowland, "Introduction: The Theology of Liberation," 1–16. See also Gutiérrez, *A Theology of Liberation*.
37 Anderson, "A Canadian Perspective."

38 Anderson, interview by author.
39 "Liberation in a Christian Perspective," *Canadian Register*, 5 September 1970. Later published in Sheridan, *Do Justice*, 197–203.
40 Ibid.
41 It is outside of the scope of this study to explore these important themes. On poverty in Canada in this time period, see Adams, *The Real Poverty Report*. The literature on First Nations issues in the same period is immense; one representative example is Cardinal, *The Unjust Society*. On the French-Canadian left and the movement for an independent Quebec, see Mills, *The Empire Within*.
42 Granatstein, *Yankee Go Home?*, 12–66; Azzi, "Nationalist Moment in English Canada," 214–15.
43 Cited in Azzi, "Nationalist Moment in English Canada," 223.
44 Azzi, "Nationalist Moment in English Canada," 223–5; Churchill, "Draft Resisters, Left Nationalism." In *Radical Ambition*, Graham and McKay argue that Grant's influence on Laxer was not as formative as Laxer had claimed (76–8).
45 Granatstein, *Yankee Go Home?*, 192–216.
46 "A Student's Garden of Politics," *Varsity*, 18 September 1972; Granatstein, *Yankee Go Home?*, 212.
47 On the Waffle, see Graham and McKay, *Radical Ambition*, 174–9; Morton, *The New Democrats*, 75–143; Owram, *Born at the Right Time*, 299–304; and Palmer, *Canada's 1960s*, 289–97. For an example of the role of left nationalism in the New Left activism of the early seventies, see Milligan, *Rebel Youth*, 127–30.
48 "Waffle Manifesto," in Cross, ed., *The Decline and Fall of a Good Idea*, 43.
49 "A Student's Garden of Politics," *Varsity*, 18 September 1972.
50 "National Council 1970," Box 84-35, Inter-Church Collections: The Student Christian Movement of Canada (Don Kirkey, 1985), United Church of Canada Archives.
51 "Canadian SCM News" (October 1970), in 82-001 C, Box 143, File Two, United Church of Canada Archives.
52 Anderson, interview.
53 Rimmer, interview.
54 Ibid.
55 Anderson, "A Canadian Perspective," 405.
56 Letter to the editor, "Ashamed of Silence on Vietnam," *Catholic Register*, 20 January 1973.
57 See chapter 6.

58 Gordon K. Stewart, "Why I Shall Join the Next Peace March," *Observer*, 1 March 1970, 36.
59 "The World Scene," *Canadian Student*, Spring 1973, in File #40 "SCM Correspondence 1972–1977," Box 2004-016/007, in LAWG Fonds.
60 Ibid.
61 The *Canadian Churchman* carried several articles on this topic in its youth section (Trend) in July/August 1970: Francie Miller, "The Churches and the Draft"; Francie Miller, "The Ordinary Kids Who Said 'No'"; "Aids Centres for Draft Dodgers"; and "Charlie McKee Will never Go Home." For the Catholic and United Church press coverage, see Michael C. Orr, "Draft Dodgers," *Canadian Register*, 18 May 1968; Robert Marjoribanks, "Draft Dodgers: What Makes Them Run?," *Observer*, 1 September 1968, 12–15; John C. Lott, "You Cannot Christianize War," *Observer*, 15 March 1970, 16–17, 25, 40; Virginia Cunningham, "Our Son, the Deserter," *Observer*, November 1970, 29.
62 "Memorandum of a meeting held on Tuesday, December 30th, 1969 concerning US Draft Age Immigrants in Canada"; Canadian Council of Churches and National Council of Churches, "Joint Consultation on Pastoral Service with US Draft-Age Immigrants in Canada: A Report to Churches and Synagogues of the United States and Canada," 3 December 1969; "Consultation on US Draft Age Immigrants to Canada," 8 May 1970; and Canadian Council of Churches, ".. ..News.. .. ..! from Canadian Churches." All documents from File 9, Box 43, Board of Evangelism and Social Service Fonds, United Church of Canada Archives.
63 Letter, Maurice P. Wilkinson to E.E. Long, 7 April 1970, File 9, Box 43, Board of Evangelism and Social Service Fonds, United Church of Canada Archives.
64 Francie Miller, "A Second Chance for Disillusioned Americans," *Canadian Churchman*, May 1971.
65 "Anglicans Fail to Help," *Canadian Churchman*, July/August 1970.
66 "Anglican Assistance Granted for American Draft Dodgers," *Canadian Churchman*, November 1970.
67 "News Release of the United Church of Canada," 2 April 1971, File 8, Box 43, Board of Evangelism and Social Services Fonds, United Church of Canada Archives.
68 See letter, Gordon Stewart to Mr C.G. Abbey, 22 July 1971; and letter, Gordon Stewart to J.M. Fraser, 19 April 1971. File 8, Box 43, Board of Evangelism and Social Service Fonds, United Church of Canada Archives.
69 Maxwell, "Religion and Politics at the Border," 829. Likewise, in *Building Sanctuary*, Squires praises Canada's churches for their "remarkable" work

in assisting draft dodgers through the Canadian Council of Churches (49–54).
70 "News Release of the United Church of Canada," 2 April 1971.
71 A 1969 survey reported in *Christian Century* that while 74 percent of Canadian clergy favoured assistance to American draft resisters, only 48 percent of Canadian church members agreed. Cited in Maxwell, "Religion and Politics at the Border," 827.
72 Leonard Epp, "Draft Refugee Assignment: Report," March 1970, in File 9, Box 43, Board of Evangelism and Social Service Fonds, United Church of Canada Archives.
73 Statement of the Toronto Anti-Draft Programme (1970?), in File 3, Box 44, Board of Evangelism and Social Service Fonds, United Church of Canada Archives.
74 "Kudos," *American Exile in Canada* 1, no. 5 (10–23 November 1968): 8.
75 See chapters 4 and 6.
76 Pietlock was an active member of St Joan of Arc Roman Catholic Church in Toronto, where he served on the parish council. St Joan of Arc Church allowed Pietlock use of its Gestetner machine to copy one of the earliest issues of the *American Exile in Canada*. See "Kudos"; and Stan Pietlock, interview with author, 13 August 2012. On Pietlock as a war resister, see *America: Love It or Leave It*. On the role of UAE and the *American Exile in Canada* (often known in abbreviation as "AMEX"), see Young, "Defining a Community in Exile."
77 Maxwell, "Religion and Politics at the Border," 818.

CHAPTER EIGHT

1 Griesinger, "Jan Griesinger," in Evans, ed., *Journeys That Opened Up the World*, 191–2.
2 Ibid., 192–5.
3 Ibid., 195.
4 Ibid., 198.
5 Ibid., 200–1. See the beginning of chapter 7 for an overview of the WSCF's 1972 quadrennial conference.
6 Ibid., 206.
7 On women's liberation and gay liberation in the context of the sexual revolution, see McLeod, *Religious Crisis of the 1960s*, 161–87; Owram, *Born at the Right Time*, 248–79; and Sethna, "'Chastity Outmoded!'"
8 See chapter 6.
9 Hanisch, "The Personal Is Political."

10 Rebick, *Ten Thousand Roses*, 19.
11 Gosse, *Rethinking the New Left*, 161–5.
12 See Kostash, *Long Way from Home*, 172–9; Rebick, *Ten Thousand Roses*, 35–46; Sethna and Hewitt, "Clandestine Operations"; and Stettner, "'We Are Forced to Declare War.'"
13 One of the Royal Commission's recommendations was a national daycare program. Rebick, *Ten Thousand Roses*, 59.
14 Ibid., 60–5; and Foster, "Sussex Day Care," 101. See also Graham and McKay, *Radical Ambition*, 153–5.
15 Bagnell's article appeared in the *Observer* on 1 May 1970, when the Abortion Caravan was underway, and was likely written before the caravan began its journey. Nevertheless, it seems surprising that an issue so central to Canadian feminists at the beginning of the seventies merited only three words in a four-page feature on feminism. Bagnell, "The Feminists," 13.
16 Ibid., 15.
17 Ibid.
18 Korinek, "No Women Need Apply."
19 Patricia Clarke, "Women's Lib Hit the Church, in a Ladylike Way," *Observer*, April 1973, 6–7.
20 Fletcher-Marsh, *Beyond the Walled Garden*, 116–17.
21 The vote was preceded by an address to the assembly on "Christianity and Feminism" by Joanne Dewart, then a Roman Catholic theologian at St Michael's College. Hayes, *Anglicans in Canada*, 188–91, 303.
22 Fletcher-Marsh, *Beyond the Walled Garden*, 150.
23 Fr R. Drake Will, "Reader Asks about Women in the Ministry," *Canadian Register*, 27 November 1971; Elizabeth Hudson, "A Woman's Dignity, Rights: A Balance Please," *Catholic Register*, 20 April 1974; Elizabeth Hudson, "Women Priests: 'Attitudes Must Change First,'" *Catholic Register*, 8 June 1974.
24 Daly, *Remembering for Tomorrow*, 78–80.
25 McLeod, *Religious Crisis of the 1960s*, 197.
26 These included Bishop Emmett Carter of London (later archbishop of Toronto) and Aloysius Ambrozic (later Carter's successor as archbishop of Toronto). Conservatives such as Carter and Ambrozic argued that the ideal role model for women was the Virgin Mary because of her submissiveness. Higgins and Letson, *My Father's Business*, 118–21.
27 Sacred Congregation for the Doctrine of the Faith, *Declaration Inter Insigniores on the Question of Admission of Women to the Ministerial Priesthood*.

28 MacGuigan, *Abortion, Conscience and Democracy*, 36–45; and Bakke, *When Children Became People*, 110–39.
29 MacGuigan, *Abortion, Conscience and Democracy*, 45–6; and United Church of Canada, *Abortion: A Study*, 13
30 Stettner and Douville, "'In the Image and Likeness of God.'"
31 MacGuigan, *Abortion, Conscience and Democracy*, 36–7; and United Church of Canada, *Abortion: A Study*, 8–9.
32 Canadian Catholic Conference, "Pastoral Statement on Proposed Change of Canadian Law on Abortion," in Sheridan, ed., *Love Kindness!*, 135–41.
33 Ibid., 136.
34 Cuneo, *Catholics against the Church*.
35 "No Deadlier Sin," *Canadian Register*, 17 May 1969.
36 Task Force on Human Life, *Abortion: An Issue for Conscience*, 41.
37 Ibid., 9–10.
38 Ibid., 42–3.
39 Ibid., 28–9, 37.
40 Ibid., 38.
41 For a fuller exploration of the United Church's evolving response to the abortion issue in these years, see Ackerman, Douville, and Stettner, "'Is Abortion Ever Right?'"
42 Rebick, *Ten Thousand Roses*, 35–46.
43 United Church of Canada, *Abortion: A Study*, iii–iv.
44 Ibid., iv; Ackerman, Douville, and Stettner, "'Is Abortion Ever Right?,'" 56.
45 United Church of Canada, *Abortion: A Study*, 39–40.
46 A.C. Forrest and Patricia Clarke, "Abortion: The United Church's Official Position Should Be Changed," *Observer*, February 1972, 10–11.
47 Letters to the editor, *Observer*, April 1972, 7–9.
48 United Church of Canada, *Twenty-Fifth General Council*, 89–91.
49 "Church Passes Quebec Report, Abortion Study," *Globe and Mail*, 22 August 1972; "No Change on Abortion: Up to Woman and Doctor," *Observer*, October 1972, 19.
50 United Church of Canada, *Twenty-Fifth General Council*, 169.
51 Ackerman, Douville, and Stettner, "'Is Abortion Ever Right?,'" 59–60.
52 Wyatt, "The 1970s," 130.
53 Ibid., 174.
54 For example, in a letter to a United Church official, a writer identified herself as a member of the Ad Hoc Committee of United Church People for Life. Kathryn Schlatter, Ancaster, ON, to Secretary, General Council, United Church of Canada, Rev. George Morrison, 12 October 1974, Accession 82.160C, Box 1, File 6: Commission on Abortion,

Correspondence, 1974, United Church of Canada Archives. See also Ackerman, Douville, and Stettner, "'Is Abortion Ever Right?,'" 60.

55 New Left groups that incorporated a women's liberationist perspective into their critique included the New Left Caucus at the University of Toronto; the Waffle faction of the NDP; and Trotskyite groups such as the League for Socialist Action. Owram, *Born at the Right Time*, 296, 302; Palmer, *Canada's 1960s*, 297–304; and Sangster, "Radical Ruptures."
56 Foster, "Notes on a Northbound Subway" (Toronto, 1969); and Foster, "Sussex Daycare," 99–108. I am thankful to John Foster for providing me with a copy of the former essay.
57 Skinner, interview.
58 *Women Unite!*, 13; Anderson, interview.
59 Leueen Macdonald, cited in Adamson, "Feminists, Libbers, Lefties, and Radicals," 262.
60 "National Council Minutes, 1974," Box 84–35, Student Christian Movement of Canada, United Church of Canada Archives.
61 Anderson, "A Canadian Perspective," 405.
62 Anderson, interview.
63 Gosse, *Rethinking the New Left*, 175; Tom Warner, *Never Going Back*, 42–6.
64 Kinsman and Gentile, *The Canadian War on Queers*, 1–220.
65 Kinsman, *The Regulation of Desire*, 213–78.
66 Ibid., 161–5.
67 Ibid., 213–78.
68 Gosse, *Rethinking the New Left*, 176–80.
69 Warner, *Never Going Back*, 59–60.
70 Kinsman, *Regulation of Desire*, 291.
71 Ibid.
72 Graham and McKay, *Radical Ambition*, 307–20; Warner, *Never Going Back*, 66–93.
73 Warner, *Never Going Back*, 92; Averill, "The Church, Gays, and Archives," 87.
74 McLeod, *Lesbian and Gay Liberation*, 172.
75 Warner, *Never Going Back*, 92.
76 "MCC Toronto Mission Opens," *Body Politic*, 1 June 1973.
77 Leviticus 18:22; Leviticus 20:13. Some theologians, such as Daniel Helminiak, claim that the Bible does not condemn homosexuality, arguing that the biblical passages pertaining to homosexuality have been misunderstood. Furthermore, the late historian John Boswell argued the Church did not condemn homosexuality prior to the twelfth century.

Such arguments have generated much controversy among biblical scholars (such as Robert Gagnon, who defends the conservative interpretation), historians, and ordinary Christians on either side of the "culture war" divide. The debates over homosexuality and the Bible, or homosexuality and the early church, are beyond the scope of this dissertation, but the following works provide an overview: Boswell, *Christianity, Social Tolerance, and Homosexuality*; Gagnon, *The Bible and Homosexual Practice*; and Helminiak, *What the Bible Really Says*. For a broader examination of Christianity and sexuality throughout history, see Kamitsuka, ed., *The Embrace of Eros*.

78 See, for example, "Homosexuality Sin; Not Crime – Church Panel," *Toronto Star*, 10 March 1964; "Church Council Aims to Aid Homosexuals," *Globe and Mail*, 2 June 1965.
79 "Hang Homosexuals, Fundamentalist Says," *Globe and Mail*, 7 January 1966; "Minister: Toronto Homosexual Centre," *Toronto Star*, 31 January 1966.
80 Rick Bébout, "1972."
81 "MCC Toronto Mission Opens," *Body Politic*, 1 June 1973.
82 That same year, Baum would also publish a gay-positive piece, "Catholic Homosexuals," in *Commonweal*, a lay Catholic journal. See McLeod, *Lesbian and Gay Liberation*, 153, 156.
83 "Don't Prejudge Homosexuals, Moderator Says," *Toronto Star*, 9 March 1974.
84 Gardner, "A Holy or a Broken Hallelujah," 145.
85 Hannum, cited in Gardner, "A Holy or a Broken Hallelujah," 171.
86 Ibid., 172–3, 181–3; Mervyn Dickinson, "The Church and the Homosexual," *Observer*, 15 November 1965, 22.
87 "Accept Homosexuals; But Don't Approve Homosexual Acts," *Observer*, December 1971, 11.
88 Sacred Congregation for the Doctrine of the Faith, *Persona Humana*, section 8. Homosexuality was only one of the matters discussed in this statement on human sexuality.
89 Jocelyn Dingman, "Takeover at the SCM," *Observer*, 15 June 1967, 10.
90 Young, *Beginnings of Gay Liberation*, 1.
91 Ibid., 1–2.
92 Ibid., 2.
93 Erlichman, interview.
94 All of my examples are male. While it is likely that there were lesbian-identified members of the SCM in the sixties and seventies, none of my interviewees mentioned any by name.

95 Lee, "Straight to Gay," in *Love's Gay Fool*; interviews with Erlichman, Caloren (9 April 2009), Lee, and Frerichs.
96 "National Council Minutes 1974," Box 84-35, Student Christian Movement, United Church of Canada Archives.
97 Interviews with Frerichs, Skinner, and Anderson.
98 Ian Young, interview by author, 21 July 2010.
99 Anderson, interview.
100 Graham and McKay *Radical Ambition*, 316-20; Kinsman and Gentile, *Canadian War on Queers*, 272-83.
101 Cathleen Kneen, "Self-Fulfilling Prophecy, or How to Approach the Saksatoon Meetings," SUPA Newsletter, 21 December 1965, "SUPA 1965-1966," B1979-0047, University of Toronto Archives. These observations are doubly ironic, since Kneen would later become heavily involved in the women's movement, which popularized the slogan "the personal is political."
102 The SCM's lack of engagement with either women's liberation or gay liberation in the early 1970s remains puzzling to me. In this matter, Canadians in the SCM lagged behind their American counterparts. The answers that I have proposed here are speculative, and more research is needed.
103 For example, see Macourt, *Towards a Theology of Gay Liberation*.
104 Bruce McLeod, "What We Think of *Your* Church," *Observer*, November 1972, 16-19, 42.

CHAPTER NINE

1 McLeod, *Religious Crisis of the 1960s*.
2 Williams, ed., *Canadian Churches and Social Justice*.
3 See chapter 6.
4 Obituary in *Winnipeg Free Press*, 16 July 2010.
5 Foster, interview.
6 Hannum, interview; Kuyek, interview. One of the products of this project was Kuyek's book, *Fighting for Hope*.
7 Hayes, *Anglicans in Canada*, 75-6.
8 Ibid., 76.
9 Treat, *Around the Sacred Fire*.
10 Higgins and Letson, *Power and Peril*; Kung and Swidler, eds, *The Church in Anguish*.
11 Bisson, "Towards a Canadian Contextual Ecclesiology"; and Leddy, *Say to the Darkness*.
12 Williams, ed., *Canadian Churches and Social Justice*, 3-8; and Wyatt, "The 1970s," 127-9.

13 Foster, interview. KAIROS is not to be confused with the earlier United Church youth organization Kairos. They are two separate entities.
14 Janice Acton and Betsy Anderson, "The LAWG Solidarity Story," available at the LAWG Hay Camino History Project.
15 Hartwell, interview.
16 Gentles, interview.
17 Chow, *My Journey: A Memoir*, 51–4.
18 Wyatt, "The 1970s," 130–2.
19 Ibid.
20 On feminism and inclusive language in the United Church, see United Church of Canada, *Guidelines for Inclusive Language*; and Whynot, "Liberating Christianity." On the hymnal, see *Voices United*; and Walker, "Diversity, Diversity, All Is Diversity."
21 By a conservative estimate, approximately 25,000 individuals left the United Church in the wake of the 1988 decision, but as Ross Bartlett notes, some may have departed for reasons other than (or in addition to) the ordination of gay and lesbian clergy. The overall decline in membership is undeniable: from 3.7 million members in 1981, to 3 million members in 1991, to 2 million members in 2011. See Riordan, *The First Stone*; Bartlett, "1990–2003," 164–8; and Clarke and Macdonald, *Leaving Christianity*, 58.
22 Michael Adams, "The Word, Unheeded," *Globe and Mail*, 15 August 2003.
23 Airhart, *Serving the Present Age*; Allen, *The Social Passion*.
24 McLeod, *Religious Crisis of the 1960s*, 161–239. These developments culminated in federal recognition of same-sex marriage in 2005.
25 Warner, *Never Going Back*, 197, 218–46.
26 Riordan, *The First Stone*, 40.
27 Ibid., 59–60.
28 One only has to peruse the monthly issues of the *Anglican Journal* over the past fifteen years to recognize the depth of division occasioned in the Anglican Church of Canada by issues of sexuality.
29 Clarke and Macdonald, *Leaving Christianity*, 34.
30 Ibid., 124–5.
31 Ibid., 138.
32 Ibid., 110–19.
33 Statistics Canada, *2001 Census: analysis series – Religions in Canada*, 7. Available at https://www12.statcan.gc.ca/access_acces/archive.action-eng.cfm?/english/census01/products/analytic/companion/rel/pdf/96F0030XIE2001015.pdf. Accessed 2 December 2019.

34 Ibid., 9. See also Clarke and Macdonald, *Leaving Christianity*, 168–73.
35 Higgins and Letson, *Power and Peril*, 269–72.
36 McLeod, *Religious Crisis of the 1960s*, 260–1.
37 On the relative success of conservative Protestant churches in Canada since the 1960s, see Clarke and Macdonald, *Leaving Christianity*, 72–121.
38 The sociologist Christian Smith argues that religious groups succeed in modern, pluralistic societies when they function as subcultures "that offer satisfying morally orienting collective identities which provide adherents meaning and belonging." The growth of evangelical denominations from the 1960s to the 1990s, especially when compared to the declining number of adherents among mainline Protestant churches, suggests that Smith's subcultural identity theory has merit. See Smith, *American Evangelicalism*, 118.
39 For a study of the spirituality of current feminist activists, see Laurel Zwissler, "Spiritual, but Religious." Ironically, Zwissler argues that for activists in the present day, "spirituality" is publicly acceptable discourse, while "religion," because of its specificity, is private. This is a reversal of the traditionally understood dichotomy between public religion and private spirituality.
40 Turner, *There Can Be No Light without Shadows*, 78.

Bibliography

ARCHIVAL COLLECTIONS

Archives of the Roman Catholic Archdiocese of Toronto, Toronto
Clara Thomas Archives, York University, Toronto
General Synod Archives, Anglican Church of Canada, Toronto
Thomas Fisher Rare Book Library, University of Toronto, Toronto
United Church of Canada Archives, Toronto
University of Toronto Archives, Toronto
William Ready Archives, McMaster University, Hamilton

CONTEMPORARY JOURNALS, MAGAZINES, AND NEWSPAPERS

American Exile in Canada (Toronto)
Anglican (Anglican Diocese of Toronto)
Body Politic (Toronto)
Canadian (Montreal)
Canadian Baptist (Baptist Convention of Ontario and Quebec)
Canadian Churchman (Anglican Church of Canada)
Canadian Register/Catholic Register (Roman Catholic Archdiocese of Toronto)
Canadian Student (Student Christian Movement of Canada)
Globe and Mail (Toronto)
Maclean's Magazine (Toronto)
Mike (St Michael's College, University of Toronto)
Observer (United Church of Canada)
Our Generation (Montreal)

Presbyterian Record (Presbyterian Church in Canada)
Sanity (Montreal)
Time Magazine (New York City)
Toronto Star
Ubyssey (University of British Columbia)
Varsity (University of Toronto)

INTERVIEWS CONDUCTED BY AUTHOR

Anderson, Betsy. 26 May 2010 (Toronto, Ontario)
Caloren, Fred. 31 March 2009 and 9 April 2009 (Markham, Ontario); 11 April 2009 (by phone)
Erlichman, Wolfe. 2 April 2009 (by phone)
Faulkner, Tom. 11 May 2010 (by Skype)
Foster, John W. 9 February 2009 (Ottawa, Ontario)
Frerichs, Eilert. 18 June 2009 (Whitby, Ontario)
Gentles, Ian. 1 February 2009 (Toronto, Ontario)
Hannum, Nancy. 4 June 2009 (by phone)
Hartwell, George. 21 August 2009 (Mississauga, Ontario)
Hyde, Richard. 2 June 2009 (by phone)
Jolly, Stan. 10 August 2009 (Markham, Ontario)
Kealey, Linda. 30 July 2009 (by phone)
Kneen, Brewster. 9 February 2009 (Ottawa, Ontario)
Kneen, Cathleen. 9 February 2009 (Ottawa, Ontario)
Kutz, Stan. 4 February 2009 (Toronto, Ontario)
Kuyek, Joan Newman. 9 February 2009 (Ottawa, Ontario)
Lee, John Alan. 24 February 2009 (Toronto, Ontario)
McKenna, Philip. 3 September 2009 (Toronto, Ontario)
Mackenzie, Ian. 19 October 2009 (by phone)
Pietlock, Stan. 13 August 2012 (Toronto, Ontario)
Rimmer, Alan. 7 August 2012 (Toronto, Ontario)
Roussopoulos, Dimitri. 11 February 2009 (Montreal, Quebec)
Schmidt, Ted. 27 April 2009 (Toronto, Ontario)
Shepherd, Harvey. 11 February 2009 (Montreal, Quebec)
Skinner, Judy. 12 May 2010 (Toronto, Ontario)
Ward, Doug. 10 February 2009 (Ottawa, Ontario)
Warrian, Peter. 4 February 2009 (by phone)
Whitla, William. 17 February 2011 (by phone)
Young, Ian. 21 July 2010 (Toronto, Ontario)

BOOKS, ARTICLES, THESES, AND OTHER MEDIA SOURCES

Abzug, Robert. *Cosmos Crumbling: American Reform and the Religious Imagination.* New York: Oxford University Press, 1994.

Ackerman, Katrina, Bruce Douville, and Shannon Stettner. "'Is Abortion Ever Right?': The United Church of Canada and the Debate over Abortion Law Reform, 1960–1980." In *No Place for the State*, edited by Christopher Dummitt and Christabelle Sethna, 52–73. Vancouver: University of British Columbia Press, 2020.

Adams, Ian. *The Real Poverty Report.* Edmonton: M.G. Hurtig Ltd, 1971.

Adamson, Nancy. "Feminists, Libbers, Lefties, and Radicals: The Emergence of the Women's Liberation Movement." In *A Diversity of Women: Ontario, 1945–1980*, edited by Joy Parr, 252–80. Toronto: University of Toronto Press, 1995.

– Linda Briskin, and Margaret McPhail. *Feminist Organizing for Change: The Contemporary Women's Movement in Canada.* Toronto: Oxford University Press, 1988.

Airhart, Phyllis. *Church with the Soul of a Nation: Making and Remaking the United Church of Canada.* Montreal & Kingston: McGill-Queen's University Press, 2014.

– "Ordering a New Nation and Reordering Protestantism, 1867–1914." In *The Canadian Protestant Experience, 1760–1990*, edited by George Rawlyk, 98–138. Montreal & Kingston: McGill-Queen's University Press, 1990.

– *Serving the Present Age: Revivalism, Progressivism, and the Methodist Tradition in Canada.* Montreal & Kingston: McGill-Queen's University Press, 1992.

Alinsky, Saul. *Reveille for Radicals.* Chicago: University of Chicago Press, 1946.

Allen, Richard. *The Social Passion: Religion and Reform in Canada, 1914–1928.* Toronto: University of Toronto Press, 1971.

– *The View from Murney Tower: Salem Bland, the Late Victorian Controversies, and the Search for a New Christianity.* Toronto: University of Toronto Press, 2008.

America: Love It or Leave It, video documentary directed by Kirwan Cox and Tom Shandel. Alioli Films, 1991.

Anderson, Betsy. "A Canadian Perspective on the WSCF North American Region." *Journal of Ecumenical Studies* 32, no. 3 (Summer 1995): 402–5.

- "The Place Where 'Men' Earn Their Bread Is to Be the Place of Holiness." *Historical Papers: Canadian Society of Church History* (2011): 129–50.
Anderson, Terry H. *The Movement and the Sixties*. New York: Oxford University Press, 1995.
Anglican Church of Canada. *Journal of Proceedings of the General Synod, Twenty-Second Session*. Toronto: Anglican Church of Canada, 1965.
Averill, Harold. "The Church, Gays, and Archives." *Archivaria* 30 (Summer 1990): 85–90.
Axelrod, Paul. *Making a Middle Class: Student Life in English Canada during the Thirties*. Montreal & Kingston: McGill-Queen's University Press, 1990.
Azzi, Stephen. "The Nationalist Moment in English Canada." In Campbell, Clément, and Kealey, *Debating Dissent*, 213–28.
Bakke, Odd Magne. *When Children Became People: The Birth of Childhood in Early Christianity*. Minneapolis: Fortress Press, 2005.
Bartlett, Ross. "1990–2003: The Church into the New Millennium." In Schweitzer, *The United Church of Canada*, 161–81.
Bass, Dorothy C. "Revolutions, Quiet and Otherwise: Protestants and Higher Education during the 1960s." In *Caring for the Commonweal: Education for Religious and Public Life*, edited by Parker J. Palmer, Barbara G. Wheeler, and James W. Fowler, 207–26. Macon: Mercer University Press, 1990.
Baum, Gregory. *Catholics and Canadian Socialism: Political Thought in the Thirties and Forties*. Toronto: James Lorimer & Company, 1980.
Beardsall, Sandra. "'And Whether Pigs Have Wings': The United Church in the 1960s." In Schweitzer, *The United Church of Canada*, 97–117.
- "Ray Hord: 'Prophet Evangelist' of the United Church." *Touchstone* 24, no. 3 (September 2006): 48–59.
Beattie, Margaret. *A Brief History of the Student Christian Movement in Canada*. Toronto: SCM Canada, 1975.
Bébout, Rick. "1972." In *Promiscuous Affections: A Life in the Bar, 1969–2000*. Available at http://rbebout.com/bar/1972.htm. Accessed 1 July 2020.
Belliveau, Joel. "Tradition, libéralisme et communautarisme durant les 'Trente glorieuses': Les étudiants de Moncton et l'entrée dans la modernité avancée des francophones du Nouveau-Brunswick, 1957–1969." PhD diss., Université de Montréal, 2008.
Bengston, Vern L. "The Generation Gap: A Review and Typology of Social-Psychological Perspectives." *Youth and Society* 2, no. 1 (September 1970): 7–32.

Berger, Peter. *The Sacred Canopy: Elements of a Sociological Theory of Religion*. Garden City: Doubleday & Company, Inc., 1967.
– Grace Davie, and Effie Fokas. *Religious America, Secular Europe? A Theme and Variations*. Aldershot: Ashgate Publishing Limited, 2008.
Berrigan, Philip, and Fred A. Wilcox. *Fighting the Lamb's War – Skirmishes with the American Empire: The Autobiography of Philip Berrigan*. Monroe, ME: Common Courage Press, 1996.
Berton, Pierre. *The Comfortable Pew*. Toronto: McClelland and Stewart Limited, 1965.
Bibby, Reginald W. *Fragmented Gods: The Poverty and Potential of Religion in Canada*. Toronto: Irwin Publishing, 1987.
Bissell, Claude. *Halfway Up Parnassus: A Personal Account of the University of Toronto, 1932–1971*. Toronto: University of Toronto Press, 1974.
Bisson, Diane. "Towards a Canadian Contextual Ecclesiology: The Contribution of *Catholic New Times* (1976–1993)." PhD diss., Toronto School of Theology, 1996.
Black, Robert Merrill. "Inwardly Renewed: The Emergence of Modernity in the Diocese of Toronto, 1939–1989." In *By Grace Co-Workers: Building the Anglican Diocese of Toronto, 1780–1989*, edited by Alan Hayes, 97–138. Toronto: Anglican Book Centre, 1989.
Bland, Salem Goldworth. *The New Christianity, or, The Religion of the New Age*. Toronto: McClelland and Stewart, 1920.
Bonhoeffer, Dietrich. *Letters and Papers from Prison*. Edited by Eberhard Bethge and translated by Reginald H. Fuller. New York: Macmillan Company, 1953.
Boswell, John. *Christianity, Social Tolerance, and Homosexuality: Gay People in Western Europe from the Beginning of the Christian Era to the Fourteenth Century*. Chicago: University of Chicago Press, 1980.
Brake, Michael. *Comparative Youth Culture: The Sociology of Youth Culture and Youth Subcultures in America, Britain and Canada*. New York: Routledge and Kegan Paul Inc., 1985.
Braunstein, Peter, and Michael William Doyle. "Historicizing the American Counterculture of the 1960s and '70s." In *Imagine Nation: The American Counterculture of the 1960s and '70s*, edited by Peter Braunstein and Michael William Doyle, 5–14. New York: Routledge, 2002.
Breines, Wini. *Community and Organization in the New Left, 1962–1968: The Great Refusal*. New Brunswick: Rutgers University Press, 1989.
Brouwer, Ruth Compton. "When Missions Became Development: Ironies of 'NGOization' in Mainstream Canadian Churches in the 1960s." *Canadian Historical Review* 91, no. 4 (December 2010): 661–93.

Brown, Callum. *The Death of Christian Britain: Understanding Secularization, 1800–2000.* 2nd ed. London and New York: Routledge, 2009.

Brushett, Kevin. "Making Shit Disturbers: The Selection and Training of the Company of Young Canadian Volunteers, 1965–1970." In Palaeologu, *The Sixties in Canada,* 246–69.

Campbell, Lara, Dominique Clément, and Gregory S. Kealey, eds. *Debating Dissent: Canada and the Sixties.* Toronto: University of Toronto Press, 2012.

Cardinal, Harold. *The Unjust Society: The Tragedy of Canada's Indians.* Edmonton: M.G. Hurtig Ltd, 1969.

Casanova, José. *Public Religions in the Modern World.* Chicago: University of Chicago Press, 1994.

Chafe, William H. *Civilities and Civil Rights: Greensboro, North Carolina, and the Black Struggle for Freedom.* Oxford: Oxford University Press, 1981.

Chow, Olivia. *My Journey: A Memoir.* Toronto: HarperCollins, 2014.

Christian, William. *George Grant: A Biography.* Toronto: University of Toronto, 1993.

Christie, Nancy, and Michael Gauvreau. "'Even the hippies were only very slowly going secular': Dechristianization and the Culture of Individualism in North America and Western Europe." In *The Sixties and Beyond: Dechristianization in North America and Western Europe, 1945–2000,* edited by Nancy Christie and Michael Gauvreau, 3–26. Toronto: University of Toronto, 2013.

– *A Full-Orbed Christianity: The Protestant Churches and Social Welfare in Canada, 1900–1940.* Montreal & Kingston: McGill-Queen's University Press, 1996.

Churchill, David. "An Ambiguous Welcome: Vietnam Draft Resistance, the Canadian State, and Cold War Containment." *Social History/Histoire Sociale* 37, no. 73 (2004): 1–25.

– "American Expatriates and the Building of Alternative Social Space in Toronto, 1965–1977." *Urban History Review* 39, no. 1 (Fall 2010): 31–44.

– "Draft Resisters, Left Nationalism, and the Politics of Anti-Imperialism." *Canadian Historical Review* 93, no. 2 (June 2012): 227–60.

– "SUPA, Selma, and Stevenson: The Politics of Solidarity in mid-1960s Toronto." *Journal of Canadian Studies* 44, no. 2 (Spring 2010): 32–69.

Claiborne, Shane, and Chris Haw. *Jesus for President: Politics for Ordinary Radicals.* Grand Rapids: Zondervan, 2008.

Clarke, Brian P. *Piety and Nationalism: Lay Voluntary Associations and the Creation of an Irish-Catholic Community in Toronto, 1850–1895.* Montreal & Kingston: McGill-Queen's University Press, 1993.

Clarke, Brian P., and Stuart Macdonald. *Leaving Christianity: Changing Allegiances in Canada since 1945.* Montreal & Kingston: McGill-Queen's University Press, 2017.

Clarke, Patricia. "Ray Hord: A Prophet ahead of His Time." *Mission Magazine*, 1981, 13–15.

Cockburn, Bruce, and Greg King. *Rumours of Glory: A Memoir.* Toronto: HarperCollins Publishers Ltd, 2014.

Comacchio, Cynthia. *The Dominion of Youth: Adolescence and the Making of Modern Canada, 1920 to 1950.* Waterloo: Wilfrid Laurier University Press, 2006.

Cook, Ramsay. *The Regenerators: Social Criticism in Late Victorian English Canada.* Toronto: University of Toronto Press, 1985.

Cox, Harvey. *The Secular City: Secularization and Urbanization in Theological Perspective.* New York: Macmillan, 1965.

Cross, Michael, ed. *The Decline and Fall of a Good Idea: CCF-NDP Manifestoes, 1932–1969.* Toronto: New Hogtown Press, 1974.

Crysdale, Stewart. *Churches Where the Action Is: Churches and People in Canadian Situations.* Toronto: United Church Publishing House, 1966.

Cuneo, Michael. *Catholics against the Church: Anti-Abortion Protest in Toronto, 1969–1985.* Toronto: University of Toronto Press, 1989.

Daly, Bernard. *Remembering for Tomorrow: A History of the Canadian Conference of Catholic Bishops, 1943–1993.* Ottawa: Canadian Conference of Catholic Bishops, 1995.

Daly, Margaret. *The Revolution Game: The Short, Unhappy Life of the Company of Young Canadians.* Toronto: New Press, 1970.

Daniels, Dan. "The Cultural Revolution." *Our Generation* 7, no. 3 (1970): 115–41.

Danielson, Leilah. "'It Is a Day of Judgment': The Peacemakers, Religion, and Radicalism in Cold War America." *Religion and American Culture: A Journal of Interpretation* 18, no. 2 (Summer 2008): 215–48.

Davis, Bob. "Before Browndale." In *This Book Is about Schools*, edited by Satu Repo, 227–239. New York: Random House, 1970.

Dickenson, Carrie A., and William J. Campbell. "'Strange Bedfellows': Youth Activists, Government Sponsorship, and the Company of Young Canadians (CYC), 1965–1970." *European Journal of Canadian Studies*, 2008, Special Issue May '68. Available at https://journals.openedition.org/ejas/2862. Accessed 18 December 2019.

Didion, Joan. "Slouching towards Bethlehem." In *Slouching towards Bethlehem*, 84–128. New York: Farrar, Straus and Giroux, 1968.

Dixon, Robert T. *We Remember, We Believe: A History of Toronto's Catholic Separate School Boards, 1841 to 1997*. Toronto: Toronto Catholic District School Board, 2008.

Douville, Bruce. "Project La Macaza: A Study of Two Canadian Peace Protests in the 1960s." In *Worth Fighting For: Canada's Tradition of War Resistance from 1812 to the War on Terror*, edited by Lara Campbell, Michael Dawson, and Catherine Gidney, 161–71. Toronto: Between the Lines, 2015.

Dubinsky, Karen, Catherine Krull, Susan Lord, Sean Mills, and Scott Rutherford, eds. *New World Coming: The Sixties and the Shaping of Global Consciousness*. Toronto: Between the Lines, 2009.

Dufresne, Michael Maurice. "'Let's Not Be Cremated Equal': The Combined Universities Campaign for Nuclear Disarmament, 1959–1967." In Palaeologu, *The Sixties in Canada*, 9–64.

Dylan, Bob. *The Times They Are a-Changin'*. Columbia Records, 1964.

Ellwood, Robert. *The Sixties Spiritual Awakening: American Religion Moving from Modern to Postmodern*. New Brunswick, NJ: Rutgers University Press, 1994.

Evans, Sara M., ed. *Journeys That Opened Up the World: Women, Student Christian Movements, and Social Justice, 1955–1975*. New Brunswick: Rutgers University Press, 2003.

– *Personal Politics: The Roots of Women's Liberation in the Civil Rights Movement and the New Left*. New York: Alfred A. Knopf, 1979.

Fay, Terence J. *A History of Canadian Catholics*. Toronto: University of Toronto Press, 2002.

Fentress, James, and Chris Wickham. *Social Memory*. Cambridge, MA: Blackwell, 1992.

Flatt, Kevin. *After Evangelicalism: The Sixties and the United Church of Canada*. Montreal & Kingston: McGill-Queen's University Press, 2013.

Fletcher-Marsh, Wendy. *Beyond the Walled Garden: Anglican Women and the Priesthood*. Dundas, ON: Artemis Enterprises, 1995.

Foster, John. "Sussex Day Care." In *Women Unite! An Anthology of the Canadian Women's Movement*, 99–108. Toronto: Canadian Women's Educational Press, 1971.

Frost, Jennifer. *"An Interracial Movement of the Poor": Community Organizing and the New Left in the 1960s*. New York: New York University Press, 2001.

Gagnon, Robert. *The Bible and Homosexual Practice: Texts and Hermeneutics.* Nashville: Abingdon Press, 2001.

Gardner, Philip. "A Holy or a Broken Hallelujah: The United Church of Canada in the 1960s Decade of Ferment." PhD diss., Toronto School of Theology, 2018.

Garrows, David. *Bearing the Cross: Martin Luther King, Jr and the Southern Christian Leadership Conference.* New York: W. Morrow, 1986.

Gauvreau, Michael. *The Catholic Origins of Quebec's Quiet Revolution, 1931–1970.* Montreal & Kingston: McGill-Queen's University Press, 2005.

– *The Evangelical Century: College and Creed in English Canada from the Great Revival to the Great Depression.* Montreal & Kingston: McGill-Queen's University Press, 1991.

– "The Protracted Birth of the Canadian 'Teenager': Work, Citizenship, and the Canadian Youth Commission, 1945–1955." In *Cultures of Citizenship in Post-war Canada*, edited by Nancy Christie and Michael Gauvreau, 201–38. Montreal & Kingston: McGill-Queen's University Press, 1996.

Ghent, Jocelyn Maynard. "Did He Fall or Was He Pushed? The Kennedy Administration and the Collapse of the Diefenbaker Government." *International History Review* 1, no. 2 (April 1979): 246–70.

Gidney, Catherine. *A Long Eclipse: The Liberal Protestant Establishment and the Canadian University, 1920–1970.* Montreal & Kingston: McGill-Queen's University Press, 2004.

– "Poisoning the Student Mind? The Student Christian Movement at the University of Toronto, 1920–1965." *Journal of the Canadian Historical Association* 7, no. 1 (1997): 147–63.

Gidney, R.D. *From Hope to Harris: The Reshaping of Ontario's Schools.* Toronto: University of Toronto, 1999.

Gidney, R.D., and W.P.J. Millar. "The Christian Recessional in Ontario's Public Schools." In Van Die, *Religion and Public Life in Canada*, 275–93.

Gitlin, Todd. *The Sixties: Years of Hope, Days of Rage.* New York: Bantam, 1993.

Goodbrand, Grant. *Therafields: The Rise and Fall of Lea Hindley-Smith's Psychoanalytic Commune.* Toronto: ECW Press, 2010.

Gosse, Van. *Rethinking the New Left: An Interpretive History.* New York: Palgrave MacMillan, 2005.

Graham, Peter, and Ian McKay. *Radical Ambition: The New Left in Toronto*. Toronto: Between the Lines, 2019.

Granatstein, J.L. *Yankee Go Home? Canadians and Anti-Americanism*. Toronto: Harper Collins, 1996.

Grant, John Webster. *The Church in the Canadian Era*. 2nd ed. Burlington, ON: Welch Publishing Company Inc., 1988.

Grayson, J. Paul. "'Remember Now Thy Creator in the Days of Thy Youth': The Quiet Religious Revolution on a Canadian Campus in the 1960s." *Historical Studies in Education* 23, no. 2 (Fall 2011): 87–112.

Griesinger, Jan. "Jan Griesinger." In Evans, *Journeys That Opened Up the World*, 191–207.

Gutierrez, Gustavo. *A Theology of Liberation: History, Politics and Salvation*. Translated and edited by Sister Caridad Inda and John Eagleson. Maryknoll: Orbis Books, 1973.

Haggart, Ron, and Aubrey E. Golden. *Rumours of War*. Toronto: New Press, 1971.

Hanisch, Carol. "The Personal Is Political." In *Notes from the Second Year: Women's Liberation*, edited by Shulamith Firestone and Anne Koedt, 76–8. New York, 1970.

Harding, James. "An Ethical Movement in Search of an Analysis: The Student Union for Peace Action in Canada." *Our Generation* 3 and 4 (May 1966): 20–9.

Harris, Ruth. "Ruth Harris." In Evans, *Journeys That Opened Up the World*, 15–44.

Harrison, Ernest Wilfrid. *A Church without God*. Philadelphia: Lippincott, 1967.

Hayden, Casey. "Onto Open Ground." In *Hands on the Freedom Plow: Personal Accounts by Women in SNCC*, edited by Faith S. Holsaert, Martha Prescod, Norman Noonan, Judy Richardson, Betty Garrman Robinson, Jean Smith Young, and Dorothy M. Zellner, 49–52. Champaign: University of Illinois Press, 2010.

Hayden, Tom. *The Port Huron Statement: The Visionary Call of the 1960s Revolution*. New York: Thunder's Mouth Press, 2005.

Hayes, Alan. *Anglicans in Canada: Controversies and Identity in Historical Perspective*. Urbana and Chicago: University of Illinois Press, 2004.

"Heap Family: An online place for memories and more for the extended family of Alice and Don Heap." Available at http://www.alicedonheap.ca. Date accessed, 29 August 2019.

Helminiak, Daniel. *What the Bible Really Says about Homosexuality*. San Francisco: Alamo Square Press, 2000.

Henderson, Stuart. *Making the Scene: Yorkville and Hip Toronto in the 1960s*. Toronto: University of Toronto Press, 2011.
– "Off the Streets and into the Fortress: Experiments in Hip Separatism at Toronto's Rochdale College, 1968–1975." *Canadian Historical Review* 92, no. 1 (March 2011): 107–33.
Herring, George. *America's Longest War: The United States and Vietnam, 1950–1975*. New York: McGraw-Hill, 2002.
Hewitt, Steve. *Spying 101: The RCMP's Secret Activities at Canadian Universities, 1917–1997*. Toronto: University of Toronto Press, 2002.
Heylin, Clinton. *Bob Dylan: Behind the Shades Revisited*. New York: William Morrow, 2001.
Higgins, Michael W., and Douglas R. Letson. *My Father's Business: A Biography of His Eminence G. Emmett Cardinal Carter*. Toronto: Macmillan of Canada, 1990.
– *Power and Peril: The Catholic Church at the Crossroads*. Toronto: HarperCollins Publishers Ltd, 2002.
Howe, Renate. *A Century of Influence: The Australian Student Christian Movement, 1896–1996*. Sydney: University of New South Wales Press, 2009.
Iacovetta, Franca. *Such Hardworking People: Italian Immigrants in Postwar Toronto*. Montreal & Kingston: McGill-Queen's University Press, 1992.
Isserman, Maurice. *If I Had A Hammer... The Death of the Old Left and the Birth of the New Left*. New York: Basic Books, Inc., Publishers, 1987.
Isserman, Maurice, and Michael Kazin. *America Divided: The Civil War of the 1960s*, 3rd ed. New York: Oxford University Press, 2008.
Jasen, Patricia. "'In Pursuit of Human Values (or Laugh When You Say That)': The Student Critique of the Arts Curriculum in the 1960s." In *Youth, University and Canadian Society: Essays in the Social History of Higher Education*, edited by Paul Axelrod and John G. Reid, 247–71. Montreal & Kingston: McGill-Queen's University Press, 1989.
Johnson, Benton. "Religion and Politics in America: The Last Twenty Years." In *The Sacred in a Secular Age: Toward Revision in the Scientific Study of Religion*, edited by Phillip E. Hammond, 301–16. Berkeley: University of California Press, 1985.
Kamitsuka, Margaret, ed. *The Embrace of Eros: Bodies, Desires, and Sexuality in Christianity*. Minneapolis: Fortress Press, 2010.
Katerberg, William H. "Redefining Evangelicalism in the Canadian Anglican Church: Wycliffe College and the Evangelical Party,

1867–1995." In *Aspects of the Canadian Evangelical Experience*, edited by George Rawlyk, 171–88. Montreal & Kingston: McGill-Queen's University Press, 1997.

Kilbourn, William, ed. *The Restless Church*. Toronto: McClelland and Stewart, 1966.

Kinsman, Gary. *The Regulation of Desire: Homo and Hetero Sexualities*. 2nd ed. Montreal: Black Rose Books, 1996.

Kinsman, Gary, and Patrizia Gentile. *The Canadian War on Queers: National Security as Sexual Regulation*. Vancouver: UBC Press, 2010.

Kneen, Brewster. *The Right Hand and the Left*. Toronto: CENSIT/Ecumenical Institute of Canada, 1970.

Korinek, V.J. "No Women Need Apply: The Ordination of Women in the United Church, 1918–1965." *Canadian Historical Review* 74, no. 4 (December 1993): 473–509.

Kostash, Myrna. *Long Way from Home: The Story of the Sixties Generation in Canada*. Toronto: James Lorimer & Company, 1980.

Kung, Hans, and Leonard Swidler, eds. *The Church in Anguish: Has the Vatican Betrayed Vatican II?* San Francisco: Harper & Row, 1987.

Kuyek, Joan. *Fighting for Hope: Organizing to Realize Our Dreams*. Montreal: Black Rose Books, 1990.

"LAWG Hay Camino History Project." Available at https://lawghistoryproject.wixsite.com/lawghaycaminohistory. Accessed 30 June 2020.

Laxer, James. *Red Diaper Baby: A Boyhood in the Age of McCarthyism*. Vancouver: Douglas & McIntyre, 2004.

Leddy, Mary Jo. *Say to the Darkness, We Beg to Differ*. Toronto: Lester & Orpen Dennys, 1990.

Lee, John Alan. *Love's Gay Fool: Autobiography of John Alan Lee*. Available at http://www.johnalanlee.com. Accessed 30 June 2020.

Lehtonen, Risto. *Story of a Storm: The Ecumenical Student Movement in the Turmoil of Revolution*. Grand Rapids: Wm. B. Eerdmans Publishing Co., 1998.

Levant, Victor. *Quiet Complicity: Canadian Involvement in the Vietnam War*. Toronto: Between the Lines, 1986.

Levin, Matthew. *Cold War University: Madison and the New Left in the Sixties*. Madison: University of Wisconsin Press, 2013.

Levitt, Cyril. *Children of Privilege: Student Revolt in the Sixties: A Study of Student Movements in Canada, the United States, and West Germany*. Toronto: University of Toronto Press, 1984.

Lexier, Roberta. "The Canadian Student Movement in the Sixties: Three Case Studies." PhD diss., University of Alberta, 2009.

Livingston, James C. *Modern Christian Thought: From the Enlightenment to Vatican II.* New York: Macmillan Publishing Co., Ltd, 1971.
McGuigan, Gerald, George Payerle, and Patricia Horrobin, eds. *Student Protest.* Toronto: Methuen, 1968.
MacGuigan, Mark. *Abortion, Conscience and Democracy.* Toronto: Hounslow Press, 1994.
McInnis, Peter S. "'Hothead Troubles': Sixties-Era Wildcat Strikes in Canada." In Campbell, Clément, and Kealey, *Debating Dissent*, 155–170.
McIntire, C.T. "Unity among Many: The Formation of the United Church of Canada, 1899–1930." In Schweitzer, *The United Church of Canada*, 97–117.
McKay, Ian. *Reasoning Otherwise: Leftists and the People's Enlightenment in Canada, 1890–1920.* Toronto: Between the Lines, 2008.
– *Rebels, Reds, Radicals: Rethinking Canada's Left History.* Toronto: Between the Lines, 2005.
McKillop, A.B. *Pierre Berton: A Biography.* Toronto: McClelland and Stewart, 2008.
McLeod, Donald. *Lesbian and Gay Liberation in Canada: A Selected Annotated Chronology, 1964–1975.* Toronto: ECW Press/Homewood Books, 1996.
MacLeod, Henry Gordon. "The Transformation of the United Church of Canada, 1946–1977." PhD diss., University of Toronto, 1980.
McLeod, Hugh. *The Religious Crisis of the 1960s.* Oxford: Oxford University Press, 2007.
McLeod, Thomas H., and Ian McLeod. *Tommy Douglas: The Road to Jerusalem.* Edmonton: Hurtig, 1987.
McLoughlin, William G. *Revivals, Awakenings, and Reform: An Essay on Religion and Social Change in America, 1607–1977.* Chicago: University of Chicago Press, 1978.
McMahon, Patricia. *Essence of Indecision: Diefenbaker's Nuclear Policy, 1957–1963.* Montreal & Kingston: McGill-Queen's University Press, 2009.
McNeal, Patricia. *Harder than War: Catholic Peacemaking in Twentieth-Century America.* New Brunswick: Rutgers University Press, 1992.
Macourt, Malcolm, ed. *Towards a Theology of Gay Liberation.* London: SCM Press, 1977.
Marchand, Philip. "Lea and Me." *Toronto Life*, September 2002, 111–20.
Marcuse, Herbert. *One-Dimensional Man.* Boston: Beacon Press, 1964.

Marks, Lynne. *Revivals and Roller Rinks: Religion, Leisure and Identity in Late-Nineteenth-Century Small-Town Ontario*. Toronto: University of Toronto Press, 1996.

Marsden, George. *Fundamentalism and American Culture*. 2nd ed. Oxford: Oxford University Press, 2006.

Marsh, Charles. *God's Long Summer: Stories of Faith and Civil Rights*. Princeton: Princeton University Press, 1997.

Marshall, David. *Secularizing the Faith: Canadian Protestant Clergy and the Crisis of Belief, 1850–1940*. Toronto: University of Toronto Press, 1992.

Martel, Marcel. "'They smell bad, have diseases and are lazy': RCMP Officers Reporting on Hippies in the Late Sixties." *Canadian Historical Review* 90, no 2 (June 2009): 215–45.

Marwick, Arthur. *The Sixties: Cultural Revolution in Britain, France, Italy, and the United States, c.1958–c.1974*. Oxford: Oxford University Press, 1998.

Matusow, Allen. *The Unraveling of America: A History of Liberalism in the 1960s*. New York: Harper & Row Publishers, 1984.

Maugans, Todd A. "The SPIRITual History." *Archives of Family Medicine* 5, no. 1 (1996): 11–16.

Maxwell, Donald W. "Religion and Politics at the Border: Canadian Church Support for American Vietnam War Resisters." *Journal of Church and State* 48, no. 4 (Autumn 2006): 807–29.

Meconis, Charles. *With Clumsy Grace: The American Catholic Left, 1961–1975*. New York: Seabury Press, 1979.

Meunier, E.-Martin, and Jean-Philippe Warren. *Sortir de la "Grande noirceur": L'horizon "personnaliste" de la Révolution tranquille*. Sillery: Septentrion, 2002.

Miedema, Gary. *For Canada's Sake: Public Religion, Centennial Celebrations, and the Re-making of Canada in the 1960s*. Montreal & Kingston: McGill-Queen's University Press, 2005.

Mietkiewicz, Henry, and Bob Mackowycz. *Dream Tower: The Life and Legacy of Rochdale College*. Toronto: McGraw-Hill Ryerson, 1988.

Miller, Ron. *Free Schools, Free People: Education and Democracy after the 1960s*. Albany: State University of New York Press, 2002.

Miller, Timothy. *The Hippies and American Values*. Knoxville: University of Tennessee Press, 1991.

Miller, William D. *A Harsh and Dreadful Love: Dorothy Day and the Catholic Worker Movement*. New York: Liveright, 1973.

Milligan, Ian. *Rebel Youth: 1960s Labour Unrest, Young Workers, and New Leftists in English Canada*. Vancouver: UBC Press, 2014.

Mills, Allen. *Fool for Christ: The Political Thought of J.S. Woodsworth.* Toronto: University of Toronto Press, 1991.
Mills, C. Wright. "The New Left." Reprinted in *Power, Politics, and People: The Collected Essays of C. Wright Mills*, edited by Irving Louis Horowitz, 247–59. New York: Oxford University Press, 1963.
Mills, Sean. *The Empire Within: Postcolonial Thought and Political Activism in Sixties Montreal.* Montreal & Kingston: McGill-Queen's University Press, 2010.
Minifie, James. *Peacemaker or Powder-Monkey: Canada's Role in a Revolutionary World.* Toronto: McClelland and Stewart, 1960.
Mintz, Steven. "Reflections on Age as a Category of Historical Analysis." *Journal of the History of Childhood and Youth* 1, no. 1 (Winter 2008): 91–4.
Moffatt, Gary. *History of the Canadian Peace Movement until 1969.* St Catharines, ON: Grape Vine Press, 1969.
Moir, J.S. "Toronto's Protestants and Their Perceptions of Their Roman Catholic Neighbours." In *Catholics at the "Gathering Place": Historical Essays on the Archdiocese of Toronto, 1841–991*, edited by Mark McGowan and Brian Clarke, 313–27. Toronto: Canadian Catholic Historical Association, 1993.
Mol, Hans. *Faith and Fragility: Religion and Identity in Canada.* Burlington, ON: Trinity Press, 1985.
Morton, Desmond. *The New Democrats, 1961–1986: The Politics of Change.* Toronto: Copp Clark Pitman Ltd., 1986.
Mutchmor, James R. *Mutchmor: The Memoirs of James Ralph Mutchmor.* Toronto: The Ryerson Press, 1965.
New Left Committee, "The Revolutionary Process: Statement of the New Left Committee – October 1967." In McGuigan, Payerle, and Hobson, *Student Protest*, 105–11.
Niebuhr, H. Richard. *Christ and Culture.* New York: Harper Torchbooks, 1951.
Noll, Mark. "What Happened to Christian Canada?" *Church History* 75, no. 2 (June 2006): 245–73.
Norris, Pippa, and Ronald Inglehart. *Sacred and Secular: Religion and Politics Worldwide.* Cambridge: Cambridge University Press, 2004.
Oppenheimer, Mark. *Knocking on Heaven's Door: American Religion in the Age of Counterculture.* New Haven: Yale University Press, 2003.
O'Toole, Roger, Douglas F. Campbell, John A. Hannigan, Peter Beyer, and John H. Simpson. "The United Church in Crisis: A Sociological Perspective on the Dilemmas of a Mainstream Denomination." *Studies in Religion* 20, no. 2 (1991): 151–63.

Owram, Doug. *Born at the Right Time: A History of the Baby Boom Generation*. Toronto: University of Toronto Press, 1996.
Palaeologu, M. Athena, ed. *The Sixties in Canada: A Turbulent and Creative Decade*. Montreal: Black Rose Books, 2009.
Palmer, Bryan. *Canada's 1960s: The Ironies of Identity in a Rebellious Era*. Toronto: University of Toronto Press, 2009.
Paul VI, *Humanae Vitae*. Vatican, 1968. Available at http://www.vatican.va/holy_father/paul_vi/encyclicals/documents/hf_p-vi_enc_25071968_humanae-vitae_en.html. Accessed 18 December 2019.
Perin, Roberto. "Das englischsprachige Kanada." In *Kirche und Katholizismus zeit 1945, Band IV: Die britischen Inseln und Nordamerika*, edited by Erwin Gatz, 71–88. Paderborn-München-Wien-Zürich: Ferdinand Schöningh, 2002.
Perry, Charles. *Haight-Ashbury, A History*. New York: Random House, 1984.
Perry, Lewis. *Radical Abolitionism: Anarchy and the Government of God in Antislavery Thought*. Ithaca: Cornell University Press, 1973.
Pius XI, *Casti Connubii*. Vatican, 1930. Available at http://w2.vatican.va/content/pius-xi/en/encyclicals/documents/hf_p-xi_enc_19301231_casti-connubii.html. Accessed 18 December 2019.
– *Quadragesimo Anno*. Vatican, 1931. Available at http://w2.vatican.va/content/pius_xi/en/encyclicals/documents/hf_p-xi_enc_19310515_quadragesimo-anno.html. Accessed 11 October 2017.
Portelli, Alessandro. *The Death of Luigi Trastulli, and Other Stories: Form and Meaning in Oral History*. Albany: State University of New York Press, 1991.
Porter, John. *The Vertical Mosaic: An Analysis of Social Class and Power in Canada*. Toronto: University of Toronto Press, 1965.
Pulker, Edward. *We Stand on Their Shoulders: The Growth of Social Concern in Canadian Anglicanism*. Toronto: Anglican Book Centre, 1986.
Quealey, Michael. *My Basilian Priesthood*. Waterloo: Wilfrid Laurier University Press, 2019.
Rebick, Judy. *Ten Thousand Roses: The Making of a Feminist Revolution*. Toronto: Penguin Canada, 2005.
Reeve, Ted. "Walking the Talk." In *Action Training in Canada: Reflections on Church-Based Education for Social Transformation*, edited by Ted Reeve and Roger Hutchinson, 13–57. Toronto: Centre for Research in Religion – Emmanuel College, 1997.
Riordan, Michael. *The First Stone: Homosexuality and the United Church*. Toronto: McClelland and Stewart, 1990.

Roberts, Thomas D., ed. *Contraception and Holiness*. New York: Herder and Herder, 1964.

Rossinow, Doug. "The New Left in the Counterculture: Hypotheses and Evidence." *Radical History Review* 67 (1997): 79–120.

– *The Politics of Authenticity: Liberalism, Christianity, and the New Left in America*. New York: Columbia University Press, 1998.

Roszak, Theodore. *The Making of a Counter Culture: Reflections on the Technocratic Society and Its Youthful Opposition*. Garden City: Doubleday & Company, Inc., 1968.

Roussopoulos, "Towards a Revolutionary Youth Movement." *Our Generation* 7, no. 2 (1970): 45–59.

Rowland, Christopher. "Introduction: The Theology of Liberation." In *Cambridge Companion to Liberation Theology*, 2nd ed., edited by Christopher Rowland, 1–16. Cambridge: Cambridge University Press, 2007.

Sacred Congregation for the Doctrine of the Faith. *Declaration Inter Insigniores on the Question of Admission of Women to the Ministerial Priesthood*. Vatican, 1976. Available at http://www.vatican.va/roman_curia/congregations/cfaith/documents/rc_con_cfaith_doc_19761015_inter-insigniores_en.html. Accessed 31 August 2017.

– *Persona Humana*. Vatican, 1975. Available at http://www.vatican.va/roman_curia/congregations/cfaith/documents/rc_con_cfaith_doc_19751229_persona_humana_en.html. Accessed 14 February 2011.

Sangster, Joan. "Radical Ruptures: Feminism, Labor, and the Left in the Long Sixties in Canada." *American Review of Canadian Studies* 40, no. 1 (March 2010): 1–21.

Schweitzer, Don, ed. *The United Church of Canada: A History*. Waterloo: Wilfrid Laurier University Press, 2012.

Second Vatican Council. *Decree on the Apostolate of the Laity: Apostolicam Actuositatem*. Vatican, 1965. Available at http://www.vatican.va/archive/hist_councils/ii_vatican_council/documents/vat-ii_decree_19651118_apostolicam-actuositatem_en.html. Accessed 28 February 2011.

– *Pastoral Constitution on the Church in the Modern World: Gaudium et Spes*. Vatican, 1965. Available at http://www.vatican.va/archive/hist_councils/ii_vatican_council/documents/vat-ii_cons_19651207_gaudium-et-spes_en.html. Accessed 28 February 2011.

Seljak, David. "Catholicism's 'Quiet Revolution': *Maintenant* and the New Public Catholicism in Quebec after 1960." In Van Die, *Religion and Public Life in Canada*, 257–74.

Selles, Johanna M. *The World Student Christian Federation, 1895–1925: Motives, Methods, and Influential Women*. Eugene, OR: Pickwick Publications, 2011.

Senate of Canada. *Speech from the Throne* (5 April 1965). Available at https://www.poltext.org/sites/poltext.org/files/discoursV2/Canada/CAN_DT_XXXX_26_03.pdf. Accessed 18 December 2019.

Sethna, Christabelle. "'Chastity Outmoded!': The *Ubyssey*, Sex, and the Single Girl, 1960–1970." In *Creating Postwar Canada: Community, Diversity, and Dissent, 1945–1975*, edited by Magda Fahrni and Robert Rutherdale, 289–314. Vancouver: University of British Columbia Press, 2007.

– "The University of Toronto Health Service, Oral Contraception and Student Demand for Birth Control, 1960–1970." *Historical Studies in Education/Revue d'histoire de l'éducation* 17, no. 2 (2005): 265–92.

Sethna, Christabelle, and Steve Hewitt. "Clandestine Operations: The Vancouver Women's Caucus, the Abortion Caravan, and the RCMP." *Canadian Historical Review* 90, no. 3 (September 2009): 463–96.

Shaull, Richard, and Carl Oglesby. *Containment and Change*. New York: MacMillan, 1967.

Sheinin, David. "Cuba's Long Shadow: The Progressive Church Movement and Canadian-Latin American Relations, 1970–1987." In *The Long Dance: Canada and Cuba in the Castro Era*, edited by Robert W. Wright and Lana Wylie, 121–43. Toronto: University of Toronto Press, 2009.

Sheinin, David, and Sara Lamble. "Discovering Dictatorship: The Shaping of a Canadian Human Rights Discourse in Regard to Latin America, 1970–1985." Presentation at the 24th International Congress of the Latin American Studies Association (Dallas, March 2003). Available at http://lasa.international.pitt.edu/Lasa2003/SheininDavid.pdf. Accessed 18 December 2019.

Sheridan, E.F, ed. *Do Justice: The Social Teaching of the Canadian Catholic Bishops (1945–1986)*. Toronto: Jesuit Centre for Social Faith and Justice, 1987.

– ed. *Love Kindness! The Social Teaching of the Canadian Catholic Bishops (1948–1989): A Second Collection*. Toronto: Jesuit Centre for Social Faith and Justice, 1991.

Simpson, John H., and Walter Phillips. "Understanding Student Protest in Canada: The University of Toronto Strike Vote." *Canadian Journal of Higher Education* 6, no. 1 (1976): 59–67.

Sinasac, Joseph. *Fateful Passages: The Life of Henry Somerville, Catholic Journalist*. Toronto: Novalis, 2003.

Smith, Christian. *American Evangelicalism: Embattled and Thriving.* Chicago: University of Chicago Press, 1998.

Smyth, William J. *Toronto, the Belfast of Canada: The Orange Order and the Shaping of Municipal Culture.* Toronto: University of Toronto Press, 2015.

Socknat, Thomas P. *Witness against War: Pacifism in Canada, 1900–1945.* Toronto: University of Toronto Press, 1987.

Squires, Jessica. *Building Sanctuary: The Movement to Support Vietnam War Resisters in Canada, 1965–1973.* Vancouver: UBC Press, 2013.

Statistics Canada. *2001 Census: analysis series – Religions in Canada.* Available at https://www12.statcan.gc.ca/access_acces/archive.action-eng.cfm?/english/census01/products/analytic/companion/rel/pdf/96F0030XIE2001015.pdf. Accessed 2 December 2019.

Stebner, Eleanor. "The 1930s." In Schweitzer, *The United Church of Canada*, 39–56.

Stein, David Lewis. *Scratch One Dreamer.* Toronto: McClelland and Stewart, 1967.

Stettner, Shannon. "'We Are Forced to Declare War': Linkages between the 1970 Abortion Caravan and Women's Anti-Vietnam War Activism." *Histoire sociale/Social History* 46, no. 92 (November 2013): 423–41.

Stettner, Shannon, and Bruce Douville. "'In the Image and Likeness of God': Christianity and Public Opinion on Abortion in the *Globe and Mail* during the 1960s." *Journal of Canadian Studies* 50, no. 1 (Winter 2016): 179–213.

Sutherland, S.L. *Patterns of Belief and Action: Measurement of Student Political Activism.* Toronto: University of Toronto Press, 1981.

Task Force on Human Life. *Abortion: An Issue for Conscience.* Edited by Phyllis Creighton. Toronto: Anglican Church of Canada, 1974.

Taylor, Charles. *A Secular Age.* Cambridge: The Belknap Press of Harvard University, 2007.

Thomas, John L. "Romantic Reform in America, 1815–1865." *American Quarterly* 17 (Winter 1965): 656–81.

Tillich, Paul. *Morality and Beyond.* New York: Harper and Row, 1963.

Treat, James. *Around the Sacred Fire: Native Religious Activism in the Red Power Movement.* New York: Palgrave Macmillan, 2003.

Trenton, Thomas. "Left-Wing Radicalism at a Canadian University: The Inapplicability of an American Model." *Interchange* 14, no. 2 (1983): 54–64.

Turner, Harry Ernest. "The Evangelical Movement in the Church of England in the Diocese of Toronto, 1839–79." MA thesis, University of Toronto, 1959.

Turner, Peter. *There Can Be No Light without Shadows*. Toronto: Rochdale College Publications, 1971.
United Church of Canada. *Abortion: A Study*. Toronto: Board of Evangelism and Social Services, 1971.
- *Guidelines for Inclusive Language*. Toronto: United Church of Canada, 1981.
- *Twenty-Third General Council: Record of Proceedings*. Toronto: United Church of Canada, 1968.
- *Twenty-Fifth General Council: Record of Proceedings*. Toronto: United Church of Canada, 1972.
- *Voices United: The Hymn and Worship Book of the United Church of Canada*. Etobicoke: United Church Publishing House, 1996.
- *Why the Sea Is Boiling Hot: A Symposium on the Church and the World*. Toronto: The Board of Evangelism and Social Service, United Church of Canada, 1965.
- *Year Book – Volume II*. Toronto: United Church of Canada, 1965.
- *Year Book – Volume II*. Toronto: United Church of Canada, 1966.
United Nations Department of Economic and Social Affairs. *World Youth Report 2007 – Young People's Transition to Adulthood: Progress and Challenges*. New York: United Nations, 2007.
US Congress. Gulf of Tonkin Resolution. 88th Congress, 2nd Session (7 August 1964). Available at http://www.ourdocuments.gov/doc.php?flash=true&doc=98. Accessed 18 December 2019.
Van Die, Marguerite. *An Evangelical Mind: Nathanael Burwash and the Methodist Tradition in Canada, 1839–1918*. Montreal & Kingston: McGill-Queen's University Press, 1989.
- ed. *Religion and Public Life in Canada*. Toronto: University of Toronto Press, 2001.
Walker, Diane M. "Diversity, Diversity, All Is Diversity: The Impact of Feminist Theology on the Women in Ministry of the United Church of Canada." DMin thesis, McMaster Divinity College, 1999.
Wallace, Anthony F.C. "Revitalization Movements." *American Anthropologist* 58, no. 2 (April 1956): 264–81.
Warner, Tom. *Never Going Back: A History of Queer Activism in Canada*. Toronto: University of Toronto Press, 2002.
Westfall, William. "Constructing Public Religions at Private Sites: The Anglican Church in the Shadow of Disestablishment." In Van Die, *Religion and Public Life in Canada*, 23–49.
- *Two Worlds: The Protestant Culture of Nineteenth-Century Ontario*. Montreal & Kingston: McGill-Queen's Press, 1989.

Whitla, William. *The Church of the Holy Trinity, 1847–1997: A Short History*. Toronto: Holy Trinity Press, 1997.

Whynot, Margie. "Liberating Christianity." In *Women, Work & Worship in the United Church of Canada*, co-ordinated by Shirley Davy, 228–35. Toronto: United Church of Canada, 1983.

Williams, John R., ed. *Canadian Churches and Social Justice*. Toronto: Anglican Book Centre, 1984.

Wilson, Bryan. *Religion in Secular Society: A Sociological Comment*. London: C.A. Watts & Co. Ltd, 1966.

Wittner, Lawrence S. *Resisting the Bomb: A History of the World Nuclear Disarmament Movement, 1954–1970*. Stanford: Stanford University Press, 1997.

Women Unite! An Anthology of the Canadian Women's Movement. Toronto: Canadian Women's Educational Press, 1971.

Wyatt, Joan. "The 1970s: Voices from the Margins." In Schweitzer, *The United Church of Canada*, 119–38.

Yablonsky, Lewis. *The Hippie Trip*. New York: Pegasus, 1968.

Young, Ian. *The Beginnings of Gay Liberation in Canada*. Toronto: Ian Young Books, n.d.

Young, Jason. "Defining a Community in Exile: Vietnam War Resister Communications and Identity in AMEX, 1968–1973." *Histoire sociale/Social History* 44, no. 87 (May 2011): 115–46.

Zwissler, Laurel. "Spiritual, but Religious: 'Spirituality' among Religiously Motivated Feminist Activists." *Culture and Religion* 8, no. 1 (2007): 51–69.

Index

abortion, 143, 152–3, 174–5, 177–82, 200; and the Anglican Church of Canada, 179–80; and the Roman Catholic Church, 177–9; traditional Christian position, 178; and the United Church of Canada, 180–2, 193
Abortion: An Issue for Conscience (Task Force on Human Life), 180
Abortion Caravan, 175, 180, 251n15
activists: identity formation, 53–61; religious upbringing as factor, 91–2. *See also* New Left; young Christian radicals
adult Christians, 147, 154–6; adopting New Left rhetoric, 131–2, 208; aid to war resisters, 164–70; long-term consequences of engagement with youth and New Left, 195–208; as mentors and supporters of young Christian radicals, 13, 80–1, 125–48; outreach to youth and New Left, 125–48, 208; reasons for outreach to youth, 126–7; and the Vietnam War, 132–7, 164–70

Affirm, 204
African-American civil rights movement: challenge to Democratic Party, 49; influence on New Left protests, 61–4; inspiration for New Left, 46–7, 58; and Selma-to-Montgomery marches, 71
Agg, Tim, 113
Alinsky, Saul, 72, 77, 90
Allende, Salvador, 149, 158
Althizer, Thomas, 75
Ambrozic, Aloysius, 251n26
American Exile in Canada, 169
American Friends' Service Committee, 87
Amex Magazine, 169
Anderson, Betsy, 154, 161, 163–4, 183–4, 192
Anglican Church of Canada, 12, 20, 31–4; on abortion, 179–80; activist clergy, 32, 81, 129, 156; aid to war resisters, 164–70; anti-institutional rhetoric, 131–2; attendance and membership, 25, 126–7, 205–8, 218n38; and Berton's *The Comfortable Pew*, 76–7; British imperial ties, 31–2;

conservatism of, 131, 156, 197–8; debates over sexuality, 205, 256n28; Diocese of Qu'Appelle, 167; in Diocese of Toronto, 31–4, 177; as "establishment" church, 31, 197–8; and gay liberation, 186–7, 205; General Synod, 113, 129, 131, 132, 165, 177, 179; "high church" vs "low church," 33; and Inter-Church Committee on Chile, 159–60; long-term consequences of engagement with youth and New Left, 197–8; National Executive Council, 167, 169; Primate's World Relief and Development Fund, 198, 201, 210; and Project North, 199; "prophetic" vs "priestly," 31–4; Public Social Responsibility Unit, 198; radical youth in, 113; Task Force on Human Life, 180; and the Vietnam War, 164–70; women's ordination, 176–7; "youth synods," 129–30. *See also* Anglican Young People's Association; Anglican Youth Movement; Church of the Holy Trinity; Heap, Dan; Integrity; Mackenzie, Ian; Trinity College; Whitla, William

Anglican Journal, 256n28

Anglican Young People's Association, 34, 82, 95, 113

Anglican Youth Movement, 7, 112, 113, 114, 123–4, 127, 198; relationship with Kairos, 113, 237n38

anti-Americanism, 162–4

anti-imperialism, 64, 105, 149–50, 153, 157–64; and Canada, 133, 162–4; and Indo-China, 118, 133, 152; and Latin America, 117–23, 153. *See also* antiwar movement; Latin American Working Group; left nationalism; liberation; liberation theology; New Left; Vietnam War

antiwar movement: broadening of, 132–3; Canadian churches and, 125, 164–70; Canadian complicity in, 108, 196; New Left solidarity with NLF and Viet Cong, 118, 149, 165–6; student protest, 73–4, 96–7, 104, 110, 132–3; student protest against Canadian complicity, 105, 116–17, 123. *See also* Vietnam War

Apostolicam Actuositatem, 78

Association for Social Knowledge, 185

avatars, youth as, 104–5

Baby Boom, 14–16, 199; and Canada's churches, 26–7, 125–7, 207; in media and popular culture in sixties, 104; and New Left, 104, 109, 123

Bagnell, Barbara, 175–6

Bagnell, Kenneth, 134

Balaguer, Joaquín, 120

Barnett, Tom, 102

Barr, Wayne, 112

Basilian Fathers, 28, 140

Bathurst Street United Church, 56, 154

Baum, Gregory, 56, 139, 244n66; on contraception, 141; on homosexuality, 187; leaves priesthood, 142

Bazoche, Placide, 161

Beardsall, Sandra, 136
Beatles, 67
Benwell, Rosemary, 177
Berger, Peter, 17
Berrigan, Daniel, 138, 230n67
Berrigan, Philip, 86, 138, 230n67
Berton, Pierre, 10, 69, 76, 208
Bibby, Reginald, 22
Bilingualism and Biculturalism Commission, 81
birth control. *See* contraception
Black, Robert Merrill, 32
Black Panthers, 185
Black Power, 185
Blanchard, Jane, 55–7, 81, 223n49
Bland, Salem, 36
"Blowin' in the Wind" (Wallace), 83
Body Politic (Toronto), 186, 191, 204
Bolioli, Oscar, 119
Bomarc missiles, 47–8, 49–50, 61
Bonhoeffer, Dietrich, 41, 52, 75, 82; influence on young Christian radicals, 87, 89–90, 231n88
Boothroyd, Peter, 87
Bradford, Douglas, 85
Brake, Michael, 15
Breines, Wini, 47, 221n7

Callwood, June, 135
Caloren, Fred, 80–1, 95–6, 100–2, 234n132
Cambodia, 152
Campbell, Heather, 183
campus chaplaincies, 98, 129
Campus Co-operative Residences, 144
campus left. *See* New Left
Canadian Churchman, 37, 76, 131; and campaign for women's ordination, 177; coverage of war resisters, 166; coverage of youth issues in sixties, 127, 130
Canadian Conference of Catholic Bishops, 161–2, 165, 175, 178, 189
Canadian Council of Churches, 13, 83, 119, 136, 159–60; aid to war resisters, 166–70
Canadian Forces Base La Macaza. *See* La Macaza, Quebec
Canadian Institute of Public Opinion, 142
Canadian Liberation Movement, 152, 162–3
Canadian Register, 30, 131, 138, 161–2; and campaign for women's ordination, 177; coverage of war resisters, 166; coverage of youth issues in sixties, 127, 130; editorial on abortion, 179. See also *Catholic Register*
Canadian Student, 154, 157, 246n23
Canadian Union of Students, 69, 86, 95, 114; role in Canada's New Left, 106, 108
Canadian Urban Training Program, 69, 77, 84, 87, 129
Canadian Women's Educational Press, 183
Canadian Young Communist League, 82
Carter, Gerald Emmett, 199, 251n26
Casti Connubii (Pius XI), 141
Castro, Fidel, 117
Catholic Information Centre (Toronto), 141

Catholic New Times, 138, 199
Catholic Register, 29–30, 37, 138, 165, 189, 199. See also *Canadian Register*
Catholic Worker movement, 30, 52, 86
Catholic Youth Organization, 79
Casanova, José, 17
Centre for the Study of Institutions and Theology (Rochdale College), 145–7, 183, 245n86–8
Charlton, Bill, 117
Chile, 149, 158–60, 200
Chile-Canada Solidarity Committee, 159
Chile Versus the Corporations, 158
Chow, Olivia, 201
Christendom: and Canadian youth in the sixties, 22–3; and church decline in the long sixties and beyond, 8–9, 24–7, 42–3, 123, 205–8, 256n21; its relative strength in the postwar years, 24–7, 42; and the Student Christian Movement of Canada, 41–2, 43
Christian existentialism, 41, 52, 57. See also existentialism
Christian Faith-and-Life Community, 52
Christianity. See Anglican Church of Canada; Christians; liberal Protestantism; religious crisis of the sixties; Roman Catholic Church; Student Christian Movement of Canada; United Church of Canada; young Christian radicals
Christian left. See adult Christians; Anglican Youth Movement; Christian Left Group (Toronto); Kairos (United Church); Latin American Working Group; New Left; "prophetic" vs "priestly" religion; Student Christian Movement of Canada; Summer of Service; young Christian radicals
Christian Left group (Toronto), 85–8, 94
Christie, Harriet, 182, 203
Churches Where the Action Is, 77
Church of the Holy Trinity (Anglican), 77; and activist parishioners, 81, 85, 129; aid to war resisters, 169; as centre of progressive activism, 32, 129, 198; support for gay and lesbian community, 187
Cincinnati Action for Peace, 171
Clarke, Patricia, 176, 181
Clergy and Laity Concerned about Vietnam (CALCAV), 167
Cockburn, Bruce, 22
Combined Universities Campaign for Nuclear Disarmament, 20, 47–8, 50, 85; and La Macaza protests, 61–6; national office, 87; origins, 47–8, 222n8; Parliament Hill protest, 48, 60; radicalization, 49–50; relationship with SCM, 59–61, 103, 200; and Student Union for Peace Action, 70. See also nuclear disarmament movement; Student Union for Peace Action
Combined University Services Overseas, 92
Comfortable Pew, The (Berton), 10, 76
Committee to Aid War Resisters (Victoria, BC), 169

Communism, 22, 39–40, 45–6, 73
Communist Party of Canada, 22, 39, 59
Community Homophile Association of Toronto, 186, 187
Company of Young Canadians, 12, 86, 92, 112, 113; funding for resource people at Rochdale College, 145; relationship with SUPA, 72–3, 96–7, 106
Confédération des syndicats nationaux, 26
Confédération des travailleurs Catholiques du Canada, 26
contraception, 116, 141–3, 199, 239n60
Cooperative Commonwealth Federation, 30, 53
Copeland, Deanna, 118
counterculture, 9, 108–9, 144–7. *See also* youth culture
Cox, Harvey, 69, 75–7, 228n29; influences on young Christian radicals, 82, 89–91, 231n88
Cram, George, 83, 94, 119
Cross, James, 151
Cuba, 117–18, 120, 157–8, 247n26

Davey, Keith, 135
Davis, Bob, 232n97
Day, Dorothy, 30
Dayton Women's Liberation, 171
Dean, Ralph, 131
"death of God" theology, 7, 34, 69, 75–6
Debray, Regis, 118
de Hueck, Catherine, 30
Democratic National Convention (1964), 49
Democratic National Convention (1968), 105

de Posadas, Ignacio, 119
Devonshire Co-op, 175
Dewart, Joanne, 251n21
Dickinson, Mervyn, 188
Diefenbaker, John, 47–8, 49–50
Dignity (Toronto), 186, 204
Dominican Republic, 120
Dostoyevsky, Fyodor, 56
Dow Chemical Company, 116–17, 133, 136
draft dodgers. *See* Toronto Anti-Draft Programme; Vietnam War; war resisters
Dufresne, Michael, 48
Dylan, Bob, 44, 67, 83, 221n2

Economic Research and Action Project, 47
Edmund Burke Society, 117
Eisenhower, Dwight, 73
Ellul, Jacques, 235n136
Ellwood, Robert, 104
Emmanuel College (University of Toronto), 37, 86
Endicott, James, 154
Endicott, Marion, 154
Episcopal Church of the USA, 129, 167
Equal Rights Amendment, 174
Erlichman, Wolfe, 54–5, 191, 234n132; migration from SCM to SUPA, 98; and nuclear disarmament activism, 62, 65
evangelical churches, success in twenty-first century relative to mainline Protestant churches, 206–7
Evans, Ruth, 180
Everdale Alternative School, 155
existentialism, 41, 56–7. *See also* Christian existentialism

Fanon, Frantz, 118
Faulkner, Tom, 112, 115–17, 123, 131, 136, 196–7; on contraception activism, 239n60; on *Manual for Draft-Age Immigrants*, 239n62
Fellowship for a Christian Social Order, 36
Fellowship of Reconciliation, 51, 85
feminism, 107, 141–3, 171–84, 203. *See also* abortion; inclusive language; women's liberation; women's ordination
File, Edgar, 77, 87, 129
First Nations, 145–6, 161–2, 198, 199
Fisk, James, 32, 129
Flahiff, George, 177
Fletcher-Marsh, Wendy, 176
Ford, Gerald, 152
Forrest, A.C., 181
Foster, John: in Christian Left group, 87–8; and Division of Mission (United Church), 155, 197; and ecumenical justice groups, 199; in Kairos, 82–3, 112–13, 196–7; and Latin American Working Group, 119; on St Calixte conference (SUPA Fall Institute), 94; on the SCM-SUPA conference in Saskatoon, 96; and women's liberation, 183; and Youth Committee on Christian Presence, 131
Frank, John, 32, 129
Freedom Summer, 49, 51
Free Speech Movement (University of California Berkeley), 50–1
Frerichs, Eilert ("Bert"): aid to war resisters, 169; as campus chaplain, 129, 154, 183, 200; and CENSIT, 146, 245n87; early involvement in SCM, 55, 60; gay identity and activism, 191, 204; and nuclear disarmament activism, 60, 62–6; on the politics of the SCM, 98
Friedan, Betty, 173
Friends Committee on National Legislation, 87
Friendship House, 30
Friends of SNCC, 46–7; connections with SCM, 58, 66, 80, 98; connections with SUPA, 71
Front de libération du Québec, 151
fundamentalist Christianity, 34

Gandhi, Mahatma, 51, 66, 161
Gardner, Philip, 188
Gardner, Robert, 167
Garry, Robert, 95–6
GATT-Fly, 199
Gaudium et Spes, 78
Gauvreau, Michael, 9
gay liberation, 21, 153, 170; and Christianity, 184–93, 195, 202–5; compared to other liberation movements, 172
Gay Liberation Front, 185
generation gap, 11, 14–16, 124, 194; and Bob Dylan, 44, 221n2. *See also* youth; youth culture
Generation X, 210–11
Gentles, Ian: at La Macaza protests, 63, 66; pacifism, 58; pro-life activism, 200; on Student Christian Movement, 40, 58, 220n75
Gidney, Catherine, 10, 110
Gitlin, Todd, 117–18

Glad Day Bookshop, 186
Glendon College, 110–11
Globe and Mail, 37, 71, 114, 133–4, 187
Goodings, Stewart, 96
Gordon, Walter, 121
Gosse, Van, 151, 221n7
Graham, Billy, 36
Graham, Peter, 9
Grant, George, 121, 162, 235n136, 245n81
Green, Howard, 49
Greenwich Village (New York), 185
Griesinger, Jan, 171–2, 183
Guevera, Che, 118
Gutiérrez, Gustavo, 160

Hamilton, William, 75
Hanisch, Carol, 174
Hannum, Nancy, 86, 196–7; and Canadian Urban Training Centre, 77, 86; and Christian Left group, 86, 88; and Church and Economic Crisis Project, 197; and the Latin American Working Group, 119; on the SCM-SUPA conference in Saskatoon, 95–7; on sexuality, 188; and Youth Committee on Christian Presence, 131
Harding, Jim, 96
Harkness, Doug, 50
Hart House (University of Toronto), 38
Hart House Farm, 154
Hartwell, George, 54, 56, 80, 94, 234n132; conversion to evangelical, charismatic Christianity, 200; migration from SCM to SUPA, 98; on religious basis of social activism, 91–2
Hayes, Alan, 32, 129, 156, 197
Heap, Alice, 81, 129
Heap, Dan ("Don"): and Church of the Holy Trinity, 129, 187; as mentor to SCM and young Christian radicals, 81, 201; nuclear disarmament activism, 63, 65–6; as politician, 201
Henderson, Larry, 199
Hindley-Smith, Lea, 139, 243n55
hippies, 108–9, 129
Hitler, Adolf, 89
Hobson, G.E., 167
Hoffman, Larry, 135
homosexuality, 172–3, 184–93, 202–5; traditional Christian position on, 186–7, 199, 253n77
Honest to God (Robinson), 34
Honey, Floyd, 159–60
Hopton, George, 55–6
Hord, J.R. ("Ray"), 36, 116, 130–1; compared to his predecessor, 36, 130, 242n17; as inspiration, 116, 132–7, 196–7; and the Vietnam War, 132–7, 155–6, 165–7, 196
Howland House (Toronto), 40, 56. 59, 154, 200
Humanae Vitae (Paul VI), 138, 142–3, 178
Hungary (invasion by Soviet Union), 45–6
Hyde, Richard, 54–6, 102

Illich, Ivan, 120
inclusive language, 203
Indo-China, 95, 152

Inn of the Unmuzzled Ox (Toronto), 190–1
Institute for Indian Studies (Rochdale College), 145–6
Integrity (Toronto), 186, 204
Inter-Church Committee on Chile, 159–60
Inter-Church Committee on Human Rights in Latin America, 200
Intervarsity Christian Fellowship, 38, 98. *See also* Varsity Christian Fellowship (University of Toronto)
Israel, 149

Jeunesse étudiantes catholiques, 95
Jews: connections with Christian left, 55, 85–8; conservative and orthodox Jewish views on sexuality, 187; involvement in the New Left, 3, 51, 91, 92, 223n31, 232n94
Job Corps, 79
John XXIII (pope), 28–9
John Paul II (pope), 198–9
Johnson, Benton, 127
Johnson, Lyndon B., 49, 73
Jolly, Stan, 100–1, 235n136

KAIROS, 200, 201, 210
Kairos (United Church of Canada), 7, 20, 69–70, 155; and the Latin American Working Group, 119, 121; membership, 237n37; and the New Left, 81–3, 93–8, 112–13, 123–4, 127, 208; and theology, 90–1
Kairos Summer Event (1966), 85, 118

Kealey, Greg, 84, 110, 139
Kealey, Linda, 84, 110–11, 139, 143; on the Newman Centre, 244n59
Kennedy, John F., 73
Kent State shootings (Ohio), 151–2
Khrushchev, Nikita, 45
Kierkegaard, Søren, 41, 56
King, Martin Luther, Jr, 46, 58
Kneen, Brewster: and Philip Berrigan, 230n67; and CENSIT at Rochdale College, 145–7, 245n86, 245n88; and Christian Left group, 85–8; and Church of the Holy Trinity, 129, 187; and Latin American Working Group, 87, 119; and St Calixte conference (SUPA Fall Institute), 94
Kneen, Cathleen: and Christian Left group, 85–8; and Church of the Holy Trinity, 129; "los muchos sombreros," 230n68; on the relationship between SCM and SUPA, 93, 97; and St Calixte conference (SUPA Fall Institute), 94; on SUPA projects, 72; and Youth Committee on Christian Presence, 131
Knowles, Stanley, 135
Kutz, Stan, 139–43, 244n66
Kuyek, Joan Newman, 72, 93, 143, 197

La Macaza, Quebec, 61–6, 110, 123, 129, 200
Lament for a Nation (Grant), 162
Laporte, Pierre, 151
Latin America, 105, 138, 149–50, 153, 200; and LAWG, 117–23, 157–61, 164. *See also* Chile;

Cuba; Dominican Republic; Latin American Working Group
Latin American Working Group, 12, 70, 87, 154, 198; beginning of LAWG and initial years, 117–23; collaboration with SCM, 119, 122, 175; 1970s–1990s, 153–6, 157–60, 164, 200; secularity of, 122–3
Laverty, Norm, 118
Lawrence Park Community Church, 85
Laxer, James, 22–3, 162–3, 232n100
Laxer, Mendel, 40
League for Industrial Democracy, 85
Leddy, Mary Jo, 199
Lee, John Alan, 53–4, 56; agnosticism/atheism, 66, 200, 234n132; homosexuality, 191; nuclear disarmament activism, 59, 62–3
left nationalism, 121–2, 133; in early 1970s, 149–50, 153, 156, 162–4
Lehtonen, Risto, 64–5
Lenin, Vladimir, 118
Leo XIII (pope), 29
Lewis, David, 163
Lexier, Roberta, 116
liberal evangelicalism, 35
liberal Protestantism, 33–4, 52, 64, 83; in Anglican Church of Canada, 34; in Student Christian Movement, 37, 64
liberation: in New Left discourse, 149–50, 153, 172, 193. *See also* anti-imperialism; antiwar movement; gay liberation; Latin American Working Group; left nationalism; liberation theology; New Left; Vietnam War; women's liberation
liberation theology, 138, 160–2, 198–9
Lockhart, Wilfred, 134
London Women's Liberation Movement, 183
Long, Ernest E., 134, 168
"long sixties": definition of term, 214n6; impact of era on Canadian Christianity, 195–208; and irony, 208; literature on religion and youth in the era, 8–10; metanarratives of the era, 14–19, 207, 209–10; the 1970s as part of the era, 150–3, 170; secularity of the era, 16–19, 208–9; sexuality in the era, 184–93. *See also* sixties
Loyalists, 162

McCullum, Hugh, 130, 131
McCurdy, Arch, 130
McDermott, Dennis, 87
MacDonald, John A., 162
McGuigan, James, 30, 243n50
McKay, Ian, 4, 9
McKay, P.A.G., 30, 138, 179
McKenna, Philip, 145–6
Mackenzie, Ian, 129, 144–6, 169, 198
McKillop, Tom, 79, 199
Maclean's Magazine, 62–4
McLeod, Hugh, 26, 126, 195, 207; and the effect of Vatican II on progressive Catholics, 177; religious crisis of the sixties, 6, 8, 195; and secularization, 18, 207

McLeod, N. Bruce, 136, 155–6, 159–60, 187
McLoughlin, William, 5, 213–14
McLuhan, Marshall, 28, 56
McNaught, Ken, 85–6
Manual for Draft-Age Immigrants to Canada (TADP), 74, 116, 239n60
Maoism, 107, 114, 152, 162, 166; and women's liberation, 183. *See also* Marxism; Stalinism; Trotskyism
March on the Pentagon, 105
Marcuse, Herbert, 86, 109, 114–15, 215n27
Martin, Paul, 134
Marx, Karl, 86, 114–15, 118
Marxism, 3, 40, 74, 114–15, 210; New Left solidarity with revolutionary Marxism, 118; and role in New Left, 105–9; spirituality, 111, 114–15, 199. *See also* liberation theology; Maoism; Stalinism; Trotskyism
Mathews, Robin, 162
Mattachine Society, 185
Maxwell, Donald, 167
Medellin, Columbia, 160
Mennonites, 52, 230n60
Methodists, 31, 34–5, 213n4
Metie, Tony, 191
Metropolitan Community Church of Toronto, 186, 187
Miedema, Gary, 19
Miller, Hugh, 118
Miller, Judy, 118
Miller, Robert ("Bob"), 40, 145, 154, 191
Milligan, Ian, 15–16, 152
Mills, C. Wright, 46, 86, 114–15

Minifie, James, 60
Mississippi Freedom Democratic Party, 49
Montreal, 27
Montreal Peace Centre, 61
Moral and Social Reform Council of Canada, 35
Morgentaler, Henry, 143
Morton, Peggy, 92
Murphy, Tom, 114
Murton, Philip, 163
Muste, A.J., 51–2, 64, 226n86
Mutchmor, James R., 36, 130, 242n17
Mylai Massacre, 165

National Council of Churches, 166–7
National Liberation Front, 118
National Organization of Women, 173
National Policy, 162
Nazism, 53, 88, 89
Nelson, Robert, 96
New Democratic Party: campus club at University of Toronto, 114, 152, 163; Waffle wing of party, 162–3
New Left: African-American civil rights movement as impetus, 46–7; and anti-imperialism, 117–23, 149–50, 153; and the antiwar movement, 73–4, 116–17, 132–3; and the Baby Boom, 104, 109, 123; Canadian churches and the New Left, 74–80, 125–37, 194; Christianity and the New Left in USA, 51–3; Christian participation in Canada's New Left, 3,

13, 58–66, 68–103, 112–23, 194, 198, 200, 208; and the counterculture, 108–9; and critique of post-secondary education, 144–5; definition of, 221n7; and the early 1970s, 150–3; ethics and action vs ideology and analysis, 232n93; and gay liberation, 184–6; identity formation of young Christian activists, 53–61; and La Macaza protests, 61–6, 110, 123; and the Latin American Working Group, 117–23; and left nationalism in Canada, 121–2; long-term consequences of Christian engagement with New Left, 195–208; on North American campuses, 50–1, 105–9, 151–3; nuclear disarmament movement as impetus for Canadian New Left, 47–50; numerical strength on Canadian campuses, 108, 236n18; origins, 45–51; participatory democracy, 47, 68, 71, 79, 81, 106; radicalization, 48–51, 105–9; religious upbringing as factor in identity formation, 91–2; second phase, 105–9; secularity, 3, 105, 109–11; as a student movement, 46, 221n7; and Student Union for Peace Action, 68, 70–4, 93–8, 105–9; values and principles, 46–7; and women's liberation, 171–3, 173–5, 253n55. *See also* activists; Students for a Democratic Society; Student Union for Peace Action; young Christian radicals

New Left Caucus (University of Toronto), 84, 107–8, 110, 139, 198
New Left Committee, 106
Newman, Joan. *See* Kuyek, Joan Newman
Newman Centre (University of Toronto), 28, 110–11, 139–41, 169, 198
Niebuhr, H. Richard, 66
Niebuhr, Reinhold, 38
Nixon, Richard, 152
Nkrumah, Kwame, 118
nonviolent civil disobedience, 61–6, 68, 161
North American Air Defence, 48, 60, 115
North American Congress on Latin America, 119
North Atlantic Treaty Organization, 48, 60
nuclear disarmament movement: Christian involvement, 58–66; La Macaza protests, 61–6; protests similar to La Macaza, 226n86; role in origins of Canadian New Left, 47–50

Observer (United Church of Canada), 37, 76, 156; on abortion, 181; coverage of war resisters, 166; coverage of youth issues in sixties, 112, 127; and the feminist movement, 175–6; on homosexuality, 188–9; and J.R. ("Ray") Hord, 130, 134; Gordon Stewart in, 165–6
Ontario Bible College, 132
Ontario Welfare Council, 133
Operation Beaver, 112

Operation St Jean Baptiste.
  See La Macaza, Quebec
Opocensky, Milan, 96
oral history, 13–14, 215n4
Owram, Doug, 92

pacifism, 51, 58–9, 61–6, 161. *See also* nonviolent civil disobedience; nuclear disarmament movement
Palestine, 149
Palmer, Bryan, 9, 106, 118
Pape, Art, 72, 232n100
Paris, Peter, 98
Paris protests (May 1968), 105, 128
Parsons, Talcott, 15
participatory democracy, 47, 68, 71, 79, 81, 106; in education, 145; in a religious context, 78–9
Paul VI (pope), 142, 177, 178, 198–9
Paulist Seminary (Baltimore, Maryland), 86
Peace Corps, 72, 79
Peacemaker or Powder-Monkey (Minifie), 60
Pearson, Lester, 37, 49–50, 72, 115; and the Vietnam War, 133–6, 165
People's Church of Toronto, 187
People's Magazine, 187
Perry, Troy, 186
Pietlock, Stan, 169, 250n76
Pinochet, Augusto, 159
Pius IX (pope), 178
Pius XI (pope), 29, 141
Pocock, Philip, 131–2, 138, 243n50
Pollution Probe, 113
Port Huron Statement (SDS), 47, 78, 118

Potter, Paul, 118
Power, William, 159–60
Prague Spring, 128
Presbyterian Church in Canada, 34–5
Presbyterians, 34–5
Project La Macaza Bulletin, 65
Project North, 199
Project Ploughshares, 199
"prophetic" vs "priestly" religion, 6–7, 125, 132–7, 147, 214n10; and Canadian Christianity up to the mid-sixties, 27–43; long-term consequences of "prophetic" religious engagement, 195–208
Proteus, myth of, 210

Quadrigesimo Anno (Pius XI), 29, 78
Quaker Medical Relief Fund, 141
Quakers. *See* Society of Friends
Quealey, Michael, 140–2
Quebec nationalism, 80, 118, 151, 162
Quentin, Edna May, 40
Quiet Revolution (Quebec), 25, 217n15

radical left, definition, 48–9
Ratzinger, Joseph, 199
Reciprocity Election of 1911, 162
Red Ensign, 26
Regina, Saskatchewan: as site for conference to establish SUPA, 70, 226–7n4
Regina Manifesto, 30
religious crisis of the sixties, 6; in Canada, 24–7, 74–7, 98–103, 126–7, 205–8, 209–10; causes,

16–19, 205–8; deepening of crisis since sixties, 205–8
Rerum Novarum (Leo XIII), 29, 78
Restless Church, The, 76, 228n33
"Revolution and Response," 74, 227n4
Rimmer, Alan, 154–5, 157, 163
Robinson, John A.T., 34
Rochdale College, 12, 125, 144–7
Roebuck, Don, 87
Roe v. Wade, 174
Roman Catholic Church, 12, 20, 27–31, 77–80; on abortion, 177–9; aid to war resisters, 169; anti-institutional rhetoric, 131–2; in Archdiocese of Toronto, 27–31, 79–80, 137–43; attempts to engage with youth and New Left, 125–32; attendance and membership, 25, 126–7, 205–8; Canadian bishops' Labour Day message, 161–2; conservatism of institution in the 1970s and 1980s, 198–9; and the debate over contraception, 141–3, 199; and "dialogue with the modern world," 29, 69, 78, 125, 195; and gay liberation, 186–90, 199; and immigration, 27–8; and Inter-Church Committee on Chile, 159–60; and "lay apostolate," 78–9, 137–8; long-term consequences of engagement with youth and New Left, 198–9; left-wing presence within, 137–43; and "personalism," 30; Project North, 199; "renewal," 29, 132, 137–43, 148; Sacred Congregation for the Doctrine of the Faith, 177, 189, 199; and socialism, 29–30; and social justice/social action, 29–31, 77–9; and the Vietnam War, 164–70; women's roles in, 176–7, 198–9. *See also* Canadian Conference of Catholic Bishops; *Catholic Register*; Catholic Worker movement; Dignity; Kutz, Stan; liberation theology; Newman Centre; Pietlock, Stan; Quealey, Michael; Roman Catholic left; Schmidt, Ted; Sheehan, Peter; St Michael's College; Vatican II; Warrian, Peter; Youth Corps
Roman Catholic left, 30, 52, 137–43, 160–2, 198–9; and church hierarchy, 156, 161–2
Ross, Murray, 59
Rossinow, Doug, 8, 52
Roussopoulos, Dimitri, 48, 60, 61–2, 82, 85; on the St Calixte conference, 233n112; speaker at gathering of Anglican and United Church youth, 232n100
Royal Canadian Airforce, 115
Royal Canadian Mounted Police, 39, 184
Royal Commission on the Status of Women, 174
Royal York Road United Church, 116, 136

St Andrew's College (University of Saskatchewan), 197
St Calixte Conference (SUPA Fall Institute), 72–3, 93–5, 233n105, 233n112
St Jerome's College (University of Waterloo), 86

St Michael's College (University of Toronto), 28, 84, 110, 139, 187
St Paul's Church, Toronto (Anglican), 31
St Thomas Aquinas, 178
Sanders, Larry, 113
Santiago, Chile, 158
Satin, Mark, 134
Schmidt, Ted, 138–9, 199
Scott, Edward, 39, 156, 159–60, 180, 197–8
Second Vatican Council. *See* Vatican II
second-wave feminism, 106–8, 171–84, 185, 202–3. *See also* abortion; feminism; inclusive language; women's liberation; women's ordination
Secular City, The (Cox), 75–7, 91, 228n29
secularization: on Canadian campuses, 110–11; causes of, 16–19, 205–8; definition, 17–19, 208–9; and irony, 208; and the secularization thesis, 16–19; from the seventies to the twenty-first century, 205–8; in the sixties, 16–19, 24–7, 110–11
secular theology, 7, 75–6, 122, 206
Selma protests in Toronto, 71, 93
Selma-to-Montgomery marches, 71
sexual revolution, 141–3, 172. *See also* contraception; gay liberation; homosexuality; women's liberation
Sharp, Mitchell, 159–60
Shaull, Richard, 121, 122
Sheehan, Peter, 169
Shepherd, Harvey, 92, 112, 227n9
Simon Fraser University, 108

sixties: irony, 208; metanarratives, 14–19, 207, 209–10; religious crisis of, 6, 24–7, 74–7, 98–103; and youth in media and popular culture, 104–5
Skinner, Judith, 87, 119, 121, 157–8, 183
Smith, Christian, 257n38
Social Gospel, 4, 8, 69, 196, 213n4; difference from liberation theology, 161; and the Student Christian Movement, 38, 161; and the United Church of Canada, 35–6, 204, 208
Socialist Party of America, 51
Social Service Council of Canada, 35
Society of Friends (Quakers), 52, 71, 87
Somerville, Henry, 30, 138
Somerville, Janet, 199
Soviet Union: invasion of Hungary, 45–6; Krushchev's "Secret Speech," 45
Spinks, Sarah, 120
spirituality, 6, 108, 111, 209–10; definition, 213n1; spirituality vs religion, 213n1, 257n39
Stalinism, 107. *See also* Maoism; Marxism; Trotskyism
Steele, James, 162
Stein, David Lewis, 62, 64
Stevenson, Adlai, 74
Stewart, Gordon, 130, 165–6
Stonewall riots, 185
Student Christian Movement (Queen's University chapter), 55, 60
Student Christian Movement (University of British Columbia chapter), 155

Student Christian Movement
  (University of Saskatchewan), 60
Student Christian Movement
  (University of Toronto chapter),
  38, 40–2, 53–61, 91, 114, 200;
  and African-American civil rights
  activism, 58; and the "Agora"
  proposal, 102; in the early 1970s,
  153–6; Inn of the Unmuzzled
  Ox, 190–2; intellectual program
  of, 56–7; and the New Left,
  80–1, 98; and nuclear disarmament activism, 58–61; numerical
  strength of chapter, 42, 114, 154,
  220n78, 238n45; Roman
  Catholic involvement, 141;
  secularity in late sixties, 114; and
  United Church chaplaincy, 129
Student Christian Movement
  (University of Waterloo chapter),
  86
Student Christian Movement (York
  University), 163, 238n47
Student Christian Movement
  Bookroom, 145
Student Christian Movement of
  Canada, 7–8, 37–42, 53–66,
  68–103, 208; the "Agora" proposal, 100–3, 235n136; alumni,
  81, 154, 156, 196–7, 200–1, 203,
  294; annual conferences in Bala,
  Ontario, 191, 232n100; anti-
  imperialism, 122; Basis and
  Aims, 38, 99–100; and
  Christendom, 41–2, 43; crisis
  of mid-sixties, 98–103; decline,
  102–3, 113–14; in early 1970s,
  153–6; financial troubles, 100–3,
  114; and gay liberation, 173,
  190–3, 255n102; and identity
  formation as activists, 53–61;
  intellectual program of, 56–7,
  91, 190; involvement of agnostics and atheists, 38, 55, 65,
  99–100, 113, 201, 226n2,
  234n132; and La Macaza protests, 61–6, 110, 123, 129, 200;
  and Latin America, 122, 157–8,
  160–1, 247n26; and the Latin
  American Working Group, 119,
  122, 157; and left nationalism,
  162–3; and liberal theology,
  37–9, 55; life trajectory of SCM
  alumni from sixties, 200–1; and
  New Left in late sixties, 112,
  113–14, 123–4; and nuclear disarmament activism, 58–66, 110;
  "Poisoning the Student Mind"
  (theme song), 39, 41; and political radicalism, 39–41, 57–66,
  80–1, 113–14; reasons for joining, 54–6; relationship with
  SUPA, 93–8, 208; rhetoric, 93;
  Roman Catholic involvement,
  86, 140–1, 198; SCM-SUPA
  conference in Saskatoon, 95–7,
  102–3, 113–14; secularity in late
  sixties, 105, 114; and the Social
  Gospel, 38; as surrogate family,
  40–1, 55–6, 80; in the twenty-
  first century, 200–2, 210; wage
  pool, 40; and women's liberation, 173, 182–4, 255n102; work
  camps, 40–1, 56, 62, 102, 190,
  191. *See also* Student Christian
  Movement National Council;
  SCM *chapters at specific
  universities*
Student Christian Movement of
  Cuba, 157–8

Student Christian Movement of Mexico (MEC), 119, 120
Student Christian Movement National Council, 113, 114, 115, 154; and left nationalism, 162; and the SCM crisis of the mid-sixties, 98, 102–3
student movement. *See* New Left
Student Nonviolent Coordinating Committee, 20, 46, 71
Students' Administrative Council (University of Toronto), 86, 108, 115–17, 136
Students for a Democratic Society, 47, 52, 85, 133; breakaway factions, 151; relationship with SUPA, 71; and women's liberation, 174
Student Union for Peace Action, 12, 68–74, 93–8, 106–8, 114; Christian participation, 80, 82–3, 85–7, 93–8, 198; community organizing projects, 71–3, 80, 84, 93–4, 112; and creation of Toronto Anti-Draft Programme, 74, 86; criticism of Christian hypocrisy, 92; demise, 106–8; and feminism, 106–8; formation, 70, 86; and Marxism, 106–8; national office, 85, 87; relationship with CYC, 72–3, 96–7, 106; relationship with Kairos, 93–8, 208; relationship with SCM, 91, 93–8, 103, 115, 208; relationship with SDS, 71; religious upbringing of participants, 91–2; St Calixte conference (SUPA Fall Institute), 72–3, 93–5, 97; SCM-SUPA conference in Saskatoon, 95–7, 113–14; Selma protest at American consulate, 71, 93, 227n9; and Vietnam War, 73–4

Student Volunteer Movement Conference (Athens, Ohio, 1959), 58, 60
Summer of Service, 7, 12, 20, 112, 119; formation and purpose, 69–70; and the New Left, 83–4, 94
Survival Day, 113
Sussex Day Care, 175, 183

Task Force on Churches and Corporate Responsibility, 199
Task Force on Human Life (Anglican Church of Canada), 180
Taylor, Charles, 17
Templeton, Charles, 36
Theología de la liberación (Gutierrez), 160
Therafields, 139, 243n55
There Can Be No Light without Shadow, 210
This Magazine Is about Schools, 144, 155
Thomas, Norman, 51, 52
Tillich, Paul, 41, 52, 82, 86, 88–90, 231n88
Time Magazine, 104
"The Times They Are a-Changin'" (Dylan), 44
Timothy Eaton Memorial United Church, 135
Toombs, Farrell, 145
Toronto: as principal site of study, 11
Toronto Anti-Draft Programme, 74, 86, 116, 134–7, 166–9
Toronto Gay Action, 153, 186, 191

Toronto Star, 37, 141–2, 187
Toronto Student Movement, 108
Toronto Women's Liberation Movement, 107, 175, 183
Trinity College (University of Toronto), 33, 129
Trotskyism, 51, 74, 107, 152–3. *See also* Maoism; Marxism; Stalinism
Trudeau, Pierre, 151, 174, 179, 185
Turner, Peter, 210

Union générale des étudiants du Quebec, 95
Union of American Exiles, 169
Union of Latin American Evangelical Youth (ULAJE), 119, 120
Union Theological Seminary (New York), 85, 86, 89
Unitarian-Universalists, 186
United Church of Canada, 12, 20–1, 34–7; attendance and membership, 24–5, 126–7, 205–8, 256n21; and Berton's *The Comfortable Pew*, 76; Board of Evangelism and Social Service, 36, 76–7, 129–30, 132–7, 155, 165–6, 180, 188, 196; Board of Women, 180, 182; Board of World Mission, 77; and Canadian Urban Training Program, 77; Caravans, 112; chaplaincy at University of Toronto, 129; Committee on Overseas Relief and Inter-Church Aid, 167; Committee on Sex and Morality, 188; Committee on the Church and International Affairs, 133, 134, 164–5; conservatism of lay membership, 134–5, 156, 166, 181, 182, 203–4; debate over abortion, 180–2, 193; Division of Mission in Canada, 155, 158, 182, 197, 203; and gay liberation, 187–9, 193, 202–4, 256n21; General Council, 134, 180–2, 189, 203, 204; and Inter-Church Committee on Chile, 159–60; Joint Committee on Abortion, 180–1; long-term consequences of engagement with youth and the New Left, 196–7, 202–4, 208, 256n21; New Curriculum, 36; "new evangelism," 77; "New Morality," 187–9; and Project North, 199; on sexuality, 187–9, 202–4; shift to the left, 136, 197; and Social Gospel, 35–6, 208; and the Student Christian Movement, 114; Task Force on Women and Partnership between Men and Women in Church and Society, 203; and the Vietnam War, 132–7, 164–70; and the women's movement, 176, 180–2, 193, 203; and women's ordination, 176. *See also* adult Christians; Affirm; Christie, Harriet; Foster, John; Frerichs, Eilert ("Bert"); Hord, J.R. ("Ray"); inclusive language; Kairos (United Church of Canada); McCurdy, Arch; *Observer* (United Church); Stewart, Gordon; Wallace, Bronwyn; young Christian radicals; Young People's Union (United Church of Canada)

United Nations Conference on Trade and Development, 158
Universal Fellowship of Metropolitan Community Churches, 186
University Christian Movement, 238n46
University of Toronto, 12, 53, 129, 140, 145; anti-Vietnam War activism at, 74, 115–17; civil rights activism at, 58, 71; day-care activism on campus, 175; disarmament activism at, 48, 58–61; Students' Administrative Council, 86, 108, 115–17, 136. *See also affiliated colleges, chapters of student organizations, and individual professors and student leaders*
University of Toronto Homophile Association, 185–6
University Placement Service (University of Toronto), 116–17

Van Buren, Paul, 75
Van Den Heuvel, Albert, 96
Varsity (University of Toronto), 114, 115–16, 132, 152–3
Varsity Christian Fellowship (University of Toronto), 54–5. *See also* Intervarsity Christian Fellowship
Vatican II, 7, 28–9, 69, 139; and *Apostolicam Actuositatem*, 78–9; and campaign for women's ordination, 177; and declining adherence since the sixties, 205–8; and "dialogue with the modern world," 29, 69, 78, 125, 195; and *Gaudium et Spes*, 78–9; and "lay apostolate," 78–9, 137–8; and liturgical changes, 29, 140; raised hopes of progressives within church, 29–30, 137–8, 141, 177, 198–9; "renewal," 29, 132, 137–43, 148. *See also* Roman Catholic Church

Venceremos Brigades, 118, 158
Victoria University (University of Toronto), 37, 115
Viet Cong, 118, 141, 157, 166
Vietminh, 73
Vietnam War, 6, 20–1, 70, 73–4, 106; broadening antiwar movement, 132–7, 152; Canadian churches and, 125, 132–7, 164–70, 150, 156, 196; Canadian complicity in, 108, 133–4, 196; Canadian support for war resisters, 134–7, 140–1; conclusion of war, 152; Gulf of Tonkin incident, 49, 116; New Left solidarity with NLF and Viet Cong, 118, 149; student protest against, 73–4, 96–7, 104, 110, 132–3; student protest against Canadian complicity in, 105, 116–17, 123; United Church and, 132–7
Voices United! (United Church of Canada), 203

Waffle, 152, 162–3
Waffle Manifesto, 162–3
Wallace, Bronwyn, 82–3, 90
Ward, Bonnie, 183
Ward, Doug, 85–6
War Measures Act, 151
Warner, Paul, 191
war resisters, 132–7, 140–1, 242n29

Warrian, Peter, 86, 96, 98, 112; on Catholic student involvement in the New Left, 139; as a Christian in the New Left, 114–15, 123; in the Latin American Working Group, 119, 120; on the Newman Centre, 141; on the secularity of the New Left, 109; and the Toronto Anti-Draft Programme, 86, 169
Washington, DC, 87
Watkins, Mel, 121
Weatherman Underground, 151
Wernick, Andy, 114
Whitla, William, 63, 65
Why the Sea Is Boiling Hot (United Church of Canada), 76
Wilson, Bryan, 17
Wilson, Don, 113
Wilson, Lois, 39, 203
Wolfenden Report, 185
Wolffe, John, 18
women's liberation, 21, 107, 141–3, 152–3; and Christianity, 170, 171–84, 193, 196, 202–3; compared to other liberation movements, 172; "personal is political," 174. *See also* abortion; feminism; inclusive language; women's ordination
women's ordination, 173, 176–8, 183, 199
Woodgreen United Church, 77
World Council of Churches: funding to aid war resisters in Canada, 167; meeting in Uppsala, Sweden (1968), 127–8
World Student Christian Federation, 39, 64–5, 122, 154; and anti-imperialism in the early 1970s, 149, 157, 161, 163–4, 165–6; and tensions between American and Canadian students, 163–4; and women's liberation, 171, 172, 183, 184; and prominent Canadian women, 203; quadrennial conference (Addis Ababa, 1972), 149, 165–6, 172
Wyatt, Joan, 182
Wycliffe College (University of Toronto), 33

York University (Toronto), 140
Yorkville (Toronto), 108–9, 113, 125, 147
Young, Ian, 190–2
young Christian radicals, 13; in Anglican Youth Movement, 113; and anti-imperialism, 117–23; in Christian Left group, 85–8; identity formation, 53–61; in Kairos, 81–3; in Latin American Working Group, 117–23; long-term consequences of engagement with churches and New Left, 195–208; older Christians as mentors and supporters, 13, 80–1, 125–43, 153–6, 196–8; relationship with churches and church leaders, 125–43, 153–6, 196–8; role in New Left, 51–66, 80–98, 112–24, 208; in Roman Catholic Church, 86, 110–11, 143; on sexuality and gender, 188, 193–4; in Student Christian Movement, 80–1; in Summer of Service, 83–4; theology, 88–93; at Uppsala, 127–8
Young Men's Christian Association (YMCA), 4, 8, 38, 52

Young People's Union (United Church of Canada), 37, 81, 83, 119
Young Socialists, 152–3
Young Women's Christian Association (YWCA), 4, 8, 38, 87
youth: adult Christian outreach to, 6, 125–43; definition, 14, 215n28; generation and "generation gap," 15–16, 104–5; literature on youth movements in sixties, 8–10; in media and popular culture in sixties, 104–5; metanarratives about youth in sixties, 14–16; role in church growth and decline, 26–7, 110, 127, 205–8; and spiritual search in the sixties, 210. *See also* Baby Boom
Youth Committee on Christian Presence, 131
Youth Corps, 7, 70, 79–80, 83, 198–9
youth culture, 15–16, 104–5, 108–9. *See also* counterculture